WELLINGTON IN INDIA

Wellington
in India

Jac Weller

LONGMAN

LONGMAN GROUP LIMITED LONDON

*Associated companies, branches and
representatives throughout the world*

First published 1972

ISBN 0 582 12784 X

*Printed in Great Britain by
The Camelot Press Ltd, London and Southampton*

To the young Englishmen like Richard, Arthur and Henry Wellesley who gave their strength, health, and sometimes lives for the British Empire

Contents

Illustrations

Maps

drawn by John Flower

Preface

The man whom the world knows as Wellington began to demonstrate his military ability in the East. We all know the bare ribs of this, but India is a long way away. The best original records still exist and are relatively easy to obtain, but thorough study of them presents problems. It is partly fascinating drudgery and partly detective work; both occupations are time-consuming. Most of us who have 'studied Wellington's whole life' have been more thorough in connection with Salamanca than Assaye. Ciudad Rodrigo is more often visited than Gawilghur. It is easier to trace the least conspicuous British regiment in the Waterloo campaign than the best known East India Company unit through any series of actions.

Biographers and others, including the Duke himself, have come to the conclusion that when he returned to Europe in 1805, his abilities were fully developed. With some reservation, I agree; in India he had done most of the things he did so well later in Europe. He did not suddenly receive, for instance, an inspiration from on high about how to cross rivers or even employ again field guns after they had been 'taken by the enemy'. In India he had used, or had been opposed with, most of the 'innovations' he employed in the Peninsula and at Waterloo. He learned his trade in an area where the stakes were not so high, nor control by antiquated superiors so likely.

I expected to find a great many instances of this military apprenticeship and found even more than I anticipated. My study led me, however, to a full understanding of something I had only half grasped before. The years the three Wellesley brothers spent in India were crucial to the development of the British Empire both in India and throughout the world. Arthur's contributions, both military and civil, were greater than I had realized. Assaye is a remarkable victory, but the quick and complete pacification of Mysore after May 1799 appears at least as important today. As I read, thought and talked to a few friends, I became conscious of more than one man. 'Wellington' in India was a member of a team. His story from 1797 to 1805 is closely related to that of his elder brother, the Earl of Mornington and later Marquess Wellesley, his younger brother, the Hon. Henry Wellesley, and many others. To some extent, the original scope of this book has been broadened to include them.

Names have been a problem, especially with the three Wellesleys: all were Wesleys in 1795, their titles did not remain the same either. There is also a technical problem. The spelling of names of places and people is difficult. Even in English, modern Indian spelling is hopeless; some towns and rivers which were important in the Wellesleys' era are recognizable now only after detailed study and map comparisons. 'Bombay' remains the same, but the 'Mahrattas' have gained and lost various letters in their collective name. I found, however, that in April 1968 a Bangalore newspaper did use my spelling. I have retained Arthur Wellesley's own spellings, save where they lead to awkwardness. Ajanta, for instance, is fairly well known because of the sculptures of some sacred caves situated nearby; there seems to be no valid reason to refer to the place as Adjuntee, the spelling current among Englishmen in 1803. All names are, I hope, consistent throughout the narrative and in the diagrams. Anyone going to India is warned, however, that in some areas English place-names have already gone, especially in the case of villages that have grown, changed sites or disappeared.

I want to thank His Grace, the 7th Duke of Wellington, for guidance, inspiration and the privilege of seeing him and his son, the Marquess Douro, both at Strathfield Saye and in their rooms at Apsley House surrounded by the Great Duke's possessions: a privilege for which My Little Wife and I are deeply grateful. I could not think of the Wellesley brothers with confidence if I had not met the present Duke who is only Arthur's great grandson. Through the present Duke my wife and I met the Earl and Countess of Longford who have given time, friendship and information that is perhaps unavailable anywhere else, for which we are very grateful.

I have many other people to thank for their help during the efforts, literally around the world, which preceded the writing of this book. Brigadier Mehta, the Indian Army Attaché in Washington, and Major Gulu Kohli, formerly of the Indian Army but now my neighbour here in Princeton, set in motion a series of visits to the modern Indian Army and arrangements for the hire of vehicles, drivers and the like. I particularly want to thank Lieutenant-General and Mrs H. K. Sibal, Major-General Virandra Singh, and Brigadier Naib and his family for their friendly co-operation, their hospitality and their answers to my questions both oral and in letters.

I appreciate the guidance in the old Mahratta area of Lieutenant-Colonel Gay, recently retired from the Indian Army, and 'Driver' who is one of the nicest human beings we have ever known. In spite of a jeep literally held together by pieces of his handkerchief and of other difficulties he managed to get us to every single topographical objective north of Poona which we had selected months before and half a world away. Having met 'Driver', we understand why British officers of the Indian Army sometimes have moist eyes when talking of their old commands. I also want to thank Brigadier Naib's people and an enterprising young 'rent-a-car' agency in Bangalore which allowed us to borrow a vehicle and drive it ourselves all over Southern India. Mysore has not only kept their public statue of Queen Victoria, but also their English road signs. Their roads are better than most Indian roads too. God bless them for all three things.

In regard to weapons which were originally used or designed for India 1799–1805 I am indebted especially to my friends Mr A. N. Kennard of the Tower, Mr Keith Neal of Warminster and Mr Gerald Stowe of the West Point Museum. The Indian Room of the Museum at Sandhurst and the Museum of the Royal Hospital at Chelsea were most generous with photographs of their exhibits and in allowing me to examine some of their priceless possessions out of their cases. General Sir Frank E. W. Simpson and Major Andrew showed us the colours of Pohlmann's Regular Battalions that were captured at Assaye and are now at the Hospital; they also allowed us to talk to British veterans of later wars. Mr Peter Mitchell of A. H. Baldwin and Sons made it possible for us to acquire the India General Service Medal with Assaye, Argaum, and Gawilghur bars issued to Sergeant Alec Macrae of the 78th.

I want to thank many British soldiers who served in India for their advice and guidance, especially Field-Marshal Sir Francis Festing, Major-General Robin Goldsmith and Colonel John Masters. Other British officers have given information and encouragement, particularly Brigadier P. H. C. Hayward of *The British Army Review* and Major-General B. P. Hughes of Woolwich. Colonel Rixon Bucknall unselfishly has shared with me his astonishingly broad military knowledge. Mr Victor Percival and the Apsley House Museum have given me time, information and photographs, all of which I truly appreciate. Mr D. W. King and the Ministry of Defence were also most helpful.

I humbly acknowledge my debt to Captain Sir Basil Liddell Hart in so many areas. I have just read of his death. Those who write military history past and present will do it better because of his techniques, his example and his many friendships. He was never too busy to help us, nor were Lady Liddell Hart's days too full to make us feel at home.

On a slightly less elevated, but no less valuable plane, I want to thank Bunny Tubbs and our fellow members of the Rowland Club, Jim Risk and Dudley Johnson, who started it all. My Little Wife, Helen Nason and Isabel Frank have had not only to put up with a tired and often exasperating author, but to find things that he has lost and correct his mistakes. For those of the latter which still survive, please blame them.

Chronology

1797	February	Colonel Arthur Wellesley and the King's 33rd Foot arrive at Calcutta (Fort William).
	August	Colonel Wellesley and the King's 33rd Foot sail for Penang.
	November	They return to Calcutta.
1798	January–March	Colonel Wellesley visits Madras.
	17 May	Richard Wellesley, Earl of Mornington, and Henry Wellesley arrive at Calcutta.
	September	Arthur Wellesley and the King's 33rd Foot join the Madras Army.
	18 December	Wellesley appointed to command an army forming at Arcot, Arnee and Vellore.
1799	29 January	He relinquishes command to General Harris personally.
	11 February	Harris begins his advance on Seringapatam.
	18 February	Wellesley and the King's 33rd Foot added to the Nizam's contingent at Amboor; Wellesley more or less in command.
	10 March	Wellesley's first combat in India; he is attacked by Tipoo's forces while on Harris's right flank.
	27 March	Battle of Malavelley.
	3 April	The British arrive near Seringapatam.
	5 April	The Sultanpetah Tope affair, Wellesley's only military defeat.
	6 April	Victorious British attack in the same place by daylight.
	26–27 April	Wellesley in command of an attack which carries all Tipoo's defences west of the South Cauvery.
	4 May	Seringapatam taken by storm.
	5 May	Wellesley appointed to command in the disorderly city.
	11 September	He is appointed to command all Mysore.
1800	May	He is appointed to command an expedition to Batavia, but refuses.

1800	24 June	The campaign against Dhoondiah Waugh begins in earnest when Wellesley crosses Tombuddra.
	10 September	Final defeat of Dhoondiah at Conaghull.
	December	Wellesley leaves Mysore to command an expeditionary force assembling at Trincomalee, Ceylon.
1801	24 January–5 February	Mornington supersedes his brother Arthur with Baird in command of the Ceylon force. (Arthur receives notice of this on 21 February 1801 while on his way to Bombay.)
	6 February	Arthur receives orders from London for an expedition to Egypt.
	March & April	He is ill with fever and Malabar itch at Bombay.
	7 May	He returns to Seringapatam and reassumes all commands.
1802	January & February	Active and successful operations against the Rajah of Bullum.
	26 September	Wellesley receives news of his promotion to Major-General in His Majesty's service. (Commission dated 29 April 1802.)
	October	Minor rebellions in Wynaad, especially at Pancoorta Cottah.
	12 November	Wellesley receives orders concerning the forming of a British army on the Tombuddra.
1803	27 February	He is appointed to command a force sent to restore the Peshwa.
	9 March	His army begins to advance from Hurryhur.
	20 April	It arrives at Poona.
	13 May	The restoration of the Peshwa.
	17 July	Wellesley receives notice of his appointment to command in the Deccan. (The Governor-General's order is dated 26 June 1803.)
	8 August	He takes the *pettah* at Ahmednuggur.
	12 August	The fort at Ahmednuggur surrenders.
	23 September	Battle of Assaye.
	16 October	Burhampoor taken by Colonel James Stevenson.
	24 October	Asseergurh surrenders to Stevenson.

1803	29 November	Battle of Argaum.
	15 December	Gawilghur taken by storm.
	17 December	Treaty of Deogaum with the Rajah of Berar.
	30 December	Similar treaty with Scindia.
1804	6 February	Action at Munkaiseer, after Wellesley's troops have marched '60 miles in 30 hours'.
	May–June	Active operations against Holkar in the Deccan are found to be impossible.
	30 May	The Governor-General orders his brother to Fort William. (This dispatch reaches Arthur on 19 June 1804.)
	24 June	Wellesley relinquishes command in the Deccan and begins journey to Seringapatam. He visits Madras before embarking for Calcutta.
	c. 12 August	He arrives at Fort William.
	10 November	He leaves Fort William.
	1 December	He arrives at Seringapatam.
1805	9 February	He leaves Seringapatam.
	10 March	He sails for home aboard H.M.S. *Trident* from Madras.
	20 June to 10 July	Sojourn in St Helena.
	10 September	Sir Arthur Wellesley returns to England.

I

Arrival in India

The Hoogley was broad and muddy brown. The new grey granite fort on its eastern shore stood out sharp against the green and white of Calcutta. Several of the East India Company's ships stood finally at anchor in the sluggish current; there were true men-of-war of the Royal Navy too. All had sun-bleached sails and standing rigging that showed signs of repairs made during the long voyage out from Britain.

There was a lot of activity on the river and ashore. These vessels had just arrived and had brought merchandise and hundreds of Britons to India for the first time. All had high hopes, whatever their station. The great Clive himself had risen from an unknown writer[1] to vast wealth and a peerage. A common Irish sailor had made himself into a prince. Men who served John Company well sometimes returned home after only a few years with tens of thousands of pounds. A King's officer who would draw 300 pounds a year at home, in India might receive 10,000 pounds or more.[2] On the other hand, Arthur Wesley, the young colonel of His Majesty's 33rd Regiment of Foot, found the fabulous East not as inviting at close quarters as he had hoped. Even two hundred yards out in the river there was an all-pervasive stench of human excrement. Frightening water-borne beggars clamoured for food or coppers. Only slightly more prepossessing boatmen vied with

---

[1] A 'writer' was a clerk.

[2] *Biddulph*, 101–2: 'General Floyd is now [including his King's pay as major-general and lieutenant-colonel of the 19th Light Dragoons, his Company pay and his allowance from the Company and the Nizam as commandant of the southern district] in the receipt of from £14,000 to £16,000.' This was undoubtedly unusual, but obviously possible. A lieutenant-colonel's pay in Britain, the highest salary that a general officer not actively employed could get, was 300 pounds: *Harris*, 134.

each other to take officers and their baggage ashore. Wesley began to recall statistics he had put together on the long voyage out. Even at the age of twenty-seven he had a gift for this sort of thing. For every ten Englishmen who came to India, less than five would return. All hoped for wealth and position, but only a fortunate few found them even in a modest way – less than one in twenty-five. The odds for a soldier favoured an Indian grave.

With these sobering thoughts Wesley went about getting his regiment ashore and reassembled. It had come out in several different vessels because in 1797 all ships were small. The voyage, including a stop-over at the Cape, had taken ten months. Wesley himself had been ill in April the year before, when the regiment embarked, but left Britain two months later in H.M.S. *Fox* and caught up because a frigate could sail faster than the Indiamen. He completed his voyage in one of the latter.

Wesley and the King's 33rd were a part of reinforcements being sent out because Britain was again at war with France. There was even more reason for conflict now than the old national rivalry: France was republican and alive with new and militant power. Under the monarchy she had lost a strong position in India in the Seven Years War and failed to win it back in the world-wide struggle which grew out of the American Revolution;[1] but more recently she had defeated a coalition of European monarchies that attacked her after the Reign of Terror. The new republic was showing the same sort of ambitions the monarchy had manifested in the past, and the Younger Pitt and his Government expected another French effort in the Far East.

Bonaparte, a Corsican artillery officer in the service of France, had already begun his unique rise to military and political power and glory. He was almost the same age as Wesley, but had already fought his magnificent first Italian campaign and in February 1798 was planning his victorious march on Vienna. The colonel of the King's 33rd was a long way behind the Corsican. No one could have guessed that both the 33rd and its commander were destined to have a part in Bonaparte's final downfall more than eighteen years later. By that time Arthur Wesley would have changed his name twice and won a score of major battles; a field-marshal and a duke, he would command an allied army in a defensive position south of a village in Flanders called Waterloo. The King's 33rd was destined to be one of those British infantry units

[1] France had been allowed to keep some 'unfortified' trading ports like Pondicherry and Mahe, but these had been taken over by the British in 1793.

that took the best that the Grand Army of France could give, staggered, recovered and drove Napoleon Bonaparte into history.

In Calcutta the weather was hot, the river traffic unpleasant, and the insects were just beginning their sucking of bright new blood. Dockage was poor and the crowds oppressive. Fort William was new and strong, but the rest of Calcutta was raw and squalid. Wesley somehow got ashore, but left his personal baggage aboard ship. There were calls to be made: British India was small then not only in area, but in the number of people who ran it.

Wesley had never met Sir John Shore, the Governor-General, but both knew something of each other. Shore was capable in some areas, if not a builder of empires. He served his two masters at home better than most – the Board of Control representing the British Parliament on one hand and the Court of Directors representing the stockholders of the East India Company (EIC) on the other.

Arthur Wesley came from a family of political importance; his elder brother Richard, the Irish Earl of Mornington, had been a member of the Board of Control and active in Indian affairs for some years. The colonel of the 33rd had been in command of his regiment since September 1793 and had won a modest military reputation in the Low Countries against the armies of Republican France during the autumn of 1794.[1] The British handling of the campaign was poor. The Duke of York, the second son of George III, who was in command, avoided disastrous defeat in the field, but gave up all the territory from which he was supposed to attack and his retreat north in mid-winter was more costly than a lost battle.[2] The Duke of York was matched against better field commanders and a more efficient and energetic military system. Wesley somehow had managed to take his own command – it was probably a small brigade – safely north to the Ems in spite of their poor equipment; most of his men had no greatcoats. He was later to say that he learned from this campaign how not to do things; he absorbed far more than that. He learned, for instance, how to handle British infantry under extreme conditions of climate and also had a vivid demonstration of the value of discipline.

[1] His first action was at Boxtel on 15 September where 'his coolness and promptitude attracted the notice of Dundas', the man who wrote the drill books and served for years as the Duke of York's number one assistant: *Hooper*, 10. *Ward*, 20, says, however, that the 33rd 'in three successful actions lost not 20 casualties' by enemy action.

[2] *Fortescue's Life*, 19: ' "Your army is destroyed," wrote the Hanoverian general, Walmoden, to the Duke of York at the end of the retreat. "The officers, their carriages, and a large [private baggage] train are safe, but the men are destroyed." It was a terrible indictment, but it was true.'

Arthur Wesley was a man slightly above middle height with a body well muscled from hard exercise. His features were perhaps not handsome, but pleasant, clear and bronzed by the sun. His nose was high-bridged, his eyes a vivid sparkling blue and his hair in those days jet black and cropped short. Even then his sense of responsibility and self-discipline imposed some severity of expression, but he smiled often and laughed easily. As he went through the portals of Fort William, he admired with a professional soldier's eye this magnificent fortification which had already become a symbol of British power in India. He remembered, however, that it was built in part on tragedy. Less than half a century before the EIC's Calcutta defences had proved inadequate against an Indian army. On 19 June 1756 the Nabob of Bengal imprisoned for a night 146 English inhabitants in an underground room eighteen feet by fifteen; all but twenty-three died of heat and thirst.[1] The new fort had been part of the British defensive reaction to their loss of the old; Clive's victory in the field at Plassey had been more valuable. In India the offensive was more important than defence, a principle the young colonel probably fully appreciated already.

Wesley was new to India, but he knew more of the country than many men who had spent their lives there. The previous spring at home he had gone even further into debt to complete his Oriental library, and the long voyage out had given him the time to read. He set up regular procedures for self-improvement and had the will to carry them out. He was particularly interested in the military history of the place where he was going. Let us review in brief outline what he learnt. For almost a century and a half, until roughly 1740, the EIC had functioned as a private trading concern. Profits had been the primary motive for corporate effort. Territory was obtained only as necessary for safe mercantile operations. The EIC's land forces were organized into companies only and performed no more extensive duties than guarding compounds and garrisoning forts. The early disputes with the other European trading companies in the East had required some preparations for war, but these were mostly naval. Indiamen were still more equipped as men-of-war than as ordinary merchantmen; each sailed with a crew large enough not only to handle the ship but manage an ample complement of cannon as well.

The wars with France, especially that of the Austrian Succession

---

[1] *Aldington*, 59–60. There are several versions of the Black Hole of Calcutta incident, but all are appalling. The frightful heat of India in summer must be experienced to be appreciated.

(1740–48), led to land fighting in India which required more than factory protection. Madras was taken by the French in September 1746. The Treaty of Aix-la-Chapelle (1748) ended the war in Europe and gave Madras back to the British in exchange for Louisburg in Nova Scotia which had been captured from the French by the Americans. But the fighting in India did not stop entirely. Early in 1748 Stringer Lawrence formed the Madras independent companies of European infantrymen employed by the EIC into a battalion. Robert Clive began to earn his military reputation soon thereafter.

This unusual fighting in India, by two European nations who were at peace at home, developed out of commercial rivalry. Britain and France backed opposing factions in local Indian disputes. Sometimes forces from both countries were present at the same battle endeavouring not to fight each other. However, conflicts led to a considerable increase in British land forces in India; King's regiments began to come out, though at the expense and in the pay of the EIC.[1]

The early land fighting of the British in India was in the Carnatic, a territory extending both north and south from Madras, one of the three major EIC Presidencies. The area of conflict briefly shifted north in 1756 because of the Nabob of Bengal's capricious attack on Calcutta. Clive's victory at Plassey (23 June 1757) was partly based on the presence of a detachment of the King's 39th Foot in his small army. One result of the war in Bengal was the acquisition of more territory than could ever be needed for trading purposes. By the time Clive left India for the last time, in 1767, the EIC was ruling over an area around Fort William larger than all of England and containing many more people. Revenue[2] collected in this area was supposed to pay all expenses of government and military protection and yield a handsome profit as well. During the Clive period the Madras Presidency too gained more territory than was needed for trading. Masulipatam was taken in 1759; most of the rest of the Circars were obtained six years later. Guntoor finally became EIC territory in 1788.[3] But the city of Madras itself continued to be surrounded by the territory of the Nabob of Arcot. This Native prince, whose ancestors had ruled the entire Carnatic – the country to the east of Mysore, between the ghauts and the sea – was

[1] See especially Wilson, *passim*. The status of these regiments and their officers changed considerably over the years.

[2] The term 'revenue' as it applied in India at that time meant a combination of land tax and rent.

[3] *Hamilton*, 292. Final possession was delayed because of negotiations with the Nizam of Hyderabad.

now dependent upon British military power, but insisted on a hollow sort of independence. The Madras Presidency also controlled two pieces of EIC territory taken from Tipoo, Sultan of Mysore, in 1792, the Baramahal and a separate area around Coimbatore. Bombay was still essentially only a British island, but a long belt of the Malabar coast containing Tellicherry and Cannanore had been added to it by Cornwallis in 1792. So long as Tipoo remained in power in Mysore, the EIC hold on Malabar would remain tenuous.

The Governor-General at Fort William was the supreme executive of British India. The Governors at Madras and Bombay were subordinate, but sometimes took advantage of poor communications to be less than fully co-operative. In spite of numerous Acts of Parliament and EIC regulations defining power and responsibility, the running of British India was subject to human personality. Clive, who began the march towards empire, and Warren Hastings, who preserved all that was entrusted to him against local enemies and a coalition of all European powers in the East, had been strong, dominant individuals. The Marquess Cornwallis was a soldier and a statesman of considerable ability and had run India as he saw fit, adding both territory and prestige.

Sir John Shore, the man to whom Colonel Wesley was soon to report, was from a different mould. He had risen by doing simple tasks well and was an authority on Indian revenue. He was not, however, a man of broad vision or strong will. In carrying out, precisely but unimaginatively, his instructions from both the Board of Control and the Court of Directors not to get involved in Indian politics, he had done the British position in India severe damage. He had taken advantage of technicalities to break the spirit of Cornwallis's treaty with the Nizam of Hyderabad and had given in to mutinous pressure from EIC army officers only the year before.[1]

In February 1797 and for years after Arthur Wesley considered himself a comparative nobody. This may well have been true at home. He had become a lieutenant-colonel at twenty-four and would rise automatically to full general if he lived long enough, but others had reached this rank as young or even younger.[2] He had done some

---

[1] This 'mutiny of the EIC officers in January and February 1796' (*Wilson*, II, 283-4) created a most difficult situation. 'Sir Robert Abercrombie who was at that time C-in-C in India and the artillery officers who did not join in the mutiny restored the situation to some extent, but Shore modified his orders from home so that he gave more than the company intended to the malcontents.'

[2] *Glover*, 46: 'Edward Paget, Charles Stuart, and Henry Fane were all lieutenant colonels at nineteen.'

Irish staff duty and sat in the Irish House of Commons, but these things were usual for his class at the time – Pitt had become Prime Minister at twenty-four. In Britain Arthur Wesley was only a younger brother of an Irish peer with financial problems and even to his intimates he may well have appeared to have no great prospects.[1]

In India his position was quite different right from the start. A full colonel in command of a King's regiment was a man of importance. He brought letters of recommendation from Cornwallis with whom he had been closely associated through the Marquess being colonel-in-chief of the 33rd, which at that time still implied some rights of ownership.[2] His elder brother had written briefly to Shore, and Mornington might easily be the next Governor of Madras, or even Governor-General. Pitt was Mornington's friend and political colleague. All this was common knowledge.

On the other hand, Arthur Wesley was perhaps at some disadvantage because he did hold a King's commission. For a long time the EIC officers had been resentful of the prerogatives granted those with Royal commissions. Even the fairness of Cornwallis who in 1788[3] had removed all precedence in rank had not entirely remedied the situation. The EIC officers who only the year before had threatened to take all members of the Bengal Council into custody and run British India themselves were in part protesting at the better situations of those in King's regiments. All EIC officers were now promoted by seniority only. Not many reached field rank with less than twenty years of service.[4] A King's colonel who was not yet twenty-eight years old would be the object of considerable professional jealousy unless he was unusually talented – men of his age in EIC employ were captains.

[1] *Lady Longford*, 33, 36 and *passim*, makes all this clearer than any of her predecessors not only because of her meticulous research, but also because of her understanding of the entire situation.

[2] Arthur Wesley's relationship with Cornwallis was not as close as it might have been. The younger man wrote on 18 December 1799: 'Colonel Cornwallis . . . not only allowed the ships to sail without settling his accounts, but . . . sold his commission. As from his former dilatoriness I had reason to apprehend that he would still delay the settlement, and that, being out of the service, the accounts might never be settled, I desired Messrs Meyricks to detain in their possession the purchase-money of his commission as a security to us all for the arrangement of our accounts.' *Supplementary Despatches*, I, 418–19.

[3] Before this date, any King's officer took precedence over all EIC officers of his rank regardless of the date of their commissions.

[4] *Wilson*, II, 280: 'of the approximately 1,000 [EIC] officers in all three Presidencies only 62 held field rank. The reason for this was that the EIC wanted to keep down expense and frequently had battalions commanded by captains.'

Shore and Wesley got on well from the start. Sir John is supposed to have said after Wesley left their first meeting that the young colonel would go far if he had the opportunity to distinguish himself.[1] More important, the Governor-General took the trouble to discover Wesley's particular talents and soon involved him in the government of the country. The older man asked him for all sorts of information and opinions and received lengthy, carefully reasoned replies, both verbal and written. From the first, he thought as a member of the government even though he had no official position in it.

Shore's early use of Wesley stemmed from the Governor-General's need to know more than came through his official dispatches about the war situation in Europe and the thoughts of the Board of Control and the Court of Directors on the war with reference to India. No record of Wesley's answers survives, but they must have been useful, or he would not have been so quickly accepted. The changes in the new and dynamic France were difficult to understand even from Whitehall. What must it have been like for those who were trying to run British India months away from communication with their masters in London? Wesley could supply the vital personal link.

Arthur Wesley found himself, perhaps to his own surprise, in the position of an expert whose opinions were requested at the highest level to be used for the public good. This brought out the very best in the young man. His sound common sense and strong self-discipline had driven him to master thoroughly the international situation as it appeared to his brother Mornington and the British Government. Because of his studies and conversations with others on the journey out – he and his regiment had stopped for several weeks at the Cape – he already knew a lot about India. He could and did think and speak with due respect, but with confidence and strength. Arthur Wesley was not as ambitious as most young men in India, but he had an all-pervasive sense of public duty.

By February 1797 overland dispatches[2] made it known in India that Spain had become France's ally the previous October. Since the Dutch

---

[1] *Pearce*, I, 307–8, says: 'On his first interview with Colonel Wellesley ... Sir John Shore evinced his characteristic prompt discernment of character. Turning quickly round to his aides-de-camp, as the young soldier retired, he remarked with prophetic sagacity, "If Colonel Wellesley – this was not yet his name – should ever have the opportunity of distinguishing himself, he will do it, and greatly." '

[2] There were throughout this period two ways of sending letters to and from India, by sea and over land. The latter was usually faster, but communications by sea were more certain of arriving.

too were under French domination, the British in India were now at war with three of the four important European powers in the East. Only Portugal retained a precarious neutrality. This situation was not unprecedented; Warren Hastings had faced an even more powerful coalition fifteen years before. But those in India who were responsible for the British position there were kept on the mark. Soon after Wesley's arrival, Shore consulted him about an expedition against Spanish Manila in the Philippines. Wesley's reply was such that he was at least considered for the command. He also commented in writing on a memorandum about horse artillery,[1] commenting on missed 'opportunities of bringing the enemy to action'. What he wrote is remarkable for so young an officer not 'regularly bred to artillery' and in a strange land, but he had obviously already considered the advantages of bullocks as well as the scarcity of suitable horses in India. He was obviously making a good impression on Shore and his associates.

Wesley was not so pressed for time during these early months in India as he was later. He did not neglect his military duties; the 33rd was considered a model of efficiency. But he had been running it for more than three years and his system of control required a minimum of his own personal attention. He appears to have played more strenuously than at any other time during his life, if we are to believe what a friend put down in his voluminous diary.[2]

During the spring and summer of 1797 Arthur Wesley was also writing at length to his elder brother. They were nine years apart in age, but still unusually affectionate. At this time each admired the other without reservation. The young Earl of Mornington had been a brilliant scholar at Harrow, Eton and Oxford, and had inherited his father's title along with his debts before his twenty-first birthday. He had risen rapidly in the Tory party and was capable of speaking well and of carrying out political assignments requiring judgment and ability. As has already been mentioned, it was common knowledge that Mornington was likely to be offered either the Governorship of Madras or the Governor-Generalship. A month after he arrived Arthur wrote to advise his brother to accept. There were opportunities in India at this time he thought would ideally suit Richard who could take full advantage of them for the public good and his own.

[1] *Supplementary Despatches*, Vol. I, p. 1.
[2] *Hickey*, IV, 160–1 and 190–1. The amounts of drink consumed in an evening are almost unbelievable. Arthur Wesley was surely a member of the company, but did he take as much as Hickey thought?

On 27 July 1797, after receiving two letters from Mornington written in March (which surely came overland) the younger brother wrote: 'I am convinced that you will retain your health. Nay, it is possible that its general state may be mended. You will have the fairest opportunities of rendering material services to the public, and of doing yourself credit, which, exclusive of other personal considerations, should induce you to come out. I shall be able to give you opinions in person upon the different subjects which you have desired me to consider.' Arthur had already written 'several letters, in which I have delivered opinions upon military and political subjects as they occurred to me'.[1]

Mornington accepted the post of Governor-General and left England (7 November 1797) probably before he received this letter, but those which had preceded it were to the same effect. As soon as Arthur Wesley knew that his brother was on his way out, he planned to write a letter to be delivered to him on his arrival giving 'my opinion of the principal men in this country, as far as I have been able to form it'.[2] The two brothers, in spite of their difference in rank, were to be partners in a joint effort to build up British India.

Arthur Wesley had a large share in fitting out the expedition to Manila but was not in fact offered the command. General St Leger had charge of the Calcutta troops which sailed early in August for Prince of Wales Island (also known as Penang). It consisted of the King's 33rd and a provisional EIC Sepoy regiment of two battalions made up of drafts of picked men from several Bengal battalions. The entire Calcutta force consisted of about 2,200 soldiers. At Penang it was to meet a similar but somewhat stronger force from Madras.[3]

The Manila expedition seems to have been well organized and staffed, but was deficient in other respects, especially in timing and secrecy. August was probably too late in the season to make the attempt. A Danish ship bound for Manila had been allowed to pass out of the river past Fort William.[4] Everyone of importance in Bengal appears to

[1] *Supplementary Despatches*, I, 17.

[2] *Supplementary Despatches*, I, 18.

[3] *Wilson*, II, 300–1, says that 461 men from the King's 12th Foot, 680 from the King's 74th Foot, 438 from the Madras Europeans, 673 Madras Native Infantry, and detachments of both Royal artillery and Madras artillery actually reached Penang, but there were other detachments aboard other Indiamen.

[4] *Supplementary Despatches*, I, 13. This letter from Arthur Wesley to his brother Richard was dated 12 July 1797.

have known about the British preparations and their destination, and Manila was surely alerted.

The King's 33rd was again aboard transports after only six months ashore. They sailed out of the Hoogley – the branch of the Ganges that flows past Fort William and Calcutta – in fine condition but were destined only for a long and boring time on board. The expedition was recalled before it had been gone a month, a decision made by Lord Hobart, Governor of Madras, under the special authority of Sir John Shore. The news from Mysore, still the most powerful single state in India, was such that these fine British units were likely to be required in India. There was also bad news from Europe; Austria had been totally defeated by Bonaparte and had made peace; veteran French armies could now be used elsewhere. The Royal Navy had suffered a serious mutiny which had been put down, but efficiency would be low in many ships for some time. Rebellion in Ireland, so often threatening, seemed actually to be breaking out. Hobart's orders quickly reached Penang, but in the days of sailing ships and prevailing winds the return voyage would be impossible for most East Indiamen before late November.

The voyage from Calcutta and the stay in Penang must have been extremely unpleasant. Enlisted men lived aboard the transports and had limited shore leave. We should note, however, that before the expedition sailed Colonel Wesley calmly insisted on keeping control of all companies of his regiment although they were divided among several East Indiamen. With the assistance of his regimental surgeon he preferred to look after his men both in sickness and in health rather than to follow the established procedure of allowing the captains of the various vessels and their surgeons to have charge of the soldiers in each ship. Even before the first parties went aboard Wesley set up rules designed to keep the 33rd in as good shape as possible. Every man was responsible for his hammock and scrubbed it every two weeks. Every soldier was kept clean by daily bathing and in good physical condition through exercise, a part of which was with dumbbells. Quarters were cramped for all but fumigated regularly and blown out by carefully directing the wind. This programme was supervised by the regular regimental chain of command; officers and NCOs were held responsible for their men. Wesley had seen how badly the old 'every ship for itself' system worked on the voyage out and was profiting by this experience.

Colonel Wesley's Regimental orders, all thirty-six of them, were complete in every detail, including target practice with ball ammunition 'twice a week at least'.[1] Wesley was scrupulously careful not to interfere with the prerogatives of the Company ship commanders, for instance in regard to where and at what hours men could smoke, but totally refused to place a man of the King's 33rd under their orders even in action; Shore hastened to revoke a part of one of his orders which infringed this prerogative.[2]

Wesley realised that there was nothing he could do about sailing winds and cramped quarters. He could see, however, that the three months spent at Penang were not wasted. He had his companies come ashore as if landing for the first time in enemy territory, and drilled them individually and as a battalion. In the days of close-order battles this exercise was of extreme importance. A well-trained unit under competent officers could form in line, go to column, move in any direction and reform into line or square precisely and without straggling even on fairly uneven ground.[3] Wesley rarely missed this drill; he was good at this sort of thing and believed that it promoted discipline and inspired confidence.

Wesley also had his soldiers practise 'dry-firing' until all motion, including even the changing of flints, became automatic. This musketry exercise was at least of equal importance. The colonel also insisted on some additional live firing at targets beyond the sixty rounds per man already expended on the way to Penang. Ammunition was expensive, but the EIC could afford the luxury and the investment would pay dividends in battle. At this stage in his career Wesley knew every man in his regiment by name and face and was familiar with his record. There were only about 680 of them,[4] but none had been with them for less than two years. Most of them remembered vividly how their young colonel had brought them through the wintry hell from the Low Countries to the Ems when other battalions were literally freezing to death. No one, however, was worried about freezing in Penang in the autumn of 1797. The place was only five degrees north of the Equator and when the breeze failed the Indiamen became intolerably hot. At least there was plenty of fresh clean water.

Wesley continued his personal studies and his writing to his elder

[1] *Supplementary Despatches*, I, 19–24.
[2] Ibid., I, 23. Shore said: 'I repeat my regret at an occurrence which appears to have afforded you any uneasiness and add my hope that revocation of that part of the instruction which has been the occasion of it will reach the ships before their departure.'
[3] See Appendix II for the details of this drill.
[4] *Wilson*, II, 300, says 682 on arrival.

brother. During the expedition he produced two more of his tightly reasoned memoranda, 'Memorandum On Pulo Penang' and 'Memorandum On Bengal'; they show an unusual grasp of complicated economic facts.[1] Wesley was developing a standard procedure for the imparting of information to others and the forceful presentation of his own conclusions; he had also discovered that the best way to learn something himself was to write about it.

We should now examine more carefully the reasons for the recall of the expedition. Sir John Shore was perhaps overcautious in allowing Lord Hobart to decide a question like this. Hobart may have been too close to his potential enemy, Tipoo, to use good judgment. But the capture of Manila might have led to tragedy in India. Cornwallis had defeated Tipoo between 1790 and 1792 and considerably reduced his territory. Tipoo became a yet more determined enemy and was trying to the limit of his considerable ability to form an active alliance with France, the strongest military power in Europe and the foremost enemy of Britain throughout the world. The total British strength in the East may not have warranted the dispersion an expedition to Manila would have entailed for the time it would probably have taken. Expeditions of this type often failed owing to poor logistics, unexpected resistance and disease.

Wesley had studied carefully all that was known in Britain about the new French armies as well as having taken a small part in fighting them. A French army could be dispatched direct to India, especially if Tipoo welcomed it at his main port of Mangalore. In the days of sail a naval blockade was at best unpredictable.[2] Hobart and Shore sensed the revival of French influence in Mysore and Hyderabad and correctly anticipated another trial of strength between France and Britain in India. Even though all territory which remained to France after the earlier wars was safely in EIC hands, the French influence in India was now based on their alliances with Native Indian princes. In both Mysore and Hyderabad French-officered infantry, organized, armed and drilled in the European manner, marched under the tricolor and had Cap of Liberty buttons on their uniforms. There was some talk of similar trends among the European-officered units in the Mahratta armies, although the British seem to have figured more importantly there at this time.

[1] *Supplementary Despatches*, I, 24–34 and 34–49.

[2] The Bantry Bay invasion of Ireland had been literally wrecked by a storm off the Irish coast in December 1796 – news of this reached Arthur Wesley before he set out for Penang – but others were to follow. Squadrons could take advantage of the weather to get out of French ports.

A coalition of Indian states under French leadership could be dangerous even without the intervention of French land forces. Hobart probably made the right decision; a secure India was more important than a tenuous grip on Manila and the Philippines.

The King's 33rd and its young colonel arrived back in Calcutta in December 1797. Everything seemed peaceful for the moment, so Arthur Wesley decided to increase his limited personal knowledge of India, especially the places that had been of military importance. He had ridden over the battlefield of Plassey and visited a few similar sites in Bengal, but at that time most British fighting had taken place in the Madras area. He wanted to see those battlefields, campaign areas and places where important sieges had occurred. He had read about the victories and defeats of Lawrence, Clive, Coote, Munro, Baillie and the rest, but reading alone was not enough. He also wanted to get to know something of the people and the terrain of the Madras Presidency. Fortunately, he had an ideal introduction to this area; he and Hobart were still friends from their service in Ireland of several years before.

Wesley quartered the 33rd in Bengal, obtained leave and set out for Madras. He was cordially received by the Governor who talked to him freely. Even though Hobart had now been recalled because of a difference of opinion as to how to treat the new Nabob of Arcot – Hobart was for the farmers and against corruption in politics in spite of an old Cornwallis treaty – he gave his young friend his time and a lot of first-hand information about his Presidency. One gathers that the Governor was exceptionally unselfish. He could hardly have liked Mornington's appointment as Governor-General which he had reasons to expect for himself. But he appears to have given Arthur Wesley all the information he had.

Some of it was depressing. Madras, also known as Fort St George, had a number of entrenched interests. The Governor and his Council, when united, were supposed to be in complete control, but the Presidency had a history of contention. In January 1798 it was in serious financial and other troubles. Madras City was sovereign EIC territory, but the much larger area surrounding it belonged to the Nabob and was only loosely under British control. The Nabob's government had become so bad that the British had partly taken over responsibility, though in a most inefficient manner. The subsidiary treaty[1] by which

---

[1] The term 'subsidiary' had a special meaning in India. An Indian state would pay a subsidy of so much money a month to support an English-officered Sepoy army to protect it against outside or foreign aggression.

the Nabob allied himself to the EIC had led to financial chaos, for the prince had been forced to borrow at exorbitant rates to pay what was due to the Company for its battalions. Some of the lenders of the money were private Englishmen who appear to have profited not only by their high rates of interest, but also because they contrived to increase the amount of the debt. These transactions were most unsavoury and remained matters of contention for years even after the entire debt was taken over by the EIC.

Arthur Wesley left Madras City with a small retinue[1] and spent five weeks examining the terrain and important military details of the Carnatic. He was often accompanied by British officers who had marched and fought in the campaigns and battles he was studying. They visited Cuddalore where Lawrence had won his first action, and Pondicherry where Boscawen had failed but others succeeded. He inspected what was left of the fortress at Arcot where Clive started his rise to military fame in 1751 and visited the battlefield of Covrepauk where that commander won his first victory in the field the next year. He went as far south as Trichinopoly following the complicated moves during the unofficial war between France and Britain when the two countries had backed different claimants to the thrones or *musnuds* of the Carnatic and the Deccan (Hyderabad).

Wesley was particularly interested in the campaigns against Hyder Ali, Sultan of Mysore, and his son Tipoo. Tipoo's armies were now deployed to the west; only six years after his defeat by Cornwallis, British officials at Fort St George judged him to be stronger than the British. He was their most dangerous single enemy in India and the most likely to be active in future. The past fighting against Mysore had included several British victories, but there were defeats as well. Wesley visited Wandewash where Eyre Coote won in 1759 and Porto Novo where he was again victorious twenty-two years later. He studied carefully the tragedy of 10 September 1780 when Colonel Baillie was defeated near Conjeveram. Baillie had 3,720 fighting men, including 86 British officers and 200 European soldiers, but the entire force was destroyed by native armies (with a few Frenchmen in them) under Hyder and Tipoo. A larger British army under Sir Hector Munro was only about two miles away but took counsel of its fears and did not go to Baillie's assistance.

[1] A King's full colonel in India, even a modest one, would undoubtedly have had what appears today to be a large collection of grooms, tentmen, cooks and personal servants, at least twenty in all. Some majors had three times this number. Arthur Wesley also probably had a small military escort, perhaps a dozen EIC Indian cavalry.

More important for what was soon to follow, Arthur Wesley reviewed Cornwallis's recent campaigns against Seringapatam, the capital and principal city of Tipoo's Mysore. During 1790 the fighting had been conducted by Major-General Meadows, but Cornwallis assumed personal command in 1791 and 1792. He advanced from Vellore through the Baramahal and the Eastern Ghauts on to the tableland of south central India and took Bangalore. Using it as a fortified base, he then moved against the capital. In 1791 he failed from want of supplies and had to destroy his siege train within sight of Seringapatam. He returned the following spring, however, and beat Tipoo in the outer fortifications north of his capital so conclusively that a most advantageous treaty was negotiated without his having to storm the actual city. Thus the British got possession of the three parcels of EIC territory around still independent Mysore.

The Baramahal was one of these tracts; it was situated south-west of Madras and contained a long narrow valley with rocky hills on either side extending west and southwest from Vellore. The shortest and easiest route from Madras to Seringapatam was through the Baramahal. Wesley visited the area in March 1797 and talked at length to EIC Lieutenant-Colonel Read, the local military commander, who had built the new road from Vellore through to Ryacotta on the border. Wesley also discussed at length the situation to the west with EIC Captain Macleod, the Collector for the area.[1] In addition to his regular duties Macleod was gathering information from various sources inside Mysore for Hobart and Lieutenant-General George Harris, the Commander-in-Chief of Madras. The Baramahal was flourishing under EIC government and contained several strong fortifications, especially in the ghauts. The term 'ghaut' had a special meaning in India. The entire peninsula of the subcontinent roughly consists of a moderately high central tableland with coastal plains on either side; the borders between these two dissimilar areas are usually long lines of rough hill country which occasionally rise to considerable heights. Both the hills themselves and the passes through them were known as ghauts. The line of the Eastern Ghauts is irregular, especially around the Baramahal, but in general lies a considerable distance inland, usually slightly more than one hundred miles. The Western Ghauts are closer to the coast.

Arthur Wesley discovered another important fact in his riding about:

[1] A 'Collector' was not only in charge of revenue but also had executive and judicial functions.

the passes through rugged hills are seldom the only ways to get through. An agile horse with a good rider can cross almost anywhere. Light infantry can move on either side of most of the well-known passes with only moderate inconvenience. This was and is particularly true in the Baramahal; neither the Ryacotta nor the Kistnagherry passes were really difficult to get around. Wesley realized, however, the importance of possessing the Baramahal, including the regular roadheads from it into Mysore. If a new advance on Seringapatam was necessary, a British army would not have to fight its way through difficult passes and take hill forts commanding them as Meadows and Cornwallis had done. If Read were able to hold his present territory, a British expeditionary force from Madras would start its invasion of Mysore from the edge of the central tableland. Read's and Macleod's units were mostly revenue soldiers, *sebundies*[1] and *peons*[2] under Indian officers, but Read did have one EIC battalion.[3] It was not likely that Tipoo would begin hostilities unless a French army of considerable size actually joined him in Mysore.

Wesley returned to Madras and heard that his brother Richard was on his way. Mornington had been appointed Governor-General on 4 October and left Britain on 7 November 1797. Cornwallis had been sworn in as Governor-General on 1 February, but as his presence in Ireland was required owing to the outbreak of a rebellion – he accepted the dual appointments of Viceroy and C-in-C in May – he could not leave for India. Arthur returned to Calcutta and his regimental duties so as to be to hand when his brother arrived, who might or might not stop at Madras on the way.

Wesley had been in India for only a bit more than a year, but his studies, his personal observations, his travels and his memoranda had given him an unusual comprehension of its problems. His political and military career still lay before him, but he and his regiment were as fully prepared for Indian responsibilities as was reasonably possible. Wesley was ready to help in any way the new Governor-General saw fit. The younger brother could absorb facts, reason logically about them and reach hardheaded, common sense conclusions. He may still have been a nobody in his own opinion, but it is doubtful that many in India who knew him well would have agreed with him.

[1] Irregular Indian soldiers, country militia employed generally in the police and revenue.
[2] Irregular infantry, armed with swords or matchlocks and employed chiefly in the defence of forts and in the collection of revenue.
[3] Read had the 2/4 (second battalion of the fourth regiment) Madras Native Infantry: *Wilson*, II, 309–13.

II

The Wellesley Brothers

Richard Wellesley, second Earl of Mornington and new Governor-General of India, arrived at Madras aboard the frigate HMS *Virginia* on 26 April 1798. Henry Wellesley, Richard's and Arthur's youngest brother, came as the Governor-General's private secretary. Both Richard and Henry had recently changed the spelling of their surname from Wesley to the older form, Wellesley. They went ashore in one of the unique Madras collapsible lighters, and the new Governor-General received for the first time the thundering salute which was his due from the deep-toned iron 18-pounders of Fort St George. Neither Mornington nor India would be the same again; each was to change the other. Mornington brought with him a sense of purpose, perhaps even a sense of destiny, also an extremely active and able intelligence and a power to lead others. He knew a lot about India and what he wanted to accomplish there.

Henry Wellesley was thirteen years younger than Richard and almost four younger than Arthur, but he was far from inexperienced. He had served in the Army, in the Diplomatic Corps and in the Irish Parliament. While he was in India he was a full partner in the undertakings of his two older brothers.

The Wellesleys – Arthur was to change the spelling of his own surname within less than a month – brought to India enthusiasm, national ambition and a spirit of rectitude in public service at complete variance with the poorly concealed and (partly, at least) socially acceptable profiteering of many who served the EIC. Mornington especially was to lead a crusade for education and an attitude of 'sacred trust' towards public service. This concept may be the greatest enduring good to come out of British rule in India.[1]

Mornington had experience and connections at home to support his own abilities. He was a friend of Pitt and Cornwallis, and his time as a member of the Board of Control had kept him in close touch with India. All three Wellesleys had the same quality of exerting themselves to the very limit, first to understand a problem and then to solve it.

It may be well to mention a personal irregularity that seems to have hindered Mornington's career more than once. He flaunted the moral conventions of the times when on 29 November 1794 he married Mademoiselle Hyacinthe Gabrielle Roland with whom he had been living for nine years. There were already five children, but by British law of the time all remained illegitimate.[2]

Mornington's voyage out to India had been broken by three weeks at the Cape of Good Hope where he was fortunate in meeting several men who knew India first-hand. Lord Hobart, Arthur Wellesley's friend and until recently Governor of Madras, had stopped off on his way home. Lord Macartney, Governor of the Cape, was himself a former Governor of Madras. Major-General David Baird had been a captain in Baillie's commnad in 1780 and was desperately wounded in the fight near Conjeveram. Taken prisoner more dead than alive, he had somehow recovered but remained in chains in Tipoo's dungeon at Seringapatam for three and a half years.[3] Baird knew India, although his ideas about the Indians were not those of the Wellesleys. He returned to India with Mornington and Henry Wellesley. EIC Lieutenant-Colonel William Kirkpatrick was on leave at the Cape for his health. He had been British Resident at Hyderabad and also served in the Mahratta States. Resident meant an official position; a resident not only conducted political negotiations with all the weight of British power behind him, but also gave general directions to EIC units in his area even though junior to some officers serving in them. Mornington

---

[1] *Misra*, 378, writes, 'Among the contributions of British rule in India the creation of the Indian Civil Service is one of the most remarkable.' In the pages immediately following this modern Indian historian then sketches Richard's contribution in this area.

[2] *Lady Longford*, 31, mentions another illegitimate son by another mistress. Mornington carried into middle age desires normally associated with youth.

[3] When Baird's mother heard that these prisoners were chained in couples, she is supposed to have said, 'I pity the man who is chained to Ma Davie!' (which became his probably posthumous nickname). Baird was large and unusually powerful.

was favourably impressed by Kirkpatrick and made him his military secretary.[1]

Most Governors and Governor-Generals who had not been out to India needed a kind of running-in period, but not Mornington. He had been not only a careful student, but a good listener. While at the Cape he even took advantage of his rank to open and carefully read a packet of the dispatches which arrived en route from Fort William to London. His first dispatch to Dundas was written from here; it was based mostly on information recently received and gave 'his own views of the course of policy which it was advisable to pursue'.[2] The Madras stopover was valuable because the two Wellesleys saw India for the first time and met most of the men of that Presidency with whom they would work in the years ahead, especially Lieutenant-General George Harris, C-in-C of Madras and acting Governor, Josiah Webbe who was secretary of the Council, Barry Close, Cockburn and John Malcolm,[3] all of whom we will meet again. Mornington also had his first personal confrontation with an Indian prince; it must have been quite a surprise. He was unable to persuade the Nabob of Arcot to mend his ways, although his actual reception of the Wellesleys at court could not have been more gracious and friendly. The acts of dissimulation and flattery were more advanced in the East than in Europe.

Mornington and Henry Wellesley sailed up the Hoogley on 17 May 1798 and anchored off Fort William as their brother had done more than a year before. Again the long iron 18-pounders, the finest artillery of the age, thundered out their welcome. The 'Governor-General of Fort William in India' began his control of British India the next day. His power was equal to that of a Roman Proconsul, a term later often associated with Mornington. The Governor-General had the legal right to overrule his entire council if he saw fit. He could do as he pleased with the EIC's vast wealth and had as much power in India as any European monarch.

The three brothers were together for the first time in many months; they had a great deal to say to each other personally and about their

---

[1] There were two Kirkpatrick brothers, both Residents at Hyderabad at different times. William was the elder and more conventional. James Achilles, an EIC captain in 1798, was one of the few Englishmen of position in India in his era who 'went native', but he appears to have done a reasonably effective job in spite of it.

[2] *Marshman*, II, 72, who adds, 'This letter afforded the clearest evidence of his [Richard's] extraordinary genius for government.'

[3] John Malcolm was not only able, but was to become the good, sincere and lifelong friend of all the Wellesleys in India, especially Arthur's.

public efforts. They were thirty-eight, twenty-nine and twenty-five years old respectively, but still bound to each other by strong ties of affection as well as common ideals and interests. Richard and Henry told Arthur the latest news from Europe, especially of France and her obvious worldwide ambitions now that resistance to her armies on the continent of Europe had crumbled. They did not yet know of Bonaparte's expedition to Egypt which started at this time – Toulon left 19 May and Malta taken 10 June 1798 – nor of his report to the Directorate (February 1798) that a cross-Channel invasion was then impractical and of his suggestion that France should strike at the sources of British power by occupying Egypt and threatening India.[1] All three of them realized, however, that France was likely to have such plans.

Arthur Wellesley told his brother what he had learned in India, especially his estimate of the British with whom he had come in personal contact. There were some men of unusual ability at Fort William; Sir Alured Clarke, military C-in-C of all British India and acting Governor-General between Shore's departure and Mornington's arrival, was surely one of these. But there were others of whom Arthur Wellesley could not approve. He may have mentioned the military commanders who were too old and set in their alcoholic ways to be efficient. He undoubtedly also named men with small selfish interests. The strict sense of public trust and personal rectitude which all three Wellesleys had was often lacking in those who had served the EIC in the past. A man could amass a large fortune, more than 100,000 pounds in some cases, in as little as ten years. Even though it was possible for an individual serving the Company to have several jobs and legitimately receive several salaries at the same time, the accumulation of large amounts of capital appears to have been possible only through illegal personal trade or by accepting presents from Indians which were actually bribes. The latter practice was neither illegal nor contrary to the usual code of proper behaviour at that time, but it was anathema to the Wellesleys.

The Wellesley brothers also brought to India extreme national ambition. Clive was an empire builder almost by accident; Warren Hastings fought for continued existence; even Cornwallis acted defensively. Mornington may have come out with a master plan for expansion in the back of his mind.

There are two aspects to the Wellesleys' ambition for India that must be understood in order to appreciate what is to follow. They

[1] This recommendation was based on the superiority of Britain at sea.

were as much empire builders as Clive and just as patriotic for Britain, but they were also prepared to work unselfishly for the people of India. Their words 'service to the public' meant not only service to the public at home, but also to the native population of India. There was no question in their minds, however, that Indians were better off under British rule than in any other condition. The Wellesleys wanted to improve the lot of Indians by bringing them good government, settled conditions and the opportunity to prosper by individual effort in agriculture, industry, commerce and public service. This aim recurs throughout the writings of Mornington and Arthur Wellesley.

Before the coming of Europeans about 1600 the vast Peninsula of India and the country to the north had been in an almost continuous state of chaos for centuries. Dynasties came and went but did not really help the people. Capricious personal power rather than justice under law and responsible control had been nearly universal. Turmoil and robbery were so frequent that they were considered normal. Even modern Indian scholars agree, although they rightly point out that feudal Europe was not exactly tranquil.

At first the arrival of Europeans in India changed the pattern of life only slightly if at all. It was not unusual to combine a little robbery with mercantile operations; profit was surely the EIC's original aim. The Wellesleys knew about this; periods of violence accompanied by extortion, robbery and murder of the weak exceeded those of local tranquillity even during the last two hundred years; the British had not yet made a real effort to improve India. These conditions existed not only at governmental but at individual level as well. Armed robbery and murder were ways of life followed by tens of thousands of Indians for generations through a kind of hereditary caste system.[1] Child murder and the burning of widows with their deceased husbands were common.[2]

There was a magnificent opportunity to fulfil for the public good – both British and Indian – a challenge the Wellesleys could never refuse. The area then known as India exceeded half of Europe in size. It contained about 140 million people; the total population of the United Kingdom in 1801 was 11,944,000. Even more remarkable, there were less than 4,000 Britons in India under the Wellesleys, including every-

[1] Thugs and Dacoits appear to have prospered for centuries, not as individual outlaws but rather as societies with some status.
[2] A baby of either sex born to a woman long childless was often sacrificed. Female children were frequently destroyed for economic reasons.

one except enlisted soldiers and sailors. We should remember, however, that British domination of the vast subcontinent was far from established. When Cornwallis went home in September 1793, everything had seemed in order, but Sir John Shore had managed to lose prestige, an ever important quality in the East. Tipoo was more dangerous than ever; the Mahrattas and the Nizam of Hyderabad had been British allies, but were no better than neutral now and the French influence in their armies was strong.

The Mahrattas had defeated the armies of the Nizam in 1795; Hyderabad had asked for British assistance which the country had every right to expect under a subsidiary treaty in which the EIC and the British Government had guaranteed the Nizam's territory against foreign aggression.[1] Hyderabad paid a monthly subsidy to the EIC to support two regular battalions of sepoys under British officers, with complete assigned artillery handled by European gunners. Surely the Nizam deserved to use these units against the Mahrattas, but Shore refused their services. The Mahrattas won at Kardla, temporarily took half the Nizam's territory and ran his government. The situation at Hyderabad was made worse by the fact that a French soldier of fortune, Monsieur or Colonel Raymond, had gradually built up in the Nizam's service a force of regular battalions officered in part by French professional soldiers and organized in the European way. These units of the Nizam's army fought reasonably well at Kardla, even though at a considerable disadvantage because they were opposed by similar, older and predominantly British-officered units in the service of the Mahrattas. It was known in May 1798 that Raymond's units were marching under tricolor flags and using Cap of Liberty buttons.

Mornington's first major objective was to restore the British position at Hyderabad. In fact, we may assume that the rough plan was already made before the Governor-General came ashore at Calcutta. The elder Kirkpatrick had an intimate knowledge of everything that had gone on in Hyderabad. The Nizam was getting old and had not reacted as strongly as he might have done against Shore's decision not to help him. The younger Kirkpatrick was still Resident in his capital and kept at least a part of his friendship.

The Nizam was in arrears in the monthly payments of 57,713 rupees for the upkeep of his two EIC battalions, but he certainly did not want to give them up. He knew more of the world than most Indians of his

[1] The word foreign meant at that time a force from outside Hyderabad, not outside India.

time. Cornwallis had been his friend; he may have understood Sir John Shore and his decision better than Shore's own subordinates. The elder Kirkpatrick wrote him at length in his own language and explained that the new Governor-General was going to be another Cornwallis, not another Shore. A favourable reply came back. Although the Nizam still had in his service twenty-three French-officered regular battalions, nearly 16,000 men, he did not trust them. Raymond had commanded this infantry for several years, but died in the spring of 1798. A Fleming called Piron – who should not be confused with the Frenchman Perron who served Scindia – took his place. The units appear not to have been so satisfactory under their new commander.

Mornington ordered Captain James Kirkpatrick to negotiate a new treaty with Hyderabad and sent him a rough draft, undoubtedly drawn in part by Colonel William Kirkpatrick. James Kirkpatrick assisted by Captain John Malcolm and Lieutenant-Colonel Dalrymple, the commander of the two EIC battalions, convinced the Nizam of the advantages of a renewed alliance with Britain, even though he would have to give up his French-officered units. He realized that these Frenchmen were no more than a group of independent adventurers with nothing behind them save vague republican principles that were unlikely to appeal to an Eastern potentate. The EIC might change from administration to administration, but it was obviously and continuously powerful in India. A comparison between the EIC battalions complete with artillery and Piron's units may also have influenced the Nizam. Although there were only two EIC battalions in Hyderabad, they were larger, better armed, better organized, better trained, and better disciplined. They contained more European officers by nearly ten to one.[1]

Even more important, the Nizam and most of his government were Muslims. The Mahrattas who had already taken half of Hyderabad (much of it not yet delivered) were Hindoos; they might decide to take over the rest of his country, and a British alliance was almost sure to prevent this. Conceivably, it might even prevent the Nizam from having to give up in fact what he had already ceded by treaty. Furthermore, the Nizam may have had more than a suspicion that Piron's French-officered units would not again fight against similar battalions in the Mahratta armies. The French on both sides might decide to unite with

[1] See Appendix II on 'Organization and Tactics' which includes details of these Regular Battalions in the service of Indian rulers.

24

his enemies. The Nizam was in desperate need of powerful friends not already closely associated with the Mahrattas.

Mornington's treaty was signed at Hyderabad on 1 September 1798 and he ratified the final draft three weeks later. The number of EIC battalions in the subsidiary force was to be six rather than two; the monthly subsidy was increased to 210,425 rupees. All Frenchmen in the Nizam's pay were to be discharged and delivered over to the British as soon as the four additional British battalions arrived.

Long before the treaty was signed, Mornington had ordered General Harris to get ready a force of four full-strength EIC battalions under a reliable officer and march them to Guntoor close to the Hyderabad border.[1] Though Harris was not only Madras C-in-C but also acting Governor – the new Governor was Lord Clive, the son of the great Clive, who did not arrive until 21 August – he had trouble with the Council over this matter. He had to pledge his personal funds to get the necessary orders issued. The Guntoor force was commanded by Lieutenant-Colonel George Roberts, Dalrymple's half-brother,[2] who had orders to be ready to move on Hyderabad City as soon as word reached him from Fort William. He began his march from Guntoor on 10 October and arrived at Hyderabad City on the 20th. All six British battalions were now concentrated at the Nizam's capital.

As often happened when an Indian prince was finally faced with carrying out an unpleasant task, the Nizam showed signs of weakening; he did not want to disband his French-officered units immediately. But Kirkpatrick, Roberts, Dalrymple and Malcolm did not let him go back on his bargain. They took advantage of some discontent in these battalions to take them over completely without killing a man on 22 October 1798.[3] The British Resident became supreme in the *durbar* (council or government) of the Nizam. Malcolm was able to reconstitute some Indian personnel from French regular battalions under British officers and NCOs from the EIC battalions and added them to the Nizam's army. A total of about a hundred French were sent home in one of the EIC Indiamen. Hyderabad was again solidly a British ally by the end of October.

[1] This order was dated 15 July 1798; the situation at Madras is discussed at length in *Harris*, 185–7 and 193–5.

[2] *Harris*, 192.

[3] Malcolm's fine account of this, quoted in *Harris*, 229–37, says that 16,000 men complete with artillery and an arsenal were taken and disarmed in six hours. He himself commanded 2,000 of the Nizam's cavalry which cooperated with Roberts and Dalrymple. Meer Allum, the Nizam's principal minister and perhaps his son, was pro-British and assisted in this complicated but entirely successful operation.

The restoration of the British position at Hyderabad was not the only or even the most important interest of the Wellesley brothers in Calcutta in the summer of 1798. A more serious situation existed in Mysore. In 1792 Cornwallis had allowed Tipoo, the Muslim ruler of this predominantly Hindoo State, to survive, partly because a total victory would have cost more British casualties and partly because of pressure from home not to increase territorial responsibility. The partial defeat had not served Tipoo as a warning. He hated the British more than ever and wanted to drive them from India, and appears to have spent most of his life planning, or rather scheming, for such a result.

After 1792 Tipoo realized that he could not do the job alone or with Indian allies only. Both Tipoo and the Wellesleys understood that in 1798 the most dangerous enemy for British India was not any Indian prince, or even a combination of them, but France. No British politician realized more fully than Mornington the strength of the reconstituted French nation under the Directory then in power, or the young General Bonaparte's potentialities for mischief. The spiritual rejuvenation of France was based on radical principles of which the Wellesley brothers did not approve, but the new order increased French resources of men and material and also made them controllable. The new leaders of France still smarted at the memory of the French defeat in India; some at least wanted to use their new strength to get back what they had lost. As we have seen, one of these was Bonaparte.

At Fort William, only twenty-two days after his arrival, Mornington read a Calcutta newspaper account of a proclamation by Governor Malartic of French Mauritius[1] announcing an alliance between Tipoo and France. French troops were to be sent to Mangalore. Additional volunteers were solicited. A few days later an actual copy of the proclamation was received by way of the Cape of Good Hope. An American sea captain who had just come from the French island told the Wellesleys of having seen Tipoo's ambassadors entertained with all honours. The French in Mauritius were obviously threatening to use Mysore as a beachhead for an attack on British India. The trouble with this conclusion was that it was not practical. Arthur Wellesley pointed out that France had no land forces of any consequence at Mauritius or elsewhere in the East at that time. Even if Malartic

[1] This island was situated 400 miles east of Madagascar and also had the name of Ile de France. It was the only French naval base worthy of the name between the Cape of Good Hope and Cape Horn.

expected reinforcements, why proclaim this? His announcement was made long before he could have known about French plans for the invasion of Egypt. The whole thing was and still is inexplicable. The only explanation that appears to be logical is that he was trying to get Tipoo involved in a war with Britain which he hoped would be advantageous to France some day.

The Wellesleys decided to ignore the hostile intentions of Tipoo for the time being. The Governor-General wrote a friendly letter to Tipoo on 14 June, five days after first receiving the news of Malartic's proclamation, and even consented to a readjustment of the Malabar border in Tipoo's favour. The danger was obvious, but nothing could be gained by a premature rupture or a policy that would cause Tipoo to begin the fight before the British were ready. The three Wellesleys realized the precarious condition of the Madras Presidency at that time.

At this stage of his Indian career, Mornington welcomed information and tolerated opposition, particularly from his brothers. The Governor-General moved most cautiously in Madras which was so close to Mysore, but all troops in that area were to be prepared for active service and redeployed into positions from which an advance on Seringapatam by way of the Baramahal would be most easily commenced. The Governor-General ordered Harris to begin actual preparations for war on 16 July 1798. He included in this dispatch: 'The growth of a French party in the councils and armies of the Native princes attracted my attention before I left England.' He was thoroughly aware of the danger of the alliance between France and Tipoo if the French did somehow manage to transport an army to India. His conciliatory policy towards Tipoo was to cover British preparations, but at the same time the Wellesleys surely did not want a war if it could be avoided without sacrificing safety. Tipoo need not be defeated, if he would give acceptable guarantees against active military cooperation with the French, but the time to ask for these had not yet come.

This dual course of 'get ready to fight, but keep Tipoo from attacking first' appears now to be the only logical one, but there were strong opinions against it in the Madras Presidency at that time. Josiah Webbe,[1]

---

[1] Webbe was to become one of the inner circle of Mornington's bright young men. Both Mornington and Arthur Wellesley probably to some extent resented Webbe's strongly expressed opinions at the time, but soon recognized both his sincerity and his ability. Long afterwards a guest at Strathfield Saye was to ask the old Duke about a small picture of Webbe. 'One of the most able and honest men I ever knew!' *Brett-James*, 63–4.

who was Secretary of the Madras Council and an able and honest man, wrote a memorandum against it which Mornington received through General Harris. Webbe thought a Cornwallis-type campaign would not succeed; it would cost a lot of money which the Presidency did not have, and he feared that preliminary preparations might cause Tipoo to attack.

Harris did not share Webbe's pessimism, although he was not without some doubts. He ran the Presidency and its army until the younger Clive, the new Governor who arrived on 21 August 1798, learned his job, a process that took several weeks. Harris not only concentrated his units in positions where they could move easily towards Tipoo's capital but also had them spread out so as to oppose an advance by the enemy along the most probable routes. He was able to write to the Governor-General on 7 August that his preliminary redeployment about Wallajabad was complete; his other preparations were proceeding as well as such matters ever did in India. Delays were inherent in the East and in the committee system used by some departments of the EIC, especially the Military Board of Madras. The most important single shift of a British force in India occurred when the Governor-General sent his brother Arthur and the King's 33rd from Bengal to Madras to reinforce Harris and also to get a sort of personal representative in the Madras Presidency.[1]

Colonel Wellesley and his regiment went aboard transports again on 16 August; they had spent more than half their time travelling during the preceding two and a half years. This journey was to be the shortest but most unfortunate of their voyages. The Indiaman in which Arthur Wellesley and about half his regiment sailed, the *Fitz William*, ran on a shoal outside the mouth of the Hoogley and was saved from going to pieces by the physical strength of soldiers who pulled her off. A thousand bags of saltpetre had to be thrown overboard, but the voyage was continued, though the pumps had to be manned for long periods each day. Twenty-five days were required for what could often be accomplished in less than five. Everyone aboard, including the colonel, had dysentery from bad water taken aboard in barrels at Calcutta. 'Fifteen of the finest men we have' died of it.

The King's 33rd went ashore through the surf at Fort St George

[1] Mornington wrote a magnificent briefing letter to Clive on 29 July outlining diplomatically the problems the new Governor would have and giving his estimates of the men Clive would have under him. Mornington included in his communication the wish that Clive would allow 'my brother, Colonel Wellesley, to state my opinions with respect to the defence of the Carnatic': *Harris*, 500–1.

in Madras on 13 September 1799. This experience was always memorable; all the diaries dealing with Madras describe it, some vividly and in detail. There was at that time no harbour nor any breakwater. Ships were unloaded from an open anchorage to an equally open beach. The waves coming in from the Bay of Bengal created a surf that was practically continuous for months on end. Only special local boats could operate in it. These boats were made of timber sufficiently buoyant for the entire vessel to float without being watertight. The relatively short and wide raft-like vessels often came down so hard on the sand that they were momentarily forced out of shape but came back to form, because they were held together by resilient rope. Their crew sprang overboard and carried the vessel, including its cargo, up the beach with the next wave. Accidents involving loss of property and sometimes loss of life were common.

In September 1798 Arthur Wellesley found the situation at Fort St George quite different from what it had been only five months before when he left. The second Lord Clive was in residence, but Harris, that strong, reliable, God-fearing Scot, was still running both the Madras army and the Government.

George Harris was born in Kent, but of Scottish parents, in 1746. He went to the then new military academy at Woolwich and earned an artillery commission, but transferred to the infantry in 1762. He began as an ensign in the 5th Foot and served with honour in the American War of Independence, the West Indies and in India.[1] He was second in command to General Meadows in the resounding victory at Vigie in St Lucia (West Indies) on 18 December 1788 when 1,300 British beat 12,000 French. He had come out to India two years later as lieutenant-colonel of the King's 76th Foot, one of the four new regiments raised especially for India.

Harris had confidence in the valour of British soldiers, but had seen a good deal of it wasted by inefficiency, poor organization and a tendency to 'tell George to do' some task and then not make sure that George did it or even understood what he was supposed to do. He mistrusted grand strategy because he had seen too many complicated plans flounder through inefficiency, mainly in logistics.

Harris and Arthur Wellesley already knew each other, of course, but they quickly became much better acquainted. There is some reason

---

[1] He was badly wounded at Bunker Hill and trepanned, a crude operation at that time. Some writers have said that he had a gold plate in his skull, but his own memoirs, quoted by Lushington, seem to refute this.

to believe that they were not at first attracted to each other, but both were too good at soldiering to allow this to affect their relationship. Wellesley remained in Fort St George for more than a month.[1] The military situation was still critical; the Madras army was being re-organized and re-equipped, but it was not yet ready for combat. The King's 33rd formed a central reserve of extreme importance if Tipoo should forestall a British movement. Harris soon appreciated Wellesley's unusual talents and took advantage of them and of his special know-ledge.

There was also an important political problem to deal with. The new Governor of Madras had to be converted to the Wellesleys' point of view. The younger Clive appears to have thought the Governor-General's preparations for war against Tipoo in the event that all else failed were offensive in nature. Arthur Wellesley had the job of convincing him otherwise. Colonel Wellesley saw Lord Clive almost daily, sometimes for several hours at a stretch. The intercourse was not at first as smooth as it might have been; Edward Clive was then forty-five and had been in politics for a quarter of a century, but at the time of his arrival at Madras he was not accustomed to considering questions of large importance. He was certainly not as brilliant as his father. Wellesley wrote to his brothers soon after the two met: 'He is a mild moderate man, remarkably reserved, having a bad delivery, and apparently a heavy understanding. I doubt whether he is as dull as he appears, or as people think he is.'[2]

Clive and Wellesley became more intimate with their daily meetings and began to cooperate more efficiently. Slightly more than a month after the above comment, Wellesley wrote much more favourably. 'Lord C. opens his mind to me freely upon all subjects. I give him my opinion, and talk as I would to M. [Mornington]. The truth is, he does not want talents, but he is very diffident of himself. Now that he has begun to find out that he has no difficulty in transacting the business of Government, he improves daily, takes more upon himself, and will very shortly have less need for the opinions and abilities of those who have long done the business of the country. A violent or harsh letter from Fort William would spoil all.'[3] Clive was learning to think for himself, but perhaps along Wellesley lines.[4]

[1] If he ever actually lived in the house now called the 'Wellesley House' in Fort William, it would have been at this time. I believe it more likely that Mornington used it and gave his name to it, although the modern guidebook definitely states that it was Arthur Wellesley. Labels of this sort in India are frequently inexact.

[2] *Supplementary Despatches*, I, 87.   [3] *Supplementary Despatches*, I, 109.

This friendly intercourse between a young colonel, a lieutenant-general and local C-in-C and a peer who was also Governor of the Presidency must be considered most unusual. Though men now seldom rise to be full colonels in their twenties they practically never speak as equals to men so far above them. But Arthur Wellesley appears to have taken his position as a matter of course. Some who have read and written about this situation have assumed that he owed such an advantage to his brother being the Governor-General; after all, both Clive and Harris must gain from a close contact with a well-informed brother of the Governor-General. This reasoning seems, however, to be faulty. Sir John Shore had reposed as much confidence in Arthur Wellesley as Mornington did; Shore may even have been more receptive of ideas from Arthur Wellesley than Mornington was. Mornington, on the other hand, was too anxious to succeed to use anyone but the best man he had; furthermore, Arthur Wellesley had to prove his value not only to his brother, but also to Clive and Harris. He appears to have done this completely and reasonably quickly.

While Arthur Wellesley was in Madras, he discussed Webbe's unfavourable memorandum about preparations for war against Tipoo with Webbe himself. Without the least rancour he answered Webbe's memorandum with one of his own.[1] The two papers are both good and in many respects agree. Essentially, Wellesley admits the difficulties that Cornwallis, Meadows and others had in operating inland. It had taken Cornwallis two and a half years to beat Mysore with greater resources than the British had in 1798. Wellesley went on to show, however, how the difficulties could be overcome. In this and in another paper written about the same time he laid the foundation of a plan to conquer Mysore more quickly, more completely and with a smaller force than was used in 1790–92.[2]

We should now briefly retrace our steps to Calcutta and the beginning of the summer of 1798 when the Wellesley brothers were considering Richard's plans for British India. We have already reviewed the Hyderabad situation, the French pressure and the coming confronta-

---

[1] 'Remarks upon Mr Josiah Webbe's Memorandum' written 22 October 1798 and found in *Supplementary Despatches*, I, 113–17.

[2] 'Reflections upon the Plan for Having the Army . . . in a State of Preparation' written 26 October 1798 and found in *Supplementary Despatches*, I, 119–25.

---

[4] Wellesley's coaching of Clive led to a five-hour conference in which he persuaded the Governor that Mornington did not want a war with Tipoo. *Lady Longford*, 56, remarks, 'If Clive's understanding had been lighter, Arthur might have taken even longer.'

tion with Tipoo. It is necessary to consider the Mahratta Confederation also. This Hindoo people, originally from western India, had unusual spirit and the brigandage by which many earned their living made them excellent light cavalry. About 1670 an exceptionally able chief named Sevajee temporarily united them, and this group of tribes, although subordinate to Mogul Delhi, continued a kind of loose national existence. By the 1790s they were ruled by five great and many lesser chiefs who fought more often among themselves than together against an outside power; they had been briefly united in 1795 against the Nizam of Hyderabad, but fell out shortly afterwards. The Mahrattas could assemble by far the largest military force in India and undoubtedly resented the new and stronger alliance between the EIC and the Nizam, especially as much of the territory given by Hyderabad to the Mahrattas in 1795 had never actually been surrendered. Presumably they would not like to see the Wellesleys defeat Tipoo.

The Governor-General found at least a temporary counterweight for the Mahrattas in Zemaun Shah and his Afghans who were threatening north-western India. The Afghans, from the high country far north of the Indian Peninsula, were the hereditary enemies of the Mahrattas.[1] Zemaun Shah had already briefly invaded northern India and was expected to do so again. He and his courageous soldiers were also dangerous to the British. The Governor-General negotiated with the Peshwa who was supposed to be the overlord in the Mahratta Confederation and obtained a kind of conditional promise of aid against Tipoo if war should occur. The Wellesleys were convinced that the Mahrattas would remain no worse than neutral for the immediate future. The British Residents at the Mahratta *durbars* wrote that all the Mahrattas were reasonably friendly and more interested in their internal problems than in fighting the British.

There remained the minor problem of Tanjore, an isolated Mahratta State in the extreme south of India. The Governor-General solved it quickly by putting one of the two principal claimants to the title of rajah on the throne, complete with a treaty and a subsidiary EIC force to back up the British Resident.

[1] Ahmed Shah had commanded an army of Afghans and Rohillas which decisively defeated the Mahrattas at the battle of Paniput on 7 January 1761. The Mahrattas are said to have lost as many as 200,000 men, including camp followers.

III

The First Action

Henry Harvey Ashton was a few months older than Arthur Wellesley and a few days senior in the grade of full colonel. Ashton was in command of the King's 12th Foot as Wellesley was of the 33rd. Both regiments came out to India at the same time; they broke their voyages to India at the Cape where they stayed together. The young colonels were friends even before leaving England and saw a good deal of each other in Africa, but Ashton and the 12th went to Madras while Wellesley and the 33rd continued on to Calcutta.

When Wellesley came ashore at Fort St George in September 1798 he joined Ashton and EIC Lieutenant-Colonel Barry Close who were hard at work for Harris getting the army redeployed, re-equipped and ready to advance against Tipoo if necessary. Harris quite rightly did not burden himself with the detailed implementation of the Governor-General's orders. Close had been Cornwallis's Deputy Adjutant General in 1891–92 and was Harris's adjutant general and acting chief of staff. He was good at this type of work and knew as much of Indian languages, customs and people as any man in India. Like most EIC officers of his rank he had been in India for more than a quarter of a century;[1] unlike most of his compatriots he had spent much of his free time in study and investigation. He was able both in military matters and in political negotiations.

Ashton, many years Close's junior, was also unusual. He was a King's officer of the best type, wealthy and socially popular even with the Prince of Wales and good at his profession. He had the somewhat

---

[1] Close came out as a cadet in 1771; his first commission in the Madras Army (Infantry) was dated 3 September 1773: *Dodwell and Miles*, Madras 28–9. His birth date is not given in the short *D.N.B.* sketch, but it was probably about 1756.

nebulous quality which Wellesley called 'respectability' and he must have added stature to Harris's small staff. While Wellesley, Ashton and Close did staff work, both the King's 12th and the King's 33rd were taken over by their next senior officers. The 12th was already inland at Arnee towards the Baramahal where Major Picton[1] was in command. The 33rd was closer to Madras, at Wallajabad, with Colonel Sherbrooke in charge.

At this time a relatively trifling argument occurred in the 12th between a Lieutenant Hartley and a Major Allen about charges for certain equipment that Hartley said he had not received. While still at Fort St George Ashton received a letter from Hartley about the issue. He replied to Hartley and wrote to Picton to handle the matter which did not then seem important. Ashton probably forgot it, especially as he was ordered forward in November to take command of the concentration of British forces being assembled at Arcot, Vellore and Arnee. Then suddenly the Hartley–Allen contention flared up again in a slightly different form. Ashton had not been as diplomatic as he might have been in his dealing with Picton.[2] We should remember how strict the gentleman's code of behaviour was at that time. An officer could not accept what he considered a severe personal slight even from his commander. Ashton appears to have been generous and kind, but he had an unusual ability to get into duels and even street fights; he inspired strong likes and dislikes and perhaps considerable jealousy. Picton did feel that his honour was involved and challenged Ashton to a duel. The colonel could have refused without loss of honour. He was Picton's commanding officer; the quarrel was obviously about official business. However, Ashton was not that sort of man. He gave Picton an opportunity to kill him, but the major's pistol misfired. Ashton then fired into the air; both firebrands were satisfied and shook hands. The encounter occurred on the morning of 16 December[3] and

---

[1] Major John Picton was the elder brother of Sir Thomas Picton, also originally in the King's 12th Foot. The brothers seem to have been much alike in temperament. The latter was to distinguish himself under Wellington in the Peninsula and die at the head of his division at Waterloo.

[2] *Elers*, 81, says that Ashton showed Arthur Wellesley his orders in this connection and asked his advice. Wellesley said, 'Don't issue them that way!' But Ashton went ahead as he planned.

[3] For the date I have followed Wellesley's letter to Mr Greenwood and his 'Memorandum on the Duel and Death of Colonel Ashton', *Supplementary Despatches*, I, 160–5, rather than Ashton's letter 'dictated to my secretary while dressing for dinner' which would place it two days earlier. Ashton was writing between the time he finally accepted the challenge and the duel with Picton.

would probably have been forgotten if nothing else had occurred.

After the duel, Ashton and Allen spent an hour and a half together, at first reasonably amicably. But their moods became less conciliatory; the two men exchanged harsh words. Again Ashton could have refused the duel with honour, but again he would not. He fought Allen only after offering him as much of an apology as was possible in those days for a man of Ashton's temperament.[1] Allen fired first, and this time the colonel was hit in the side. Ashton refused to kill Allen – he could easily have done so, for he was a superb shot, and the range was short – and again fired in the air. News of the duel and of Ashton's severe wound – said to be through the liver – arrived in Fort St George late on the 17th.

Lord Clive and General Harris agreed that someone other than the next senior officer, who appears to have been Picton, must be sent to take over Ashton's command at Arnee, Arcot and Vellore. Arthur Wellesley was the man for the job and was under orders to go within the hour. He left on horseback almost immediately and alone. The road was good and the route well-known to him. He rode all night and arrived at Arnee on the morning of the 18th. Ashton was pale and obviously seriously injured but calm and rational. At first everyone hoped that he would recover. Wellesley saw him every day; all that medical science could then do was done, but to no avail. As the end approached – peritonitis almost surely – both men were visibly moved. What a completely wasteful way to die! Ashton gave Wellesley his Arab horse Diomed, perhaps the finest charger in India. On 23 December 1798 the colonel of the King's 12th breathed his last, the victim of a stupid system of honour and the mutual bad temper of officers far from home in a wretched climate and often under the influence of alcohol.

We will briefly leave Wellesley with his first extensive military command and have a look at the larger developments. The Governor-General had Hyderabad in order; his other Indian problems were safely on the way to solutions, or at least sufficiently patched up not to be pressing at the moment. But the Governor-General and Tipoo were on collision courses, and war was probably inevitable. The Wellesleys thought they were honestly trying to avoid an armed conflict, but this may have only meant that British diplomacy was being exerted to get the ruler of Mysore to conform to British wishes without

[1] The stupid affair was based on Ashton having said in a private communication to Hartley that Allen had behaved 'illiberally' and apparently on too much alcohol.

a fight. The Wellesleys wanted Tipoo specifically to send away all his French advisers, receive a British Resident and perhaps give up his sea-coast.[1]

During the early autumn of 1798 the Governor-General continued to deal with Tipoo as if he did not know of the Muslim ruler's intentions with regard to the French and of his hatred of the British.[2] The whole situation became acute, however, on 18 October 1798 when the Governor-General and his brother Henry learned of Bonaparte's invasion of Egypt. Full and complete details of Nelson's great victory at the Nile arrived on 30 October. Although this magnificent action crippled the French navy in the Mediterranean, it had no immediate influence further east. There was no way for even a rowing boat to get across the Suez isthmus at that time. It was obviously possible for Bonaparte and part of his army to sail down the Red Sea and land at Mangalore using either local shipping or French men-of-war and privateers from Mauritius. Bonaparte did consider such a move, but realized that he was likely to find most of the British Far East naval strength off the Mysore sea-coast. Actually Admiral Ranier was there with ships-of-line and frigates for months.

The Governor-General began to lose patience with Mysore. He had heard of Tipoo's rather stupid adoption of French republican principles. The French at his capital now called him Citizen Tipoo, they had planted a Tree of Liberty and were holding radical meetings. On 8 November the Governor-General took a sterner tone and wrote: 'It is impossible that you should suppose me to be ignorant of the intercourse which subsists between you and the French, whom you know to be the inveterate enemies of the Company, and to be now engaged in an unjust war with the British nation. You cannot imagine me to be indifferent to the transactions which have passed between you and the enemies of my country; nor does it appear necessary, or proper, that

[1] Arthur to Henry Wellesley, 2 January 1799, *Supplementary Despatches*, I, 158, felt that the giving up of sea-coast was impractical without a war and unnecessary. He never seems to have taken a French seaborne invasion as seriously as Mornington.

[2] On 12 August 1798 Mornington wrote in his journal, 'Since the conclusion of the peace of Seringapatam, the Sultan has received the most unequivocal proofs of the disposition of the Company to acknowledge and confirm all his just rights, and to remove every cause of jealousy which might tend to interrupt the continuance of peace; although the servants of the Company in India had not been ignorant of the implacable sentiments of revenge which he had preserved without abatement since the hour of his last defeat. He having prepared the means and instruments of a war of extermination against us, and of annihilating our empire, the present is not merely the case of an injury to be repaired, but of the public safety to be secured against the present and future designs of an irreconcilable, desperate, and treacherous enemy.' *Owen*, 19.

I should any longer conceal from you the surprise and concern with which I perceived you disposed to involve yourself in all the ruinous consequences of a connexion, which threatens not only to subvert the foundations of friendship between you and the Company, but to introduce into the heart of your kingdom the principles of anarchy and confusion, to shake your own authority, to weaken the obedience of your subjects, and to destroy the religion which you revere.'[1] In the same letter the Governor-General proposed to send EIC Major Gabriel Doveton as an ambassador to improve relations between Mysore and Great Britain. Doveton was both known and liked by Tipoo and his family. He had been in charge of two of Tipoo's sons taken as hostages by Cornwallis in 1792 and returned two years later. These two young men were genuinely fond of Doveton because he had treated them with respect and consideration.

A letter took several weeks to travel from Seringapatam in Mysore to Fort William in Bengal; the time in transit depended on wind, weather and other factors. This delay was ideal for Tipoo who was counting on assistance from the French which he had already been promised, although the French were probably not sincere. However, Arthur Wellesley persuaded his brothers to move from Calcutta to Madras[2] which brought them to about ten days' journey from Seringapatam. The Governor-General and his staff arrived in Madras on the last day of 1798, two weeks after Arthur Wellesley had been sent west to take the dead Ashton's place. Mornington was most considerate to Clive and insisted that he continue to run the Madras government as if the Governor-General were still in Bengal. The Governor-General's presence in the Madras Presidency helped greatly, however, to get a proper army together at Vellore and to bring the Mysore situation to a head. There appeared little chance of a peaceful solution, but the effort had to be made.

Now back to Colonel Wellesley and his command at the entrance to the Baramahal where the British forces were fast becoming an effective field army. He had arrived on the morning of 18 December without even an Indian servant, but he took over completely. It was his first real opportunity to put into practice some of his ideas about

[1] *Pearce*, I, 213.
[2] Wellesley wrote to Mornington on 22 November 1798, *Supplementary Despatches*, I, 133, 'In short, there is every reason why you should come, and none why you should not, excepting that you will suffer a little personal inconvenience, which I put out of the question. I don't conceive that anything in Bengal can require your presence so much as it will be required here pending the negotiation with Tippoo.'

running more than a single battalion. It should be borne firmly in mind, however, that Wellesley never meant to change the system radically, he only wanted to bend it a little and make it work.

The most glaring weaknesses of the British military system in India were transport and supply, partly because of similar weaknesses at home. There was no proper military commissariat in the British Army during any part of the eighteenth century. Where the Navy could not provide what was needed, civilian representatives of the Treasury tried to buy it locally and carry it as required in rented vehicles. The EIC merchants had seen no reason to change this practice. Their idea of an army had always been of a sort of police force to keep their warehouses safe from robbers. The expense of a continuing system of logistics in peace as well as in war was frightening; in 1798 the British in India just did not have one.

On the other hand, armies had been living, marching long distances and fighting in the East for thousands of years. They all depended on either buying or taking by force what they required, or perhaps on a combination of the two. Arthur Wellesley was familiar with all this because of his study of Indian military history and because of his conversations with British officers with actual experience of such operations, especially during Cornwallis's campaigns. Lawrence, Clive and Coote had achieved their victories mostly because their enemies came and fought battles close to where British armies happened to be stationed. Wellesley observed that even when British armies had won in the pre-Cornwallis era, they had never been able to take full advantage of their victories because of lack of mobility.

The change during the Mysore War of 1789–92 was considerable. Cornwallis marched more men further than any previous British commander. He succeeded in 1792, but the fiasco of 1791 was still fresh in the minds of many officers in India. Cornwallis had beaten Tipoo in a battle almost under the walls of Seringapatam, but then had to destroy his siege train and retreat because of lack of food.

Wellesley was essentially carrying out plans that Mornington, Harris, Close, Ashton and he himself had made weeks before, but he was also bringing the kind of order into his entire area of responsibility that later became almost a personal trademark. Subsistence was and still is the most important single problem. Indian soldiers in barracks bought their food in the local bazaar. By modern standards their pay appears low, but it was then sufficient for a relatively high standard of living.[1] European soldiers required rather more attention, though they still paid for what they ate and in peace much of it was purchased locally. Such arrangements would not work in the field, not even in the concentration area of Arnee–Vellore–Arcot. The local bazaars could not support many thousands of additional purchasers and were quickly exhausted. Conceivably the best answer would have been for the army to take over feeding all troops as is done today. Instead, Wellesley preferred to enlarge and encourage the Indian bazaars and use them as his distribution system. He spent hours talking, writing and cajoling, and in surprisingly few days plenty of everything was being brought in by privately owned bullocks for a private profit. The bazaars were in complete discipline and order, and the prices reasonable. All this cost the EIC not a single rupee.

If and when the army advanced west, these bazaars would go too and at their own expense and responsibility. This system of merchandising was as old as the East and more efficient than it seems to us. An Indian bazaar contained merchants who could supply rice, other grains and almost anything else. There were craftsmen capable of making a soup tureen from silver coin or repairing a fine pistol by adding a newly forged main spring.

But other transport would also be needed. This problem had occupied Harris's staff for months. An army in enemy country could not, of course, depend entirely on local or travelling bazaars. Besides, there was the siege train and much other public property like medicines, salt beef and arrack[2] for the European soldiers. These things would have to be carried forward by the army. This transport was unusually difficult for several reasons. First, roads were so poor in India that large horse-drawn wagons like those used in England were not practical, even if the vehicles and horses had been available which they were not. Camels and elephants were used for special tasks and had advantages;

---

[1] At that time pay in the EIC armies was approximately as follows:

	Native	European
Private soldier	6 rupees/month	1s/day
Corporal (Naique)	8 rupees/month	1s 4d/day
Sergeant (Havildar)	10 rupees/month	1s 10d/day
Officers	16 to 60 rupees/month	4s/day and up

A rupee was worth about two shillings.

[2] In India at this time arrack meant any ardent spirit, the distillate from any fermented grain. It probably resembled modern rum and may have been mostly prepared from sugar cane. It remained a favourite with Arthur Wellesley throughout his life.

human porters were also used. But bullocks did most of the work. Some draft animals were used to pull artillery pieces, ammunition tumbrils and a few carts, but most of them carried their loads in simple panniers on their backs. A pack bullock could go wherever a man could walk; it cost little and lived on the country. In 1798, the EIC owned virtually no bullocks; they and their drivers had to be rented and many thousands of each would be needed. Wellesley began to hire and organize them into the several different departments required by the regulations of his joint services, but he lacked both the intimate knowledge of this subject and the time to do a complete job.

There was another possible compromise between having the bazaar merchants take forward what they would sell and carrying public property on rented bullocks. Though the merchants lacked the capital, the animals and the know-how to handle a considerable transport, they had the advantages of close personal supervision to eliminate pilfering and an established system of distribution. Wellesley looked about for a way to have these men supplied wholesale with the grain and the other things they sold.

The answer was nothing new; it was a unique Indian institution that had been used for centuries, the Brinjarries, hereditary wholesale grain merchants who kept enormous herds of pack (not draft) bullocks. They were neither Hindoos nor Muslim, but rather a separate people similar to European gypsies. They had developed a semi-secret system of self-government and could defend themselves when necessary. A Brinjarrie chief handled all disciplinary problems within his own group. The thieving common in all Indian camps of that era was not due to these merchants who in peacetime lived by buying grain or other merchandise where it was cheap, transporting it hundreds of miles and selling it where it was more valuable. They policed their own camps more effectively than outsiders of any type could have done. By contemporary Indian standards they were exceptionally truthful and trustworthy. By proper inducements both financial and diplomatic Wellesley assembled thousands of Brinjarries and tens of thousands of their bullocks to carry grain forward with the army. Contracts of hire were such, however, that the grain they carried was sufficiently their own property for them to protect it. In the main the Brinjarries bought grain from the EIC and sold it to the bazaar merchants, although there were several variations. Even more important, they were bullock drivers almost from birth; they bred their own beasts and knew how to take care of them.

Wellesley's third major problem was the siege train. No one appears to have been in charge of providing it. As often happened during his life, he picked up the responsibility because it was lying around loose. Major military expenditures like the assembling of a siege train were made by the Military Boards of each Presidency. The gentlemen who composed the Madras Board were old, sedentary, poorly informed, inefficient and parsimonious.[1] Worse still, in the loose administrative system then prevalent in British India, they came under no one's direct control.

As Arthur Wellesley found out, the Military Board of Madras had not even begun to do anything about the siege train, and he took charge of its assembly complete with ammunition. He wrote letters and delivered respectful lectures, procedures which he was later to develop into something resembling priority orders today. He won because of the bulk of his communications and because of their obvious logic. He did not need to call on the Governor-General or Harris for any backing in his controversy with the Military Board; early in 1799 he had at Vellore two 24-pounders, thirty 18-pounders and eight long iron 12-pounders complete on their travelling and (presumably) firing carriages[2] with 1,200 rounds of battering ammunition for each piece.

Arthur Wellesley was using his relatively new knowledge of military matters in India and his common sense. The army now coming into being was not remotely to resemble that of the Duke of York in 1794–95, or even those of Meadows and Cornwallis in India. Even its motivation was changed. The Wellesleys brought with them to India not only their ability to strive, but to make their effort popular with others, even perhaps 'respectable'. There was more to do, however, than just improve motivation and attitude to military tasks. Many EIC battalions had not been assembled as a unit for years; individual companies were often spread about over a hundred miles. Hardly any battalion had drilled with other similar units. Wellesley

[1] Wellesley, *Supplementary Despatches*, I, 126, wrote to Henry, 'The vague calculations of a parcel of blockheads, who know nothing, and have no data.' He also wrote, ibid., I, 118, 'I don't think that it is advisable to let M. [Mornington] know that the Military Board have caused the delay in sending the train, as it will serve only to exasperate him still more against people here, which I don't think necessary. The fact that the train is not gone must come to his knowledge; but as he never desired that it might be sent forward, and as the intention of sending it originated with this Government, upon a suggestion of mine, I don't think that he can well attack them for it as a disobedience of his orders, although he may for stupidity. I leave it to you to do what you please about it.'

[2] See Appendix I for details of these weapons and their carriages.

insisted on daily battalion drill and also assembled brigades which operated together. The young colonel again introduced live fire target practice, something unheard of before him.

When the Governor-General arrived at Madras, he had an army nearly ready to move. He did not, however, have anyone to command it. His first choice would have been Sir Alured Clarke, but he had been forced to leave Clarke, the C-in-C of all British armies in India, in Bengal. Clarke was the best man to run the Presidency in the Governor-General's absence and would surely be needed in the north in the event of another Afghan invasion. Harris was next in line but apparently not ideal. He lacked both flair and confidence. As a matter of fact, the Governor-General thought Harris more capable than Harris did himself. The C-in-C in Madras appears not to have expected the offer of this command and did not at first accept it when it was offered.[1] Harris seems to have been a capable commander without realizing it. He had perhaps experienced too much frustration in America early in his career and under Meadows, his old chief, in India. George Harris probably all too vividly remembered Webbe's able prediction of disaster and the troubles that Meadows and Cornwallis had in the early stages of the 1789–92 war. He was a warm, righteous, industrious individual who lacked arrogance, selfishness and high personal ambition. He spent a night of thought and rest when he considered the other candidates and then accepted as much for Britain as for himself.[2]

The Mysore situation had deteriorated further. The Governor-General had not received a reply from Tipoo to his frank and forceful communication of 18 November 1798. We now know that Tipoo had received a letter from Bonaparte; the prince was playing for time.

Tipoo was now at the height of his rather exceptional powers. He was short, corpulent and darker than his father Hyder Ali who had been half Afghan. He had been brought up to command, exposed to a good deal of education and throughout his life retained smatterings of knowledge, much of it incorrect. He was a bigoted Muslim and claimed descent from the Prophet, but was not so sure of his religion that he would forsake the chance that purchased Hindoo rites might help him. The Sultan was courageous but lacked his father's ability in

[1] The situation of a senior general not wanting a field command is unusual, but Wellesley refers to Harris as lacking 'respectability'. Perhaps he was not fashionable, but no one seems to have doubted his ability. Mornington wrote Wellesley, 'I wish to God the whole were under your direction.' *Supplementary Despatches*, I, 188.

[2] *Harris*, 243: Lushington writes that Harris, his father-in-law, hesitated through modesty and lack of self-interest.

military strategy, organization and leadership. His worst traits were his tendency to surround himself with sycophants and to lose himself in details of procedures that could not be carried out. He was energetic without plan or common sense and cruel without personal gratification. Both his own people and his enemies who displeased him suffered horribly.

As long as Tipoo procrastinated, British preparations for war continued. The army forming at Vellore was the strongest but by no means the only force to be used against the enemy. Arthur Wellesley was in communication with Harris and his staff at Madras and also with his friend Lieutenant-Colonel Read, who still commanded in the Baramahal and whose outposts were on the Mysore side of the Eastern Ghauts. Major-General Floyd commanded to the south towards Coimbatore and Trichinopoly, but would move to Vellore if an advance was to be made into Mysore. Lieutenant-Colonel Archibald Brown would continue to operate from Coimbatore; a Bombay Presidency army would move in from the west coast.

The Governor-General wondered whether or not to accompany the army. Although he was not professionally trained as a soldier, it was chiefly his idea to concentrate the forces about to be used if Tipoo did not accept at least two of the three conditions necessary to keep peace. He had profited by advice from Arthur Wellesley, Harris and others, but evolved the main plan himself. He wanted to go into the field 'to assist' Harris and asked Arthur's opinion of such a move. The younger brother sent back a firm negative: 'All I can say is that if I were Harris, and you joined the army, I should quit it!'[1] Could there have been a more difficult military situation than commanding an offensive army, but being accompanied every step of the way by a forceful Governor-General who thought himself, perhaps correctly, an able strategist?

Arthur Wellesley's independent status at Vellore ended on 29 January 1799 when Harris finally arrived to begin active field command. The C-in-C at Madras brought with him four other general officers; Major-General Floyd also joined about this time and took over command of the cavalry. Colonel Wellesley went from Number 1 to Number 7; he was not even placed in command of a brigade, although this omission was obviously because he was to be used for a more important task. It is important to know what Harris thought of Wellesley's achievements in six and a half weeks of independent command.

---

[1] *Supplementary Despatches*, I, 187.

Harris appears to have been extremely pleased. He wrote to the Governor-General to this effect on 2 February and added special praise for Wellesley's 'discipline' and 'masterly arrangements in respect to supplies'.[1] Could words be more prophetic? Harris expressed to Wellesley 'his approbation and adopted as his own all orders and regulations I had made, and then said that he should mention his approbation publicly, only that he was afraid others would be displeased and jealous'.[2] Harris was, I believe, entirely right. He was among the first to appreciate Arthur Wellesley's unusual ability, but he also knew the tendency among both King's and EIC officers to believe the worst of the young colonel.[3] Praise from the C-in-C to the Governor-General's brother for obscure services – not many Englishmen in India knew or cared 'precisely what is meant by commissariat' – would not have helped Wellesley.

Harris's main army consisted of more than 20,000 fighting men, including 4,300 European soldiers. Of the three other co-operating British forces under Harris the army from the Bombay Presidency, under Lieutenant-General James Stuart,[4] had a total strength of 1,600 European and 4,800 Indian fighting men along with some pioneers, gun lascars and attached irregulars. Read and Brown had forces with fighting strengths of about 2,000 and 2,500 respectively; they were to protect British territory and gather supplies and then to join at Cauveryporam. The strengths and organizations of all these forces are given in Appendix III: British Order of Battle Against Tipoo, Sultan of Mysore.

After more diplomatic manœuvring with Tipoo, which had no definite result,[5] the Governor-General on 3 February 1799 sent orders to both Harris and Stuart to begin their advances from different sides of the peninsula towards Mysore. The Governor-General was not

[1] *Harris*, 250.

[2] *Supplementary Despatches*, I, 199. In this communication Wellesley expressed acute displeasure in not having this 'public approbation'.

[3] *Lady Longford*, 57, points out the omission from *Supplementary Despatches*, I, 110, of a paragraph in which Wellesley wrote that 'others [considered] me as very little better than a spy'.

[4] Stuart's rank was at this time local and confined to 'the coast of Malabar'. Wellesley wrote to Mornington about Stuart's and Floyd's relative rank on Harris's behalf on 2 February 1799: *Supplementary Despatches*, I, 189–91. Stuart became a Lieutenant-General in the King's Army on 29 April 1802.

[5] There was Tipoo's well-known communication containing the sentences: 'Being frequently disposed to make excursions and hunt, I am "going hunting". You will be pleased to dispatch Major Doveton slightly attended.' *Pearce*, I, 248. This message did not reach Madras until 5 February 1799. It was, of course, unsatisfactory.

yet declaring war, but he was moving to prevent Tipoo from gaining the entire monsoon season by his procrastination. If Seringapatam were not taken by about 15 May, it could not be attacked for at least six months.

Harris moved from Vellore on the 11th. His route lay, of course, through the irregular U-shaped valley of the Baramahal. Fertile flat plains were surrounded and sometimes interrupted by steep rocky hills. The distance from Vellore to the Eastern Ghauts (all in British territory) was about 120 miles and would take more than three weeks. Stuart was ordered to stop at the Mysore border. Tipoo had plenty of time to mend his ways and retain his throne (musnud). However, the French emphasized the presence in Egypt of Bonaparte and a French army and the promised seaborne expedition down the Red Sea to Mangalore.[1] The Governor-General did not actually 'declare war' until 23 February, but even then he left the door open for Tipoo to choose peace if he wanted it.

Harris's force reached Amboor on the 18th and there joined an army from Hyderabad. The Nizam, once more the firm ally of the British had sent his subsidiary force of six fine EIC battalions and other units as well.[2] Captain John Malcolm had reorganized the personnel formerly commanded by French officers into four battalions, each now commanded by English officers. Some Indian officers and NCOs from the EIC units had also been added. There were also 'really about 10,000'[3] semi-regular Mogul cavalry under Captain Walker. This force had twenty-six field pieces, probably all assigned directly to the infantry battalions and cavalry units.

The entire Hyderabad army was commanded by Meer Allum who was perhaps the Nizam's son and at this time his principal minister.[4] When the army arrived its senior British officer was EIC Colonel George Roberts (commission dated 12 October 1798) who had commanded the six Hyderabad EIC battalions the previous October when they disarmed the French force. He had asked, however, to be relieved of this command and had already been appointed to take over a brigade

[1] *Pearce*, James Mill and others feel that Bonaparte had either abandoned this idea or never considered it seriously, but it was surely expected at Seringapatam and Madras.

[2] The strength and organization of this force, so far as it can be determined, is given in Appendix III.

[3] The number of these cavalry is variously stated, but Wellesley made this estimate, *Supplementary Despatches*, I, 203, and added, 'some good, some bad'.

[4] The father-son relationship is not mentioned by some authorities in India at the time, so it probably was not definite. Adoptions as well as illegitimate births were common in the East.

in Harris's army. There had been at least rumours that a King's infantry battalion would be added to the Nizam's army with a colonel senior to Roberts.[1] The Nizam's army appears to have been as large in numbers as Harris's own, but it needed two things: a European unit of infantry to stiffen it and a British officer able to exercise control. We should not forget, however, that Meer Allum was and would remain both the nominal and to a considerable extent the actual commander. The King's colonel who took this job would have to be both 'respectable' and tactful. Harris had a long time to consider this appointment, but now that Ashton was gone, there was really only one answer:[2] Arthur Wellesley and the King's 33rd. Meer Allum made the final announcement easier by actually requesting Wellesley.

Arthur Wellesley's appoinmtent to the Hyderabad army led to immediate controversy. Of the four major-generals whom Harris had brought with him from Madras, three had considerable commands, but the most junior, David Baird, had only a brigade. Though Baird's brigade did consist of three European battalions, he had essentially the same responsibility as five colonels and two lieutenant-colonels, some of them EIC officers. Baird was strong, brave and a sound professional soldier. He was also a squabbler with limited political and diplomatic abilities. Late in 1795 and in 1796 he had handled badly a position requiring such abilities in Tanjore and had to be removed from his military command. He disliked most Indians and got on with them less well than almost any other contemporary senior British officer in India.

Characteristically, Baird protested to Harris and demanded that in accordance with seniority he should have been assigned to the Nizam's army. He even wanted Lieutentant-Colonel Browne's semi-independent command in Coimbatore.[3] It would have been hard to find a worse man than Baird for assisting Meer Allum with the Hyderabad command. Even if the Nizam's chief minister had not requested Wellesley, Harris would almost surely have chosen him. Among many other things, there was an EIC regulation about full colonel being the top rank in any subsidiary force. Arthur Wellesley had already proven his ability to control efficiently a large mixed command and get on with people; Baird had made a good start at proving the opposite. Wellesley treated Indians as equals because he thought of them as

---

[1] All commanders of King's regiments in Harris's army were senior to Roberts, *Supplementary Despatches*, I, 139.

[2] *Lady Longford*, 57, writes that Ashton had originally been considered for this post.

[3] *Harris*, 408.

1 A hill fort in the Baramahal

2 Vellore

3 The battlefield of Malavelley at approximately the spot where the 33rd received the attack of Tipoo's infantry

4 Sultanpetah Tope below the central *nullah* or aqueduct

such. There was mutual respect and sometimes friendship between him and the Indians with whom he worked, although he understood their weaknesses. Baird was the type of man who made British rule in India more difficult. Harris made the right decision.

Before following the journey towards Seringapatam from Amboor where Harris's armies stayed for two days, we should note that the Governor-General appointed a Mysore Commission to assist General Harris with political decisions, in particular to help him decide what to do should Tipoo offer less than complete compliance with British demands. This first commission was composed of Close, Malcolm, Agnew (Harris's Military Secretary), and Arthur Wellesley; all except Wellesley were EIC officers and had devoted at least a part of their time to political relations.

Harris began to advance west from Amboor on 21 February. The valley was broad and flat; the British army was in column on the right, with the Nizam's force similarly deployed on the left about three miles away. Between them was a slowly moving stream of more than 100,000 non-combatants of all descriptions, including merchants and the families of sepoys. There were even more animals than human beings, at least 100,000 bullocks and thousands of mules, camels, horses and elephants. On the march through the Baramahal the expeditionary force resembled a migrating people rather than an army. Progress was slow, on the average less than ten miles a marching day. The whole combination stopped in camp about one day in three.[1] This rate of progress was maintained without incident through the British territory of the Baramahal. For the country and the time the road was good; Lieutenant-Colonel Read had it in excellent condition, especially the stretch through the Ryacotta ghaut or pass which was better than that used by Cornwallis through Kistnagherry, a town and fort of considerable importance. Harris and his massive command arrived at the entrance to the pass below Ryacotta on 3 March 1799. The slow-moving rectangle changed into a number of straggling columns. All wheeled vehicles, including the heavy carriages of the siege pieces drawn by as many as sixty bullocks harnessed four abreast used the road, but pack animals found their way up the ghaut both north and south of the road.[2]

[1] *Harris*, 523–4, gives a dated itinerary with the exact distance marched each day for the entire journey.

[2] The Ryacotta pass now is unimpressive. An unencumbered man, even one in his middle 50s, can walk up and down in a dozen places parallel to the modern road which is presumably coincident with Read's old one.

On 5 March the major portion of Harris's army stayed in camp at Ryacotta while some light troops took minor hill-forts guarding Tipoo's border. The next day the main force began its march through enemy territory. Harris was advancing on Bangalore as Cornwallis had done in 1791. The latter, however, had laid siege to and captured the place in order to use it as a fortified base for his further advance on Seringapatam. Harris already knew that Tipoo had destroyed most of Bangalore and demolished its defences. The Sultan adopted a strategy of defending his capital with maximum force – Harris had abundant information of new walls and new big guns – but destroying everything else of value to his enemies. This included not only Bangalore, but also a wide band of territory through which Tipoo thought Harris's armies would move.

The scorched-earth concept was sound. The British and Hyderabad armies could carry enough food for men to last for about three months, but they were dependent upon the country for most of their animals.[1] If Tipoo's cavalry could destroy enough bullock food for a considerable percentage of animals to die of starvation, the entire conglomeration of men, animals and baggage, including the siege train, would come to a resounding halt. The British army was probably unbeatable in battle, but could be turned back easily if it could not feed its animals. The strategy was, of course, two-edged. The inhabitants of the areas where the forage was destroyed and stores of grain taken away would certainly lose their own animals and perhaps starve themselves. But Tipoo appears to have cared little about his people and would willingly sacrifice them by the thousand. It was, however, difficult to destroy all food for bullocks. These beasts ate many things, most of them growing wild. Enormous amounts of human labour would have been required to strip an area of all natural grasses; it was impossible to do it indiscriminately over many square miles. This part of India cannot just be set on fire.

Harris's route was of extreme importance. If he moved predictably, his army would be in a long narrow corridor of devastated territory and surrounded by an elastic ring of Tipoo's fine light cavalry. His bullocks could not support themselves for long. Indeed, as soon as the border was crossed and the armies were headed for Bangalore, Mysore cavalry were in sight almost continuously. Forage was in short supply, although even here there were some small parcels of unburnt grass, straw and

---

[1] Some grain was carried for horses, but other animals, especially the vast multitude of bullocks, ate only locally procured forage.

hay. The country was wild and not fully cultivated, but it was not real jungle. On 9 March the entire force camped near the village of Kelamangalam, no more than about fifteen miles from the border. Some 4,000 of Meer Allum's Hyderabad troops, though none of the EIC subsidiary force, were detached to stay with Read. Even at this time Harris was worrying about a resupply of food; Read's most important mission was to collect grain and move it to Cauveryporam.

Soon after dawn on the 10th the great conglomeration began to move out; Arthur Wellesley and Meer Allum now were on the right while Harris's own army was on the left, closer to the centre of Mysore. The country was ideal for harassing movements by enemy cavalry, open enough to give proper footing, but with *topes* (groves of trees) spread about for cover. Within two hours Wellesley's guns were in action three times, once at the head of the column and twice towards the rear. The enemy was trying to break through to the central baggage. Wellesley understood their objectives and deployed both his advance and rear guards to extend inward. They were each composed essentially of a half company of the 33rd, a half company from each of his six EIC battalions, and a similar force from each of Malcolm's four units. Detachments of Mogul (Hyderabad) cavalry were with each of the two forces.

Suddenly firing broke out in earnest in the rear. Wellesley spurred Diomed towards the threatened point. An enemy column of 2,000 horsemen had used a covered approach route and charged one section of his rear guard. Wellesley quickly took counteraction. The two 6-pounders with the 'pickets of the day before',[1] went into action with the surviving infantry which now had time to form. Grape from the cannon and regular volleys from forty muskets of the 33rd and about five hundred of Colonel Wellesley's Indian units emptied saddles and killed horses. Wellesley personally led the rear-guard cavalry in a bloody counter-attack which completed a costly defeat for the enemy. Harris's armies were to march all the way to Seringapatam, but opposing cavalry was not again to try anything similar in this strength or actually close with British troops at all. Although Mysore casualties were considerably larger, Wellesley's force did not escape unscathed. The half company of 1/11 Madras Native Infantry (MNI) under Lieutenant Reynolds was overrun before it was properly formed into line. Reynolds was severely wounded, and all of his men were either

---

[1] In the review of the actions of 1803 this picket procedure will be discussed more thoroughly (see chs X and XI).

killed or wounded. Total British casualties, nearly all of them in this unfortunate unit, were twenty killed and thirty-seven wounded.

Harris continued north in a man-made semi-desert as far as Achel. Enemy horsemen were thick in front and to either flank so that only a strong foraging party could leave the line of march. There were other problems. Both grain and ammunition were disappearing. Gunpowder, lead projectiles for small arms and even cannon balls were stolen. They were valuable objects in India. Even the Brinjarries were having troubles. If Harris had continued to Bangalore, all these problems would have accompanied him and he would have lost thousands of bullocks. On the 19th, however, he turned abruptly south-west towards Cankanelli on the most direct route to Seringapatam. Within two miles he was in untouched territory. Forage stood in abundance along this route and was harvested in various ways, often directly by the animals themselves. Tipoo's cavalry was not even sighted in strength for two days.

Apart from the rearguard action outside Kelamangalam there had so far been no real fighting. Floyd's disciplined and organized European and Indian cavalry were in front and too powerful for the Mysore cavalry. The lighter, less disciplined enemy horsemen would not stand and fight, but they could not be caught. A few stragglers from both sides were cut off, but nothing more serious occurred. No enemy infantry or artillery had as yet been seen. On the other hand, Harris was moving in a near vacuum. He was cut off from regular dispatches both from the Governor-General at Madras and from Stuart on the west coast, although some were soon to be brought in secretly.

But in spite of plenty of forage and the relative absence of all enemy action, the progress of Harris's army north-east of Cankanelli was unsatisfactory. It took five days to cover the distance that Cornwallis in 1791 had marched in two.[1] The cause is easy to determine, labour trouble. The contractors who rented bullocks to the EIC and their Indian drivers were dissatisfied with new regulations. Both were exercising 'all their ingenuity, notwithstanding their large means of transport, in opposing a thousand obstacles to every advance'.[2]

We should now leave Harris and join Stuart. As has been mentioned, the British strategy as it had perhaps first been put into concrete

---

[1] *Wilks*, III, 389–90. He points out too that the earlier British army had just completed the arduous and exhausting siege of Bangalore.

[2] *Alexander*, 52, but the exact reasons appear to be lost.

form by Arthur Wellesley months before called for movements against Seringapatam from both coasts.[1] Tipoo could be defeated most easily and quickly by taking his capital at Seringapatam. Separate but co-ordinated thrusts from Madras and Malabar were best. There were, of course, compensating disadvantages, those referred to by military strategists in the context of 'interior lines'. Tipoo just might be able to defeat one army or the other by using all his forces against it. Harris's army was big and powerful, but perhaps Stuart's to the west was not. Both the Governor-General and Harris had taken this into consideration. Stuart, who had no adequate cavalry, had been ordered to move from Cannanore only as far as the top of the Western Ghauts. He was to wait for a cavalry escort from the main army before moving the last fifty miles through the open plain to Seringapatam.

Stuart moved from Cannanore on 21 February 1799 and reached the Western Ghauts on 2 March. He was in the principality of Koorg; the Rajah of Koorg was a firm friend of British India and had joined Stuart with his irregular troops. The Bombay army was to take up a strong defensive position 'above the ghauts' and wait for further orders. Stuart and his second-in-command, General Hartley, found these directions almost impossible to carry out. Aided by the Rajah of Koorg, they established a lookout with a position for two EIC battalions under Colonel Montresor to support it, but not a place for the whole army. If the entire army came up the ten-mile pass, it could be cut off from the Malabar coast fairly easily. Stuart therefore left the rest of his army in a more secure position twelve miles away 'below the ghauts'.

On 5 March the Rajah of Koorg and others on the lookout station saw unusual activity in the direction of Periapatam and Seringapatam. Contemporary accounts claim that from this point it was possible to see east 'almost to Seringapatam'. In the flat land below, the Rajah saw the erection of a large green tent and recognized it as Tipoo's. An attack the next day was obviously possible. Stuart and Montresor immediately realized their danger, but a precipitate retreat back down the ghaut was undesirable. Stuart ordered forward another battalion of Bombay Indian infantry which arrived early in the evening. Montresor had his entire command under arms and ready an hour before dawn.

Tipoo attacked about nine o'clock on the 6th. His troops hit the three British battalions from both front and rear. Montresor, apparently

[1] Wellesley's 'Reflections' of 26 October 1798 in *Supplementary Despatches*, I, 119–24. But this whole strategy was used by Cornwallis in 1791 and 1792.

one of the best British officers in India,[1] had cleared his long, narrow camp area as best he could three days before. He had, however, no field fortifications. He formed his men so as to use mobile controlled firepower against both attacks and employed his six 6-pounders advantageously. Grape from these was particularly effective; it had a range of more than 300 yards and could tear through thickets of scrub. British artillery in India – the gunners were all European – was extremely skilful.

The fight went on for hours against heavy odds, but Montresor's men were never even close to defeat. In spite of a numerical superiority of about five to one, Tipoo accomplished nothing. Montresor kept his forces flexible and was able to reinforce where necessary as well as rest some of his companies from time to time. Each enemy thrust that made headway and progressed through the artillery fire was met by sepoys in line who fired precise volleys and then came forward with their bayonets.

Stuart personally brought the King's 77th Foot and the flank companies of the King's 75th up the pass and arrived about three o'clock in the afternoon. The fresh European infantry hit the rear of Tipoo's troops who were still attacking Montresor's rear. The soldiers of Mysore broke completely and carried away in their panic their companions who had been attacking Montresor in front. The Bombay army was left in undisputed possession of a bloody battlefield said to contain the bodies of 2,000 of the enemy. During the night, however, Stuart pulled back down the ghaut to consolidate his entire force in one place and avoid the risk of having his communications with Cannanore cut off.

Tipoo stayed briefly in the area and then retired to the east without firing another shot. His strategy was certainly sound; he was trying to take advantage of his 'interior lines'. He may have been following the advice of French professional soldiers in his employ;[2] but the execution was faulty. Rumours about the battle of Sedaseer (the name of the closest village) reached Harris's army on 15 March. They were confirmed by prisoners taken by Floyd's cavalry on the 18th. Harris heard directly from Stuart on 24 March when Tipoo and his main army were known to have moved back east.

[1] John Montresor was a King's officer, apparently a lieutenant-colonel of the 80th Foot. He was serving as one of Stuart's brigade commanders. There will be further references to his abilities and Arthur Wellesley's recognition of them.

[2] *Fortescue*, IV, ii, 718, writes that the force sent from Mauritius included 'one general of the land forces'.

After his sudden shift of direction north of Anicul Harris's army had moved freely. In spite of its labour problems, it was making fair progress along the main Bangalore–Seringapatam road. This route was bordered by 'thick jungle', though it was not as thick as the nearly impenetrable vegetation 'below the ghauts'. Arthur Wellesley and others were later to exclaim: 'If Tipoo had resisted with his infantry in this thick area we could not have got through before the monsoon!' Before giving battle, however, the Sultan of Mysore appears to have waited for more open territory where his control of his forces would be better.

The main British army was at Cankanelli on 21 March 1799 and moved through nearly continuous tope country for four days – a total of about twenty miles. On the 26th they came out on cleared, almost flat land east of the considerable village of Malavelley. Before evening the British saw some of Tipoo's artillery and infantry in the distance. There were elephants and cannon on a skyline.

Soon after daybreak on 27 March the allied armies began their slow plodding towards Seringapatam. Malavelley was six miles away; it was the next campsite at which there was ample water. The order of march was about the same as in the Baramahal, the British and the Hyderabad armies in column to each side with the vast conglomeration of baggage between them. Each army was preceded by cavalry and the infantry pickets. Contacts between the allied cavalry advance guards and the enemy were heavier than normal; when the heads of the main infantry columns were no more than a mile from Malavelley, they came under long-range artillery fire for the first time in the campaign. Tipoo's guns, said to be brass 18-pounders, were in position on some low hills a mile west of the village.[1] The enemy was not attacking, but they did seem to be solidly in position and ready to fight defensively.

The day was well advanced and the Quartermaster-General's party was already laying out the Malavelley camp. Harris felt, however, that the opportunity to defeat Tipoo in the field was so valuable that he made every effort to close. His two armies were not fatigued and in superb condition; the terrain would give no considerable advantage to the enemy. In the open Tipoo could not possibly match British discipline, firepower and controlled mobility.

Soon after the Mysore guns opened, both the 25th Dragoons under

---

[1] Captain Sydenham's Sketch with a sheet of explanations given in *Harris* is the best contemporary map of the battle, but in March 1968 I found a number of inconsistencies between it and the terrain around Malavelley.

Stapleton Cotton and the British pickets of the day under John Sherbrooke were engaged north-west of Malavelley.[1] The cavalry held in check a larger body of Mysore light horse by using their new 'galloper' 6-pounders;[2] the infantry drove back some rocket boys and their supporting horsemen.

Bridges's right wing led the British infantry column; it passed just to the north of the village of Malavelley without halting. This unit was formed 5th Brigade, 1st Brigade and finally 3rd Brigade. Harris ordered it into line en echelon left in front, which meant that Baird's all-European Brigade should have been in the centre of the line. Somehow the 1st Brigade got ahead of the 5th Brigade; the actual formation appears to have been an arrowhead V with one brigade up and two back. All were moving at speed; less than two hours of daylight remained.

The Hyderabad army under Meer Allum and Arthur Wellesley was level with Harris's but at least a mile further south. Initially Wellesley had an infantry column of eleven battalions, led by the King's 33rd. About 3.30 p.m. he received Harris's order to continue his advance and endeavour to force the enemy to fight. In order to save time, he also formed line from column en echelon to the south on the 33rd which continued to advance. This meant an oblique line of battalions still in column of half companies at quarter distance each about 200 yards behind the one on its right and about 200 yards south. It is likely that only the King's 33rd and six EIC battalions were in this formation. Malcolm's four Hyderabad units probably formed a reserve. In Wellesley's area the terrain had been a trifle more open than in Baird's; the movements of the southern army are less confused.

Wellesley galloped to the south – he was mounted on Diomed – to make sure all his units were properly spaced. The six EIC battalions were to go from column into line simultaneously with the 33rd and continue their advance. Then he quickly returned to the 33rd. He was pleased to see that his army was now about a quarter mile ahead of Baird's brigade of the main force. Everybody realized that Tipoo might not remain for long in a position where he could be attacked. As Wellesley and the 33rd approached the low ridge where the enemy could be clearly seen, he ordered his regiment to form line from column to the left. The first half company continued as it was, but slowed its pace; the others obliqued various distances to the left and double-

---

[1] Both were to fight under Wellington in the Peninsula.
[2] See Appendix I for a description.

timed to catch up. In less than two minutes the whole battalion was in a two-deep line about 350[1] files long. The EIC units to the south-east also executed this manœuvre. What a thrill it must have been for a young colonel to see his command perform in this manner. He had been in the Army for twelve years, but had not yet taken part in a real battle.

Tipoo's line was still mostly to be identified by the sudden puffs of cotton white which preceded the sound of each artillery discharge. Occasionally a ball would pass close enough for men involuntarily to bob their heads. Suddenly Wellesley saw a heavy column of Mysore infantry, between 2,000 and 3,000 soldiers, emerge from Tipoo's hilltop line and advance toward the centre of the 33rd with unusual bravery.[2] Every man in the 33rd must have realized that this was their moment of truth. For nearly six years they had drilled and practised under their present commander. This was their first opportunity to use their experience for maximum advantage in battle. The enemy column was still coming straight for the British colours; they were not much more than a hundred yards away. An incisive, well-known voice rang out: 'Thirty-third, Halt! Half-right, Face! Make ready!'

The enemy column was more numerous by three to one and moving fast. Surely the heavy mass could penetrate the thin red line, even though it extended further on both flanks. The last time the veterans of this British regiment had fought in earnest had been more than four years before in cramped frozen country against the French. Now there was no congestion; the formation allowed every man to fire with perfect ease at the head of the approaching column. There were no cold fingers either. The clamour from the enemy was almost deafening; they were so close together that they seemed able to exert shock by sheer mass in motion. The incisive voice came again: 'Present!' Up came two lines of polished brown wood stocks and bright steel barrels. The muzzles of the rear rank muskets projected well past the faces of the soldiers in front. The glittering bayonets were probably already fixed.[3] Outwardly Wellesley was calm and steady as a rock, but he

---

[1] The total strength, rank and file, of the King's 33rd was below 670 when it arrived at Madras, but Wellesley received about 130 replacements. *Wilson*, ii, 301, gives its strength as of 1 February 1799 as 788. Two half companies, however, were probably detached to the pickets.

[2] They behaved sufficiently well for rumours that they were 'under the influence of stimulants' to gain credence in the British camps.

[3] I believe that British infantry in Europe rarely fixed bayonets until after their firing was completed. It is much more difficult to load a bayoneted musket than an unbayoneted one; fixing a bayonet requires only two seconds. In India, however, the plan was usually to fire once and charge.

must have asked himself, 'Are they close enough?' Surely! He could see clearly the frenzied dark faces. The enemy was no more than sixty yards away.

'Fire!' Seven hundred cocks drove flint against hard serrated steel frizzens. Flame spurted from every pan; a line of fire and then white smoke jumped from the muzzles. There was the single resounding crash of a well delivered volley. The head of Tipoo's column collapsed almost to a man from the impact of heavy British bullets. Those behind were brought to a stand; men in column could not advance over their own dead and wounded. The 33rd, still completely under control, recovered, faced back to the front and advanced in a disciplined formation. The flanks moved a bit faster to cup round the head of the enemy column. Tipoo's men had displayed exceptional courage in opposing disciplined European soldiers in the open, but as Wellesley said later they 'did not quite stand' to receive the bayonets.[1] As the unfortunate Mysore infantry streamed back in disorder, they were overtaken by the 1st Brigade of Floyd's cavalry under Colonel James Stevenson. It was the type of action where disciplined horsemen with long practice with the sabre could be most damaging.[2] Tipoo failed to support his brave men; they were nearly exterminated.

While Wellesley's army had been engaged as described, Baird's brigade of the main force had been attacked first by Mysore cavalry trying to get at the British baggage and later perhaps by infantry. The King's 74th, Baird's central regiment, momentarily got itself into a little trouble by being too impetuous, but Baird personally corrected this. To the north the enemy was repulsed as completely as it had been to the south.

Tipoo made these attacks on Harris's army to gain time for the retreat of the rest of his forces, especially the artillery. The sight of Harris's army and of Wellesley's coming forward en echelon probably caused the Mysore commander to change his mind about fighting a battle. It is interesting to note that Colonels Sherbrooke and Cotton were already moving around Tipoo's left flank and were soon in a position to attack his rear or cut off his retreat, had he actually fought. However, the enemy went back too fast and too far for this to be effective. A British pursuit could not be carried far because of the approach of

[1] *Burton*, 15.
[2] Pursuing practice was one part of the sword exercise, or perhaps a separate exercise, regularly done by all British cavalry in India. It consisted of slashes only, first on one side and then on the other.

darkness and the presence of still unbroken masses of enemy cavalry.

Malavelley was not large as battles go. The 33rd lost just two men, and even Baird's brigade lost only twenty-nine. But it was surely creditable from the British point of view. They could hardly have gained more from it considering the enemy commander's early change of heart and the mobility of his forces, including his artillery drawn by fine big white bullocks. Sedaseer and Malavelley together were so disheartening to Tipoo that he lost confidence in himself, his forces, and his military ability.

IV

The Storming of Seringapatam

At Malavelley Tipoo rediscovered what he must already have known;
in spite of some training by French officers and NCOs, his soldiers
could not stand against a British force in battle. He reverted to his
scorched-earth defence. When on 28 March Harris continued from
Malavelley towards Seringapatam, he found his line of march stripped
bare of forage. The cavalry grass cutters could get enough roots to
supplement the regular issue of gram (horse 'corn' like coarse dried
peas) for their animals,[1] but the bullocks would soon die.

Harris had no intention, however, of making a predictable advance
on Seringapatam. He marched west along the main road for less than
four miles and camped. At the same time he sent a detachment under
Major Allan,[2] his Assistant Quartermaster-General, south towards the
large village of Sirsoli on the Cauvery; they reached their destination
before sunset and found sheep, goats and grain as well as some 5,000
bullocks. Hundreds of people, driven away from their homes by Tipoo's
cavalry, were cowering under the shadow of a mud fort. Harris
bought what he needed and posted a battalion of Sepoys to prevent his
camp followers from molesting the villagers or their property. On
the 29th the army turned south and in two days crossed the broad
shallow river at a good ford.

Again Harris had shifted his direction more than ninety degrees and

---

[1] Each cavalry horse had a grass cutter and a groom. The collection of grass roots
required a lot of labour, but allowed horses to remain in good shape.
[2] This was not the Major Allan of the King's 12th who killed Ashton and died while
still under arrest within three months of the duel: Elers, 81.

completely surprised his enemies.[1] The country south of the river was full of forage and held some other food as well. After this shift Tipoo abandoned hope of stopping the British army short of Seringapatam. He retreated to his capital to wait for Harris. He and his French advisers assumed, however, that the attack would come from the south or south-east. The Mysore army was settled into a system of field fortifications on the island and across the South Cauvery. This position covered the Arrakerry ford and included the village of Chendgal (now Chandagala). It appears to have been strong and Tipoo and his principal chiefs decided to win or die there.[2]

On 4 April 1799 Harris's combined armies moved past Tipoo's flank and did not turn north until the head of their massive columns was even with Tipoo's capital. Harris camped at Nova Shaher (now Naganahalli?) two miles due south of Seringapatam.

Central Mysore is a fertile, almost flat plain broken occasionally by magnificent outcroppings of rock. The Cauvery rises in the Western Ghauts and flows east and then south-east, splitting into two branches around Seringapatam Island. There is no swamp; the area enclosed is high and dry and about three miles long by one mile wide. Tipoo and his French advisers hoped to keep Harris's force away until the coming of the monsoon made both rivers unfordable. If Harris did not get on Seringapatam Island by 20 May, he would have to retreat, for the North and South Cauvery would remain too deep to wade across and too swift for boats until at least mid-November.

Wellesley had first examined the city and its fortifications from the south-east of the island on the afternoon of the 3rd. Even from five miles away the place was impressive. On the downstream side of the city the twin white minarets of the Mosque rose slender and tall against a clear blue sky. To the west the single, bulkier tower of the Hindoo Temple of Vishnu was equally magnificent. From afar the whole island was beautiful, a white jewel in a lush green setting. On the afternoon of the 4th Wellesley came close enough to make out the defences around the city. The walls were chiefly made of solid granite well cut and mortared with some occasional brick. The place was large and obviously strong. Through his telescope Wellesley counted

---

[1] *Beatson*, 82, says that Harris always intended to cross the Cauvery here. It would appear that the Madras C-in-C not only had a carefully thought-out plan based on his earlier experience in Mysore, but kept his own council and carried it out flawlessly.

[2] *Wilks*, III, 414. He is perhaps the best source for this information because he wrote his *Historical Sketches* while serving as Resident at Mysore.

nearly a hundred guns on the south face and in the south cavaliers[1] alone. But the design was of the Eastern type; the defenders could not deliver flanking fire against an assaulting column, save imperfectly from cavaliers.[2]

Colonel Wellesley already knew Harris's siege plan. The combined armies were to march past the island on the south side of the Cauvery, turn north and then approach Seringapatam from the west. If all went well, the British would establish a secure fortified camp and then deliver an assault across the South Cauvery against the city itself which occupied the western tip of the island. There was to be no siege in the sense of cutting off the place from the surrounding country; the island was too large and the Mysore armies too powerful and mobile. The selection of the point of attack had already been made tentatively, though it was to remain a well-kept secret. Anywhere on the west or north faces, however, would have the advantage that a single attack could be immediately decisive. If an assault was to be made on the south or east, the British armies would first have to gain a foothold on the island. Tipoo's army was known to have established a line of earthworks entirely surrounding the area.

On the night of 4 April Harris sent a probing force under Baird, the brigade commander of the day, to see what lay in the area of the permanent British camp and between it and Seringapatam. This thrust was not opposed and at first progressed well in a bright moonlit night. This force crossed an aqueduct[3] that was to play an important part in the siege and got into a wooded area . . . where the entire force lost its collective sense of direction and very nearly retreated north-east towards Seringapatam. The mistake was rectified by an officer under Baird's command who later became an astronomer and a surveyor of note and who could tell direction by the stars.[4] Some Mysore cavalry that blundered into Baird's column was severely handled.

On the 5th the combined armies completed their long march. Since crossing the border the main British force had covered 153·5

---

[1] Cavalier: a raised part of fortifications usually mounting guns.

[2] The great advantage of European fortifications of that time, often referred to as the Vauban type, was that their angularity did give the defenders the capability of directing flanking fire against almost any attack.

[3] An aqueduct in India was usually a canal which often ran in a channel in a long artificial mound of earth higher than the adjacent areas. It did, however, carry water for irrigation and other purposes.

[4] *Harris*, 290, gives the name of Lieutenant Lambton. The author treats a rudimentary knowledge of the stars as unusual. Lambton is also referred to by *Wilks*, III, *passim*, as a captain and brigade major for Baird.

miles (measured by the perambulator) in thirty-one days (twenty-three of them marching days). Harris had managed to negotiate a lot of difficult terrain in the presence of a numerically superior enemy whose cavalry was probably the best in India. Losses in men, material and even in anmials had been remarkably small considering the vast mass of baggage and the enormous siege train. In spite of pilfering on the way, Harris still had, for instance, 36,395 18-pound shot which required more than 6,000 bullocks.[1]

The area which Harris had chosen, apparently months before, for his enormous semi-fortified camp was south of the Cauvery and west of the island; it was covered by the river to the north and by broken ground to the west. The C-in-C placed the Nizam's army, now completely controlled by Colonel Wellesley, on the south.[2] Thus Wellesley would be responsible for the long unprotected southern flank. He did what he could to establish a line of posts on the afternoon of the 5th.

Harris had shown the enemy the general direction from which he would attack. The 'siege' would obviously resolve itself into a race between British operations and the breaking of the monsoon. Tipoo or his French advisers would surely realize that anything they could do to hold Harris back, like defending the line of the aqueduct, would win time. Harris had been using the 'brigade commander of the day' for special services and would continue to use him regardless of who he happened to be. The appointment alternated between six officers in his army; as the joint camp was established, Wellesley was to be a seventh, although he would continue in 'advisory' command of the Nizam's contingent. He was to follow Baird in this rotation.

Early in the afternoon of the 5th Harris ordered Wellesley to deliver a sunset and night attack to clear the village of Sultanpetah, the aqueduct and 'Sultanpetah Tope'. The last of these objectives was not precisely defined, but more of this presently. Colonel Wellesley was to

[1] *Beatson*, cxx, for a table of ordnance which arrived, was expended during the siege, and which remained at the end. A few bullocks could carry eight 18-pounder shot, a load including saddle of at least 160 pounds, but most could not; six shot of this size were normal, amounting to a total of slightly more than 120 pounds.

[2] Wellesley wrote to Mornington on 8 May 1799: 'I do not mean that Dalrymple [the most senior British officer after Wellesley] and I are not upon the very best terms, but on one or two occasions he sent me orders which he said came from Meer Allum, and which never could have entered his [Meer Allum's] head. If I had obeyed I should probably have lost part of the detachment.' *Supplementary Despatches*, I, 215–16. Wellesley was diplomatic with both Meer Allum and Dalrymple, but ran the force precisely as he saw fit.

use his King's 33rd supported by two of his EIC battalions, apparently the 1/11 and 2/11 Madras Native Infantry.[1]

Lieutenant-Colonel Shawe with the King's 12th supported by the 1/1 and the 2/3 Madras Native Infantry was to advance in a similar direction towards the same aqueduct, but from Harris's camp rather than from the Hyderabad position. Shawe's objective was also the aqueduct and a village contained within a loop of it.

When Baird had penetrated this area the night before, most of Tipoo's army was in trenches south-east of the capital still waiting to be attacked there. But early on the 5th they withdrew to the island and then moved south-west as far as the aqueduct from which they were firing rockets into the British camp during the afternoon.

The orders to Wellesley and Shawe seem simple, but they were not. No one then had a precise knowledge of the area into which the two commands were to penetrate. At that time the aqueduct originated miles to the west at Kanambaddy; in April 1799 it was about fifteen yards wide and as much as six feet deep.[2] The aqueduct, or *nullah* as Wellesley called it, remains confusing because it is located on top of high ground, not at the bottom of a valley. There are still incredibly small rice fields and a system of tiny canals leading outward and down from the aqueduct on both sides.

Sultanpetah, the village, was south by south-west of Seringapatam. It is marked definitely on some contemporary plans but not on all. In his Diary Harris refers to it as a ruined village only. By inference Sultanpetah Tope, although not marked on any contemporary map, is the wooded area north-west of the village which is shown on most diagrams. At the risk of confusing everyone, I should add that later on during the siege the *tope* in question was known as the Engineer's Tope. A careful investigation of this area today is inconclusive. I have found no village or ruins where Sultanpetah once stood. The Tope is gone also and there is hardly a tree anywhere around the aqueduct.

Wellesley appears to have been on his horse establishing the eastern end of his line of posts when he received his orders for the attack. He did not know precisely what he was to do and hastened to ask Harris for clarification. He said, 'I do not know where you mean . . . do me the

---

[1] I am following *Wilson*, II, 319–21, but *Beatson*, 90, gives the 1/10 and 2/10 Bengal Native Infantry. All four battalions were in Wellesley's Hyderabad command.

[2] The aqueduct still follows the old path in the area where fighting occurred, but issues from the Cauvery much further east and is shallower and narrower. The old Kanambaddy site was destroyed by a large dam and lake installed before the end of the nineteenth century.

favour to meet me in front of the lines . . . when you get possession of the nullah you have the tope.'[1] There is no record of Harris complying with this request, but Wellesley could not protest further. He knew all about subordinates who created unnecessary problems about details. At sundown he moved east from his camp with the 33rd in column supported by two of his EIC battalions. He personally rode at the head of this force and ran into hostile rocket fire as he approached the aqueduct. The 33rd went *up* to the watercourse with fixed bayonets and forced the enemy to retreat *down* the other side. There was some fighting, but casualties were light. Wellesley had his section of the aqueduct, but it was clear now that the Sultanpetah Tope was on the Seringapatam side of the embanked *nullah*.

Wellesley led forward the flank companies of the 33rd, with the battalion companies at first close behind under Major Shee, a contentious and alcoholic officer.[2] It was dark as pitch below the aqueduct in the *tope*, but the Europeans may have been silhouetted against the skyline for they received a straggling but heavy fire. There was nothing to do but press on even though the immediate surroundings could not have been worse. Wellesley and his soldiers ran into tiny canals, dykes, trees and clumps of bamboo. They had no guides and no idea what their area looked like in daylight because the aqueduct was higher than the country on either side of it.

On the other hand, Tipoo's rocket boys and musket men knew the ground and could probably see better. British pupils were being contracted by Mysore rockets which came arching through the blackness towards them. The light infantry of Mysore would have been at a hopeless disadvantage against the 33rd in daylight, but here they were formidable. They delivered at least one savage hand-to-hand attack and killed Lieutenant Fitzgerald with a bayonet thrust;[3] eight men from the Grenadier company were captured, but perhaps not all at the same time. The flank companies of the 33rd were blundering around in darkness and became separated from the rest of the battalion. Major Shee pulled back his battalion companies across the aqueduct although he may have penetrated entirely across the *tope* and recrossed

---

[1] *Supplementary Despatches*, I, 23. Wellesley thought the group of trees he was to attack were on his side of the aqueduct, but contemporary maps indicate that he was wrong.

[2] John Shee's major's commission in the regiment is dated 1 December 1794. I would not use these adjectives if *Lady Longford*, 61 and 83–4, had not arrived at essentially the same conclusions.

[3] Fitzgerald had already been wounded by a rocket 'which nearly carried away his arm': *Supplementary Despatches*, I, 210.

the aqueduct at another place. The Sepoys in support never got into action at all. We really have no idea exactly what happened; I believe that Wellesley was never sure about it himself. Shee and five battalion companies finally reappeared about a mile to the north and joined Shawe. Captain Francis Ralph West and some of his Grenadier company were so badly lost that they went south into Wellesley's main picket in the village of Sultanpetah.

For a while at least, Wellesley wandered about either alone or in the company of a young engineer officer, Colin Mackenzie.[1] The colonel had been hit on the knee by a bullet, but was not badly wounded. Somehow he, or they, found the way back to the aqueduct and re-crossed. Once reoriented, Wellesley learnt as much as possible about his own attack and the one made by Shawe. This officer and the King's 12th had gone forward supported by two EIC battalions at about the same time as Wellesley and the 33rd and much in the same way. Shawe took his village without firing a shot and probably carried a section of the aqueduct as well, although contemporary records do not agree.

Shawe's two supporting EIC battalions, however, appear to have run into perhaps imaginary trouble from the start; they probably received hostile rocket fire from long range, fired back and then each mistook each other for the enemy. The 2/3 Madras, temporarily under Major Colin Campbell, 'paid no attention to orders' and with their shooting killed their commanding officer. The 1/1 Madras under Lieutenant-Colonel David Campbell did not do much better. Neither battalion could be controlled, though Shawe tried and failed, after which he returned to his own regiment. Major Shee with his five battalion companies of the King's 33rd came up during the night with Shawe and the King's 12th about 10 o'clock. Shee's part of the 33rd then apparently took unopposed possession of a part of the aqueduct south-west of Shawe's village and held it for the rest of the night.

Once Wellesley had the information about Shawe, Shee and most of the survivors of his own flank companies – Lieutenant Fitzgerald, although mortally wounded, was carried back by some of his grenadiers – he found his horse and rode to Harris's headquarters to report his lack of success. He reached headquarters about midnight, when Harris had neither retired nor fallen asleep at his dining table. Harris

---

[1] We are fortunate in having a number of independent accounts of what happened, both original and secondary, but they do not always agree. See *Vibert*, I, 300; *Wilson*, II, 319; *Harris*, 291; and *Beatson*, 90.

recorded that the young colonel 'came to my tent in a good deal of agitation to say that he had not carried the tope'.[1]

The entire Sultanpetah Tope affair has been magnified out of all proportion because it was the only action in which the Duke of Wellington ever suffered a military reverse. Even at the time there were camp rumours; Wellesley had not yet risen above professional jealousy. The victor of Waterloo was later to defend his conduct at Sultanpetah Tope more vigorously, perhaps, than was necessary. The whole thing was regrettable but relatively small; the total casualties, including the eight prisoners, did not reach twenty-five.

I resist the obvious temptation to blame Harris more than his subordinate. The line of the aqueduct is all that was militarily important. To send the 33rd blundering down the other side in darkness just does not seem to make sense, least of all after one has climbed about among postage-stamp rice fields and Japanese garden canals by daylight in the same area 170 years later. Neither at this time nor later did Wellesley try to shift his responsibility to anyone else, but he did decide 'never to attack an enemy who is prepared and strongly posted, and whose posts have not been reconnoitred by daylight'.[2] Actually, he was not to undertake many more night operations during his military career. What is more important, Wellesley would never again get personally so far forward in an attack that he lost control of his force as a whole. That night he probably fought with his own sword for one of the few times in his career. He may have found the experience exhilarating because almost certainly he handled the weapon well.[3] But a man who fights cannot think to maximum advantage.

On the morning of 6 April Harris had a clear idea of what had occurred the night before because of Wellesley's midnight visit. On the evenings of 4 and 5 April the British had failed to get and hold the area between their camp and Seringapatam, or even any considerable part of it. Harris told Barry Close to lay on another attack to carry the entire aqueduct and Sultanpetah Tope. A fresh King's infantry battalion was to be used, the Scotch Brigade, supported by two new

[1] This is from Harris's private diary quoted by his son-in-law and biographer: *Harris*, 294–5.

[2] *Supplementary Despatches*, I, 209.

[3] Many British officers in India practised daily with all their weapons. I have found no specific reference to Wellesley doing this, but I believe it to be extremely likely. Sword exercise was so common among all officers that it would not have caused any comment, especially if undertaken as part of his daily riding. He was agile, muscular and unusually fit.

EIC units and four 12-pounder brass field guns. Wellesley was again to have command.[1] Cotton with his King's 25th Dragoons and the 2nd Native Cavalry was in support on the open right flank. Wallace with the grenadier company of the King's 74th Foot and four companies of Sepoys were to go forward on the north next to the newly established post of Shawe.

Close was a remarkably good adjutant-general and immediately dispatched the necessary orders to most of the units involved. Unfortunately there was a delay in sending off an order to Wellesley. The assaulting column was ready to move out and the preliminary artillery fire had already begun. But Wellesley had not yet arrived. Harris probably considered giving the command to Baird who was on hand as a spectator and perhaps also because the Scotch Brigade was one of Baird's three battalions. The C-in-C, however, either did not give it, or if he did, countermanded the order before Baird moved out.[2] Suddenly a cloud of dust was seen approaching: Wellesley had Diomed in a full gallop. He had just received his orders.

The daylight attack then went off without a hitch. The sight of the British troops assembling and the preliminary artillery fire – in India 12-pounder field guns often used shell[3] – caused the enemy to begin their retreat. Wellesley took the entire aqueduct and the Sultanpetah Tope area without the loss of a man.

It should be mentioned that there exists another version of this incident in the continuing Baird–Wellesley confrontation. Baird married an heiress who after his death hired a biographer to set down her own view of her husband. Mr Hook, who is now known to be the author, says that Wellesley was late – as he was – and that Harris ordered Baird to take over the attack. Baird is said to have refused, however, out of kindness for Wellesley's feelings after his unpleasant experience of the night before. No soldier, least of all Baird who was particularly noted for his fiery personal courage, would act like this under any circumstances. Everyone expected a tough fight in the *tope* and if Baird had been ordered to go in, he would have gone claymore in hand.

---

[1] He was brigade commander of the day until noon.

[2] *Harris*, 296–9. Lushington says the order was given and recalled – he was ill in his tent, however, at the time. Wellington wrote to Gurwood in 1833: 'I never knew that in my absence General Baird had been appointed to command. Indeed I should doubt from General Harris's papers that General Baird ever did receive such orders.' *Maxwell*, I, 33, quoting an Apsley House MS.

[3] These were the same shells as used in 4.5-inch howitzers. For details see Appendix I.

Harris's army now occupied the irregular line of the aqueduct and the part of the ground between this line and Seringapatam. After less than 48 hours the British were in a strong position and would soon make it stronger. The village taken by Shawe on the night of the 5th was made the key to a sort of 'first line' of siege works. Shawe's post became the forward command post of the British army and was thereafter occupied by the brigade commander of the day. A battery of two iron 12-pounders was established behind the bank of the *nullah* or aqueduct at this point. They had a fine field of fire which included various enemy positions west of the South Cauvery; Shawe's post was about 1,500 yards from the north-west corner of the Seringapatam fortifications.

After the daylight attack of 6 April Wellesley had more time for his own string of posts which extended from Sultanpetah in a flat arc about eleven miles long to the Cauvery; they were held by more than half his entire force of infantry, cavalry and artillery.[1]

Even before the aqueduct and Sultanpetah Tope were carried Harris sent Floyd with a mixed force of cavalry, infantry and artillery to fetch in Stuart and his Bombay army. This army consisted of the King's 19th Dragoons, the 1st, 3rd, and 4th Native Cavalry, the King's 73rd Foot, the 1st, 2nd, and 3rd Bengal Volunteers and twenty field guns. Floyd and Stuart met at Periapatam on the 10th and moved towards Seringapatam. Throughout this movement Floyd's army was observed by masses of enemy cavalry waiting for an opportunity to do damage to the British units, but none was presented. At precisely 7.30 p.m. on the 13th, Floyd fired two guns in succession. According to a code established before Floyd left the British camp at Seringapatam this signal meant: 'I am one day's march away.' Exactly ten minutes later, Harris replied with two guns also fired in succession which meant: 'Message received and understood.'[2] The next morning Harris took the King's 25th Dragoons, the 2nd Native Cavalry and some Mogul mounted units under Meer Allum and marched towards Floyd and Stuart to prevent any last-minute effort by Tipoo to defeat the British armies in detail. All arrived safely in camp at sundown on the 14th.

After a day of rest Stuart and his Bombay army were ordered to the

---

[1] *Dispatches*, I, 27 and 28. 'Not enough men left to give a relief.' 'I have fourteen 6-pounders, of which eight are out with the outposts and pickets.'

[2] *Biddulph*, 110; many different messages could be sent by varying the time and the number of guns. More important, I have had to choose between a variety of dates, distances and other details in working out this march. Several conflicts exist in original and secondary records.

north side of the Cauvery. They crossed well to the west of Seringapatam Island and then marched back eastward on the north side of the river. On the 16th their camp was established to the west of Seringapatam Island, but Stuart pushed forward patrols towards what he knew to be his future combat area.[1] Harris now controlled both banks of the river west of Seringapatam. Batteries could be mounted south of the Cauvery without fear of enfilade fire from the north side. The time between 6 April and 16 April had been spent in moving solidly into the main camp area, properly storing the siege train and assembling siege materials. On the 17th the British armies delivered sharp attacks both north and south of the river.

Let us first consider the southern attack. Here the situation remained essentially as it was on the afternoon of the 6th. EIC Colonel William Gent, Harris's able chief engineer, had fortified the village between the aqueduct and the Cauvery that had been taken by Wallace, Shawe's post, the line of the aqueduct, a post in front of the Engineer's Tope (the old Sultanpetah Tope), and Sultanpetah itself. The enemy had moved forward in strength, however, and still occupied a third branch of the Cauvery, known as the Little Cauvery.

At sunset on the 17th Major Macdonald led the 2/12 Madras Native Infantry out from Shawe's post and carried the north–south stretch of the Little Cauvery. He struck by surprise and so swiftly that the issue was never in doubt. The Little Cauvery here was virtually a natural parallel for 500 yards. It became known as Macdonald's Post and was situated only 1,000 yards from the main defences of Seringapatam.

At about the same time Stuart, aided by the King's 74th and one EIC battalion from Harris's army, attacked on the north side of the river and took possession of a ruined village and the old redoubt at Agra, or Agrarum. The Bombay army worked all night to throw up trenches around the whole position and to erect a battery according to a 1792 survey to enfilade the west face of the Seringapatam defences. The labour for the battery was mostly wasted, however, because daylight revealed it to be too far west.

Before continuing with the siege, we should briefly consider what at the time appeared to be an extremely serious shortage of food. An accurate check of all grain, biscuit and meat available showed only enough to provide half rations for all fighting men for twenty-three

---

[1] Actually towards the Delhi bridge, but this was in ruins according to contemporary maps. It was apparently still usable by foot traffic. There is a similar structure there today.

days. Only a few days before the army was thought to have enough for full rations for forty-three days. In spite of some captures and supplies brought by Stuart and Floyd, the food supply had shrunk by thousands of bullock loads, and rice in particular appears to have been stolen in large quantities. Harris found himself in the position of having to capture Seringapatam quickly or give up the attempt as Cornwallis had done in 1791. On 22 April, however, the food situation was better; there was enough until the middle of May.[1] Floyd had already gone off with a second force similar, but not identical to the one he had taken to bring back Stuart.[2] He was moving to Cauveryporam to bring back Read and Brown with the supplies they had collected.

The siege operations were being carried on by EIC Colonel William Gent and his engineers, ably and unselfishly supported by George Harris. The engineers were professionals with many years' experience in India. There was an ample siege train, a great number of Indian pioneers organized into four units, some European pioneers (who were more effective with their greater size and strength) and working parties from infantry units. The siege was carried forward on scientific principles by men who had all they required, but who realized that they could take no liberties with the opposition since the enemy had Frenchmen who knew as much as they did. Their progress from step to step was based on efficiency and security. Speed was secondary.

Macdonald's capture of the South Cauvery on the night of the 17th had been improved. It was now connected with Shawe's Post by a *sap*, or covered way. An effort was made to establish a battery at the southern end of Macdonald's position, but Tipoo had established a fortified position in the ruins of a powder mill on the bank of the Cauvery 300 yards in front of Macdonald's new line. The powder mill fort was taken by Sherbrooke (acting major-general of the day) in a well delivered sunset attack by artillery, pioneers, the King's

---

[1] Harris's diary gives the bare facts of this scarcity and its relief: *Harris*, 318. There are hints, especially in *Wilks*, III, 422, that this situation was caused by improper behaviour. My copy of this volume contains a long marginal note clearly written in pencil as follows: 'Major Hart, who had charge of the grain department with the army, offered these 1,200 loads of rice for sale. He alleged that they were a private venture of his own. He was charged with having them surreptitiously from the public store. The question became a party question, and begat a great deal of that dissention that party questions generally do beget. Even if it was a private venture, it was one that Major Hart, in his position, had no business to be engaged in.'

[2] This time Floyd took all the regular cavalry and Lieutenant-Colonel Gowdie's brigade composed of the 1/1, 1/6, and 1/12 Madras Native Infantry. He finally left on the 19th although he had been encamped some distance to the south for four days: *Wilson*, II, 322, and other sources.

73rd and a battalion of Bengal Sepoys. Casualties appear to have been the almost unbelievable total of one man killed and four wounded in the assaulting force to 250 killed among the defenders. As sometimes happened in India, British audacity temporarily paralysed the enemy. Lieutenant-Colonels Monypenny and St John of the 73rd and Gardiner of the EIC Bengal Army distinguished themselves. During the night of the 20th the engineers, pioneers and infantry working parties constructed a battery near the powder mill and a parallel from behind it to the Little Cauvery. The battery was armed with six 18-pounders, the best artillery of the time, early on the morning of the 21st.

North of the stream Stuart was improving his position. Shortly before sunset on the 22nd a new battery was laid out precisely in line with the west face of the Seringapatam defences, but this activity led to a considerable enemy reaction. First, heavy fire was brought on the British position; later it was attacked in force with Lally's old Corps of Frenchmen in the lead.[1] Stuart repulsed this assault with heavy losses to the enemy and completed a new, properly located battery the next night.

Work now progressed steadily and securely on both sides of the Cauvery. During the night of the 25th a four-gun battery was constructed at the southern end of the diagonal trench extending from the rear of the powder mill battery towards the Little Cauvery. Early the following morning it opened against Tipoo's cannon in the two round towers and the single square tower half way down the western defences of Seringapatam. The range was nearly 900 yards, but the four British 18-pounders were astonishingly effective. The enemy guns were silenced – actually they were in part removed – 'in half an hour'.[2] By noon of the 26th all the guns on the walls of Seringapatam and most of those in the elevated calivers and bastions that could fire effectively at the British batteries either north and south of the river had been silenced. Stuart's batteries north of the river and the powder mill battery had blasted an old and a new bastion at the north-west corner of the main wall; the shots that were too high passed down the north and west wall clearing away men, guns and anything else in the area.

However, in the vital section south-west of the South Cauvery there remained a line of entrenchments, including some brick and stone

[1] This unit had been in the service of Mysore for almost twenty years and was sadly depleted in strength, but fought valiantly. Frenchmen were killed with bayonets both inside and outside the British field fortifications.

[2] *Vibart*, 311. His details of the siege itself are the best available.

70

outworks at the high-water margin of the river. They were connected with the main defences by the Periapatam bridge and protected for most of their length by a 'water course' which branched north from the Little Cauvery before the latter stream turned south to form Macdonald's Post. This 'water course' once provided power for the powder mill and, in combination with the Periapatam bridge, water to fill the outer ditch or moat around Seringapatam. There were also some additional works at the southern end of this line of outer fortifications and to cover the 'Stone Bridge' across the Little Cauvery.

Arthur Wellesley became brigade commander of the day at noon on the 26th. He had already received orders to attack Tipoo's line of outer fortifications at or soon after sunset. This was not to be another Sultan-petah Tope. Wellesley knew exactly what the position of the enemy was and how it was defended. There were to be no surprises, at least not for the British. Wellesley used a simple assault plan with two columns and fully discussed with his subordinate commanders what they were to do.

On the left, next to the Cauvery, Major Skelly was to lead four companies of his Scotch Brigade and four of the 2nd Bengal Native Infantry forward from the British trenches into the northern anchor of Tipoo's line of defences and work south. Lieutenant-Colonel Monypenny was to move forward as close as possible to the Little Cauvery with four companies of his 73rd and four more of the 2nd Bengal, to enter the line of defences near its middle and move south. The two columns easily carried this line of low fortifications. Most of the defenders just left their positions and walked back across the river which in late April was fordable at almost any place. Tipoo's troops were giving up not just the sections of their position actually attacked, but the rest too even before Skelly and Monypenny reached them.

Wellesley also had under his command a reserve consisting of 'the relief from the trenches' – the troops who had garrisoned the trenches for the previous twenty-four hours – under his friend Colonel Sher-brooke, also of the 33rd. This reserve consisted of the King's 74th and the Regiment De Meuron plus some EIC units. Wellesley's initial attacks had succeeded so well that he sent Sherbrooke's men forward against the Stone Bridge across the Little Cauvery and against two works behind it usually referred to as the Ravelin and the Circular or three-gun Battery. All three were taken almost as easily as the line of works closer to the South Cauvery. Support for these enemy positions had come from the recently abandoned trenches.

All the objectives were achieved so easily that without orders to do so Lieutenant-Colonel Campbell of the 74th led some of his own regiment and most of the Regiment De Meuron across the Periapatam Bridge to the island of Seringapatam. Fortunately they did not try to go through the Mysore Gate into the main defences. They captured a couple of field guns south of the main walls inside Tipoo's strong fortified camp, used them briefly against the enemy, spiked them and returned across the Periapatam Bridge. Somewhere in this attack Campbell lost his shoes, probably in crossing the Little Cauvery, and had his feet cut so badly subsequently that he had to report himself a casualty. His place was taken by Lieutenant-Colonel William Wallace, an officer of whom we shall see a lot more.

The rest of this attack on the night of the 26th was not quite so favourable to the British. Both the Ravelin and the Circular Battery were open to fire from guns mounted in the main defences of Seringapatam, a design of obviously French origin. Most of the enemy guns mounted around the Mysore Gate and in the southern cavaliers were still undamaged because they were out of the line of fire of the British batteries then in existence. These pieces may even have been loaded and aimed in daylight, after the French fashion, but left for use at night. Wallace and his men were subjected to accurate and heavy artillery fire and a few minutes later to showers of small arms bullets and rockets from the units of Tipoo's army holding the area between the Little Cauvery and the South Cauvery not yet attacked. Wallace and/or Wellesley wisely decided to pull back into the eastern strip of the Little Cauvery where their men would be protected by the embankment, temporarily giving up the Stone Bridge, the Ravelin and the Circular Battery.

The fire from the walls was renewed at dawn, but Wellesley attacked again. His units quickly tumbled every Mysore soldier out of the entire area between the Cauverys. Every man appears to have had a musket and bayonet in one hand and a pickaxe or shovel in the other. As soon as the enemy was driven out, they dug in. Wellesley's entire force was fully protected by trenches or other defences by 10 a.m. The long assault had finally succeeded beyond its original objectives, but it had been costly. Seventy-two men were killed in the action, 226 wounded and nineteen reported missing. The fire from the walls of Seringapatam was the main cause of the casualties.

Harris now had all the territory he could use in his future operations on his side of the river. Breaching batteries were constructed at a distance less than 400 yards from the main ramparts of Seringapatam. But this was done carefully and in a manner to conceal from the enemy the exact point of attack. On the night of 28 April the first actual breaching battery was begun and filled with six 18-pounders. It opened fire on the 29th, but at the north-west corner bastions, not at the walls to be breached. Battery No. 6, also called the Nizam's Battery, was added along with Nos 7, 8 and 9 for various purposes, including the silencing of the guns in the southern cavaliers during the next two nights. Thirty-nine of the forty siege guns originally assembled by Wellesley at Vellore (one 18-pounder had been destroyed), plus some big howitzers and field pieces were all in place somewhere in the siege works. There were also fieldpieces south of the river and in a secondary battery of Stuart's, north of it.

Early in the morning of 2 May 1799 the Powder Mill, the Nizam's and No. 5 Batteries suddenly concentrated all their fire on the walls where an actual breach was to be made. Two of the three batteries were 380 and 340 yards from their targets. The point chosen was in the west wall just south of the already destroyed north-west bastions. At this point the glacis which protected the entire northern wall and the north-west corner after a fashion – it was too low to protect completely – was replaced by a forward curtain or vertical wall which kept water in the outer ditch.

Solid cast-iron 18-pound balls, varied occasionally with 24-pound balls from the two larger pieces, tore up both curtains for more than sixty yards. Save for a few inches, the water in the elevated outer ditch ran into the South Cauvery. Here the main or outer wall of the city was smashed back into the terreplein, or paved area, behind the rampart. The breach was tentatively pronounced practical on the evening of the 3rd; in the technical language of the day this meant that a man, encumbered only by a musket, bayonet and cartridge box would be able to climb it. Such a conclusion is not always easy to establish from a distance even with a telescope. There were the additional difficulties of crossing the South Cauvery and the outer ditch. Everyone thought that enough water had drained out of the latter to render it useless, but no one was sure.

That night Arthur Wellesley was again in command in the trenches and batteries. He and his command took on a heavy work load and accomplished it all save for filling some sandbags.[1] Some of his active young officers carefully reconnoitred the South Cauvery over the

[1] At 7 a.m. on 3 May 1799 Wellesley wrote to General Harris, 'We did all our work last

entire front below the breach and marked unobtrusively safe areas for fording. Enough space was also provided and covered to allow a large assaulting force to be assembled within the trenches and breast-works without revealing its presence to the enemy.

Harris was determined that, if humanly possible, his first assault should be successful. If necessary he was ready to throw his entire army into the effort. His soldiers, both European and Indian, had been on somewhat short rations for two weeks. The C-in-C was probably over-conscious of the food situation; Floyd was to bring back Read and Brown with supplies from the Baramahal and Coimbatoor right on schedule. The coming of the monsoon was much more dangerous and beyond human control. The rains would quickly fill all branches of the Cauvery and Seringapatam would be safe seventy-two hours after they began.[1] It was high time the British armies completed their work.

Tipoo had 30,000 fighting men in and around Seringapatam; there was but a single breach through which to get at them after fording a rocky stream 200 yards wide. The assault should be delivered at maximum power, but too many men would get in each other's way and would lead to more severe casualties, and perhaps to failure. Throughout the campaign, Harris utilized the abilities of his fine staff, but the master design was his own. He gave Barry Close the essential details for a simple but flawless attack using all available British man-power. Baird had volunteered to lead the assault; Harris accepted his offer. The major-general's height, strength and gallant personality made him a favourite with all European troops who, when available, always led assaults in British operations in India. They knew that he had spent forty-four months in Tipoo's dungeon without losing his spirit. No one in the assembled allied armies was as suited to the task as Baird.

He would have two columns, each with its own commander and objectives. The left column, led by Lieutenant-Colonel Dunlop from Stuart's army, would consist of all six flank companies from Stuart's King's regiments, the whole of the King's 12th and the King's 33rd, and finally ten companies of Bengal Sepoy flankers. There were fifty European artillerymen with a proportion of gun Lascars attached to

[1] The extent and the regularity from year to year of Eastern Monsoons are difficult for those who have not lived there to understand. At Seringapatam they generally began about 20 May, but could be four or five days early or late.

---

night except filling the sandbags... I shall have them filled in the course of the morning... Lt Lalor found the retaining wall of the glacis [actually the outer wall of the outer ditch] to be seven feet high and the water 14 inches deep': *Dispatches*, I, 29–30.

this column. There were also pioneers, fascines (in this case, bundles of bamboo) and scaling ladders. The right column under Colonel Sherbrooke consisted of the flank companies of the Scotch Brigade, followed by those of the Regiment de Meuron, the entire King's 73rd and 74th, eight companies of Madras Sepoy flankers from the Hyderabad contingent and six companies of Bombay Sepoy flankers. The column also included 200 men from Meer Allum's Hyderabad army. It had the same number of artillerymen and gun Lascars assigned as on the left; pioneers, scaling ladders and fascines were distributed in the same way.

Harris's plan called for the two columns to remain concealed in the trenches until Baird ordered the attack, probably at 1 p.m. They would then come out, form, cross the river side by side and go up the breach together. In the event that both columns could not cross the South Cauvery or ascend the breach at the same time – unlikely after Wellesley's careful investigation on the night following 2 May – the left was to be in front.[1] Once up the breach and into the defences, the columns were not to enter the city but to turn left and right respectively and circle the defences to the north and to the south until they met somewhere on the opposite or east side. The idea was to get possession of the entire defences before entering the city. Each cavalier or bastion was to be taken and then garrisoned by a battalion company from a European regiment before the column proceeded. Each column would advance in formation of half companies at quarter distance, but would be preceded by 'forlorn hopes'. In those days these small all-volunteer groups led the way. Each was to consist of a sergeant with the colours and twelve lightly armed volunteer privates followed by a lieutenant and twenty-five men noted for their personal fighting prowess.

There was a third force in the trenches with the other two, but to the rear. It was commanded by Arthur Wellesley and consisted of the eight battalion companies of the EIC Swiss Regiment de Meuron and four EIC battalions.[2] As soon as the two main columns had crossed, Wellesley would advance his force to the river. He was then to do everything possible to reinforce any part of the attack that did not succeed, but was not needlessly to crowd into the assaults. It may be significant that Wellesley was the only subordinate commander

[1] There are three large coloured prints of 'The Storming of Seringapatam' at Sandhurst and the Royal Hospital which show this assault in detail. The artist appears to have the details of uniform and individuals correct. There is a key to identities; 45 men are named and located. The original appears to have been produced in India and at the time.

[2] *Wilson*, II, 327, says these were the 2/5, 2/7, 1/8 and 2/9 Madras.

authorized to use his own judgment. The total strengths of these three commands were about 3,000 for Dunlop, about 2,800 for Sherbrooke and at least 4,400 for Wellesley. Harris and Stuart were reduced to nearly the minimum for holding their camps should Tipoo's external forces attack.

Throughout the morning of the 4th the British guns continued to play on the breach as if to improve it further – actually to prevent the defenders from making it more difficult. There was little to indicate to an observer inside Seringapatam that an attack was to be launched that day, although a senior officer in Tipoo's service who had begun his military career with the British, Seyed Goffhar, did correctly interpret what he saw and warned his chief of the impending assault.

Baird and his entire force had been in the trenches since before dawn. The attackers were crowded together under a pitiless sun as the morning wore on, and the heat must have become nearly unbearable. Not a man stirred, however, until it was 1 p.m. by Baird's watch. Only then did the huge Scot rouse himself. Although his sweat-soddened uniform stuck to him, he climbed out of the foremost trench and drew his regimental claymore. 'Now, my brave fellows!' Baird said in his strong, deep voice. 'Follow me and prove yourselves worthy of the name British soldiers!'

The two columns quickly formed abreast in line of platoons and began to move forward with Baird in front. Only the two forlorn hopes, a total of seventy-six young men, were ahead of him. Baird was in his forty-second year, worn by hardship and climate, and perhaps rather heavy for scrambling about on wet rocks, but he kept in front and was ready to fight. His face which never suntanned properly was as red as his uniform. As he reached the top of the breach, he glanced towards the dungeon where he had spent forty-four months. To his surprise he saw a new ditch filled with water and a second wall.[1]

As long as they dared the British batteries had continued to fire to keep the enemy off the main Seringapatam walls and away from the breach. They fell silent, however, as the assailants masked their line of fire. The two forlorn hopes mounted the slippery debris that choked the breach and began to split apart to the north and south respectively, but they were met by a fair number of defenders who appeared and fought in the breach itself. In the brief combat which ensued before all the enemy were killed, there were two British casualties of more than

---

[1] This second ditch and probably the wall behind it were begun after 1792; *Supplementary Despatches*, II, 477. They were, however, still incomplete.

usual interest. Sergeant Graham of Dunlop's forlorn hope, presumably the first man to climb the breach, was shot dead as he unfurled his colours and announced himself 'Lieutenant Graham!' According to the custom of the times he had won himself a commission. Dunlop himself was badly wounded in the hand in a brief duel with a Mysore swordsman.

The European flankers who followed Graham, Baird and Dunlop were too numerous and too impassioned to be stopped. With a viciousness some officers had never seen before, they swept the enemy right out of the breach itself and off the battlement at the top. It took only six or seven minutes. Both columns continued to cross the Cauvery in water up to four feet deep, but without difficulty save for receiving some long-range artillery fire.[1] The climb up the breach was relatively easy compared to what some had expected, but there was considerable confusion at the top. There was not enough space to deploy properly for all who crowded up.

Baird, not realizing that Dunlop was badly wounded, went with Sherbrooke's column which at that time appeared to have the more difficult job. They moved towards the west wall towers and the heavy defences around the Mysore Gate. Dunlop's force minus its commander went around the north-west corner of the outer wall – no one in the assaulting army had crossed the inner ditch yet – and was immediately involved in a serious fight. They were opposed in front by a frenzied group under a short fat officer that defended every traverse. The officer himself kept firing loaded weapons that were handed to him by his hunting servants. One of those who fell by this accurate fire was Lieutenant Lalor of the King's 73rd, the guide who on the night of 3 May did most for Wellesley in exploring the ford and breach.

Dunlop's men were not only meeting severe opposition in front, but were also subjected to intense small arms fire from the inner wall which was inaccessible to them because of the inner ditch. Even though the European flankers of the Bombay army surged east along the outer wall through and over a mass of broken guns, carriages and masonry, and over the new brick traverses in the outer bastion, they were finally stopped by this fire from the inner wall. It was particularly effective because the English on the inner side of the outer wall were exposed and the enemy protected by the parapet on the outer side of theirs.

[1] All of Tipoo's guns near to the point of attack had been silenced, but pieces from as far away as the round tower at the south-east corner of the city's main defences were firing at the two red columns crossing the river.

Captain Goodall of the King's 12th, the first unit behind the Bombay army flankers in the northern column, saw the difficulty and discovered a narrow way across the inner ditch.[1] He led his company across, obviously one by one. For a time it was probably touch and go in bloody hand-to-hand combat, but every few seconds another Englishman came into the fight. Goodall's men began to make headway faster and finally opposition collapsed.

On the outer wall, the situation suddenly changed drastically. The Bombay European flankers were no longer being fired on from the flank, but their enemies were and after a few minutes gave way. They tried to make a stand at the Sultan Battery, which surrounded Tipoo's dungeons, but were swept out of that also and forced into an area between the walls and the North Cauvery. Here the fortifications are irregular; there was and is an entrance into Seringapatam known as the Water Gate, actually a long tunnel through an earth and masonry wall. This was soon being attacked from both ends by British infantry firing platoon volleys. Some hand-to-hand fighting also occurred.

Meanwhile Sherbrooke's column had taken the Mysore Gate and continued eastward against irregular opposition. Some strong points were defended with considerable resolution, others were easily taken. Sherbrooke secured both the inner and outer walls of Seringapatam on the south side and reached the Bangalore Gate to the east within an hour. The left column originally under Dunlop did equally well in the north. At the beginning they were held up near the Water Gate, but they made faster progress thereafter. The outer defences of Seringapatam were taken; however, about half of Tipoo's fighting men in and around the island had not yet been engaged. There was the possibility that the enemy troops within the town might retreat into the palace, which was a kind of incomplete citadel.

The idea of continued resistance at the palace seems to have occurred to several British officers independently at about the same time, among others to Majors Allan, the deputy Quartermaster-General, and Beatson, the engineer and later historian. Resistance there would have been deplorable for several reasons. In India prisoners were rarely taken in assaults, Tipoo's women would inevitably be maltreated and treasure would probably be lost. Allan and Beatson briefly conferred with Baird and were ordered to go to the palace and see if they could

---

[1] This is variously described as a narrow scaffolding, a piece of terreplein, and a *batardeau* (cofferdam). The latter (*Beatson*, 129) appears to me to be most likely. The author was an engineer and certainly saw it. The others may not have known what they were looking at.

5 Seringapatam from the north-west: the Mosque and the Wellesley Bridge over the North Cauvery

6 Seringapatam from the north near the junction of North and South Cauvery

7 Seringapatam from the west, seen from the new bridge over the South Cauvery. The monument (centre-left) marks the site of the breach

8 The site of the breach: the assault came between the camera and the monument, the only repairs since having been the terreplein in the foreground and the removal of rubble. Note the scars from glancing shot below the monument

9 The northern fortifications of Seringapatam with the inner curtain gun
  emplacements facing across the North Cauvery

10 The inner ditch now partially filled up. The traverses in the background are
   those defended by Tipoo along the north wall

11 Seringapatam: the inner side of the Water Gate where Tipoo was killed

12 Hyder Ali's and Tipoo's 'dungeon'

persuade the enemy to surrender.[1] The two officers who left immediately were just in time to prevent Major Shee with some companies of the King's 33rd from attacking the palace. The two young British officers went in and managed to persuade the *killadar*, commandant of Seringapatam, and two of Tipoo's sons to surrender. The Sultan, however, was not there. After a delay a search was made, but no Tipoo.

Back to Colonel Wellesley and his supporting force in the trenches. He had his battalions ready in column at quarter distance to cross the river, if either Dunlop or Sherbrooke needed assistance. Since neither was held up for any appreciable time, no physical support was necessary. When this became obvious Wellesley ordered his five battalions to break ranks and rest easy. He sent some men to assist wounded who lay in the ford and posted a cordon of Swiss infantrymen to seal off the breach. His sepoys were all from Madras which had suffered a great deal from Mysore troops under Tipoo and his father, Hyder Ali. Wellesley, however, wanted no vengeance or plundering of the city.

This subject is important enough to be considered in more detail. In Europe a town which refused to surrender after a breach into it was practical belonged to the assaulting troops who took it. The soldiers who incurred the risk of mounting a defended breach under fire and defeating the garrison had a right to all the city contained, including its female inhabitants.[2] The Wellesleys were completely against this concept, especially in India where the civilian population had nothing to do with political and military decisions. Arthur Wellesley could do nothing about the troops already in Seringapatam; he was not in command of them. But he was certainly not going to allow his Madras sepoys the opportunity of participating in a brutal orgy. The Regiment De Meuron was unusually well disciplined and could be trusted to obey his orders.

Wellesley and half a dozen of his officers climbed the breach and entered the city. The firing had died down to occasional bursts from small arms. Some artillery fire from the eastern towers and cavaliers was not directed towards British targets; the artillerymen who accompanied both Dunlop's and Sherbrooke's columns had turned undamaged guns in these works against Mysore infantry in Tipoo's fortified camp outside the walls proper and were forcing the enemy to leave the island by the Corighaut ford.

---

[1] *Beatson*, cxxvii–cxxxi, gives Allan's complete account of this mission.
[2] Even a man as gallant as James Wolfe, the conqueror of Quebec, insisted on this if an assault was necessary.

Not 300 yards away, Wellesley caught sight of a familiar formation. Major Shee had the 33rd, or most of it, drawn up in front of Tipoo's inner palace. Baird and several other officers were impatiently awaiting the reappearance of Allan and Beatson. Wellesley and his small group joined them and heard the most recent news. The city was taken; organized resistance by large units of the enemy appeared to be at an end.

Just then Allan and Beatson came out of the palace by the main door; they had climbed in above ground level. The palace and several hundred armed men would surrender, but Tipoo was not there. An informal conference spontaneously came into being. Allan and Beatson communicated what they had learnt inside, and Baird had just heard that Tipoo had murdered thirteen English prisoners, including Wellesley's eight grenadiers from the thirty-third.[1] In spite of this, the palace and those in it were not to be harmed if there was no resistance. Tipoo, however, must be found before he was able to escape and begin operations again in one of his outlying territories.

Finally one of Tipoo's officers revealed that he knew where the Sultan was. Shee and the 33rd less the Grenadier company were left to guard the palace both to prevent those inside from getting out and the victorious British soldiers from getting at Tipoo's women and treasure. In the quickly gathering shadows of an approaching Indian night Baird and his officers and the Grenadier company followed their guide the short distance to the Water Gate. Tipoo had fallen in the fighting there after taking a personal part in the defence of the northern wall. He had been the short fat officer who fired a succession of hunting weapons at the commanders of British units.

The tunnel-like passage was choked with dead and wounded, and dozens of bodies were removed. Finally, a man dressed better than most was brought out. He seemed relatively unhurt and could still be alive.[2] Wellesley put his hand over the man's heart; there was no beat. The body was short and corpulent with small hands and feet and dark skin, darker than usual for an upper-class Indian. By torchlight the body was tentatively identified as Tipoo and taken back to the palace in

[1] According to Macleod's report given by *Beatson*, 166–7, there were thirteen Europeans executed in all, including '8 Grenadiers of the 33rd'. These were killed either by 'Jetties, a caste who perform feats of strength' by 'twisting heads to break necks' or 'by having nails driven into their skulls' (other sources). These murders occurred 25–28 April 1799.

[2] Surviving accounts of Tipoo's wounds conflict, but he had at least three, one of them from a musket ball through the side of his head. *Wilks*, III, 444–5, mentions, 'four wounds, the last a musket ball at close range through the temple'.

the Sultan's palanquin. There a dozen people who knew him well confirmed that it was truly the Sultan.

The assault was over; Tipoo was dead. No organized unit of his army appeared to remain on Seringapatam Island. Two of Tipoo's sons were on their way to Harris's camp escorted by the Light company of the 33rd. The city was filled with extreme disorder, but this was not Wellesley's responsibility. He returned through the breach to his battalions still waiting outside and took them back to their quarters. Having reported personally to Harris, he then returned to his own tent. He had been in the same clothes for nearly sixty hours during which he had had less than ten hours of sleep. Cold food, soap and water, and a narrow camp bed were sheer luxury. He had done his jobs as well as he was able; sleep came quickly. It was not even disturbed by the sporadic firing, screams and snatches of drunken song which came through the glorious Indian night from the newly-captured city.

V

Command in Mysore

Two of Tipoo's four adult sons were taken into protective custody on the night of 4 May 1799 and sent off to Harris's camp under guard of the light company of the 33rd. Early on the morning of the 5th Abdul Khalick, the second son and the elder of the two delivered as hostages to Cornwallis, came in voluntarily and gave himself up to Dalrymple and Baird. There were other indications that the war was over.

Tipoo and his father before him had made Seringapatum a strong capital. There were 287 mounted cannons on the walls and in the calivers with a total of 929 more in storage. There was the incredible store of 99,000 muskets, 13,000 of them of British manufacture, although they were mostly in poor condition. There was also a large accumulation of correspondence and records. The rest of Mysore contained little of these things.

On 4 May the garrison in Seringapatam consisted of 13,737 troops, with 8,100 more on the island in the fortified camp south and east of the city defences. The extent of Tipoo's defeat may be measured by the fact that of these troops the British buried 9,000.[1] There remained only two Mysore forces of importance in the field. One of them was just to the north around French Rocks. It was commanded by the Sultan's eldest son, Futteh Hyder, assisted by Tipoo's only high-ranking Hindoo subordinate, a Brahmin named Purneah. This army with at least one cannon had attacked Stuart on 3 May. The other

[1] *Harris*, 419. *Burton*, 23, gives 8,000 soldiers, but both totals seem high. The units in the fortified camp suffered only from long-range artillery fire; many in the fortress must have been able to get out. On the other hand, the assailants were in a vicious mood and were ordered not to take prisoners during the actual fighting.

force, which had gone off after Floyd, was commanded by Cummer U Deen, said to be Tipoo's best surviving general – an astonishing number of his generals had been killed or had died of wounds at Sedaseer, Malavelley and during the siege. By 10 May both forces and their commanders had surrendered believing the British would deal liberally with them; perhaps they had an unofficial promise that they would continue to receive full pay and allowances.[1]

On the morning of 5 May, however, Harris had an extremely unpleasant situation on his hands. His victorious army was still mostly plundering Seringapatam, a populous oriental city with many narrow twisting streets and full of treasure. Baird seems not to have been the man to put a stop to the continuing misbehaviour. Fortunately he had asked in writing to be relieved because of physical exhaustion, a request, he insisted later, that he had countermanded. When Harris received it, he ordered the next major-general of the day to be placed in orders to take over in the city. The adjutant-general's department first thought of Colonel Roberts, the man who did not want to 'command' the Nizam's contingent, but Barry Close decided it should be Colonel Wellesley.[2] Wellesley went from Harris's headquarters through the city of Seringapatam to the Dowlut Baugh, the palace outside the walls where Baird had established himself. He presented his orders and proceeded to take command while Baird and his military family were having breakfast.[3]

When he requested relief Baird apparently failed to realize that the man in command on Seringapatam Island might become the permanent commandant. A few hours later, however, he thought of this possibility and sent a verbal message by 'Captain Young, deputy adjutant general of his Majesty's troops'.[4] After being superseded,

---

[1] Modern Indian historians consider Purneah and some other of Tipoo's officers to have behaved honourably, but others, including Mir Jaffar, that he 'betrayed Tipoo to the British'; a letter of 6 February 1969 to the author from Brigadier V. P. Naib, Indian Army.

[2] The order of duty of the brigade commanders had been interrupted when Baird commanded the assault out of turn; it should have been Roberts on 4 May. Since he had been superseded by Baird, he was logically the man for duty on the 5th. But we may safely assume that Close knew Wellesley to be better suited to this particular job. Wellesley regularly followed Baird so this choice was almost equally proper.

[3] Wellesley's first dispatch to Harris after he assumed command is marked 'Ten a.m.: *Dispatches*, I, 36. He wrote: 'We are in much confusion still . . .' implying that he had been in command for some time. The story that Baird said to his military family, 'Come, Gentlemen, we are not wanted here', is probably true. Wellesley is said to have replied, 'Oh! Finish your breakfast': *Elers*, 103.

[4] *Hook*, I, 237.

Baird remonstrated with Harris at such length, with such vehemence and, in Harris's opinion, so improperly that the C-in-C lost patience and gave Baird the alternatives of withdrawing his letters or leaving the army.[1] Militarily Baird's conduct was intolerable. Harris could send into Seringapatam anyone he considered best for the job and he had the right to keep him there as long as he liked.

On 5 May Harris probably did not mean to make Wellesley permanent commandant. But he surely wanted to get Baird out; British soldiers undoubtedly thought that Baird was in favour of punishing the city, and he may have been too fond of his popularity with King's troops to be severe.[2] Wellesley was not. As soon as he was in command, he took the 33rd and some other reliable units into Seringapatam and hanged and flogged as much as was necessary. The total number of those punished is not available; I have found no record of a European soldier being hanged, but it may have happened. There were four executions, probably at least two of which were of Bengal sepoys.[3] Flogging was much more common. In situations like this summary examples work better than arrests. Wellesley quickly imposed discipline not only on those under his command, but also on British soldiers and camp followers from outside and on Mysore civilians as well. A good deal of minor disorder appears to have come from the actual inhabitants of Seringapatam.

On the 6th Harris sent in no relief for Wellesley. He may have decided before he received Baird's violent communication to leave Wellesley in charge, but it is possible that he was prompted by Baird's behaviour. More important, Wellesley was obviously doing a good job. The Governor-General had told Harris clearly that if and when Tipoo was disposed of or came to terms, the British policy in Mysore would be one of conciliation. Arthur Wellesley was already carrying this policy through on Seringapatam Island. The people who

[1] Baird wrote, in part: 'I should have been permitted to retain the command of Seringapatam, or, at least, that I should not be superseded by a junior officer. I request that copies of this letter may be transmitted to his Highness the Duke of York, Commander-in-Chief, for the information of his Majesty': Ibid., 235-7.

[2] Many years later Wellesley was to write of him: 'Baird was a gallant, hard-headed, lionhearted officer, but he had no talent, no tact; had strong prejudices against the natives; and he was peculiarly disqualified from his manners, habits, etc., and it was supposed his temper, for the management of them. He had been Tipoo's prisoner for years. He had a strong feeling of the bad usage he had received during his captivity . . .' Croker, II, 102-3.

[3] Vibart, 321. Beatson, 168, gives four exactly. Wellesley wrote: 'I came in to take command on the morning of the 5th, and by hanging, flogging, etc., restored order among the troops. I hope I have gained the confidence of the people': Dispatches, I, 212.

had fled from the city returned; in less than a week the bazaars were open as if nothing had happened.

The Governor-General from afar and Harris on the spot had won a war of extreme difficulty in less than three months. Harris had moved a total distance of 256⅞ miles from Vellore to Seringapatam with about as unwieldy an army as can be imagined. He had taken the capital of Mysore at a total cost of 825 European (181 dead, 622 wounded and 22 missing) and 639 Indian casualties (119, 420 and 100 respectively). The final assault had cost only 389 casualties of all sorts, 343 European and 46 Indian.[1] The comparative percentage of losses in the two attacking columns is interesting because the right one under Sherbrooke suffered more – a total of 180 out of 2,009 or a percentage of 8·9, not counting the Nizam's contingent which probably had few casualties. Dunlop's command lost 176 out of 2,449 or 7·2 per cent.[2]

On the other hand, twenty-two English officers were killed and forty-five wounded during the entire siege, a comparatively high price. Twenty-five of these seventy-seven casualties occurred on 4 May. In India European soldiers suffered more in assaults than their Indian companions, and officers proportionately more than other ranks. But soldiers must ultimately pay with their lives for most political aspirations which lead to combat. Once the war had begun, the campaign was essentially the efficient execution of a simple effective plan. Two British and one composite army (Hyderabad) moved safely from dispersed points to concentrate for appropriate action at Seringapatam.

On the evening of the 4th Harris sent off a short dispatch to Mornington acquainting him with the death of Tipoo and the capture of his capital. The Governor-General, who received it late on 11 May, sent Henry Wellesley and the older Kirkpatrick with a reply on the 12th.[3] Obviously the Governor-General had already made his plans to follow up a victory of this sort. He created a Second Commission consisting of Harris (if he could spare the time), Close, Kirkpatrick, Henry Wellesley and Arthur Wellesley, with Malcolm and Munro as secretaries. Lieutenant-Colonel Agnew was dropped from the First Commission, presumably because his duties as Harris's military secretary did not allow him sufficient extra time; Henry Wellesley and Kirkpatrick were added. The Governor-General set out in broad outline what he

[1] Casualties of British forces with which Wellesley was associated are given in detail in *Burton*, Appendix XI, 171 ff.

[2] *Harris*, 551. The total strengths of the columns given here appear to be too low. I have used larger approximations in the preceding chapter.

[3] *Harris*, 344–61, quotes this correspondence.

wanted the commission to do. He had, of course, already discussed this at length with the two new members.

On 13 May, before receiving any orders from Madras, Harris had sent Stuart and the Bombay army back to Malabar and Canara. On the 14th Floyd and his associates brought in the convoy from Coimbatore. On 17 May Harris sent Read to Bangalore and adjacent territories, and Brown back to Coimbatore on the 22nd. The C-in-C had enough to do with his military responsibilities; until news of the Second Commission arrived he left the political matters in the hands of the first.

Since Mornington first sat on the Board of Control in 1794 and Arthur began his voyage out in June 1796 the Wellesleys had learned a lot about India and its inhabitants. The resettlement of Mysore was their finest opportunity to put into practice all they had evolved in theory. Mornington controlled from a distance; his brothers guided what was actually done at Seringapatam. The meetings were held at Dowlut Baugh, Arthur's headquarters and now also his home. In accordance with instructions, Tipoo's four elder sons were sent off to Vellore in the charge of Lieutenant-Colonel Doveton.[1] The families of the Sultan and Hyder Ali were to follow. Mornington wanted them all out of Mysore as soon as possible.

The Governor-General had decided to restore the ancient line of Hindoo rulers who had been displaced, though not exterminated, by Hyder Ali and Tipoo. The change from a Muslim to a Hindoo ruler would be popular, for most of the people were Hindoos. No announcement was made about this, however, until the Tigers left Seringapatam with a strong British military escort suitable to their station and the damage they might do if they escaped. Once this was accomplished, a five-year-old boy, the closest surviving descendant of the old rajahs, was proclaimed ruler of a new and smaller Mysore.[2] Obviously someone must run the country for him; tentatively the committee decided on Purneah, a man noted for honesty as well as unusual military and political abilities. Hindoo himself, he was used to dealing with Muslims and had occupied several important posts under Hyder Ali and Tipoo.

Purneah was born in a village in Coimbatore in March 1746 and moved into Mysore with his family in 1760 when he became a clerk

[1] There were about eleven more, but the eldest of this second group was at that time no more than eleven. The older sons were collectively called by British officers 'the Tigers'; they were not an admirable lot.

[2] The new Mysore was larger, however, than the country had been under the boy rajah's ancestors because of the territorial acquisitions of Hyder Ali and Tipoo.

to a local merchant – he had already received a good basic education – and began to rise through his pleasing manners, sharp intelligence and exceptional trustworthiness. While still very young he came into contact with Hyder Ali's finance minister who appointed him, entirely on his merits, a clerk of the Treasury. Hyder Ali also liked the young man and took advantage of his great talents by making him into something like his commissary general.[1]

As mentioned, Futteh Hyder and Purneah commanded the army that attacked Stuart on 3 May; the latter was actually in charge of the operations since the eldest Tiger lacked any great ability. Whether Purneah had military genius or not is debatable, but he certainly had other talents.[2] In 1798 he was both Tipoo's treasurer and one of his few trusted subordinates. Acting on the advice of the Second Committee Harris appointed Purneah the Dewan (principal minister) of Mysore and left the running of the new state to the Commission and Purneah.

Meanwhile Wellesley's own job had taken shape. As was to be the case for most of the rest of his life, it was partly military and partly political. At first his military duties were confined to Seringapatam Island; but even before his brother Richard's orders arrived for the Second Commission, he was handling most of Harris's political responsibilities as senior officer or president of the first. He was careful to point out to Mornington on 8 May 1799 that he wanted from Harris 'all the [political] power he has himself till you can give your orders upon the subject'.[3]

With the arrival of Henry and Kirkpatrick, who had no military duties, Arthur Wellesley and Barry Close appear to have taken a less active part, but Arthur was still the principal force within this group not only through seniority, but because of his natural ascendancy. While he and his fellow committee members were launching the new ship of state, the military take-over proceeded smoothly. All units of the Sultan's forces were accounted for before the monsoon arrived. Here we should note that on the evening of 5 May, when Tipoo was buried with full military honours by the British army, a violent storm broke which killed some of Stuart's officers and men by lightning

---

[1] Under Purneah the commissariat functioned better than similar EIC departments. Hyder Ali defeated his British opponents more often than other princes because his forces could rely more on their own supplies.

[2] Again I am indebted to Brigadier Naib of the Indian Army for these biographical details.

[3] *Supplementary Despatches*, I, 215.

and made the Cauvery unfordable for forty-eight hours. It was not, however, the beginning of the monsoon. The rivers fell again to their former level.

While Wellesley was settling in Seringapatam, providing the town with new hospitals, clean and airy barracks and fresh water, and caring properly for both British and captured ordnance,[1] an unfortunate incident occurred. During or shortly after the final assault one of the prisoners in Tipoo's dungeons either was released or escaped. He was Dhoondiah Waugh, a Patan trooper who had risen in the service of the Sultans to a position of some authority. He preferred a life beyond even Tipoo's law, however, and on 4 May 1799 was in prison, perhaps awaiting execution. Once free, Dhoondiah enlisted a small following from among fellow prisoners and recently demobilized soldiers. He gained strength so rapidly that during July Harris found it necessary to move against him. Even though Mornington's plans included pensions for all senior officers in the Mysore armies, there were no provisions for feeding the rank and file. EIC Colonel James Stevenson was in charge of one light force which pursued Dhoondiah. EIC Lieutenant-Colonel Dalrymple – Simon, not James who was Wellesley's somewhat unsatisfactory deputy commander of the Nizam's force – was in command of another. They defeated Dhoondiah in small actions and after a bloody fight near Shikapoor on 17 August finally drove him back in extreme disorder. Stevenson and Dalrymple had begun their operations well to the north of Seringapatam and were now close to the irregular Mahratta border which they had strict orders not to cross. Goklah, the local Mahratta commander, completed the job the British had begun. On 20 August Dhoondiah's force was destroyed. He himself escaped and took service with the Rajah of Kolapoor, a minor but not subordinate Mahratta chieftain who made his living partly by piracy. In the course of this pursuit units of Harris's army took Sera and Chittledroog in northern Mysore.

Meanwhile, Arthur Wellesley and Purneah were setting up an efficient dependent government in the name of the young Hindoo prince usually known as Krishna Wodeyar. This period shows British colonialism at its best. Purneah and his subordinates – most of whom he chose himself – had a background of inefficiency, bribery and peculation, but Wellesley and other members of the Political Committee, assisted no doubt by officers like Captain Macleod, a former

---

[1] Two lists of things to be done appear in *Supplementary Despatches*, I, 217–18. One was apparently a note to himself, but the other is signed and approved by Harris.

Collector[1] of the Baramahal and Harris's chief of intelligence, soon 'licked them into shape'. The EIC had been in India for generations and knew its way about. Understanding and procedures for working with the people of India had been developed. But Wellesley and his team, unlike some of their predecessors, gave more than know-how to the new government. They managed to inspire a spirit of honesty, integrity and public service; it would be beyond belief if the new attitude had established itself fully grown immediately, but a start was surely made. Under the new regime people were quick to appreciate a change for the better; Wellesley and Purneah were obviously superior to Tipoo.

While Stevenson and Dalrymple were still pursuing Dhoondiah, Harris was withdrawing most of his main army down the Eastern Ghauts to Madras. Wellesley was soon not only head of the commission, but senior military officer between the ghauts in Southern India; Harris's General Order of 11 September clearly appointed him 'to command the troops serving above the Ghauts'.[2] Wellesley was also in charge of political affairs. When the commission was dissolved, he continued to exercise its power. He refused to accept a civilian (EIC) colleague or anyone else not subject to his orders: in a letter to the Governor-General he insisted that such a situation could only lead to chaos and corruption.[3] On the other hand, he was delighted when Barry Close, who returned with Harris to Madras, was appointed Resident in Mysore. As early as 23 September 1798, he said of Close, 'He is by far the ablest man in the company's army.'[4] Save for Malcolm, Wellesley never changed his opinion. He and Close were unlikely ever to see anything except in the same light, but even if they had differed Wellesley was the senior in rank.

In the autumn of 1799 British control over Mysore extended no further, however, than the central plain, an area about 120 miles east to west by 200 miles north to south. Even this extent was subject to some question. Hindoo hereditary *polygars* – natives who considered themselves independent and who, armed with pikes and matchlocks,

---

[1] A Collector was the chief executive officer of an EIC area as well as a tax collector; the term still survives in modern India with roughly the same meaning.

[2] *Dispatches*, I, 41–2.

[3] Wellesley wrote to Mornington: 'I intend to ask to be brought away with the army if any civil servant of the Company is to be here, or any person with civil authority who is not under my orders. I know that the whole is a system of job and corruption.' *Petrie*, 44.

[4] *Supplementary Despatches*, I, 95.

inhabited forts, hills and woods – had been forced to submit to Hyder Ali and Tipoo, but would rebel if given the chance. Wellesley's mission was to pacify by political action if possible, but to resort to force if necessary. He was in his first truly independent command and planned to make the most of it. Characteristically, he immersed himself in detail without losing sight of the larger picture. He travelled over his entire area of responsibility without losing control of any subordinate post. His dispatches to all these places are astonishingly minute and display a realistic appreciation of the basic aims of British India as he and his brothers conceived them.

As often happens when a man does one task well, he is given others in the same area, in this case in addition to the first. In the original division of Mysore the Mahrattas had been rewarded for their neutrality with the territories of Soonda and Bednore, on the condition that they would allow the British to arbitrate between them and the Nizam and banish all French from their service. Both conditions were unacceptable so Wellesley was ordered to take this territory back. He used a combination of open force and tactful consideration to accomplish his mission. In March 1800 he took over Malabar and Canara on the west coast, even though these had been formerly Bombay Presidency territories. Soon another even more nebulous responsibility landed in his lap. Mainly as a result of the discovery of Tipoo's correspondence with Bonaparte and others about a French landing on the west coast of India, the Governor-General sent a Bombay force under Sir William Clarke to 'reinforce' the Portuguese garrison of Goa. There was never any actual take-over and Clarke acted only as Resident. But command from Bombay was completely inefficient and by degrees it was given to Wellesley. Canara, Malabar and Goa were formally made over to him on 9 September.[1] Towards the end of 1800 he was given the task of recovering some former Mysore territory which was now ceded back to the EIC by virtue of a new and even more conclusive treaty with the Nizam. This involved extending his command hundreds of miles to the north.

While studying this slow extension of the authority of a full colonel, one must ask oneself how it happened. There were major-generals aplenty in India, but Mornington, Clive and Harris kept them out of Mysore and its environs. They must have agreed with Arthur Wellesley that these senior officers were 'confoundedly inefficient'.[2] The extensions of Wellesley's authority were made partly because of his political

[1] *Wilson*, III, 29.　　　[2] *Supplementary Despatches*, I, 250.

ability and his tact; he seems never to have fallen out with anyone, not even Baird or the ass who was the EIC engineer in Seringapatam.

Wellesley was also competent in combat. The resettlement of Mysore involved almost continuous exertion, not just a demonstration, of military force. There was no single war, just an unbroken series of irregular fights which began as soon as Harris returned to Madras. Although central Mysore presented no problem – here Purneah's newly raised forces could dominate with a minimum of British help – there were three areas where 'guerilla' bands began to operate and a fourth where a potential enemy only waited for a good opportunity. The enemy had advantages in the jungle, mountains, and a desert-like terrain to offset the greater regular strength of British units.

Wellesley's activities in Mysore are of extreme interest today because he used a combination of military strength and political action to achieve a decisive victory, something the Anglo-Saxon nations have recently been unable to do. To understand it, however, we need to note certain facts about fighting in the East at that time.

First, the British victories in India, like most of those won by Europeans in colonial areas, were not, as is sometimes maintained, solely dependent on better weapons. Native armies often had more small arms of the first quality than their opponents. Their artillery was frequently as good and nearly always more numerous than that of the British. The weapons that Wellesley's irregular opposition had in Mysore were relatively at least as effective as those of the Viet Cong 170 years later.

Second, Wellesley and other British commanders in India never had a European majority in their armies. Most 'British' units were made up of Indian soldiers who were only partly officered by the English. During his first year and a half in Mysore Wellesley's command changed, but it never contained more than 4,000 Europeans.

Third, the transport and supply used by Wellesley and his contemporaries were essentially Indian. Bullocks and other animals usually carried on their backs food, ammunition and most other things needed by fighting men. Furthermore, almost all supplies were procured or manufactured locally since Britain was 20,000 sailing miles away – six months in the small slow ships of that day. In 1799, bullocks and rice were much the same for both sides.

In these three areas British commanders in India did not have much advantage over the enemy. As I have said Hyder Ali's commissariat under Purneah was better than that of the British commanders he fought. In spite of Wellesley's efforts to organize and equip Harris's army, it could move neither easily nor at speed.

On the other hand, there was almost no nationalism in India in 1799 nor for many years thereafter. There was anti-British feeling, but it was confined to a tiny portion of the people. The concept of India and Indians as a single nation did not then exist. The various groups of people residing in India or the East Indies – these two were then inter-changeable [1] – were so different from one another that at that time they were seldom, perhaps never, referred to as 'Indians'. The nationalisms that after 1945 were finally to expel almost all colonial powers just did not exist in India in 1799.

In the autumn of that year Wellesley's immediate problems in Mysore stemmed from three major opponents located south-west, west and north-west of Seringapatam. These were the Pyche[2] Rajah in Wynaad on the route to Tellicherry and Cannanore, the Rajah of Bullum who controlled a vast wilderness of jungle and mountains north-west of the capital towards the important port of Mangalore, and Dhoondiah Waugh, the brigand whose force was almost com-pletely wiped out in August 1799, but who returned stronger than ever in 1800; Dhoondiah operated in the semi-desert country towards Mahratta territory. Wellesley also had to deal with the unfriendly group of Hindoo *polygars* to the north-east who were prevented from open rebellion by realizing what the British armies had done to Tipoo and the fact that their country was favourable for regular troop move-ments, including cavalry operating in formation with organic artillery support.

All four of Wellesley's enemies were in correspondence with each other and attempting to make common cause against the British. They were receiving at least the good wishes and perhaps promises of help from the French. Bonaparte was in Egypt until 22 August 1799 but his army remained there until it was finally defeated by Britain during the summer of 1801, and the French in Mauritius were trying to co-ordinate opposition to the British in India.

In Bullum and Wynaad important roads ran through jungles. These routes connected Seringapatam and Mysore to Canara and Malabar; if they were closed, Wellesley's unity of command would have been destroyed. At first British columns were at a disadvantage in using them because irregular enemy infantry could attack suddenly and from

---

[1] In 1815 Harris 'Baron of Seringapatam and Mysore in the East Indies.'
[2] Pyche is a town in this area.

concealment. But Wellesley ordered his subordinates to clear away the jungle on either side of all roads they wanted to use. There were no bulldozers in India then, but thousands of woodcutters who knew their jobs could move through even the thickest areas at a pace of several hundred yards a day. They left isolated large trees, but removed the undergrowth.

British infantry in India depended not only on their muskets and bayonets, but on field guns as well. As has been mentioned, each battalion normally had two 6-pounder guns; even in EIC battalions, the gunners were Europeans. Charges of grape at ranges of 100 to 400 yards were remarkably effective. The individual projectiles were big enough and travelled at high enough velocity to smash through scrub, vines and even some bamboo. And Indians of that era, especially the more primitive, were mortally afraid of artillery.

Once a band of open country on both sides was cleared, a road could easily be kept almost ambush-proof, there was space to manœuvre and take advantage of superior discipline, organization and firepower. Roads thus opened could be used by suitably protected convoys of thousands of bullocks each carrying 120–140 pounds eight miles per day. A similar idea is now being used in Vietnam with trucks moving fifteen times as fast and carrying 150 times as much load.

This concept of security through mobility and firepower is strong because an essentially defensive position is protected by offensive means. A long road cannot be successfully defended by fortified posts; no commander ever has enough men. If he had, there would be no continuing war. But if he can maintain control with a relatively small convoy guard that can move offensively when required, all is well. This arrangement can be effective, however, only if there are continuous cleared strips for quick and powerful reactions. An irregular, jungle-oriented enemy was and is at a serious disadvantage when forced to fight in them. He can do no damage from the edge of such strips.

This offensive control of the roads through Bullum and Wynaad did not automatically reduce the enemy to impotence. Both rulers were to achieve small local victories. The Rajah of Bullum won and then lost small actions at Munserabad, and also took some advantage of the defection of 150 sepoys from an EIC battalion at Jemalabad, but this place was retaken.[1] The Pyche Rajah caused some similar trouble at Cotaparamba.

---

[1] A confusion of names exists, and is made worse by Jemalabad being improperly placed on the map in *Supplementary Despatches*, I, where it is located in Wynaad instead of Bullum.

Another technique used by Wellesley against irregular enemies was to destroy food or prevent them from receiving it. Guerrilla country seldom produces a great deal of food and military activity, which includes the destruction of crops, reduces it further. Insurgents usually have to bring in supplies. In south-west India at that time local merchants controlled the flow of rice inland from the coastal regions to Bullum and Wynaad and were not above selling to the 'enemy' for a fat profit, even though they lived in a British area. Wellesley, however, was able to discourage this traffic. He wrote to a local subordinate: 'A hint might be given to him [the fellow at Tellicherry who supplied the Pyche Rajah with rice] that I am in the habit of hanging those whom I find living under the protection of the Company and dealing treacherously towards [our] interests. I spare neither rank nor riches.'[1] This threat worked because Wellesley could and would carry it out and the enemies of the British in both Bullum and Wynaad were pinched by a food shortage.

The Nundydroog area held one of the largest and strongest hill forts in India. As I have said, the complete defeat of Tipoo did a great deal for British prestige in southern India. In the new Wellesley era British armies no longer came to a grinding halt when their transport and supplies failed. Everyone saw that British forces could move as required and win in the open with mobility and firepower. The Company was benevolent and conscious of 'the public good', but a detachment of appropriate size could be sent out to fight at a moment's notice.

Wellesley could have occupied Nundydroog as a bastion of British power on a defensive basis. He did not, even though it was nearly impregnable against an Indian army; instead he kept there reaction forces capable of immediately dealing with anything short of a general uprising. The net of posts throughout his area allowed a flow of reinforcements, especially from Sera and Bangalore, as needed for offensive action. The *polygars* of north-eastern Mysore decided they could do without a demonstration of such powers for their personal benefit. They did not openly rebel and were slowly absorbed into Purneah's new state.

In some respects Wellesley's operations against Dhoondiah in 1800 are the most remarkable of his military accomplishments. As we have seen, Dhoondiah's band was completely destroyed in August 1799 but early in 1800 he reappeared as the leader of a growing force of free-

[1] *Supplementary Despatches*, II, 167–8.

booters in the 'no-man's-land' where Hyderabad, Mysore and the various Mahratta territories join. Wellesley had come to know this area in the autumn of 1799, due to his operation for the recovery of Soonda and Bednore, although the country was nearly useless.

Dhoondiah was an able cavalry commander with a flair for taking advantage of circumstances. He was an efficient brigand, but he was more than that. His sudden rise to power – he is said to have had 50,000 fighting men under his standard in the early summer of 1800 – was due only in part to the unsettled conditions of the times and the country. Even early in his career Dhoondiah was after more than plunder, and he displayed some qualities of a high order. In this part of India men began with a band of robbers and founded dynasties. Both Sevajee[1] and Hyder Ali came from humble backgrounds, but within a short space of years were rulers of millions. Dhoondiah planned to do the same. These three commanders took full advantage of the cavalry country of central India. It was neither jungle nor rugged mountain country, mostly just open plains with occasional hill forts. Dhoondiah's area lay roughly 250 miles north of Seringapatam, which was almost ideal because he was a long way from Poona, the Mahratta capital, and from Hyderabad City as well. He might easily have carved out a kingdom for himself because he was too far away for most people in authority to worry about.

Early in 1800, however, as Dhoondiah's power increased Wellesley watched him carefully from Seringapatam. He did not want to move too quickly, but made sure the Governor-General and Clive realized the possible danger. He ordered a subordinate in the north to do nothing drastic, but added, 'You may depend on it that if matters become serious, or are at all likely to be so, I shall not sit here and look on. I will come north myself.'[2]

Arthur Wellesley was developing an ability, unusual for his time, of being in one place and running operations in several other places. He often moved about his area of command, but never relinquished his communications with any subordinate. Today his means of sending and receiving dispatches seem primitive, but they worked remarkably well. The *hircarrahs* of India, generally brahmins, formed a profession to themselves, almost a separate race like the *brinjarries*. They were employed as messengers to carry letters and also used as guides and to gain intelligence. They were usually mounted on camels and were

[1] A seventeenth-century Mahratta to be discussed in Chapter VII.
[2] *Supplementary Despatches*, I, 540.

able to travel long distances remarkably quickly. There also existed lines of posts with runners called *tappals* or *dawks*. Runners were cheaper, but the territory through which they passed had to be secure. Throughout his area of responsibility Wellesley had carefully established his fighting forces and logistic support for them. He did this in such a way that he could take appropriate action promptly anywhere without fatally weakening other areas. His central reserve was, of course, stationed at Seringapatam. With the probability of military operations against Dhoondiah in the north, he strengthened his posts at Sera and Chittledroog and established a new one at Hurryhur.

Though still only a year out of prison, Dhoondiah was gaining power and endeavouring to unite all opposition to Britain and the East India Company in south India under his own leadership. He was carefully building up a myth of invincibility, calling himself the King of Two Worlds, and was communicating with the French.[1] Threats came from him like, 'I demand that you liberate and deliver up to me Tipoo's sons or I will lay waste the country from Seringapatam to Madras'.[2] Dhoondiah probably planned to set up one of the sons as his temporary colleague in establishing a new and greater Mysore. There is some evidence that the Tigers did not object.

This sort of bravado had a dramatic appeal to tens of thousands of discharged soldiers and freebooters in this region of India. An essentially unstable economic structure and confidence in a new and violent movement can have a snowball effect. Dhoondiah and his men did not need the usual kind of support because they lived mostly on the country. Since nearly all of them were mounted, they could move twice as far in a day as a regular force. As Dhoondiah and his more intelligent subordinates realized, no British commander in India had ever been able to catch one of these irregular cavalry forces; they were playing for high stakes.

To British India Dhoondiah, the upstart who both demanded and threatened, was intolerable. The Governor-General ordered Wellesley to 'hang him to the first tree'[3] and, even more important, allowed his brother to enter Mahratta territory to accomplish his mission.[4] Colonel

---

[1] *Supplementary Despatches*, II, 221. Dhoondiah informed 'the French that he was in arms, at the head of a powerful army': The French should 'send out an army to act in conjunction with him to restore the government and country of Tipoo to his sons'.

[2] *Supplementary Despatches*, II, 29.

[3] This order came, however, through Lord Clive's Council Secretary and was dated 24 May 1800. It reached Wellesley at Seringapatam about 1 June: *Dispatches*, I, 128.

[4] *Supplementary Despatches*, II, 2–3.

James Stevenson who now commanded at Hyderabad was ordered to co-operate with Wellesley, who was his senior in date of commission. Purneah would send along some light cavalry.

Wellesley left Seringapatam early in June 1800 and crossed the Tombuddra into Dhoondiah's territory on the 24th. He had under his immediate personal command two King's and five EIC battalions of infantry and two King's and three EIC regiments of regular cavalry.[1]

Lieutenant-Colonel John Montresor of the King's 80th was Wellesley's senior brigade commander. He had been a long time in India and had defeated Tipoo at Sedaseer in March 1799. Wellesley had carefully selected the units of this force and his subordinate officers. There were the usual two 6-pounders with their highly competent crews in each battalion and regiment. His army was composed of soldiers who were trained professionals. Wellesley took Rannee Bednore from Dhoondiah's garrison by escalade on the 27th. This success was made possible by British discipline and the deficiencies of many of the forts. Their walls were frequently no more than twelve feet tall in places, with poorly designed loopholes and no means of delivering flanking fire.[2] Lieutenant-Colonel Michael Monypenny of the 73rd superintended the attack and was thanked by Wellesley in his General Order for the following day.[3]

Wellesley was co-operating fully with the Mahrattas. On the very day he took Rannee Bednore he handed it over at 6 p.m. to Ball Kishen Bhow, the Peshwa's local representative. Unfortunately, the Peshwa's southern army of 10,000 cavalry, 5,000 infantry and 8 guns under Goklah, the man who had defeated Dhoondiah in the previous year, was surprised and routed by him on 30 June. Dhoondiah is said to have dyed his moustache in Goklah's heart's blood in fulfilment of a vow he had taken the year before.

Dhoondiah and Wellesley appeared to be heading for a decisive

---

[1] *Biddulph*, 117. *Burton*, 30, enumerates the King's 73rd and 77th Foot, the 1/1, 2/4, 1/8 and 1/12 Madras, the 2/2 and 1/4 Bombay Native Infantry and the King's 19th and 25th Dragoons, and the 1st, 2nd and 4th Native Cavalry. The apparent discrepancy comes because the 1/8 Madras was already north of the river.

[2] Many of these forts remain virtually as they were 170 years ago. A variety of slits and loopholes can still be examined. Usually they must have favoured the more audacious infantry regardless of which side of the wall they stood. Such openings sometimes tended to funnel a musket ball from outside into the face of a defender; the men inside could not see any considerable area unless they had the courage to look over the wall which was dangerous because of the covering fire.

[3] *Supplementary Despatches*, II, 35.

encounter early in July, but the Pathan refused to give battle. Once he did this, his image of invincibility might suffer. Wellesley continued to manœuvre and easily took most of the places held by the enemy. Dhoondiah could do nothing to save them. On 26 July Wellesley finally reached Dummul. Colonel Stevenson, who commanded the cavalry, isolated the place which was Dhoondiah's last stronghold; if it fell, the King of Two Worlds would have no base left, at least not in this world. Dummul was not like Rannee Bednore, but a real fortress with thirty-foot walls and a garrison of 1,000 men. Wellesley offered *cowle* or terms and gave the defenders an hour to decide. When they refused, he attacked. Three assaults were made simultaneously, two against specific spots on the walls and the third on a gate between. Each attack on the walls was delivered by the flank companies of a King's battalion with an EIC battalion in support. The Europeans went up by scaling ladders while the sepoys covered them with close-range fire.

The attack on the gate was made by the pickets of the day supported by two additional companies of sepoys. A 6-pounder loaded with a double charge of powder but no ball was to be run up close against the gate and discharged to blow it open. This manœuvre failed, but all three attacks succeeded in scaling the walls. In situations like this, audacity worked well for the British. They seldom suffered severe casualties and usually took the places in less than an hour. At Dummul they succeeded in half that time. Most of their casualties were due to the breaking of an overcrowded ladder.

After the capture of Dummul Dhoondiah was once again a foot-loose brigand. He had to divide his army into three in order to avoid starvation. One of them was located by Wellesley's system of intelligence; on 30 July a British force marched twenty-six miles in nine hours and caught this portion of Dhoondiah's army in camp. The extremely effective action which followed was more an execution than a battle and the enemy was almost totally destroyed. In this effort Wellesley used entire units of both horse and foot with their organic artillery.

The main campaign was over. Wellesley divided his total force into two parts and gave one of them to Stevenson. Dhoondiah could move faster than either, but he was in obvious danger of blundering into one while running from the other, particularly in the monsoon season when the country was cut up by swollen, often unfordable rivers. Wellesley was waging psychological war as well. He offered 30,000 rupees for Dhoondiah dead or alive and treated the local people, even recent deserters from Dhoondiah's forces, honestly and kindly. He also made sure that the Rajah of Kolapoor did not shelter Dhoondiah a second time by telling him that if he did, the British forces would enter his territory as enemies. Dhoondiah was not yet caught, but the brigand chief had lost his reputation of being invincible.

Dhoondiah lost so many men by desertion that he reunited his command. It was now entirely cavalry with almost no baggage or artillery. Wellesley divided his forces further and took advantage of unfordable rivers which he could cross by boat, though Dhoondiah could not. The enemy could still move faster but was unable to cope with at least four separate British forces controlled by Wellesley. In retreating from Stevenson, Dhoondiah fell in with Wellesley himself near Conaghull on 10 September. The British commander had only two regiments of European dragoons and two of Indian cavalry, about 1,400 troopers in all. Dhoondiah's shrunken army was still far larger than the British force; he had at least 5,000 fighting men. Wellesley formed his entire army into a single line with no reserve and led the charge himself. The King of Two Worlds was killed and his army destroyed. Wellesley's Conaghull tactics would have been extremely dangerous if used against a European opponent. But Dhoondiah's men were not Europeans and Wellesley's troopers, both Indian and European, were professionals who had spent thousands of hours at sword exercise. Every slash and thrust could kill or severely wound one of their opponents. Wellesley had his second opportunity to profit by his own hours of sword practice. He now left his irregular cavalry in the area for weeks to make sure that Dhoondiah's soldiers did not reunite under another leader. The rebel force was either destroyed or finally dispersed.

The whole campaign must have been intensely gratifying to Wellesley. It certainly made his reputation in India. British commanders had often won battles, but none had ever trapped a force such as Dhoondiah's. The cavalry charge at Conaghull was well executed, but the final victory was based as much on Wellesley's unique ability to supply his armies in the field as on strategy and tactics combined. No other British commander in India had marched so far or so fast. For two and a half months he and his armies had moved in a desolate region without serious inconvenience because of their well developed supply and transport. At 31 Wellesley had evolved a way of feeding men and animals that was better than all previous systems. The great slow-moving multitude that Harris took with him to Seringapatam was gone. When necessary British units complete with artillery could move at three miles an hour for more than twenty-five miles. For the first time Wellesley used extensively the white Mysore bullocks taken from Tipoo which he and Purneah had carefully preserved. They were a special breed that was larger, stronger and faster than any other Indian type. A 6-pounder field gun complete with carriage and limber could be drawn by five or six pairs of them as fast and as far in a day as infantry could march. They were equally good as carriage animals.

Wellesley destroyed Dhoondiah's victorious image in the minds of his own soldiers and also hurt Dhoondiah's confidence in himself. He accomplished this mainly with audacity. A fortified city was taken out of hand. A British army, no matter how small, always moved to the attack. The enemy had either to receive it or retreat. Dhoondiah's first retreat was inevitably followed by others. The Pathan lost the initiative and could not regain it even in small actions. He lost more men by desertion than he would have done in a full-scale battle. Another major element of Wellesley's strategy against Dhoondiah was the division of his own forces, 'flooding the area' in modern terminology. Wellesley, Stevenson and other subordinate commanders moved against the common enemy so that Dhoondiah was worn down by fast marching and finally caught because he could not keep track of his enemies. This strategy has often proved valuable in irregular warfare, although it has obvious dangers; a poor commander risks being beaten in detail. But if organization, control and intelligence are good, and if the initiative can be maintained, an army like Wellesley's can sometimes destroy a force like Dhoondiah's, a notable military achievement. These elements of anti-irregular strategy are now well known and were fairly obvious even then. But their effective employment required a professional competence, a knowledge of India and a practical system of intelligence of a high order. Wellesley had developed them by continuous hard work. He campaigned without luxury, but with all that was necessary for his personal efficiency.

VI

A Disappointment

Arthur Wellesley, Close and Purneah guided Mysore through the critical first eighteen months of existence as a dependent state. An area larger and much more populous than the British Isles was pacified in spite of an enemy coalition. Wellesley's total victory over Dhoon-diah established his military reputation in India, and even the Governor-General now realized that his brother was as capable a soldier as in other things. For a month and a half after the battle at Conaghull Arthur Wellesley remained in Mahratta territory building political fences. He got to know many of the subordinate chiefs and acquired much firsthand knowledge of conditions in this loose confederation. He left Savanore on 7 November 1800 and was back in Seringapatam on the 30th.

We now need to look again at the global situation. Britain and France were still at war. The Governor-General was eager to support the national interests. Early in 1800 he set about implementing vague orders from home to send a force against the French-controlled colonies of the Netherlands in the East Indies; later he added an additional objective, the French island of Mauritius. The latter was the only significant French naval base east of the Cape.

The Governor-General wanted Arthur Wellesley for the command of this expedition. He refused, however, to send a definite order direct to his brother to change posts because he appreciated what he was accomplishing in Mysore and also out of consideration for Lord Clive, the Governor of Madras who was now responsible for most of southern

India.[1] The defeat of Dhoondiah changed the situation. Mysore was likely to be relatively quiet for many months. India was like that: a resounding victory even on a small scale would bring tranquillity just as a small defeat would have the opposite effect.

The Governor-General still needed a man to execute the Batavia project. The Wellesleys never underestimated the French danger. The Netherlands had become an ally of France so the Dutch colonies could be used as a base for a new French effort in India. Even more important, French privateers and other raiders of commerce based on Mauritius had recently been doing damage to EIC trade. The island was probably too far away to be a satisfactory base for a sea-borne attack on British India, but Batavia (Java) was larger and far more convenient at some times of the year. If the British did not take both places, they might be used against them.

Arthur Wellesley received his orders on the way south from Savanore;[2] this time Clive agreed. The young colonel was well acquainted with earlier British expeditions, which had been crude affairs at best. The man appointed to command usually did the organizing, but had little help and no trained professional logistic support. The entire effort depended upon him and a small staff. In 1800 specialists in planning, procurement, shiploading, etc., were not available in the British or the EIC armies. Expeditions sometimes failed miserably through a lack of food, or from some other equally foreseeable weakness. The military system of Britain was one of divided responsibility; civilians who were subordinate only to the Treasury held key posts. Successful expeditions were usually of short duration and remained close to the ocean where the Navy could furnish what was required.

On the other hand, both the Governor-General and Arthur Wellesley realized that between them they had certain advantages, especially EIC money and credit. Wellesley had already done most of the preparatory work for the ill-fated Manila venture of 1797; he had helped to organize Harris's advance on Seringapatam; most important of all, he had fed, clothed and housed or tented a larger force in Mysore

---

[1] The offer and ultimate refusal can be traced in a four-way exchange of letters between the Governor-General, Wellesley, Clive and Josiah Webbe, the Secretary of the Madras Council. The decision to refuse appears to have been made by all of them in concert, but Clive was the most outspoken. He wrote to Wellesley on 26 May 1800 that in sending the offer of the command, he requested him to stay: 'I should find it impossible to replace you'; *Dispatches*, I, 129–30.

[2] The official order came from Clive and was dated 9 November 1800. Arthur received it on 15 November: *Supplementary Despatches*, II, 263.

than he was now to take overseas and had actually gone into the field against Dhoondiah with over 8,000 fighting men in a region as hostile and difficult as any in the world.

Colonel Wellesley was junior in rank to at least twenty officers in the country, several of them major-generals on the Staff. But at that time seniority was all-important in theory only. The trouble was that after a British officer became a lieutenant-colonel, sometimes by purchase at the age of nineteen, he was sure eventually to be the senior full general in the Army if he lived long enough. The system could have led to field commanders in their 90s.

Means for circumventing the system were relatively simple and well established. Prime Ministers and others responsible for major military operations regularly selected a man for a command and then made sure that no one senior to him was assigned to active duty in the same area. This happened often in India, for instance in Mysore after Harris took all his major-generals back to Madras. The same arrangements were made at lower levels also. A capable captain could be placed in command of a battalion destined for a difficult mission by temporarily assigning all senior officers in it to other duty. Independent expeditions were especially likely to be handled in this way and once Wellesley was appointed to command this force, there was no reason for him to believe that anyone his senior would be ordered to join it.

The Governor-General told his brother frankly that the appointment was going to be unpopular, but then went on to say, 'I employ you because I rely on your good sense, discretion, activity, and spirit. I cannot find all those qualities united in any other officer in India.'[1] At this time or for three weeks thereafter the Governor-General said nothing to indicate that Arthur's new posting was temporary, or that he would be used just to get the force ready and that someone else would later be given the command.

Wellesley's first care was to see that his Seringapatam domain was put in order. He wanted to return, if possible, and felt a strong sense of achievement in the progress already made. Barry Close would continue as Resident and handle the political side of their joint government flawlessly. Close could not, however, take over the military command because he was only an EIC lieutenant-colonel. Colonel James Stevenson would replace Wellesley in a military capacity; his responsibilities were the same and would stretch from the Arabian Sea to the Baramahal. Other things had also to be arranged, like the proper

[1] Richard to Arthur, private, 1 December, *Supplementary Despatches*, II, 315.

policing of Seringapatam Island which was EIC, not Mysore, territory. The rebuilding programme in and around the town and manufactures at the arsenal had also to be continued. There was last-minute advice for Stevenson about the prosecution of the small wars in Bullum and Wynaad and the taking over of the territory recently ceded by Hyderabad; these parts of Mysore had been given to the Nizam in 1792 and 1799, but now were being returned to the British in return for an increase in the subsidiary force, which Hyderabad no longer had to support financially. Actually, much of the area had resisted Hyderabad and had never been incorporated in it.

The new treaty was negotiated and signed on 12 October 1800; it called for an increase in EIC battalions from six to eight, two new regiments of EIC Native cavalry, and the usual allotment of two guns with European gunners per unit, a force of about 10,000 fighting men.[1]

Arthur Wellesley also had to choose his staff and some officers perhaps had to be persuaded to leave pleasant and rewarding posts. In those days, service on such expeditions was voluntary. Even though a commander's staff was pitifully small, his success was as much dependent on their collective ability and activity as in the twentieth century. Montresor came first; he would probably be Wellesley's second-in-command. Then there was an able and amiable EIC captain, William Barclay from the Shetland Islands, who was to have the responsibilities of adjutant-general. The ADC was Captain Francis Ralph West of the King's 33rd. The Persian interpreter (also secretary) was EIC Major Samuel William Ogg. EIC Captain James George Scott of the Seringapatam arsenal was to be in charge of stores.[2] There were probably one or two more officers, but I have been unable to find out their identities.

On 2 December 1800 Wellesley and his newly formed staff left Seringapatam and began the journey back along the road towards Vellore and Madras. The last twenty months had changed this country considerably. Eastern Mysore, the EIC Baramahal and the Carnatic, now all EIC territory, were peaceful and prosperous. The Wellesleys' plans for India seemed to be going forward smoothly.

Arthur Wellesley himself had changed as much as the country. When he took over the advisory command of the Nizam's army in February 1799, he was both capable and professionally competent, but

[1] *Wilson*, III, 24.
[2] I am indebted to Lady Longford's scholarship for Scott's name and position; the proof is in a letter from Arthur to Wilks, 6 June 1801, *Supplementary Despatches*, II, 426–7.

few people were sure of how well he would actually do with the opportunities ahead; perhaps he was not even sure himself. Now he had demonstrated to himself and others that his particular combination of common sense, hard work, courteous treatment of everyone and scrupulous rectitude would achieve success. He had not yet commanded or even been present at a major battle in the field, but Malavelley and Conaghull had given him some experience. He had taken a prominent part in one of the two most successful sieges of his entire career.[1] He knew how to keep a considerable force of all arms efficient and unified, even when spread over a large area, and to use parts of it to achieve local victories. A perceptive few had seen signs of considerable ability in 1798 and before. Now, only two years later, Wellesley was started on the road of positive achievements which were recognizable by almost everyone.

Wellesley stopped briefly in Madras to see Lord Clive and Josiah Webbe, the secretary to the Madras Council. There was no Madras C-in-C appointed between Harris, who left on 22 January 1800, and Lieutenant-General James Stuart, who arrived on 1 August 1801, but Wellesley undoubtedly also saw the senior officers at Fort St George. He and his staff then sailed for Ceylon and arrived at Trincomalee on 28 December 1800. There were more than 5,000 troops assembled and awaiting his command. These units, however, were still living aboard their transports and consuming the limited supplies of food which they had brought with them from Madras and Calcutta.

Ceylon was under a separate governor, the Hon. Frederick North, who had his own C-in-C. The island had been taken from the Dutch by an EIC expedition in 1795–96. North had arrived in October 1798, but was cut off from the Wellesleys by distance and a different set of problems. Ceylon became a Crown Colony in 1802. North and his subordinates did practically nothing for the expeditionary force which was assembling at Trincomalee, probably because they were themselves short of food, barracks and parade grounds. Arthur Wellesley and his small staff had to do everything themselves, but it was probably the way the young colonel wanted it. He and his friends struggled with military and related problems for fourteen hours each day. Independent units had to be organized into brigades and trained on shore to act together. Officers had to be instructed in their new duties and then given practice in doing them. Supplies of all types had to be found; Wellesley

---

[1] The other was Ciudad Rodrigo, taken in twelve days in January 1812 with moderate casualties and some insubordination among those who made the assault.

was writing for specific quantities, types and packages of salt beef, biscuit, arrack, rice, ammunition, medicines and much else. He considered it utter folly to send men anywhere without sufficient food,[1] and no one can fight effectively without weapons and proper ammunition. He was fortunate in having the EIC's vast resources to call on, but to ensure delivery was a matter of continuous effort, essentially the application of common sense aided by personal appeals to the men who had charge of the supplies and to their superiors.

Wellesley had the complete co-operation of Lord Clive and those under him at Madras. The Governor-General in Calcutta was even more important, but he was further away and more removed from the men who actually did things. At this stage Bombay appeared willing to contribute its full share, but it was on the wrong side of India.

Arthur Wellesley turned all his tact, courtesy and common sense on to North and his C-in-C, but failed to get as much co-operation as he usually obtained. Perhaps at this time Ceylon did not have much to give. A further complication was that the Royal Navy under Admiral Rainier was independent of all shore-based authority, save when the Admiral's inclinations happened to coincide with the Governor-General's plans. The expedition as originally conceived was to be sent against Batavia in Java, which Rainier found satisfactory because he had received relevant orders from home.[2] But when Mauritius was substituted for the Dutch base, or at least added as a second objective, he refused to consider going there without specific instructions from the Admiralty in London. This decision by an able naval commander seems strange in view of the serious British losses of shipping to French privateers operating from Mauritius, a major concern of Rainier's, but he and the Governor-General sometimes did not get on well.

There was another possible destination for the expedition which in global terms was more important than Java or Mauritius. A French army was still in Egypt, though Bonaparte had returned to France, and the British in India knew that the Government at home thought of sending an expedition from Britain to Egypt and might also order

[1] 'Articles of provision are not to be trifled with, or left to chance. There is nothing more clear than that the subsistance of troops must be certain . . . or the proposed service relinquished': *Dispatches*, I, 295.

[2] *Supplementary Despatches*, II, 332. The Governor-General was to be nominated by letters patent 'Captain General of all Forces of the Crown serving in the East' on 26 February 1801, *Torrens*, 226. This command, however, appears, not to have included control of the Royal Navy.

a co-operating force from India to go there.[1] But such an attack by a British force from India would require special orders from London even for the Wellesleys who were exceptionally prone to stretch authority. If such orders arrived, however, the force that Wellesley and his staff were fitting out would obviously be used there.

Meanwhile, the expedition was taking shape and would soon be ready to depart. It would not starve during the probable time required to achieve its objectives. The *Dispatches* and *Supplementary Despatches* for this period are full of lists and calculations. The man who was to become the Duke of Wellington less than fourteen years later was uniquely gifted in his care for the men he commanded, but common sense and hard work were more important than genius.

Let us now return to the Governor-General in Calcutta. As we know, he anticipated 'Great jealousy [from] the general officers in consequence of my employing you'. Time proved his prophecy only too true, especially in David Baird. This brave Scot was not the kind of man to suffer injustice silently. He protested first to Sir Alured Clarke, the C-in-C of all British India, and received his permission to take the matter up with the Governor-General who had three long and stormy interviews with Baird who vigorously urged his claims to command in Arthur Wellesley's place. He had enlisted not only Clarke but other senior officers on his behalf.

The first of these interviews occurred about 20 December 1800.[2] Either this interview or a rumour of the attitude of his senior officers caused the Governor-General to write to his brother on 21 December, 'If circumstances should ultimately determine me to attempt the expedition to Egypt, that attempt will require so large a force as to occasion the necessity of employing some one or two of his Majesty's General officers now in India.'[3]

This letter reached Arthur Wellesley on 7 January 1801. He replied the next day, protesting vigorously. In essence he said, 'You have changed your mind!'[4] It is difficult for anyone reading the Governor-General's letters, especially those of 1 December and 21 December, not

[1] The Governor-General mentioned this in his public dispatch to Wellesley of 1 December 1800; 'if the armament should proceed to the Red Sea, I should certainly be of the opinion that it ought not to move without six months' provisions and water'. *Supplementary Despatches*, II, 311. We should note particularly that he writes of the Red Sea expedition with no reference to anyone but his brother in command.

[2] Hook would have us believe that they occurred later and were spaced close together: *Baird*, I, 256-7.

[3] *Supplementary Despatches*, II, 324.   [4] *Supplementary Despatches*, II, 325.

to reach the same conclusion. But the Governor-General probably had to do this. Only five years previously an association of EIC officers had defied Sir John Shore and won the support of the authorities at home. The Marquess Wellesley – he had been raised in the Irish peerage for the defeat of Tipoo and conquest of Mysore – was preparing for the inevitable. A civilian Governor-General could not disregard what his C-in-C and most, if not all, of his senior officers thought. The problem was not so much one of seniority; that was regularly being ignored. But the Governor-General was using his own brother, which made the appointment unpopular, perhaps to the verge of mutiny. The Governor-General felt compelled to name Baird to the chief command of the expeditionary force on 24 January 1801.[1] It should be clearly understood, however, that he added no troops to those already assembling in Ceylon under his brother and still intended the expedition for Java. He was not making the change for either of the two reasons mentioned in his earlier letter.

For reasons no longer apparent, the Governor-General delayed giving Baird the actual order to proceed to Trincomalee until 5 February. Before news of this change in commanders could reach Arthur – the dispatch of 24 January reached him on 21 February – the younger brother was faced with a major problem. Clive sent him a copy of orders from home to the Governor-General to dispatch an army immediately by the Red Sea to Egypt. These had come out by sea and reached Madras before Calcutta. Usually dispatches were faster overland, but there were exceptions. Important messages were sent in duplicate, one by sea and the other by land. The time involved usually ranged from four to eight months, but fast passages and fortuitous journeys overland were not unknown. Moreover, an overland dispatch was less secure and more costly.[2]

Arthur Wellesley received Dundas's dispatch on 6 February, four days before the Governor-General did. Previous communications and common sense made it obvious that the expedition now fitting out in Ceylon would go to Egypt. Thus Wellesley knew beyond reasonable doubt that Egypt was his likely destination fifteen days before he received the first positive news that he had been superseded. Dundas had actually specified Bombay as the concentration point.

[1] *Supplementary Despatches*, II, 333.
[2] The best place to find actual times both for passages round the Cape and partly overland dispatches via Egypt or Syria is the magnificent volume referred to as *The House of Commons Account*.

The question was whether to proceed to Bombay or wait for orders. An early start was imperative if the Indian force was to arrive in Egypt in time to achieve anything. The main expedition from Britain had been scheduled to leave months ago and every day that could be saved by anticipating the Governor-General's orders to move towards the Red Sea might be valuable. There was another and more compelling reason for an immediate start. In the days of sail seasonal changes in wind directions were of extreme importance, especially in the Red Sea. Wellesley had absorbed this kind of information so that it formed part of his 'fingertip' knowledge. If the vessels which carried the expedition to Egypt did not leave Aden on the 1,000-mile passage north through the narrow Red Sea by about the middle of May, they would be unable to move for several months.

On, or slightly before, 9 February Wellesley on his own responsibility made a decision to dispatch every transport assembled at Trincomalee to Bombay, which was closer to Aden by about 600 miles. It is possible to sail directly from Ceylon to Aden and save all of this distance, but the best nautical advice was against it. At this time of the year sailing vessels from Trincomalee would probably have to go north past Bombay before turning west for the Red Sea. Wellesley had asked the opinion of the senior officer of the Royal Navy in Ceylon waters and received unqualified support.[1] A further consideration in favour of an early start, as already mentioned by the Governor-General, was that a Red Sea expedition would need six full months' food and water. The supplies assembled in Ceylon were sufficient for Java, but not for Egypt; Bombay was the only British port on the west coast of India which could provide enough. Wellesley wanted his supplies on board the ships which carried his troops, not on others perhaps hundreds of miles away. Haphazard arrangements like this had often led to disaster in recent British expeditions.

The magnitude of Wellesley's independent decision can hardly be stressed. Only a colonel, he knew that he might be superseded and got no encouragement from the Governor of Ceylon or the local C-in-C. North and General Macdowall warned him publicly – their letters were entered on the official records of the Ceylon Presidency – against going to Bombay without orders from the Governor-General,

---

[1] Captain Pulteney Malcolm, John Malcolm's brother, who wrote, 'I perfectly agree that you ... should ... proceed to the rendezvous pointed out by the Secretary of State. I will take upon me to accompany [the transports]': *Supplementary Despatches*, II, 337.

but Wellesley was not subject to their authority.[1] To wait for the Governor-General's orders would obviously have been the safe course. But throughout his long life Arthur Wellesley never hesitated to incur personal risk in order to further what he considered to be the public good. He realized, of course, that in any case the expedition from India might not arrive in Egypt in time, or that it might have extra months in which to complete its journey. But these factors were beyond his control; making an immediate start was not.

Wellesley was at sea aboard H.M.S. *Suffolk* when on 21 February he received the Governor-General's orders of 24 January appointing Baird to the principal command. Wellesley wrote Baird a handsome letter of explanation, but continued to Bombay. Baird received it when he reached Trincomalee several days later. He and Arthur Wellesley remained personal friends for thirty years, but the situation must have been a severe strain. The gallant Scot can hardly have been pleased to be separated from the force now theoretically under his command for another 1,000 miles.

This turn of events was equally confusing to the Governor-General. Had his brother taken the expedition away so he could continue to command it? Would Baird catch up? Commendably, however, he refused to express an opinion until he heard from his brother. In those days men in high positions were more used than they are today to decisions made by subordinates because of slow communications.

The end of this unusual sequence of events was simpler than the beginning. The ships from Trincomalee arrived in Bombay about the middle of March. Wellesley was still in command and continued his preparations for Egypt. Baird finally caught up on 3 April, and most of the transports sailed for the Red Sea before the end of the month. Baird approved of all that Wellesley had done and treated the younger man with marked consideration. Wellesley had done his best for the public good and got on better with Baird than he expected to do.[2] His carefully reasoned memoranda about the expedition, based on all available intelligence, became the basis of Baird's thinking.

Colonel Wellesley was prevented from leaving Bombay with Baird and the last of the transports by a severe bout of fever and the

---

[1] Wellesley to North, 18 February 1801: 'I conceive the grounds upon which I have determined to go to Bombay are so strong and the urgency of the measure so great . . . that I persist. I still hope it will meet with your approbation and that of General Macdowall': *Dispatches*, I, 297.

[2] Wellesley later wrote to Baird about the 'kind, candid, and handsome manner in which you have behaved towards me': *Dispatches*, I, 313.

13 The old *(right)* and the new (c.1900) road to Nundydroog, Wellesley's north-eastern base in the pacification of Mysore

14 Nundydroog, the two curtain walls across the only accessible side

15 The fortifications of Chittledroog, one of Wellesley's bases against Dhoondiah Waugh

16 The upper fortifications of Chittledroog

17 *(Above)* Inside the upper town of Chittledroog; note the 'tank' and the mud walls of old barracks.

18 *(Left)* Old road surface, negotiable by bullocks but not by wheeled vehicles

19 Little Bhore Ghaut

20 The ghauts south of the Taptee from the plains below

Malabar itch. He planned to catch up in a fast sailer, the *Susannah*, which was to come on ten days later, but though his fever got better, the itch got worse. It had been contracted from the bedding in a berth on the passage to Bombay and was of an unusually virulent type that resisted the normal lard and sulphur treatment. A Bombay surgeon finally began to cure it by means of a series of baths in dilute nitric acid.[1] Wellesley improved slowly, but the treatments were obviously impractical aboard a small, crowded sailing vessel as this type of itch was extremely contagious and could easily have spread to everyone aboard during a long cramped voyage.

The *Susannah* sailed without Colonel Wellesley; it had been his last chance to join the expedition. To go on later by another vessel would only lead to useless months spent at Aden, so he abandoned the whole idea with some honest regret. As he told Baird, he had really wanted to go; besides, according to his brother's order he was officially 'second in command'. A man in this position had often inherited complete responsibility and made a name for himself in the past. It was fortunate for his country, however, that Wellesley did not sail on the *Susannah*; she was lost at sea with all hands.

At Bombay Arthur Wellesley slowly recovered his health. He explained in detail to his brother why he had decided to take his entire command from Trincomalee to Bombay. The Governor-General approved. Indeed, the expedition would probably have been useless if Arthur Wellesley had acted differently.[2] On the other hand, he felt strongly that his supersession was 'the most unfortunate for me that could have occurred'.[3] With some logic, he felt that his superiors in Britain would believe that he had not done well. But the shift of commanders had not ruined all his prospects. His future and prestige in India were obviously not damaged. He had been given permission by the Governor-General not to go to Egypt if he so desired, but had been cautioned that his reputation in regard to 'the service to the public'

[1] Few people today realize how serious a really bad case of itch can be, especially in a hot climate. The eruptions can cover most of the body and make normal activity and sleep impossible. Sometimes even victims of common itch run temperatures and have alimentary troubles. *Lady Longford*, 75, points out that Malabar itch was almost certainly a form of ringworm which is worse.

[2] As it was, Baird was able to proceed only as far as Kosseir up the Red Sea before 'the lateness of the season' made it impossible 'to proceed to Suez'. With commendable initiative he marched overland through the desert to the Nile and descended the river by boat. A few days more at Trincomalee, and the expedition would not have reached northern Egypt until the end of the year.

[3] A letter to Henry Wellesley of 23 March 1801: *Dispatches*, I, 305.

might be damaged if he refused. The fever and the itch had made the decision for him. He knew unofficially that Lord Clive would welcome him back to administer Mysore and its adjacent territories from Seringapatam, although he was careful to say only that he would return to his duties as commanding officer in India of the King's 33rd Foot.

One change over the last six months was truly regrettable. The mutual affection, respect and confidence that Richard and Arthur had for each other were badly damaged. The blame cannot be said to have lain entirely with one or the other. Richard was surely right in preferring Arthur over Baird for the chief command of any expedition, no matter where it went. There cannot be much question about this now. Throughout his mature life the victor of Waterloo handled the most demanding assignments of all types; Baird was not outstanding save in strength and courage. On the other hand, it was the Governor-General's public duty to run India as efficiently as he could. To do this he needed the co-operation of his C-in-C and his general officers. Once Baird managed to get Clarke and most of the Staff on his side, the Governor-General had to use him; Baird's colleagues would have accepted the appointment of a colonel to an independent command, even over the heads of generals, but they would not stand for what they considered to be flagrant nepotism. Wolfe was junior to 200 officers when he conquered Canada, but he was not the Prime Minister's brother.

Arthur thought that his brother had given him permanent command of the expedition unless he did something to deserve to be superseded. This was the Governor-General's intention when he wrote his private letter of 1 December 1800; no other construction is possible. Arthur would not have left Seringapatam on any other basis, nor persuaded his staff to leave choice posts on his behalf. The rub was not that the Marquess changed his mind under pressure, but that he was not big enough to admit it. He did not handle his able younger brother as well as he might. The Marquess Wellesley was both brilliant and capable, but not above the human tendency to expect total obedience without explanation from subordinates he felt to be in his debt. If he had explained to his brother why he had to place Baird over him, and had apologized for doing so, there would probably have been no ill feeling. [1]

But Arthur was not altogether blameless. He certainly resented a

---

[1] I would not dare to say this if *Ward*, 28, had not written: 'If only Mornington had communicated his difficulties confidentially to his brother and appealed to his generosity, Wellesley would never have taken the disappointment so hard. Why then did he not? The only reason one can suggest is Mornington's temperamental inability at times to dismount from "the high horse he loved so well to ride".'

senior in rank taking over his command more strongly than an officer should, though in this case there was some justification. He and his staff had worked hard and brought order out of chaos. In spite of his personal regard for Baird, he must have been exasperated by his claims to commands for which he was not suited. He must also have been bored with Baird's contention that he was advanced only because he was the Governor-General's brother. Baird had many good points, but he was also a quarrelsome blockhead.

The breach between the Wellesleys was not going to be repaired easily. On 4 June 1801 Arthur wrote to Henry who had just returned to India and had rejoined the Marquess: 'I certainly never intended to annoy him [Richard] with my private grievances. He cannot expect, however, that I should have no feeling regarding what has happened: if he does, he must suppose that I feel differently from what he does upon these occasions. I only ask what would he have felt and have said if such a thing had happened to him?'[1]

In April 1800, after being created marquess, Richard had written, 'I cannot conceal my anguish of mind and disappointment at receiving an Irish rather than an English marquessate. I will confess openly that I was confident there had been nothing Irish or pinchbeck in my conduct or its results. I felt an equal confidence that I should find nothing Irish or pinchbeck in my reward.'[2] The two brothers were ready to speak out when either felt that he had received less than his due. Arthur's extreme sense of personal rectitude rebelled at Richard's efforts at self-justification even more than at the demotion itself. They were fine competitors and had great pride. Each felt himself aggrieved, and the total respect that they had for each other over many years was destroyed.

When Arthur was well enough, he went south to Mangalore by a sailing vessel and then overland through still disturbed Wynaad to Seringapatam. According to his friend, Captain George Elers of the King's 12th Foot – the two men had come out to India at the same time and journeyed through Koorg together – the colonel had greyed at the temples. He did not laugh as often or so explosively as before. Cares and responsibilities that lasted twenty-four hours a day, 365 days a year had changed his personal habits. Every project had to be considered on the basis of the time he had available. He was young for such self-denial, but duty came first. He may already have forgotten how to play.

[1] *Supplementary Despatches*, II, 425.
[2] *Roberts*, 70–1, quoting Wellesley's Papers, I, 120–1.

VII
Administration

Wellesley rode towards Seringapatam through the country where Harris's army had camped in April and May 1799. He crossed the aqueduct by the stone bridge near the still ruined village once known as Shawe's Post. It was mid-afternoon 7 May 1801, and a pre-monsoon thundery shower which had been brewing for some time suddenly swept the area. The small party of horsemen were wet to the skin before they reached the Little Cauvery. They crossed by the bridge Skelly and Wallace had used on the night of 26 April two years before early in Wellesley's total attack, night and morning, which had sealed the fate of Tipoo's city.

Wellesley felt cool, without fever or itch. As often happens in southern India at this season, the sun reappeared almost immediately and its rays slanting from the west under dark clouds revealed Seringapatam City sharp and bright. The massive grey-brown walls were topped by the intricately ornamented pinnacles of a Hindoo temple to the west, and to the east by the gleaming white and blue twin minarets of a mosque. To his left Wellesley could see the ruins of the Ravelin, and on his right those of the three-gun Circular Battery. Memories good and bad came back: the eighteen-hour operation had been his most successful, from a military point of view, although British casualties had been almost as heavy as in the final assault a week later (317 against 389). He still felt, however, the agony of Sultanpetah Tope.

Wellesley and his companions[1] were less than a mile from the nearest

---

[1] *Elers*, 115, says that Wellesley invited him to join the party on its trip from Cannonore. In addition to the two of them there were Captain West of the 33rd, Major Ogg and six troopers. Where was Barclay? He may have come on ahead, or perhaps not gone to Bombay.

thing to a permanent home Wellesley had known. It was good to be coming back. A touch of the spur and Diomed brought him over the Periapatam Bridge[1] and past the Mysore Gate. The south walls of the city and the south-eastern round tower were undamaged. The horsemen then rode north-east towards the Dowlut Baugh, Tipoo's spacious palace outside the walls.[2] Europeans seldom found India beautiful then, but this was one of those rare times and places. The monsoon, whose life-giving rain Mysore needed, was not far away but on Seringapatam Island Tipoo's gardens had magnificent trees and still produced fruit and vegetables. The clouds were piled high in the western sky, but the sun continued to pierce them with a vivid unearthly light which shone on glorious greens and golds and browns, and even a bit of scarlet, the tunic of the single sepoy sentry beside the palace entrance.

Wellesley reined in at the corner and rode slowly east along the quarter-mile of compound wall. He recognized the sentry and turned his grey charger into the large central courtyard. Familiar faces greeted him: an old servant took his bridle as he dismounted; Close, Purneah, Stevenson and Barclay rushed out to welcome him; Mrs Stevenson sat in a comfortable wicker chair. All had been awaiting Arthur Wellesley's arrival, for in those days news travelled faster than horses. Wellesley's family was reunited. In India a commander, even a bachelor, always had a family. It consisted of his staff for whom he provided food and other necessaries. Guests often came for indefinite stays. There was plenty of room and provisions; only wine was moderately expensive.

After quick, affectionate greetings, Wellesley retired briefly to change his clothes. Though his light jacket, shirt and pantaloons were soaked, he felt a new man. Thank God, the itch was gone, although his skin was still sensitive from the nitric acid baths. His old head servant Vingetty, superintended his bath. Wellesley felt the luxury of cool water, of a great dry towel and clean comfortable clothes left behind in December. He was hungry and thirsty and had so much to relate.

[1] This bridge was also called the Mysore or Mysore City Bridge and was the only one leading to the island across either the North or South Cauvery over which a horse could canter. It also brought fresh water to the city through the masonry-lined 'watercourse'.

[2] The palace was taken over by Baird and his staff on 4 May 1799. Wellesley and his staff began to use it the next day and the arrangement became permanent. The Dowlut Baugh remained Wellesley's home and headquarters until he left India. Some of his servants and all his personal possessions which did not accompany him to Ceylon and Bombay stayed here.

Friends, even an attractive woman, awaited him.[1] He found them having a glass of sherry. Dinner followed with his favourite dishes, well-cooked saddle of mutton in a rich brown sauce and a green salad. There was Madeira with dinner and Port afterwards. The Colonel did not eat and drink to excess even by modern standards – many of his contemporaries ate and drank enormously – but he enjoyed a good meal with appropriate wine. He also appreciated conversation with friends about all the personal news of the last six months. They had the same background and the same experience; they knew India and had worked hard for a jointly conceived ideal. They were moderately proud of what they had accomplished, but there was still much to do. Now that Wellesley was back, things would go better. The next morning they continued their efforts towards a Pax Britannica from the Baramahal to the Arabian Sea. For Wellesley the expedition to Egypt was soon only an unpleasant memory. However, he stored in his orderly mind pieces of information from it that might be useful in future.

Wellesley's second eighteen-month period in Mysore and adjacent territories was much like the first. There were problems great and small, both military and political. One of the first and most unpleasant was the court-martial of three EIC artillery officers for dishonesty; after the fall of Seringapatam they had stolen from the Company and from those entitled to prize money. Further, they probably placed modern and efficient small arms in the hands of potential enemies of British India. Wellesley carried through the distasteful proceedings remorselessly and strictly according to regulations. A verdict of 'guilty' was obtained and the defendants stripped of their ill-gotten gains, their rank and their hope of pensions. Then, purely in a personal capacity, Wellesley recommended that the oldest of the three be granted means to live because of his long and for many years honest service. This was to be charity, however, not a pension.[2]

In Wellesley's absence no one had bothered to touch the city's

---

[1] *Elers*, 122 and 126, refers to Mrs Stevenson, the wife of Wellesley's best subordinate in India, as if the relationship were improper, but Elers was a gossip. The Stevensons did have a son for whom Wellesley stood godfather. All three were certainly good friends, but in matters like this Lady Longford is by far the most reliable guide. She concludes (102–3) that another godson, Arthur Freese, who later lived in Wellesley's house in England, gave no indication of immoral behaviour.

[2] None of the three culprits are named in *Dispatches* and *Supplementary Despatches*, but they were Lieutenant-Colonel George Saxon, an elderly man who rose from the ranks (*Elers*, 125) and was finally allowed to retire, Lieutenant-Colonel F. Mandeville and Captain Andrew Macintire. The last two were 'Dismissed by Court Martial': *Dodwell and Miles*, Madras, *passim*.

defences, including the second or inner ditch, which was still full of water, dead animals and sewage. In building it, the sultan's 'engineers' had broken through the old drains from the city to the river so that the ditch was now practically a long narrow cesspool. The breach was still as open as on the day of Baird's assault and the area enclosed by the north-west walls was full of rubble from the breaching operations.

Wellesley's voluminous correspondence indicates that he did not attach much importance to the restoration of Seringapatam's defences; he was never a man for stone walls and heavy cannon. But the ditch was endangering the health of everyone, and piles of rubble were an insult to British efficiency. Wellesley's plan for a better Seringapatam also included proper barracks, carefully repaired powder magazines and an improved and expanded arsenal. He would need, however, to get Scot back from Egypt; progress in such matters still involved laborious battles by correspondence with the Ordnance Board at Madras. Those 'old gentlemen' had come to realize, however, that Wellesley, for all his politeness and tact, was likely to get his way, and they had to admit that for a line officer he did his administrative work astonishingly well. The Military Boards in each Presidency were the products of the desire for decentralization common among British civilians and London merchants. Individual members were honest and on occasion reasonably intelligent, but when acting together they displayed every fault of decentralized bureaucracy. If they had been more efficient, their capacity to obstruct Wellesley would have been greater.

During Wellesley's absence the economic progress of Mysore had continued under Close and Purneah. Before the end of the year the Governor-General transferred Close to Poona,[1] but Mysore's prosperity still increased. 'There is plenty of everything, and it appears that all the necessary articles will be more plentiful in the next year than they are in this. Commerce is still wanted to take off our superfluities and to throw some money into the country, and this I think that you would have established before long.'[2] Commerce depended, however, on transport. Since Mysore was an inland area with no useful water-

---

[1] Close's transfer which occurred in August 1801 is indicative of the growing importance the Governor-General attached to the Mahratta capital. He called Close his best man for such tasks. Both John Malcolm and Josiah Webbe were appointed to the Mysore Residency, but neither went there for years because there was really no need for a senior man in addition to Wellesley. A man by the name of Piele was Wellesley's unofficial deputy for a while and got on well with Purneah.

[2] Wellesley to Close, 10 October 1801: *Supplementary Despatches*, II, 576.

ways, the construction of roads and bridges was of extreme importance; they would also be of value for military operations. A proper
bridge across the North Cauvery from Seringapatam Island towards
Bangalore, Vellore and Madras was certainly important;[1] it was proposed at least as early as February 1802, and in July Purneah offered to
build it at the sole expense of Mysore and to name it in honour of
Lord Wellesley.

There was considerable discussion as to the location of this new
bridge. After the siege of 1792 Tipoo had blocked a large gate into the
city near the north-western tip of the island, which was replaced by the
'Water Gate' or tunnel where the Sultan was killed. The road from
the old Delhi bridge passed along the northern glacis for almost its
entire length, skirted the eastern fortifications and then either entered
Seringapatam through the reinforced Bangalore gate in the eastern
wall or continued to Mysore City by the Periapatam bridge. The new
Wellesley bridge could be built anywhere between the ruins of the
old Delhi bridge and the Corighaut Ford half-way down the northern
shore of the island. After careful deliberations, Wellesley and Purneah
decided on a site just north-east of Seringapatam between the town and
the Dowlut Baugh. The bridge would be within close range of the
guns on the fortifications and could also, because it was to be built
after the Indian style, be easily disassembled.[2]

Roads were a more difficult problem. Before the British arrived
almost everything throughout the vast sub-continent was carried on
the backs of porters or animals. Wheeled traffic could rarely negotiate
the Indian 'roads' and in those days there were not even many oxcarts.
But an animal can draw five to ten times as much in a wheeled vehicle
as it can carry, and for longer distances. This advantage applied to
civilian commerce and military transport.

Even in Europe road building was rather simple at that time. The
main roads of British India were narrow and surfaced only with com-
pacted earth. Local Collectors and others could be urged to mend
potholes and repair damage by rain or flood, processes of no great
difficulty. In the ghauts or passes, more was necessary. Here some roads
had been cobbled years or even centuries before, but the stones used
were uneven, some of them being so large that wheels could not pass

[1] Colonel William Gent's 'Plan of . . . Seringapatam, May 1799' shows 'Ruins of
Delhi Bridge', but this was certainly not passable by wheeled vehicles and probably not in
use at all in 1802. The original records are not as clear for this area as one would like.

[2] There were removable cross members of stone cut to fit between simple monolithic
pillars set substantially in the river bottom.

over them. Such roads were originally designed for pack animals only and could be repaired more easily than replaced. As Wellesley pointed out in one of his numerous dispatches in this connection, if projecting stones were removed and smaller pieces substituted, wheeled vehicles could use the improved surface.

Wellesley's interest in transport included draft and carriage animals. As we know, the white Mysore bullocks had given him an advantage over Dhoondiah. The breeding of these animals was now Purneah's responsibility on condition that a certain number of young males would be delivered to the EIC each year. The problem was the age at which training should begin. The Indians said two years; some Englishmen said that three would be better. Wellesley had appointed one of his best EIC officers, Captain Hugh Mackay of the 4th Native Cavalry, to command the entire military bullock establishment. He had Purneah send Mackay twelve two-year-old and twelve three-year-old animals. Mackay was to determine by experiment which age gave better results. Camels, horses and mules were also employed for carriage and draft. Elephants were in a class by themselves because of their strength and intelligence. They were extremely expensive to buy and to maintain: they were fed as a standard ration twenty seers (about forty pounds) of rice, half a seer of ghee, half a seer of goor (date-palm juice), and forty large coconut palm leaves per day or the equivalent.[1] As the temptation to steal these valuable commodities was great, the keepers required supervision.[2]

Wheeled vehicles, though obviously they offered advantages if roads and bridges could be built and maintained, were complicated and poorly understood by Indian mechanics. However, Captain Scott at the arsenal knew how to pass on his skill. He needed properly seasoned teak timber, a commodity which was very expensive in the market. Instead of buying it, Wellesley had it cut, seasoned and transported on improvised timber wagons made from limbers left over from the 1799 campaign.[3] The arsenal had a problem in connection

---

[1] *Supplementary Despatches*, II, 524,

[2] Wellesley wrote to Stuart on 17 September 1802, 'I know the people who have charge of them perfectly well, and I assure you that they are not to be trusted in the care of these valuable animals without European superintendence. I have worked them more probably than any officer in the army, and I never saw them out of condition when they were under the eye of the agent; but whenever they have been detached they have fallen off in condition, and some have died, and frequent instances of frauds and thefts in feeding them have been discovered.' *Supplementary Despatches*, III, 307.

[3] 'Two of these limbers are fastened together by a perch: the distance between each can be made greater or smaller, in proportion to the length of the timber which they are to

with pit sawing, which was the only means then used in that part of India to get parallel cut timbers and boards. The Indians lacked the physical strength and will for this exhausting work on large beams, but Wellesley provided an easy solution: 'You should have European sawers. There are some excellent drunken fellows in my regiment who are capital workmen in that line.'[1]

Wellesley's brief absence from Mysore had brought him closer to the international situation, more particularly as it applied to India. Some of his responsibilities – especially the fair-sized Portuguese colony of Goa with its exceptionally large Eurasian population (the Portuguese intermarried more with Indians than the other Europeans) – were directly connected with events in Europe. Like Tipoo's Magalore further south, now safely in EIC hands, Goa would make an almost ideal bridgehead for a French seaborne attack on British India. Such an effort might be backed by the Portuguese Government in Europe.

The Wellesley brothers and their team of young Englishmen never forgot that France was still the only real, world-wide enemy. Sir William Clarke commanded a fair-sized British force at Goa, but if the Portuguese governor, the garrison and the partly Portuguese population actually wanted the French to come, he would need help in a hurry. Arthur Wellesley had control of the British military forces in Goa during his first tour of duty in Seringapatam, although the units involved were from the Bombay Presidency. The Goa force was removed from Stevenson's command during Arthur's absence, but now returned to him. The Wellesleys did not place much confidence in the Bombay Presidency.[2] Madras encroached on Bombay in both territory and authority and was to continue to do so.

We should observe briefly other lines of responsibility. Arthur Wellesley's immediate military superior was the C-in-C in Madras,

[1] To Scott, 16 August 1802: *Supplementary Despatches*, III, 271.

[2] Jonathan Duncan (1756–1811) was a sound administrator; his C-in-C from January 1800 to February 1807 was Major-General Oliver Nicolls, a King's officer. But neither appears to have been outstanding either academically or socially or 'accustomed to consider questions of considerable magnitude'.

carry, as the perch is fastened in the hinder limber by a pin, and it is moveable. On each limber is laid a bed to receive the timber, of such a height as that the wheels of the front limber will turn under the timber. The bed of the front limber traverses so that the carriage can turn. The timber is fastened on this carriage, as it must be on every other, by ropes, and it has been tried on the worst roads here and has been found to answer. Its expense is nothing excepting the timber for the beds and for the perch, and a small quantity of iron.' *Supplementary Despatches*, III, 266.

but Harris had returned home in January 1800. As we have seen, there was no officer with full authority for a year and a half, and during the early summer of 1801 Wellesley was still reporting to EIC Major-General Brathwaite,[1] a man more intimately connected with the early wars against Hyder Ali and Tipoo than with Harris, Clive and the Wellesleys. On 1 August 1801, however, Lieutenant-General James Stuart took over as the regularly appointed C-in-C in Madras. Stuart was a King's officer and had commanded the Bombay contingent during the Seringapatam campaigns of 1792 and 1799. He already knew of Arthur Wellesley's abilities and was even more willing than his predecessors to keep major-generals out of Mysore. Wellesley was also, of course, reporting to Clive. The Governor and Council of Madras by-passed their military C-in-C in the same way as the Prime Minister and Secretary for War did in London.

Wellesley's most delicate position was in connection with his reporting both to Clive and to the Governor-General. The estrangement between Arthur and his brother may not have been a bad thing for his relations with Clive who was quite willing to back the younger brother against the elder.

Enough of the larger picture. There were still military problems not far from Seringapatam. To the north-west the Rajah of Bullum was unconquered and capable of interrupting communications with Malabar. The *polygars* of the Nundydroog area still had to be watched. Seringapatam Island, only a mile wide by three and a half long, was in a minor turmoil. It was EIC territory, but completely surrounded by Mysore; thieves frequently came on the island and got off safe again with stolen property, and Purneah's police, though willing to help, were ineffective. The new courts, criminal and civil, continued to need support; evildoers have had to be caught before they could be tried and punished.

Even more important to the Wellesley concept for India were the crimes committed by British against Indians, references to which are particularly common in Wellesley's dispatches during his second tour of duty in Seringapatam. Europeans of all classes were too likely to beat Indians or have them beaten. 'The practice is very irregular and illegal', Wellesley wrote on 6 September 1802. 'If it is not speedily put a stop to, it will tend to the injury of the troops. In this country, as in England, no man has a right to take the law into his own hand,

---

[1] John Braithwaite was commissioned major in the Madras Army on 21 June 1776 and major-general on 20 December 1793: *Dodwell and Miles*, Madras 6–7.

or to punish another. There are magistrates who have full authority to whom, if necessary, complaint ought to be made.'[1] He admonished, made officers pay damages, and made senior commanders responsible. When an assistant surgeon, convicted in part of cruelty and extortion by a court martial, got off with a reprimand Wellesley appealed to Brathwaite for stiffer punishment. He wrote, 'I never can agree in opinion with the court martial that this scandalous conduct is not unbecoming the character of a British officer and gentleman, and I never can approve a sentence which describes it in other terms than those of the strongest reprobation.'[2]

Even worse, an EIC Lieutenant, William Dodd, stationed at Seedese-gur had a goldsmith beaten so badly that he died; financial irregularities were also discovered. The young officer was tried by a court martial and found guilty, but was sentenced only to six months without pay and loss of seniority. In the pre-Wellesley era such lenient sentences were not unusual in India, but Arthur was furious, reproved the court-martial scathingly and practically insisted that they change their punishment to a dishonourable discharge. He was taking no chances on Brathwaite approving this sentence also. The court martial did reconsider; Dodd was to be dishonourably discharged, but this sen-tence required the approval of the C-in-C in India. Once Dodd had lost his military status, Wellesley planned to try him for murder before a civilian court. Dodd, however, heard of the new sentence before-hand and deserted. He sought safety and fortune in the European Officered Regular Battalions which served the Mahratta princes and got away in spite of efforts to apprehend him. But every English soldier and civilian in southern India got the message. The days of blatant petty tyranny towards defenceless Indians were over, at least while a Wellesley was at hand.

A problem more closely related to Arthur Wellesley's military duties was the health of his soldiers, European and Indian. They were subject to sickness and death which sometimes came quickly from the diseases of the East. Contemporary medical knowledge did not include, for instance, an understanding of the relationship of bad water to some of the more fatal types of illness. The proper hygienic preparation of food even as it was then understood was almost impossible because Indian

[1] *Supplementary Despatches*, III, 296.
[2] *Supplementary Despatches*, II, 440. From *Lady Longford*, 82, we learn that the assistant-surgeon was Captain Shuttleworth who had Chimbassa Chitty tied up and flogged for not giving him straw. Brathwaite confirmed the lenient sentence; he was of the eighteenth century.

cooks just would not abide by instructions. But Wellesley had the common sense to appreciate the importance of clean dry airy barracks, properly placed latrines with adequate drainage, wholesome food, fresh clear running water and similar things.

Health depended on personal cleanliness, exercise and diet. There can be no question that many – perhaps even most – Europeans in India at that time drank too much. Alcoholism frequently contributed to deaths from disease. Officers and men appear to have been almost equally intemperate, but officers generally did not drink local alcoholic beverages which were sometimes more than mildly poisonous, nor were they so likely to let their drinking interfere directly with their duties as some enlisted men.

The handling of the illness of the Nizam of Hyderabad is interesting. He was ill, probably with an incurable complaint, and asked Wellesley to send him a supply of the bark and leaves of two different types of trees, both rare. Wellesley made sure that they were found; he then had large quantities packed up and set off with a message that shows that he could write the diplomatic idiom of the period almost as well as his elder brother. 'The desire of my heart, the seat of constancy, is that the exalted Presence will confidently regard and esteem this bark as an instance of the loyalty, and well wishes, and the testimony of the anxiety of British officers who strive to effect all arrangements which may be desired by, or beneficial to, the noble Presence. May the God of his slaves grant that the orb of your Prosperity may shine and glitter from the eternal horizon like the sun in the zenith!'[1]

Wellesley's wider political and military duties did not change his sense of responsibility for his own regiment, the King's 33rd Foot. The Marquess Cornwallis remained its titular commander and still had the regimental accounts in disorder, but he was far away in Britain; Wellesley had taken his place. Active day-to-day command had passed to Major Shee in the spring of 1799 when Arthur and Sherbrooke received brigade commands. There was the matter of 130 recruits who came in from Britain and needed two uniforms for a single year. According to regulations, every man should pay for both, but Wellesley decided that a deduction would considerably reduce their modest earnings and perhaps impair their health. He decided not to charge them for their India uniform, although the extra cost would have to be borne by the Regiment. Shee himself was a problem. He drank too much and was contentious besides, as has been mentioned

[1] *Supplementary Despatches*, III, 310.

earlier. Wellesley was endeavouring to get a replacement – which was possible but required delicate handling – when Shee died of a fit in March 1802. Arthur Gore took his place and did a creditable job.

We should not get the impression that at this time Wellesley was more of a political and military administrator than a soldier. On 29 April 1802 he was promoted major-general, but he did not know about it until 26 September; he was no longer a newcomer to India and deserved the promotion, although merit had nothing to do with it. He was almost continuously involved in minor military operations. There were two small wars, one against the Pyche Rajah and his associates in Wynaad, and the other against Kisnapah Naig in Bullum.

As we have seen, Wellesley drove roads with wide borders through Bullum and Wynaad during his first command at Seringapatam. The roads were militarily effective if they were annually cleared and given some attention, especially in the ghauts, after each monsoon season. While Montresor was in command in Canara and Wellesley at Seringapatam, the Rajah of Bullum did not recover from his initial defeats. However, he began to set up an independent state of his own in 1801, and claimed to be a sovereign prince.

In January and February 1802 Wellesley personally commanded an expedition which finally destroyed the Rajah of Bullum, whose territory lay within the new and definite boundaries of Mysore.

Purneah and his troops co-operated in the effort. The conflict actually arose because the Mysore collectors of revenue could not enter the Bullum villages; Purneah's forces were not strong enough to establish normal civil control. Wellesley's combined force marched from Seringapatam on 5 January and reached the Bullum country on the 13th. The small British army consisted of the King's 77th, the Regiment de Meuron and four EIC Native Infantry battalions with ten guns, four mortars, and 500 pioneers.[1] The King's 19th Dragoons and the 5th Native Cavalry complete with their guns joined on the way. Considering the strength of the opposition, this force of about 6,000 fighting men and eighteen pieces of artillery was extremely powerful. The Rajah of Bullum had been a thorn in the British side for much too long.

Wellesley rode about the Arrakerry area for three days to get the feel of the situation. The Rajah's impressive main stronghold was

[1] The King's 77th was reduced to 300 men and the Regiment de Meuron to 'about 240': *Supplementary Despatches*, III, 33. *Wilson*, III, 53, says that the sepoy battalions were the 1/1, 1/2, 1/5 and 2/10 Madras N.I.

located in a jungle. The rest of his people who were relatively industrious and could rely on the exceptionally productive soil lived in strongly fortified villages. Frequently two or more villages had been built to give some joint protection; they were always to take full advantage of natural strength and were surrounded by formidable mud walls, ditches and thorn hedges. There were dozens of such villages, but the Rajah Kisnapah Naig and his military subordinates relied too much on their static defences. Even though Arrakerry was powerful and built in nearly impenetrable jungle, it constituted a military objective of great importance. Wellesley concluded that if he took Arrakerry and perhaps the Rajah as well, the other villages would not offer strenuous resistance.

There were three paths into the forest of Arrakerry; each was defended by hedges, elaborate ditches and sharpened stakes. The Rajah's troops were only countrymen imperfectly disciplined and armed mainly with bows and arrows. The passages into the stronghold were in daily use by the inhabitants; even carriage bullocks could pass through them. Wellesley divided his infantry into three columns and attacked Arrakerry from three different directions. Each column was led by Europeans – a detachment from the King's 77th and the Regiment de Meuron in each – who smashed straight down the clearly marked 'roads' through the jungle and through or over the primitive defences. The Bullum people were unable to stop these human avalanches; the three British columns reached the centre of the stronghold almost simultaneously. The Rajah and some of his men were able to get away because the cavalry Wellesley had posted between Arrakerry and the ghauts did not do a proper job of preventing an escape although they cut down scores of the enemy.

Wellesley and Purneah now set in motion a twofold programme for reducing the area to order. The villages were offered peace, or 'cowle' as it was called in India, in return for razing their walls, filling up their ditches and cutting down their hedges. They were also required to give up their few matchlock muskets and other arms. If they complied, they were welcome to become part of Mysore. If villages refused, they were to be taken by storm. Their defences were never too high to be scaled with ladders, nor were their gates too strong to be blown in with a cannon. Once the Rajah of Bullum was defeated, his people realized they had no chance against disciplined sepoys under British officers backed by artillery. If Arrakerry had fallen in half an hour, what chance did lesser places have?

The second part of the programme was to take the Rajah; so long as he remained alive and free, there could be no permanent peace. He received numerous hints that if he gave himself up he would be liberally treated, but he refused. Now Wellesley offered a reward for him dead or alive. Kisnapah Naig lost confidence in most of his people and reduced his party to only a few men who soon found themselves isolated from the civilian population because of their fear of betrayal.

Wellesley used his system of intelligence to get an idea where the Rajah was and then heavily patrolled the area. Neatly and with a minimum of trouble, Wellesley managed to exchange the role of a regular commander opposed everywhere by irregular enemies for that of a hunter after a single quarry. The Rajah and his few retainers ran into a British patrol and were taken on 8 February 1802. The system of Wellesley's justice and the rule of law in British India did not extend to those who rebelled against the East India Company or the allies of the Company. The Rajah and his principal subordinates were hanged on the 9th. There really was no alternative. The Rajah and his government were the only bars to tranquillity in the area. Once he was destroyed, his system disappeared.

We should again notice the lack of any widespread spirit of nationalism. There was no danger of Kisnapah Naig becoming a martyr because there was not enough feeling of unity among the people of India to resent the imposition of a foreign will, and there was no firm racial divide at that time. Besides, Purneah's Hindoo government, not the East India Company, would take over the administration of Bullum.

Wellesley had used maximum force to achieve speedy victory with a minimum of casualties on both sides. The long-continued disturbances in Bullum were over and Purneah easily reestablished Mysore rule, although precautions were taken against a renewal of rebellion by leaving a force in every major village. To demonstrate that British power backed the Rajah of Mysore, Wellesley left a captain and 500 EIC sepoys with two 6-pounders to support the local detachments.

Wellesley's other minor war was in Wynaad south-west of Seringapatam, an area which formed part of Malabar, a possession of the East India Company, extending from the Arabian Sea well past the Western Ghauts into the central tableland. Wynaad was mostly covered by jungle, but Wellesley had pacified the area during his first Mysore command by widening the roads and using infantry-artillery teams to patrol them at irregular intervals. Stevenson had used the same general tactics to drive the Pyche Rajah out of this area into a vast wilderness to the south that nominally was part of the Indian state of Travancore. Wynaad remained quiet for several months after Wellesley's return; Stevenson was still in command at Malabar and Canara. Lieutenant-Colonel J. C. Sartorius of the Bombay Army was his subordinate for this region. Sartorious died of the climate (unusually bad even for India) on 10 December 1801;[1] Stevenson went to command the Hyderabad Contingent in February 1802. Malabar and Wynaad temporarily became the responsibility of Lieutenant-Colonel Barnaby Bowles, a man of moderate initiative and understanding; he failed entirely to grasp Wellesley's concept of protecting an area by offensive rather than defensive means. Indians were quick to discover the weaknesses of their European opponents. Before Wellesley was able to get his old friend Colonel Montresor into Stevenson's old post, trouble flared in Wynaad. On 11 October 1802 a small military station at Pancoorta Cottah was attacked by surprise; two British officers and twenty-four sepoys were killed or burned to death. The weapons of an entire company were lost, but with little or no ammunition, for in accordance with the general practice, almost all the cartridges were stored for security in the commanding officer's bungalow, and they exploded when that structure went up in flames.

This small reverse was unfortunate, but perhaps unavoidable. Posts could rarely be located inside fortifications, even if this were desirable from the point of view of morale.[2] But the conduct of the rest of the 1/4 Bombay N.I. in the same general area could certainly have been avoided; so far as Wellesley was concerned, it was unpardonable. Major James Drummond who commanded the battalion was only nine miles from Pancoorta Cottah. When most of the surviving sepoys from the surprised company came in, Drummond took counsel of his fears, imagined thousands of enemies and barricaded himself in a defensive position. He sent off hysterical appeals for help, but included little in the way of intelligence because he sent out no patrols and did not even talk with trustworthy Indians. The road from Tellicherry and Cannanore, the principal towns of Malabar, to

---

[1] This Bombay engineer was first commissioned on 12 January 1775: *Dodwell and Miles*, Bombay, 72–3. He appears to have been more able than many of his contemporaries.

[2] There were many hill forts throughout India, but they were usually unhealthy. An inspection of some of them suggests that informal latrines drained into the common reservoir called the tank, but this conclusion rests in part on conjecture and probably could not be applied to all of the forts.

Seringapatam was closed; the Pyche Rajah or some other leader might or might not be in heavy strength in Wynaad. Wellesley was furious. He wrote to Bowles, 'Major Drummond, instead of putting the battalion under arms and moving quickly upon the rebels, sits quietly in his cantonment. After such supine conduct, I should not be astonished if Drummond and the remainder of the battalion were cut off likewise.'[1] Gradually, the situation became clearer. The Pyche Rajah was not directly responsible and the isolated action was little more than a raid. A force of *nairs* about 400 strong had attacked in accordance with a well conceived plan.[2] There had been no general rebellion and, if Drummond had moved out immediately, the whole thing might have been over within hours.

As it was, the Pyche Rajah's former adherents had taken heart and were gaining strength, but not so rapidly as to warrant Wellesley's personal attention, at least not yet. He sent one of his favourite EIC battalions, the 1/8 Madras, and some of Purneah's cavalry into Wynaad from Mysore. He also sent a similar force from Malabar. There was some fighting, but the situation was sufficiently restored for him to cancel orders for a part of the King's 33rd and the 1/14 Madras to move into the combat area. Before the end of the month the road from Seringapatam to Cannanore and Tellicherry was open again. Drummond and his men were saved. Montresor left Seringapatam for Cannanore on 17 November 1802 to take command in Malabar and Canara. He was more capable than most officers then in India and soon had the disturbed area under control. The defeat of a single company plus the 'supine conduct' of nine others, however, was to have a lasting bad effect in Wynaad and Malabar.

Before leaving the Pancoorta Cottah affair we should listen briefly to Wellesley's advice to Bowles; it has a modern ring. 'I beg that you will urge the officers to active measures. Let them make long and frequent marches, and let them move, not in the column style, but with the flanks covered, particularly where danger is apprehended. When an attack is to be made in paddy grounds or other places where

---

[1] *Supplementary Despatches*, III, 327. Arthur wrote privately and more scathingly to his old friend Major Macleod that Drummond's battalion were 'feeding upon damaged rice and I hope they will never feed upon anything else, if they choose to shut themselves up and remain till their throats are cut, or they are starved.' *Ibid.*, 343–4.

[2] The assault was made in three parts against the armoury, the sepoys' and the officers' bungalows under the command of Coongan Nair who committed suicide before the end of the year: *Wilson*, III, *passim*.

the enemy may be posted, let a party get round upon their flank.'[1]

Wellesley had been planning to go south from Seringapatam to Wynaad, but did not do so because of orders from Madras. On 12 November 1802 he heard from Webbe and from Stuart – the letters were both dated 9 November – of recent events among the Mahrattas. One of their chiefs, Holkar, had decisively defeated two others, Scindia and the Peshwa, in a large and bloody battle outside Poona on 25 October 1802. The same dispatches indicated the necessity for the immediate formation of a British army in northern Mysore or Ceded Districts to restore the Peshwa to his throne, if necessary by force. All senior men in British India knew that Barry Close had gone as Resident to Poona to negotiate a subsidiary treaty with the Peshwa. Webbe wrote in his 9 November dispatch, 'Colonel Close has appraised this government [that] we shall be required immediately to send a force across the Tombuddra.'[2] Clive and Stuart were forming an army even before receiving the Governor-General's orders to do so.

Wellesley was immediately involved in the developing situation. He was the only senior English officer in India with experience in command of a British army in Mahratta territory; he had deliberately increased his knowledge of the country and his Mahratta contacts, with the possibility of a command in this area clearly in mind. The Peshwa's restoration and further action against the Mahrattas were to give the young major-general his greatest Indian opportunities. These will be discussed in the following chapters. We need now to summarize briefly what he had accomplished in southern India by his two tours of duty at Seringapatam.

He had pacified his area as much as can ever be done in a territory so extended and so rough. He had defeated his enemies and firmly established his friends in power. How had this been achieved?

First and foremost, there was a completely unified command both military and political under a single strong, practical mind.

Second, Wellesley took full advantage of the abilities of Indians and he was exceptionally fortunate in receiving valuable and faithful service from them. Purneah was the best, but by no means the only one. Sepoys under English officers constituted the principal part of British military strength. Indians brought in intelligence, handled the thousands of bullocks on which depended logistical support, and did most of

---

[1] *Supplementary Despatches*, III, 331–2. The tactics are almost precisely those employed by Captain Gornell and the 1/8 Madras in their successful action at Sangaloo.
[2] *Supplementary Despatches*, III, 381.

the other work both in peace and in war. They were often inefficient, but Wellesley made allowances. He managed to create a competent and practical organization with a minimum of European participation throughout his entire area.

Third, Wellesley and his team managed their pacification magnificently. Territory taken from Tipoo only three and a half years ago was now loyal either to the new Mysore or the EIC because the British promises of security and prosperity were credible. British power was obvious and permanent; Wellesley and his subordinates were not supporting Mysore on a temporary basis. People lived better as soon as the EIC took over an area, and were unlikely to leave. Indians had confidence in the Wellesleys, in Britain and in their plans for India.

Fourth, Wellesley had advantages in administering summary punishment when necessary. The execution of the insurgent Rajah of Bullum would be contrary to enlightened public opinion today, but it was effective. A riot in Seringapatam was put down by the immediate application of military force.[1] But justice was as swift for European soldiers or sepoys who flagrantly misbehaved. The decisions were based on whether they would achieve the desired result, not on how they would influence international opinion the next morning.

It should be stressed that British control in India was not unnecessarily harsh or unusual for that time. The Wellesleys fully realized British dependence on the native population. Common sense dictated not only justice and decent treatment for Indians, but also prompt, fair and sure payments in all business transactions. Britain could continue in India only so long as she gave the Indians a better life than they had before or would have without the British. 'If we lose our character for truth and good faith, we shall have but little to stand upon in this country.'[2] On the military side, Arthur Wellesley included in his command all the troops he could use. There were enough European soldiers to leaven the whole and make it effective.[3] The East India

[1] On the morning of 17 March 1800 'mobs of cook boys went about the streets threatening the inhabitants if they opened their shops or sold anything till their leaders were released. They went to the different fords and stopped the people bringing provisions and supplies to the market. No efforts of the police could disperse the mobs.' But Wellesley's troops cleared them quickly; four of the rioters were killed. 'I attribute their [initial] obstinacy to the success they have had [with similar tactics] in the Carnatic, but I could not suffer it to happen here.' *Supplementary Despatches*, I, 484–5.

[2] *Dispatches*, II, 309.

[3] British armies in India with too few European troops were likely to be ineffective, even though the quality of Indian soldiers under British officers was unquestioned. A proportion of from three to five sepoys to one European enlisted man seems to have been about right from 1745 to 1945.

Company supplied money for the troops to be efficient and (relatively) healthy. There was enough of everything including ammunition for target practice. British soldiers, both Indian and European, were volunteers who often had many years of experience. They were doing work for which they had applied and on which their lives and families depended. The new men who joined quickly learned the relatively simple contemporary fighting tasks from the veterans who fought beside them. Practice improves human ability, especially in irregular warfare. Wellesley's European soldiers were not sent home after thirteen months.

The situation in India in 1799 allowed Wellesley to use a tactical audacity seldom equalled in military history. He took strong forts by immediate assault. He charged Dhoondiah's superior force with British cavalry in a single line, even though he had no reserves. He gained quickly and retained the image of victory throughout his years in India. His systems of supply and communication were well organized as early as 1800. His communications outward from Seringapatam stretched over hundreds of miles of roads on which even oxcarts could not travel without accompanying pioneers. But local purchases and convoys kept Wellesley's soldiers fully supplied and dispatches travelled to and from every post in his whole area with astonishing rapidity.

Wellesley's personal contribution to the military efficiency of his team cannot be overlooked. He acted as his own chief of intelligence and understood the general situation throughout his sphere of India. He knew more about his local enemies than they did about him and controlled his whole system with unusual ability. The man who won a great victory at Waterloo managed to win small victories in India between July 1799 and December 1802 by the immediate application of ample force. He kept alive the image of British invincibility by audacity.

VIII

The Restoration of the Peshwa

The Mahrattas were and are a Hindoo people, with a separate family of languages and customs, who occupy a large area of west central India. Physically small and hardy, they were generally good horsemen and lived in part by plundering those around them. The villages of the common people were all fortified, but innumerable feudal chiefs preyed on the holdings of their neighbours when there was nothing to be had more easily elsewhere. Social advancement seems always to have depended on successful robbery.

In the sixteenth century the Mahrattas bowed to the Moguls, but were not destroyed. About 1670 Sevajee, the greatest of his race, established something like a cohesive Mahratta empire. After his death on 5 April 1680 this empire became an elaborate confederation. In the course of the next hundred years this restless warlike people maintained a semblance of unity in a most unusual way. One of Sevajee's descendants, the Rajah of Satar, was nominally all-powerful, but he was kept a prisoner in his own palace. A chief minister, Bajee Rao I, took over the real power and made his position of Peshwa hereditary about 1750.[1]

By the end of the eighteenth century the Mahratta Confederation was the most powerful political entity in India after the EIC. It stretched from Soonda in the south to Delhi in the north, a distance of 900 miles. East and west it spread from coast to coast. However, the then Peshwa, Bajee Rao II, was a young man of little real talent who had succeeded in 1795 at the age of eighteen. He was supposed to

[1] For these facts about Mahratta history I have relied mainly on *Wellesley* Notes, Appendix I.

control four major and many minor feudal subordinates; in 1802 the two most important were Scindia and Holkar. Their own territories and areas occupied by other chiefs in Hindostan and the Deccan over-lapped.[1] Scindia and Holkar were more powerful in the north, for the Peshwa himself and the Rajah of Berar controlled large tracts in the south.

The fifth large Mahratta landholder was the Gaikwar of Baroda whose territory lay to the west around the Gulf of Cambay. There were no definite boundaries in Mahratta domains or even beyond them; without reference to geographical location, one village would belong to one chief and the next to another. Both Scindia and Holkar had fortresses south of the Nerbudda river. Holkar's were at Chandore and around it; Scindia held Ahmednuggur, Burhampoor, Asseergurh and a few others.

We should notice that nearly continuous fighting in Mahratta terri-tory, especially after 1795, had led to misery for the people because the armies of both sides lived by marauder. Their depredations always caused hunger and often led to starvation. People were robbed even of their brass and copper cooking and water vessels.

Bajee Rao II was dominated by an older minister, Nana Furnavese, and then by Scindia whose armies decisively defeated Holkar at Indore on 14 October 1801. Indore, Holkar's ancestral capital, was plundered and destroyed by Scindia's victorious troops. The Governor-General knew about these Mahratta troubles and sent the elder Kirk-patrick early in 1801 to negotiate a subsidiary treaty with the Peshwa. Later that year Barry Close succeeded Kirkpatrick as Resident at Poona with the same instructions. A treaty like those already in force with the Nizam of Hyderabad and other Indian princes would have obvious advantages for the British, but the Peshwa would only accept it in extremity.[2]

Such a situation arose when Holkar won a resounding victory at Poona on 25 October 1802. The Peshwa and Scindia suffered a bloody and complete defeat. Holkar was braver and a better soldier than either

---

[1] The two terms are not definite, but the Nerbudda river can be said to divide them, with the Deccan to the south and Hindostan to the north.

[2] The Peshwa objected because Close insisted that the British have the right to mediate the points at issue between the Mahrattas and the Nizam of Hyderabad and that the Peshwa expel all French from his personal dominions. These were the same unacceptable demands made earlier in regard to Soonda. The Peshwa also wanted to use his subsidiary battalions for internal operations such as the suppression of rebellion, but this was refused by the British.

of them, but all three princes depended on the Regular Battalions, Indian soldiers trained, armed and organized according to western ideas and partly officered by Europeans. More than 50 per cent of these officers were from the British Isles or of British extraction, many of them from King's or EIC units.[1] Holkar's infantry had organic artillery in each battalion in much the same way as EIC units. Most of the Mahratta cavalry was still irregular, although some of it was attached to the Regular Battalions.

The Peshwa fled before the battle at Poona was over; he could not stand the thought of being hit at long range by a cannon ball and took with him, for his personal protection, a force large enough to have had a decisive effect on the outcome of the battle. For a time Captain Dawes who commanded four of Scindia's Regular Battalions and all his efficient artillery nearly won, but Holkar with a Major Harding finally carried the day with a fine cavalry charge. Both Dawes and Harding were killed.

Barry Close maintained his own and his country's dignity during the difficult period before and after the battle of Poona. He proudly flew his new-pattern Union Jack and kept his considerable bodyguard complete with some artillery in a position of defence, almost as if he were in command of a small neutral army. He did not follow the Peshwa in flight and was asked by Holkar to continue as British Resident to his new government at Poona.

Holkar's original objective was not to destroy the Peshwa, but only to replace Scindia as the power behind him and to set up a double figurehead of government in the Confederacy with the Rajah of Satar first and the Peshwa second, but with himself in command of all military forces and wielding most of the actual power. However, when Holkar was unable to capture the Peshwa, or to persuade him to return to Poona, he decided to replace Bajee Rao II with a man of his own selection. He wanted the young son of Amrut Rao, an adopted son of Bajee Rao's father, on the throne. Amrut Rao himself was to be chief minister.

The Governor-General had given Close general instructions that covered a situation like this. Close and several of his countrymen in India realized that the defeat at Poona was likely to drive the Peshwa into their camp. He was no longer in a position to refuse conditions,

---

[1] Wellesley wrote, *Dispatches*, I, 372, 'The infantry establishments of Holkar, Scindia and the Peshwa were in the year 1800 principally officered by Europeans, three-fourths of whom were natives of France.' *Regular Corps, passim*, and *Military Adventurers*, the alphabetical appendix, indicate that Frenchmen were in the minority.

or to bargain. The Governor-General and Close were willing to restore the Peshwa, but on their own terms. Bajee Rao II first took refuge in a hill fort in Konton and then made for the west coast. After several changes of residence he went to Bassein, either in an EIC ship or escorted by one along the coast from Cowle.[1] In the meantime Close left Poona for Bombay. He met the Peshwa at Bassein and proceeded to arrange what was perhaps the most advantageous treaty that the British ever made in India. It was signed on the last day of 1802.

The important provisions of the Treaty of Bassein were that the British guaranteed to restore Bajee Rao and to supply a subsidiary force of six EIC battalions complete with artillery. These troops were to be maintained by a direct EIC collection of revenue which actually meant the taking over of some Mahratta territory. The Peshwa finally allowed the British to arbitrate all his disputes with the Nizam of Hyderabad; most of the territorial changes which were supposed to have been made after the Mahratta victory of Kardla in 1795 were never to be consummated. The Peshwa also agreed to banish Frenchmen from his service.

On 12 November 1802 Arthur Wellesley received two letters from his superiors at Madras. They told him in effect that Close thought the Governor-General would send orders to restore the Peshwa by force. They were anticipating his instructions and starting immediately to concentrate a considerable military force in northern Mysore. Even if these orders were not forthcoming, a British 'observation' force on the Tombuddra could do no harm. Wellesley responded wholeheartedly to such suggestions. For more than three years he had taken a considerable interest in Mahratta politics. He applied unofficially for the command of a force to restore the Peshwa the day he received Webbe's preliminary order.[2]

Once the Treaty of Bassein was signed, the major military problem of British India was to effect the Peshwa's restoration. No one wanted

[1] The ship was the EIC *Herculean*, Captain Kennedy. The 'voyage' lasted from 1 to 16 December, but was interrupted for trips ashore to eat because the Peshwa's religious principles prevented his eating or drinking afloat. Kennedy wrote, 'Sailed on Tuesday with his Highness the Peshwa and all his fleet in company. We passed Bombay on the 15th, between 4 and 5 p.m. We hoisted the Union jack at the mizzen-topmast head, as a signal that his Highness was not on board the *Herculean*.' *House of Commons Account*, 387. Bassein was a small town in EIC territory just north of Bombay island.

[2] 'You have not told me what part I am to act in this business. I think I can be more useful in it than anybody else. Independent of the experience I have of the country, the principal Sidars [minor chiefs] are acquainted with me, and I have kept up a communication with them ever since I was there before [against Dhoondiah]. This will be of great conse-

war but there was at least a chance that a properly handled expeditionary force could achieve its objective by peaceful means. Holkar remained friendly with the British; the Bombay to Madras overland mail or *tappall* which for hundreds of miles ran through Mahratta territory remained undisturbed. The Treaty of Bassein was not antagonistic to the rights of the Mahratta chiefs apart from its aim to prevent Holkar from gaining control of the entire Confederation through the Peshwa. Scindia had at first been strongly in favour of a British restoration of the Peshwa. The Gaikwar of Baroda already was under partial British control because of a comparable treaty which he had accepted in order to re-establish himself against a local rival in Guzerat. On 17 March and 30 April 1802 the Bombay Army had won two minor battles for him and in December had retaken his capital.

The Gaikwar's restoration had been accomplished with a few units only. The force sent to Poona to restore the Peshwa obviously had to be strong enough to defeat Holkar in battle, if this was necessary. Early in 1803 Stuart, under orders from both Clive and the Governor-General, began assembling an army at Hurryhur that was larger than any other in the history of British India except for those against Tipoo. One portion of this force came direct from Madras, another was organized, equipped and brought north from Seringapatam by Wellesley. The last units, from Hyderabad City, would probably join the main body north of the Mysore–Mahratta border.

By the end of 1802 Stuart and Arthur Wellesley had been working together for seventeen months without a single problem. They saw eye-to-eye, they were able professionals and they had tact. When news of Wellesley's promotion to major-general reached Madras, Stuart immediately appointed him to the Staff of the Presidency. Staff designations were of extreme importance, but were usually made in London. An appointment made in India could always be superseded by the arrival of a Horse Guards nominee. In November 1800 the Duke of York had promised Wellesley a permanent position 'on the Staff' as soon as he became a major-general,[1] but this staff appointment was never made.

---

[1] *Dispatches*, I, 301. Stuart's appointment was temporary only. But a general officer without it could not have an independent command.

---

quence in our operations. It will not be inconvenient that I should quit Mysore, as I have been so long accustomed to the business and have so perfect a knowledge of the country that I could conduct the details of the service [in Mysore] even though at a great distance from it.' *Supplementary Despatches*, III, 381–2.

Stuart gave Wellesley unusual latitude in making up his part of the force which was to assemble at Hurryhur, but he did not reveal who was to go forward. Wellesley realized, of course, that he might be selected to command the expedition to restore the Peshwa. He had been preparing himself, his army and his logistics system for such a possibility ever since the Dhoondiah campaign more than two years before. He had maintained his communications with minor chiefs south of Poona, especially with his friend Goklah the Younger who commanded the Peshwa's forces in that area.[1]

Past knowledge and present contact were not enough. Wellesley developed new plans and an organization, and trained his units carefully. Fortunately, his responsibilities in Mysore took only a part of his time. Montresor was now in Malabar and could handle any disturbances there. Each day Wellesley spent hours preparing for a major campaign to the north, basing his plans on his experience in that part of the country and the gleanings of a wide-flung intelligence net.

Wellesley accepted the fact that a British army operating in Mahratta country would be heavily laden.[2] A part-European army had to carry, among other things, salt beef, biscuit, arrack and medicines as well as ammunition. In the Indian climate tents and some furniture could not be dispensed with for long without damage to health. All these would impair mobility, but Wellesley decided that the difficulties were not insurmountable. The heart and soul of his proposed strategy was the ability to march.

Wellesley's common-sense approach never worked better; he made no drastic changes, just eliminated a few animals here and improved the quality of wheeled vehicles there. He accepted four iron 12-pounders to be used for breaching walls, but tactfully declined 8-inch howitzers and brass 12-pounders for his cavalry gallopers.[3] He had,

[1] This Goklah lost an eye in the battle in which his uncle was killed. It will be recalled that Dhoondiah dyed his moustache in the elder Goklah's blood. Wellesley wrote on 27 November 1802 that the southern *jaghirdars* he knew best 'have become in some degree independent' from the Peshwa. *Supplementary Despatches*, III, 435.

[2] Food for horses had in part to be carried; each cavalry horse generally had one or even two Indian attendants who walked. Wellesley to Stuart, 27 November 1802, *Supplementary Despatches*, III, 432–3.

[3] Wellesley wrote to Stuart on 28 January 1803, 'It will take as many gun bullocks to draw one of these howitzers as for a brigade [four?] of 6-pounders. I take the liberty of suggesting that I may be permitted to leave them behind': *Supplementary Despatches*, III, 564. I am not sure how many 6-pounders formed a brigade, but each 6-pounder was normally drawn by ten or twelve Mysore bullocks. See Appendix I for other technical details of this artillery.

of course, the fine white Mysore bullocks, enough for all draft requirements, and skilled men to handle them. Mackay was a specialist in this
and a good cavalryman as well. The bullocks were to be harnessed to
new carriages and tumbrils carefully made from properly seasoned
teak; there were spare wheels and even extra carriages. Wellesley,
Mackay and a few others knew how well EIC artillery could do with
those bullocks and the new carriages.[1]

Wellesley considerably increased the mobility of his entire force by
prohibiting bullock-drawn private wheeled vehicles. He wanted no
officers travelling in such style that his baggage column would become
unduly long. Pack animals took up far less room because they did not
have to use the road. One of the few bullock-drawn vehicles not carrying
a gun or ammunition was 'the tumbril for the commanders' papers'; the
papers of other general officers would not have required so much space.

We should devote a few words to Wellesley's plans for the vital
question of feeding his army. He sent the usual supplies north to
Chittledroog, Hullihall and Hurryhur. There was an abundance of
everything; the EIC had the money to pay for it. Movement inside
Mysore and EIC territory was easy. But beyond the border, local
supplies of grain would be near useless. Mahrattas and their horses ate
jowarry, a type of coarse grain unacceptable to men and even animals
from Madras and Mysore.[2] Rice was needed for humans and grain for
horses. These and other supplies would have to come from Canara and
Mysore. A system of protected convoys would be needed to maintain
continuous traffic to the north. Wellesley was again planning to depend
on the brinjarries and a similar folk to transport most of the supplies
for his Indian troops, but it would be dangerous not to have his own
system as well. He worked out the details[3] with his usual forethought.

Once more there was a problem about General Baird. He returned
late in 1802 from Egypt where he had done well up to a point. He led

---

[1] 'In our former wars in India great complaints had always been made of the inefficiency
of bullocks attached to the guns, but in this campaign the guns could outmarch the
infantry.' *Blackiston*, I, 95.

[2] *Jowarry* could be fed to horses from Mysore, but it had to be cooked first. Apart from
rice and wheat the different grains in India are difficult to identify even in a grain-store.
There are at least eight different varieties. All can be ground to flour and made into bread,
biscuits or chapatties, but men used to rice did not like grain flour. A shift from one food
to another often caused short periods of illness.

[3] One finds remarks like 'small bags to hold 72 pounds would be best [particularly]
if made of the best gunny', *Dispatches*, II, 85; 'send from Goa 400 kegs of about four gallons
each – about 30,000 pounds of salt provisions packed in small kegs each containing 50
pounds with the liquor and pickel': *Supplementary Despatches*, III, 405.

a British Indian army from the Red Sea across the desert to the Nile and down the river to aid in the final defeat of the French army in Egypt. But then he had his usual squabbles about rank and independent command. Baird was permanently on the Staff of the Madras Presidency and Wellesley's senior still, although both now held the same rank. Baird sensed that the army assembling at Hurryhur was likely to have opportunities and demanded to go there. Stuart acquiesced and sent him north. Wellesley came under Baird's command early in 1803, this time gracefully and without friction.[1]

There was some apprehension among Wellesley's friends that Baird would again supersede him. Wellesley did not share this fear for he guessed what Stuart might do.[2] Stuart left Madras for Hurryhur late in January and was half way there on 1 February. He took over the command from Baird a few days later. As a matter of fact, Baird was not the only major-general with Stuart senior to Wellesley; there was Dugald Campbell whose first EIC commission was dated 3 November 1767, almost two years before Wellesley was born.

On 5 March 1803 Stuart received a dispatch from the Governor-General to send whomever he pleased with whatever force and instructions he deemed necessary for the restoration of the Peshwa. Meanwhile, Wellesley had begun his march from French Rocks on 9 February and would join Stuart and his army early in March. He had equipped, organized and trained his units so that man for man they were perhaps the finest and most formidable force ever assembled in India. Stuart could have combined Wellesley's army with his own and then selected units from both to be sent forward under Baird or Campbell. Instead, he ordered Wellesley to go on with his own force undisturbed.[3] Wellesley was selected for this command to the surprise of no one save perhaps Baird.

[1] Wellesley to Baird, 26 January 1803, *Supplementary Despatches*, III, 557–9.

[2] He wrote to Webbe, 1 January 1803, *Supplementary Despatches*, III, 507, 'If I have not mistaken General Stuart's character, his object will be to uphold the government [i.e. the Governor-General, Clive and their team, including Wellesley]. In the meantime, while General Baird is in command, I will do all in my power to conciliate him.'

[3] Clive to Stuart, 7 March 1803: 'I have had every reason to be highly satisfied with the mode in which the intercourse with the Mahratta jaghirdars has been hitherto carried on through the medium of Major-General Wellesley. The same factors induce me to suggest to your Excellency the expediency of employing that officer in the command of the detachment destined to advance in co-operation with the southern jaghirdars, and lead me to recommend your continuing to take every advantage of that officer's personal influence with these chiefs, and of his extensive knowledge of their views and sentiments, in order to carry the intentions of the Governor-General into full execution . . .': *Dispatches*, I, 419. But this dispatch cannot have reached Stuart before he had already made the same decision.

Stuart gave Wellesley detailed instructions which amounted to 'Restore Bajee Rao, but don't involve us in a war!' If Stuart had not already been firmly convinced that Wellesley was the man to command his own force, the young Major-General's masterly memorandum of 3 March 1803 could have left little doubt of it.[1] Wellesley wrote his memorandum as much to clear and crystallize his own thinking as to impart information to others, but to anyone reading it at the time or later on it surely proved his special aptitude for responsibility in the areas it covered. No thoughtful person can reasonably argue that Baird should have had control of the force. Assuming that both were equal as commanders on the battlefield – something that had not yet been disproven – Baird would have had almost immediate trouble with logistics and with the minor Mahratta chiefs whom he did not know and would not have liked. He might have had to fight his way forward; he and his army would probably have starved.

Arthur Wellesley halted briefly with Stuart and moved six miles further north on 8 March. His force was constituted as follows:[2]

Cavalry under EIC Lt-Col Thomas Dallas, 4th Native Cavalry

King's 19th Dragoon's (Lt-Col Patrick Maxwell)	413
4th, 5th, and 7th Native Cavalry	1,297

First Brigade of Infantry under Lt-Col William Wallace, King's 74th Foot

King's 74th Foot (Major Samuel Swinton)	754
1/2nd, 1/3rd, and 2/3rd Madras Native Infantry	3,112

Second Brigade of Infantry under Lt-Col William Harness, King's 80th Foot

King's Scotch Brigade (Lt-Col James Ferrier)	1,013
1/8th, 2/12th, and 2/18th Madras Native Infantry	3,011

Artillery under EIC Captain Michael Beaumont

[1] *Dispatches*, I, 413–15. The covering letter contains the sentences, 'If you should take command yourself, I hope you will allow me to accompany you in any capacity whatever. I shall do everything in my power to make myself useful to you.' This dispatch crossed with one from Stuart appointing Wellesley.

[2] These figures are taken from *Dispatches*, I, 416. Unit strengths are higher than in some other sources.

4 – Iron 12-pdrs	Europeans	300
2 – Brass 12-pdrs	Gun lascars and pioneers	1,000
16 – Brass 6-pdrs		
4 – Galloper 6-pdrs with infantry		
8 – Galloper 6-pdrs with cavalry		

Mysore Silladar cavalry[1] under Bisnapah Pundit	2,500
	————
Grand Total	14,700

Wellesley had two regrets. His own beloved King's 33rd was not part of his command, and Montresor who was among the few military subordinates he trusted completely remained in Malabar.[2] However, he had the co-operation of two of his closest friends: Barry Close was still British Resident with the Peshwa; the lovable and very capable Major John Malcolm was to be Wellesley's civil and political assistant.[3] Wellesley, Close and Malcom had worked together on the Governor-General's two Seringapatam Commissions and were the most knowledgeable and experienced British team in India. Wellesley would also have Colonel James Stevenson and the entire Hyderabad subsidiary force under his command, as well as a numerous army of the Nizam's troops. Stevenson's subsidiary force is shown below:[4]

Cavalry:	3rd Native Cavalry	516
	6th Native Cavalry	502
		1,018

[1] A superior type of cavalry composed of men who came into the army with their own horses and weapons.

[2] Wellesley wrote in a 'private and confidential' letter to Montresor on 7 March 1803, 'I wish I had you with me.' *Supplementary Despatches*, IV, 35.

[3] Malcolm had been the Governor-General's Private Secretary as well as his political 'trouble shooter'. He was now officially British Resident at Mysore, but he never went there at this time. He sailed from Calcutta to Madras and then went straight to Hurryhur to join Wellesley, almost certainly under the Governor-General's orders. Malcolm and his party were two days late at Hurryhur, but caught up at Hoobly on 19 March 1803: *Malcolm*, I, 212. The author [Kaye] is, I believe, unduly concerned with Malcolm's dubious position at this time. He was certainly one of the inner circle of the Wellesley hierarchy and from his recent intimacy with the Governor-General knew his mind better than either Wellesley or Close.

[4] I have again used *Dispatches*, I, 417, for most of these facts, but point out that Stevenson was not in complete command of the Nizam's own army. He wrote to Close on 20 March 1803 saying, 'I have been informed by the Resident at Hyderabad that I shall be joined on the frontier [by the Nizam's force] who are to co-operate with me.' *House of Commons Account*, 431. This communication also gives the field artillery enumeration shown. I have been unable to discover the brigading of this force at this time.

Infantry: 2/4 Madras Native Infantry   1,275
1/6 Madras Native Infantry   1,288
2/7 Madras Native Infantry   1,290
2/9 Madras Native Infantry   1,286
1/11 Madras Native Infantry   1,008
2/11 Madras Native Infantry   1,035

    7,182

Others: Artillerymen   168
Gun lascars   276
Pioneers   212

    656

Grand Total   8,856

Field Artillery Pieces: 16 6-pounders and 12-pounders bullock-drawn (probably 12 and 4 respectively)
4 3-pounder gallopers (with cavalry)
2 6-pounder gallopers

The Nizam's army may as well be set down at 9,000 Mogul cavalry, 6,000 infantry and 40 guns, although there are other enumerations both above and below this total. The fighting potential of the infantry and artillery was hardly great. To give equal strength to both British armies Stuart and Wellesley had decided to turn over the Scotch Brigade to Stevenson. Stevenson was at Parianda on 25 March; Wellesley ordered him to move forward for a meeting at or near Aklooss.

Even though Major-General Wellesley was in complete command of both armies, Stevenson's was logistically independent. The forces from Hyderabad City were to be supplied from their home area. Both small armies had the enormous advantage of plenty of hard money and sound credit. The Marquess Wellesley was later to suffer censure for misappropriating EIC funds, but his use of Company wealth, especially at the end of the pipeline hundreds of miles from Seringapatam and Hyderabad City, contributed a great deal to the success of his military operations.

When Wellesley crossed the Tombuddra on 12 March, he issued strict instructions that this Mahratta territory was to be considered friendly. Anyone caught stealing would not have the benefits of justice

21 Ahmednuggur and the Wellington gun

22 Ahmednuggur: details of the fortifications showing practically no European influence

25 The River Godavery near Rakisbaum

26 Naulniah from north of the River Purna

27 Peepulgaon from the north

28 Waroor and the ford across the River Kaitna

under law, but would immediately be flogged or hanged in accordance
with the commander's sole decision. The army, Europeans and Indians
alike, knew Wellesley and realized that he did not make idle threats.
Besides, there was no compelling reason for misbehaviour. Everyone
had all he wanted to eat and pay was up to date. The army behaved
well and continued to do so to the astonishment of people used to
plunder by armies for generations. The commander himself controlled
down to the last detail the collection of fodder and the few other
useful supplies the country could furnish; it was all paid for fairly in
coins current in each area.

There was a problem almost immediately. The strong Mahratta
fortress town of Darwar lay in Wellesley's path. He knew the *killadar*,
Bappojee Scindia, personally, but had no confidence that he would
surrender the place because at this time he and his garrison were not
loyal to the Peshwa. If Darwar, summoned to surrender, should
refuse, Wellesley would have to take it. But the siege would 'occasion
the loss of lives and some wounded. It would be necessary to establish
a hospital and [put] a garrison in it.'[1] Relying on the presence of
Stuart's army at Hurryhur to keep these Mahrattas in order and to
keep his communications with Mysore open, Wellesley bypassed
Darwar. From this point the expedition was operating partly on bluff.
If the southern chiefs had the courage and ability to unite against the
British lines of communication, they could cut Wellesley's army off
from its base. If he lost in the north, they would undoubtedly turn
against him, but so long as he remained undefeated they were no
worse than neutral. His own and Malcolm's friendly intercourse with
the southern *jaghirdars* and the good behaviour of his entire force had
won 'the confidence and respect of every class in the provinces to the
south of the Kistna. [This] is in a great degree personal to Maj. Gen.
Wellesley. The admiration which the Mahratta chiefs entertain of that
officer's military character, and the firm reliance which the inhabitants
place on his justice and protection [accounts for] the extraordinary
success which has hitherto attended the progress of this force.'[2] One
wonders what might have occurred with Baird in command.

Wellesley's army was moving fast but smoothly and well within its
capacity for sustained effort. Mackay's bullocks were even exceeding
their reputations, although the limitation on private baggage helped.
The army's health was good, an easy movement of supplies supported

[1] Wellesley to Stuart, 15 March 1803: *Dispatches*, I, 437–8.
[2] Malcolm to Clive, 3 April 1803: *Dispatches*, I, 463–4.

the entire effort and in the rear all was tranquil. The news from the north was encouraging: Holkar was still friendly and apparently not preparing for war.

There was one worry, however, which Wellesley felt he should take up directly with his brother. Even though he had been detached from Stuart's army in the Madras Presidency and sent north to Poona which came within the sphere of Bombay, as far as he knew he was still in command of Mysore, Malabar and Canara. He wanted to be sure, however, that he retained his command for his own maximum logistic support. The properly guarded convoys of supplies on which his army depended would continue to leave on time and contain all that was required only so long as the people who sent them were responsible to himself. The Marquess's affirmative answer came back loud and clear.[1]

The armies of Wellesley and Stevenson approached one another at Aklooss on 15 April, but did not unite. Wellesley rode over to see his old friend and to discuss the campaign. For the time being at least he preferred to leave the Hyderabad contingent to operate as a separate army as he and Stevenson had done during the last weeks of the campaign against Dhoondiah. This was especially desirable as a new report from the north indicated that Holkar had already retreated towards Chandore, his only hereditary stronghold in the Deccan.

Stevenson now had with him not only the EIC subsidiary force, but also the Nizam's own army which needed constant watching for plundering. The Hyderabad army was sent back into their home territory around Gardoor; Stevenson with his EIC units plus the Scotch Brigade was ordered to move north to a position about twenty-five miles east of Poona on the Beemah river.

Soon there was more news from Poona; Wellesley's systems of intelligence were working well. Holkar had definitely reached Chandore. Only Amrut Rao[2] remained at Poona and he was said to be preparing to plunder and destroy the town by fire before retreating from it.

---

[1] 'The Governor-General in council considers Major-General Wellesley's continuance in the military command in Mysore to be essentially necessary.... If any other officer shall have been appointed... restore [the command] to Major-General Wellesley immediately.' *House of Commons Account*, 95.

[2] Amrut Rao was abler than the Peshwa and somewhat more decent. He refused to accept Holkar's offer either for himself or his son, partly because he did not want to plunge the country into civil war. He was no more considerate in his treatment of civilians, however, than most other Indian rulers of his day.

On 19 April Wellesley's army as usual marched about twenty miles between 6 a.m. and 1 p.m. and encamped. After a five-hour rest Wellesley, Malcolm, the cavalry and one EIC battalion moved forward again with a full complement of cavalry gallopers. The night was glorious with a brilliant moon and stars. One needs to see the hours of darkness in the Deccan under such circumstances in order to appreciate the intensity of light. The cavalry arrived at Poona in the early afternoon of 20 April after marching sixty miles in thirty-two hours, even though the gallopers stuck in Little Bhore Ghaut and delayed the march for at least four hours.[1] The sepoy battalion, the 2/12 Madras under Lieutenant-Colonel Macleod, remained at the foot of the ghaut. Wellesley later said that Amrut Rao left by one gate as the British came in by another. No fighting took place and the city was left intact. The rest of Wellesley's army arrived two or three days later. A strong British force from Bombay brought Bajee Rao to the vicinity of Poona early in May. After a considerable delay occasioned by the Peshwa's superstitions – he wanted to re-enter his capital when the stars were properly positioned – he resumed his seat on the munsud on 13 May 1803. Wellesley had accomplished his primary mission.

The situation in Poona, however, was far from ideal. The Peshwa was not likely to prove a blessing for his own people. Misgovernment was more firmly established here than was usual even in India. Wellesley remarked, 'It could not be expected that even a government regularly organized would be able to resume its functions and its powers immediately after a revolution such as that effected by the victories of Jeswunt Rao Holkar, preceded as they were by the long usurpation of Dowlut Rao Scindia, much less one conducted by a man so weak as Bajee Rao. But it may be reasonably expected this state of affairs will improve with the assistance of the British Government, and that the Peshwa will have an authority for which there will be some respect.'[2]

Bajee Rao was no blessing for the British either. He signed the Treaty of Bassein in order to recover power, but continued to conspire secretly against the EIC with Scindia, the Rajah of Berar and even with

---

[1] Wellesley's note from the 'Bottom of Bhore Ghaut 20 April 1803, 8 a.m.' to Lieutenant-Colonel Harness who was in command of the main force (*Dispatches*, I, 504–5) is most interesting. The road down the ghaut must have been ghastly for wheeled vehicles, even light 3-pounder carriages. Where did 3-pounder gallopers come from? Perhaps Stevenson's army. In March 1968 the road was 'jeeps only'. Bangalore–Poona traffic no longer uses the 'Little Bhore Ghaut', but a modern road to the north-east.

[2] *Dispatches*, II, 122.

Holkar whom he should have considered his worst enemy. Most of these things were known to Malcolm, Close and Wellesley at the time; the Peshwa could not even keep his dealings with others secret. Arthur called him, 'A prince, the only principle of whose character is insincerity'.[1]

The Peshwa had no more feeling against the British, however, than against his fellow-countrymen. After his fashion he probably admired the former and certainly behaved with extreme cruelty to many of the latter. Many years later the Duke of Wellington remembered that the Peshwa had once remarked, 'I have only three friends in the world – Malcolm, Close, and yourself.'[2]

In May Holkar decided to go to war. He advanced from Chandore into the Nizam's dominions past Dowlutabad and levied a contribution from Aurungabad. Wellesley moved north-west with his army and had Stevenson do likewise, but he also wrote Holkar a civil letter of remonstrance. The Mahratta general replied with equal courtesy and explained that the Nizam owed him money. He 'had done the country no injury and was about to depart'.[3] Holkar appears to have been disgusted with the intrigues of his fellow chiefs and was determined to take no part in them. Meanwhile, one of his important subordinates, Meer Khan, was negotiating with the Nizam's Government to change sides. Wellesley advised the Resident at Hyderabad and Stevenson to forward this in every way possible. Hyderabad itself presented a problem. The Nizam was in extremely poor health and would not live long. Stuart had sent two of his EIC battalions to Hyderabad City in place of the units on active duty to the west. They might be needed to maintain order when the Nizam died.

Scindia was developing into the most serious opponent the British had. Soon after his southern army and the Peshwa's lost to Holkar at Poona, he had been as anxious as any for Bajee Rao to get help from the British. At the time of the battle he had been hundreds of miles to the north and had more than 80 per cent of his Regular Battalions intact, but he did not relish moving south against Holkar; Scindia was no braver than the Peshwa,[4] nor was he a really good military commander. Once the Peshwa had been restored, however, Scindia realized that his own influence at Poona was gone. Barry Close had taken his place. So Scindia secretly negotiated with all the Mahratta chiefs for a combined effort against the British. He tried to convince not only

---

[1] *Dispatches*, II, 36.   [2] *Brett-James*, 48.   [3] *Supplementary Despatches*, IV, 79.
[4] He remained with his women while Colonel Sutherland won for him at Indore.

Holkar and the Rajah of Berar, but also the Gaikwar and the Peshwa, both of whom were firmly bound by subsidiary treaties to the EIC.

Scindia was not being openly antagonistic. On 27 February he received Colonel John Collins as Resident in his camp and treated him with respect. To Collins he pretended to be wholly neutral. The situation was unclear, neither peace nor war. Wellesley's army was fit and ready to fight. The approaching monsoon would severely handicap the Mahrattas, but do the British little harm because they could cross rivers that Indian armies could not. Wellesley was able to make, use, and keep secure basket-boats which could be maintained under guard at each likely river crossing-point.

Meanwhile, Wellesley's convoys from the south continued to get through 400 miles of Mahratta territory without trouble. There was always the possibility, however, that the route might suddenly be closed. If the southern *jaghirdars* should join Scindia, Wellesley's system of supply would be in severe difficulties. For months he had considered a partial shift of base from Mysore to Bombay and had written to Governor Jonathan Duncan of Bombay about this matter on 20 January 1803 while still at Seringapatam. Bombay was the finest port on the west coast of India and only seventy-five miles from Poona; Panwell on the mainland would be an almost perfect place for a supply depot. 'We shall carry on the war at Poona with the resources of Bombay and shorten our line of communication many hundred miles.'[1]

In spite of its obvious advantages, however, Bombay was a far from satisfactory base. The inefficient handling of Wellesley's requisitions for supplies which came from there to Panwell by water and were then transported by bullocks up the Big Bhore Ghaut to Poona could have been disastrous had anything disturbed the far longer line of communication with the south. For weeks, the army received nothing that had been ordered, but hundreds of bullock loads of supplies of marginal usefulness. After 600 miles of atrocious roads wheels were needed but did not arrive. Wellesley's army had to make new ones at Poona. To crown the whole poor show, pontoons which Wellesley had wanted for weeks to make his river crossing easier were sent off during a heavy rainstorm, and all the carriages broke down during the first day.[2]

---

[1] *Dispatches*, I, 394 and 395.

[2] Bombay's performance made Wellesley lose some of his accustomed forbearance; he said, 'Only think of these stupid creatures sending off these carriages in the midst of that heavy rain.' 21 June 1803: *Dispatches*, II, 27.

There were other problems; what military movement in history has been without them? On the short march beyond Poona the usually honest brinjarries made off with a good deal of rice. The rank and file bullocks, not the fine Mysore draft beasts, suffered from a lack of forage in a country already devastated over several years by Mahratta armies and the chronic laziness of those who were supposed to look after them. The animals died by dozens, but there were replacements. Coins current in Mysore were unknown in Poona, but Wellesley did some judicious money-changing.[1]

Even from this distance there were still details to be handled and decisions to be made concerning Seringapatam. These were the inseparable consequences of Wellesley's two commands. The arsenal needed a form of incentive pay to get efficient production. The best way of stopping minor robberies in the Ryacotta–Kistnagherry section was to hire at least some of the thieves and make them into police. The rebellion led by the Pyche Rajah in Wynaad was still going on, but Montresor was doing a good job. Purneah wanted new small arms rather than captured stuff which was 'not worth having'.

On the other hand, both British armies could hardly have been in better condition. Wellesley and Stevenson were exercising cavalry, infantry and artillery in drill, target practice, small unit manœuvres and the indispensable forming of multiple unit lines so necessary in those days and so difficult to do in unfamiliar terrain.'[2]

If the Mahrattas should attack, the British forces were ready. As early as 5 May 1803 Wellesley wrote to Stevenson that their potential enemies 'may attempt an invasion of the Nizam's territories by Holkar while Scindia advances towards Poona. The defence of the Nizam's territories must depend upon you and the Nizam's army. I shall deal with Scindia. If both parties invade the Nizam's territories, your force and mine must combine, leaving at Poona a sufficient force for the protection of the Peshwa's person. If both parties advance together towards Poona, your force and mine must join in this quarter.'[3]

We should take advantage of the lull to have a look at what was

[1] The gold coins of India at that time were mainly of two types, *mohurs* in the north and *pagodas* and *fanams* in the south. Mysore used both, but the *pagoda* was not current at Poona. Silver rupees were common in most places, but they varied in weight, fineness and appearance.

[2] Wellesley had placed a high priority on this practice and had begun it as soon as his army came together north of Seringapatam before he marched for Hurryhur: *Welsh*, I, 147. Also General Order, 4 February 1803, at French Rocks: *Supplementary Despatches*, III, 578.

[3] *Dispatches*, I, 545.

happening elsewhere in India. Baird went home to England in disgust. Stuart returned to Madras to be on hand if he were needed to deal with the two French forces which arrived in India after the Peace of Amiens to reclaim Pondicherry and other French possessions taken by the British in 1793. The Governor-General did not want this turn of events to interfere with the Mahratta negotiations.[1]

Stuart left Campbell in charge of the army which had been at Hurryhur but was now moved about one hundred miles further north to Moodgul. Since Campbell was years senior to Wellesley, special instructions were necessary. Campbell was personally to remain in the Ceded Districts south of the Kistna so as not to interfere with Wellesley's carrying out his duties further north, but he was to send to Wellesley any forces for which he received 'an application'. In other words, Stuart left Wellesley in sole charge above the Kistna with authority to requisition reinforcements from his senior at Moodgul if he should require them.[2]

On the international scene, the Treaty of Amiens, which for a time at least brought peace between Britain and France, was signed on 27 March 1802; the news reached Madras on 4 September. Pondicherry, Mahe and other small possessions taken from the French in 1793 were to be given back, but nothing further was heard for months. Finally on 15 June 1803 the French frigate *La Belle Poule* arrived at Madras with 150 officers and men to take back Pondicherry and was followed, on 12 August, by General De Caen with more troops in the *Marengo*, a ship-of-the-line. The French were waving copies of the treaty and clamouring for their small colonies. The Governor-General decided not to give them up 'pending direct orders from home even though he had already received instructions issued in May 1802 to do so'. He passed his decision to Clive who on 28 July in turn ordered Stuart to return to the coast with an appropriate force. The Madras C-in-C came

[1] The Governor-General to Wellesley, 27 June 1803, 'Although a division of the French troops is already arrived at Pondicherry, and the remainder may be soon expected, I desire that you will not be induced, by that event, to precipitate an accommodation with any of the Mahratta powers. The effectual security of our interests in the Mahratta empire is the strongest barrier which can be opposed to the progress of the French interests in India; the early reduction of Scindia (if that chief should compel us to resort to hostilities) is certain, and would prove a fatal blow to the views of France. An imperfect arrangement with the Mahratta powers, or a delay of active measures, might open to France the means of engaging, with advantage, in the affairs of the Mahratta empire.' *Dispatches*, II, 56.

[2] *Dispatches*, II, 190, Stuart to Marquess Wellesley: 'Major-General Campbell has been directed to detach the force under his command, or part of it, to join the troops in advance on receiving an application to that effect from Major-General Wellesley . . .' but to stay south of the Kistna himself.

with three King's units, the 25th Dragoons, the 73rd Foot and part of the 80th Foot. He also brought a regiment of Native Cavalry.[1]

Meanwhile, on 12 August, a French corvette joined the *Marengo* and her escorts; within an hour, the entire small fleet weighed anchor and sailed. It was the first indication in India of the reopening of the war with France. The 150 French who had come ashore from *La Belle Poule* were taken prisoner. The Marquess Wellesley had certainly saved himself and Britain the trouble, expense and casualties of retaking a strong position at Pondicherry. A few days after he had the satisfaction of receiving orders from London to do exactly as he had done – make excuses, but not give anything back.

About the same time the Governor-General made another remarkable decision. He realized his complete inability to control the situation in and around Poona. He was several weeks' journey away from negotiations in which his potential enemies were gaining by procrastinating. There were able men in the area; Collins, Malcolm, Close and Wellesley were good at political negotiations, but none of them was in charge. Duncan at Bombay, their senior, was useful, 'but no good in a crisis'.[2] His many years in India – he had come out first in 1772 – hardly fitted him for the new order of things. The Marquess appointed his brother Arthur to supreme command both military and political of all British personnel involved in the Mahratta effort, with full power to negotiate treaties with friends and enemies. He could go to war or not as he thought best, subject only to a provision in regard to General Stuart which we will presently discuss. This enlarged responsibility gave Wellesley what amounted to the command of the military forces of Bombay, a situation that would have been relatively easy for Stuart since he was senior to all officers in that Presidency and had been Bombay C-in-C before he moved to Madras.

The Marquess's order of 26 June did not reach Arthur until 17 July. The younger brother immediately assumed full military and political authority and sent off a flood of letters, in particular to Close at Poona, Collins at Scindia's capital, Kirkpatrick at Hyderabad and Duncan in Bombay and Gujerat. Scindia was still the principal problem; he wanted time to continue trying to form his anti-British coalition, but his own army of about 40,000 men and eighty guns was only a few miles north of the Nizam's town and fortress of Ajanta, situated at the top of the principal ghaut between the Taptee and the Godavery.

---

[1] *House of Commons Account*, 337.
[2] *Malcolm*, I, 188.

The Rajah of Berar was moving towards Scindia with an additional 20,000 horse, 6,000 infantry and 40 guns.

Soon after he received his new orders, Wellesley told Collins not to mince words with Scindia and Berar and to allow them no further time. The British Resident was to explain the Treaty of Bassein and demand to know what specifically was objectionable in it. Wellesley was prepared to make concessions, but the two chiefs would have to withdraw their forces from the very brink of the Nizam's territory. There were to be no further delays.

Collins conducted his diplomatic manœuvres precisely in accordance with his instructions. He demanded an audience and spoke frankly. Scindia and Berar could not single out any specific pieces of the treaty that were unfair. Their real objection was to the British presence at Poona, but they did not dare to say so against the new firm attitude of the Resident. Since they could give no reasonable excuse for their full-strength military presence so close to the Nizam's territory, they were told to withdraw.

Some sparring took place in which the Mahrattas endeavoured to negotiate a mutual withdrawal. For a few days peace seemed possible, although Wellesley had moved in two stages to a position close to Scindia's strong fortress of Ahmednuggur. If war did come, Ahmednuggur would make a fine base for further British operations. It was said to contain an abundance of all simple supplies. Scindia, Berar and their armies were to the north in the Taptee valley, about one hundred miles away. The local garrison appeared of good quality, but too small for the fortress and town it was supposed to defend.

Before continuing with the coming of the war, however, we should observe one of the outstanding examples of unselfishness in military history. Stuart could have taken Wellesley's place with all the authority, military and political, that Arthur had just received; he refused. His reply to the Governor-General contains the following sentence, 'The experience gained by Major-General Wellesley during his former operations in the Mahratta territories, the extensive knowledge and influence which he has acquired in the present campaign, and his eminent military talents, enable him better than any other officer to prosecute with success the service which he has hitherto conducted with so much ability; and I have chosen to relinquish the gratification which I should derive from the command of an army, probably destined to undertake very distinguished services, in order to continue that important charge in the hands of the officer best qualified in my judgment to exercise it with advantage to the public.'[1]

During July Wellesley had with him the same units with which he began the march from Hurryhur in March except that he had given Stevenson the Scotch Brigade and exchanged the 2/3 Madras N.I. now at Poona for the King's 78th Foot. This unit was the only kilted regiment then in India and was to be of extreme value to Wellesley's small army. It had been with Harris at Seringapatam, but had returned to Bengal. The Governor-General sent it off to Bombay on 7 February 1803 where it arrived in time to help escort the Peshwa back to Poona.[2]

Meanwhile, Collins was unable to pin Scindia and the Rajah of Berar down. They tried to procrastinate; he was firm. He reported to Wellesley that he did not receive the satisfactions he demanded and left Scindia's camp north of Ajanta on 3 August. With a considerable bodyguard he marched south for the Nizam's city of Aurungabad.

Wellesley issued the following statement which amounted to a local declaration of war: 'Major-General Wellesley offered to Dowlut Rao Scindia and the Rajah of Berar peace on terms of equality, and honourable to all parties. They have preferred war, and they alone must be considered responsible for the consequences. Under these circumstances Major-General Wellesley is obliged to commence operations against them, in order to secure the interests of the British Government and its allies.[3] Messages in all directions alerted British India to the fact that war was declared.

---

[1] *Dispatches*, II, 191.   [2] *House of Commons Account*, 226: *Wilson*, III, 62.
[3] *Dispatches*, II, 183.

IX

The Mahratta War Begins

Wellesley's orders were issued for the morning of 7 August 1803: at sunrise the army was to march the seven miles to Ahmednuggur. The monsoon of 1803 was irregular and generally light, but 7 August was a day of hard rain. It began so early that the commander cancelled his marching orders. He did not want to take his fine new army into the field for its first day of real campaigning in a downpour.

The 8th was clear, however, so the head of the British column reached the vicinity of Ahmednuggur in two hours. As was usual in India at the time, this fortified city consisted of a fort and a town or *pettah* nearby for civilians dependent upon the fort for employment. Both were surrounded by defences, but the walls and bastions of the fortress were higher, stronger and more carefully designed.

On several occasions during his daily rides for exercise Wellesley had examined carefully fort and town through his telescope. On the 8th he rode ahead of his army, accompanied only by Bisnapah and a squadron of the 19th Dragoons. He had the *pettah* and the fort summoned to surrender while his infantry pickets were still two miles away. He received the expected refusal, but was prepared to take the town by assault without a preliminary bombardment.

Wellesley already knew the composition of the garrisons of both *pettah* and fort. One of Scindia's Regular Battalions had been encamped just outside the town for some time and had now entered. It consisted of '1,000 sepoys in white jackets, with five brass guns, smaller than our 6-pounders, commanded by three French officers, a little dark-coloured, who wear blue clothes. They have twelve one-pole tents.'[1] There were also 1,000 Arab mercenaries in the town. These men were noted for their courage and their good faith to those who employed them, the latter an unusual attribute in India at that time. But they fought as individuals, and were rarely well organized and disciplined.

Wellesley felt sure that the place could be carried by escalade because there was but a single relatively low wall far too long to be properly held by only 2,000 professional soldiers. The town might have some sort of militia, but undoubtedly poorly armed and nearly useless. The wall had forty bastions and a total length of near 4,000 yards. Wellesley immediately issued his instructions for three separate, but mutually supporting assaults. The composite battalion of infantry, the pickets of the day, consisted as usual of a half company from each King's and EIC infantry battalion in the army, a total of one company of Europeans and two and a half of sepoys under the field officer of the day. It was to assault the wall to the left of a gateway with the assistance of the flank companies of the King's 78th; Lieutenant-Colonel Harness was in command. The gateway itself was to be attacked by the battalion companies of the 74th supported by the 1/8 Madras all under Lieutenant-Colonel Wallace. They were to take a gun forward with them and, if possible, blow open the door; this required the muzzle to be placed in contact with the outer surface of the heavy wooden gate. The theory of this was the same as that of the European petard, but seems not to have been thoroughly understood by Wellesley's artillery officers. On the right, the flank companies of the 74th plus the 1/3 Madras was to attack the wall under the command of Captain Vesey of the EIC unit. The two outer columns were supplied with scaling ladders, although apparently not enough of them.[2]

This assault out of hand was audacious in the extreme. The *pettah* walls were probably constructed of brick, mud and masonry and were about twenty feet tall.[3] Around the entire circumference there were circular bastions with wall pieces mounted in each at regular intervals and with tiers of loopholes.

The flank companies of the King's 78th and, of course, the pickets were well up in the column of march; Harness appears to have begun his assault immediately, before the other two columns were in position.

---

[1] *Supplementary Despatches*, IV, 101.

[2] Vesey's command appears to have had only two: *Fortescue*, V, 17.

[3] The town of Ahmednuggur has grown so much that only a single small ruined section of the *pettah* walls remain, but other similar fortifications survive.

The pickets advanced and formed line sixty yards from the wall and the flanking bastions that were to be attacked. The kilted Scots of the 78th carried forward their ladders and placed them midway between the bastions. The wall was undefended, although both bastions – manned by Arabs who came under heavy platoon fire from the pickets – were spouting flame and smoke.

The Highlanders were in for a surprise. The wall they assaulted had no banquette or place behind the parapet to stand on, but a rounded top with a sheer drop on the inside. The men at the top of the ladders hesitated. The garrison in the bastions on either flank were not firing accurately because the pickets shot at anyone who exposed himself, but the Scots at the top of the ladders were also being shot at by some of Scindia's professionals who were deployed behind the wall on the ground and were not under British fire. To drop down inside of the wall under these circumstances was not only to risk being killed by fire or injured in the descent, but also to court almost certain capture. This section of the assault was beaten back.

Harness and his Highlanders were not, however, so easily defeated. He launched the two flank companies of the 78th still covered by the fire of the pickets at one of the two enemy bastions next to the wall they had failed to carry. The first man up was a young lieutenant of the grenadier company, Colin Campbell. Wellesley was watching this assault and saw Campbell go up sword in hand; he was wounded and thrown off the ladder. The men behind were cleared away by a shower of heavy stones and pikes. The young lieutenant was not incapacitated; he bounded to his feet and remounted the ladder, but was again wounded and thrown off. Campbell was brave and strong, but he could also think. On the first two occasions he had gone up claymore in hand. In his third attempt he allowed his weapon to hang from his wrist by a scarf so that both hands were free for use on the ladder. The covering fire from the pickets was keeping the bastion garrison from looking over the wall. Campbell told his men to follow fast once he started and gathered himself for a sprint up the ladder. This time he mounted quickly and leaped into the middle of the bastion over the heads of the Arab defenders at the parapet. He recovered his claymore during the leap and laid about with abandon.

Wellesley saw flashes of light from Campbell's claymore; the kilted grenadiers of the 78th, man after man, were following their young leader up the ladder. From a distance they looked like a stream of angry red ants. Once Campbell and his claymore had gained a foothold, the bastion was quickly cleared. Every Arab inside appears to have been killed. The flank companies of the 78th had no sooner emerged from the inner doorway of the bastion, however, when they were charged by another unit of Arabs. Again it was touch and go, but Campbell's claymore plus the still loaded muskets of some of his men and the bayonets of all of them prevailed. Harness soon had the half companies of infantry from the pickets flowing over the un-banquetted wall by pairs of ladders.

The right-hand attack, by the flank companies of the 74th and the 1/3 Madras under Captain Vesey, had been delayed by the panic of a wounded artillery elephant. They also appear to have learned about the difficulty of getting over the unbanquetted wall and placed their two ladders at a re-entrant angle next to a bastion. One broke from over-loading, but about 300 men got over by the other before it too was smashed by an enemy cannon ball. The Scots in trews and the sepoys already inside were attacked in the cleared space behind the wall by part of Scindia's Regular Battalion. Vesey formed up his miscellaneous command and won a short, sharp fight.

Resistance began to collapse in the area of the *pettah* that was attacked and Scindia's soldiers retreated back into the sprawling town. Vesey and perhaps Campbell led their men to the gate which was still being assaulted by Wallace's force. They removed the bar and began to swing open the heavy wooden door, only to have the British 6-pounder go off in their faces, burning clothing and singeing hair. A sepoy of the 1/3 Madras was practically torn in two by the shot, but no one else was badly hurt.

The *pettah* garrison was able to get out on the opposite side, but was prevented by the British and allied cavalry from retreating into the fort;[1] they were forced to the north and severely harassed. The town had fallen in less than twenty minutes. There was some plundering and rape, but Wellesley hanged one of Vesey's sepoys on the side of the captured gate as an example to others, both European and Indian. If this sort of indiscipline was allowed to get a start, the Mahratta people could not be kept friendly to the British, or even neutral.[2] It must be remembered that under the Wellesleys the British in India were

---

[1] About one hundred Arabs may have got into the fortress from the town; they appear among the garrison of that place when it surrendered later.

[2] *Blackiston*, I, 141, describes this summary justice as 'a measure which, it must be confessed, created some disgust at the moment, but was a proper vindication of the British character for justice and good faith'.

sincerely on the side of the common people and trying to bring them reasonably decent living conditions.

A considerable company of British officers returned to Wellesley's sizeable dining tent – put up during the assault, no doubt – for their first real meal of the day. Wellesley joined them after he had spoken a few words of commendation to young Campbell whose two wounds had finally laid him low.[1]

The victorious assault, followed by breakfast in a normal manner, led to one of the more interesting British Indian quotations still commemorated outside Ahmednuggur on a tablet set into the mounting of an old cannon. The younger Goklah, one of the two Mahratta chieftains[2] who actually joined Wellesley with his troops and remained with him throughout the war, wrote to a friend, 'These English are a strange people, and their General a wonderful man. They came here in the morning, looked at the *pettah* wall, walked over it, killed all the garrison, and returned to breakfast! What can withstand them?'

In this remark we see the result of Wellesley's careful thought and planning. He was using audacity to build a legend of invincibility. In future it was to be of extreme importance to the British in India. This magnificent assault was not, however, without its 'butcher bill'. Six officers and about fifty other Europeans as well as a smaller number of Indian soldiers were killed and wounded;[3] the 78th suffered most.

Even though the *pettah* had fallen, the fortress of Ahmednuggur remained. It was and is an enormous circular work of stone with round bastions at close intervals.[4] The walls and bastions are of solid masonry, several times as strong as those of the *pettah*. There was a deep ditch all around which at that time contained water; the two entrances, one large and the other small, could be reached only through additional

[1] This was their first meeting: *D.N.B.*, III, 803. Colin Campbell's career was thereafter bound up with Arthur's. He became a major-general in 1825 and died in June 1847, a few days after returning from 'eight years as Governor of Ceylon'.

[2] Goklah and Appah Dessaye were nominally the Peshwa's officers and commanded about 4,000 cavalry, but they were paid by Wellesley. They and their men were not professionally competent, nor perhaps as loyal as Gurkas were later, but they were better than nothing: *Dispatches*, II, 259, 260, and 314.

[3] Casualties are given only for the entire operation against both *pettah* and fort, 8–12 August 1803, but most actually occurred on the 8th in the storming of the *pettah*: *Dispatches*, II, 195–6.

[4] This magnificent fortress is still in use as the HQ of the Indian Army Armoured Corps. It has weathered a bit; the old guns are gone and the moat mostly filled in, but the different bastions, thirty in all, show varying amounts of subsequent European reconstruction. In August 1803 they mounted a variety of cannon, some of large size, on different types of carriages.

outer defences. The place was a real fortification that could not be taken by any form of escalade. A formal siege like that of Seringapatam was required, but the *killadar* was short of men; he had only about 1,500. Wellesley's efforts to prevent the *pettah* garrison from escaping into the fort had been important.

Today Ahmednuggur appears to have been beyond the power of Wellesley's small siege train; he only had four iron 12-pounders. But even then the walls had stood for almost 300 years and had probably been weakened by heat, sun and lack of proper repair. Solid shot from 12-pounders could be extremely destructive if the range was short and full charges of four to six pounds of powder were used.

At Seringapatam Tipoo had the advantages of unlimited troops and expert French advice on scientific defence in depth. The *killadar* of Ahmednuggur had neither. He allowed a British battery to be opened without preliminary parallels during the night following the successful assault on the *pettah*. He made no effort to protect the territory beyond the moat with even a picket line and did not fire effectively at British working parties. Large guns loaded with grape – he had plenty of artillery and ammunition – aimed in the general vicinity of the initial digging could have been extremely destructive, but the British battery was completed without the loss of a man. It opened fire the next day, but a few rounds showed that the range, 700 yards, was too great.

On the night of the 9th Wellesley took even greater liberties. A heavy covering force of infantry was paraded at dusk; all pioneers in the army were also mustered complete with their implements. A new battery was constructed only 300 yards from a section of wall carefully selected after inspection by telescope. It was completed during the night and offered exceptionally good protection to both guns and gunners. Early on the 10th the four iron 12-pounders opened from their new position. Their fire was much more effective and the wall began to crumble about noon. At this short range the shot smashed the old weathered masonry, tumbling debris down into the ditch. Every round was slowly and carefully loaded, aimed and fired; the new carriages built at Seringapatam stood up well to the recoil from full charges. But four guns were not really enough. A practical[1] breach did not begin to appear until the late afternoon of the 11th when the guns were running out of ammunition.

---

[1] The term 'practical' in reference to a breach meant that a soldier with musket, bayonet and ammunition only could mount unaided by ladders, fascines and the techniques of escalade used by professional soldiers in assaults for hundreds of years.

An assault was sure to be costly, although Wellesley had brass 12-pounder field guns in flanking batteries ready to sweep the breach from the side during the forthcoming attack. On the morning of the 12th the British troops selected to storm the place were formed and moved forward. It was attack now, or wait two weeks for more 12-pound solid shot.

The *killadar* had been negotiating for a capitulation since the afternoon of the 10th. This kind of psychological delaying action was normal in India. Wellesley had agreed to allow the garrison to march out with all their private property, but the *killadar* had not yet acquiesced or refused. The sight of the assaulting columns forming, however, was too much, for everyone inside Ahmednuggur had seen the British storm the *pettah*. The *killadar* sent out hostages and abandoned the fort soon afterwards. He took with him a good deal of public property, but this was not discovered until later.

Wellesley could have gained nothing worthwhile by taking Ahmednuggur by storm; in India prisoners were a burden only. The capitulation undoubtedly saved many lives on both sides. The taking of a fort which surrenders is never so dramatic as when it falls under assault, but the escalade of the *pettah* had provided enough drama. Ahmednuggur was impregnable for three centuries, but then succumbed to four iron 12-pounders in four and a half days. This fine achievement was based partly on bluff, but was also furthered by professional ability in the whole attacking army from the commanding general to the most junior Indian pioneer.

Wellesley and his team immediately began to take over all Scindia's possessions south of the Godavery. An EIC garrison was installed in Ahmednuggur, initially one EIC battalion and a detail of artillerymen.[1] Captain Graham was appointed Collector; a semi-military force of revenue men, both horse and foot, was organized for his use. These *peons* and *sebundies* were important in India because they could defend the civil administrators and impose local order. They freed EIC troops for more important duty elsewhere. If such units were defeated, there was little or no damage done to military reputation since no British were involved in them.

Wellesley's instructions to Graham show how his mind was

[1] 'This was composed of the 2/3 Madras [Major Kennet], a platoon from the King's 84th Foot [to assist in handling guns], and artillerymen for a brigade of guns', all brought forward from Poona, apparently; they were not taken from the field army: Wellesley to Stuart, 19 August 1803, *Dispatches*, II, 216.

working: 'The officer commanding in Ahmednuggur will have orders to afford you every assistance in his power which you may require; and I have given directions that a body of horse, and a body of peons, shall be raised, who are to be under your orders. You have already so much experience in the revenue duties, that I cannot think it necessary to send you any detailed instructions. I should wish that the accounts may be kept according to the forms which are in use with the government of Fort St. George, and have been approved of by Government; and you will transmit them to me at the regular periods. Bear in mind the facts, that to keep this country in a state of tranquillity, and to secure for the use of the troops under my command its resources, and a free communication through it with Poonah and Bombay, are objects of far greater importance than to collect at present a large revenue from it.'[1]

Scindia's territory around Ahmednuggur and a contiguous large village belonging to Berar[2] were being taken over in the name of Bajee Rao, but the Peshwa who by now was more inclined to help his former enemies than his new allies[3] tried to cause trouble for the administration that Wellesley was setting up in his name. Late in August he received a curt warning from the general through Close, 'I shall be obliged to you if you will tell the Peshwa that he ought not to interfere in [my] arrangement of this country in any manner. If he is not satisfied, let him state his wishes, and I will let him know whether I can comply with them. But if there should be any more of this underhand opposition to the management after it has been approved, I shall be obliged to alter my proclamation and to take possession of the country solely in the name of the company.'[4]

The fortress of Ahmednuggur was quickly repaired and became an ideal base for Wellesley's contemplated operations to the north. A garrison of no great size could hold the place until the rivers became fordable again in about two months. Here supplies from Bombay and Mysore could accumulate in security and be sent on to the army as they were needed. Wellesley and his field units were ready for the second part of his plan, to 'cross the Godavery and bring the enemy to action'.

[1] Wellesley to Graham, 14 August 1803, *Dispatches*, II, 200-1.

[2] 'Nimgaum, about 30 miles south east from Ahmednuggur': *Dispatches*, II, 218.

[3] 'During the period of suspense, the Peshwa was engaged in constant communications with Scindia, urging him to make no concession; but to advance at once to Poona. The Peshwa was lavish in his promises to Close, but took care to perform nothing.' *Marshman*, II, 145-6.

[4] *Dispatches*, II, 240.

On the 14th an advance party and all the cavalry were sent off to Toka on the Godavery to begin making round leather-covered wicker boats which were ready on the 20th. The entire army was over the river by the 22nd. Wellesley had with him the same units of cavalry, the King's 74th and 78th Foot, and the same EIC battalions; only the 2/3 Madras was missing from the six he led across the Tombuddra five months before. He had, however, noticed certain weaknesses in the EIC units. Desertion was particularly bad in the 2/18 Madras – as many as eighty in a single month – although the commanding officer, Lieutenant-Colonel Chalmers, appears not to have been at fault. Lieutenant-Colonel Griffin of the 1/2 Madras was unfit for active service 'through incapacity and sickness'. Wellesley asked Stuart for permission to shift these two officers so when the rivers became fordable again and Poona would need reinforcements he could get rid of Griffin and the 2/18 at the same time.

Wellesley knew that two convoys of supplies, each guarded by an EIC battalion, were on their way to him by different routes. They were the 1/4 Madras under Major Joseph Hill and 1/10 Madras under Major P. Dallas. At this time Wellesley considered Macleod (2/12), Dallas and perhaps Chalmers his best EIC battalion commanders.[1] There was only one change in brigade commanders; T. Dallas of the cavalry who was in Bombay, probably because of his health, had been replaced by Maxwell of the King's 19th Dragoons. Total strength was approximately 2,200 European and 5,000 Indian soldiers, including pioneers and gun lascars. Additionally there were, of course, Bisnapah's fine Mysore light cavalry, now reduced to about 2,200, and the 4,000 Mahrattas under Goklah and Appah Dessaye. The army was small, but of high quality. Every man was a volunteer and many had served in India for more than ten years. They were excellently equipped, carefully trained for the war they had finally begun to fight and well organized. This army had already proved its mobility and its stamina; if the assault on the *pettah* of Ahmednuggur was any indication, it would be able to fight also.

Stevenson and his army had been opposite the forces of Scindia and Berar in the Aurungabad region of north-west Hyderabad since May. In accordance with Wellesley's instructions he was protecting the 'line

---

[1] The tracing of units and commanders and finding out Wellesley's evaluation of both is a difficult but fascinating task. I know of no single source but have built up a chart on *Dispatches*, I, 416, 417; *Dispatches*, II, 245–6; *Dispatches*, III, 115–16; *Welsh*, I, 149–51; and *Supplementary Despatches*, IV, 245–6.

of the ghauts', roughly the Mahratta–Hyderabad border. Wellesley had suggested the exciting possibility of catching one or both Mahratta armies as they were coming up one of the three steep narrow passes. Stevenson had moved close to the top of the Ajanta Ghaut as soon as he heard that Collins had left Scindia and Berar.

The main danger to be anticipated in a war against Mahratta armies was a plundering expedition deep into the territory of the Peshwa or the Nizam. Wellesley already appreciated, however, that Scindia would find such an action difficult because of his numerous Regular Battalions. A swarm of Mahratta cavalry could travel fast and light, but a force containing infantry and artillery was likely to be caught by Wellesley's army that probably had greater mobility.

After crossing the Godavery, an extensive operation which took most of three days, Wellesley moved towards Aurungabad. About this time Stevenson received erroneous intelligence that his enemies were ascending the Badowly Ghaut to the east and moved in that direction. Scindia and Berar then came up the Ajanta Ghaut[1] on the 24th. When Wellesley heard of this on 28 August he was one march from Aurungabad. The Nizam's territory was being invaded, although no great damage had been reported so far.

Wellesley arrived at Aurungabad on the 29th and found that Scindia's *pindarries* – Muslim independent mercenary brigands, under their own more-or-less hereditary chiefs – had been there the day before. This irregular light cavalry had come almost up to the walls, but the Nizam's *killadar* had remained confident because he knew help was at hand. This fellow had a good deal of information and was anxious to talk; Wellesley confirmed some of his own sources of intelligence. Scindia and probably Berar were only forty miles to the east. They were encamped with their cavalry, but no Regular Battalions, at Jalna, a fortified place belonging to Scindia though fifty miles south of the supposed border between Hyderabad and the Mahratta

[1] The 'line of ghauts' which separates the valley of the Taptee from the upland plain of Hyderabad is not high, a rise of 600 to 800 feet, but the hills are steep, especially when approached from the north, and continuous. There were many ascents for a few men on foot or even mounted, but not for an army. The three main passes were Ferdapoor in the west, Ajanta and Badowly. The pass north of Ajanta was and is much the best, the only one of importance in this campaign. A 'new' road built about 1900 which follows a slightly different route has left the old one as it was for centuries, complete with a fortification at the top. The old ghaut is excessively narrow and steep by modern standards, but appears to have been no worse early in the nineteenth century than the Roman road across the Pyrenees between St Jean Pied-de-Port and Pamplona. Both were used for thousands of years, but were abandoned at about the same time.

Confederacy. Boundaries were most irregular in India at that time.

On their way to Jalna Scindia and Berar had attacked the Nizam's fortified village of Budnapoor but had not taken it. They had no artillery worthy of the name; cavalry alone could accomplish little against determined resistance even by revenue *peons* if they were behind solid village walls.[1] Matchlock muskets and bows and arrows were better than *tulwars* in a situation like this. Horses could not get over walls.

Accompanied by some officers, Wellesley found time to see Colonel Collins who was camped just north of Aurungabad. War was not so serious in 1803 as it is now. Wellesley's party was riding for pleasure and exercise. They were received with a salute from the colonel's artillery, a part of a bodyguard larger than Close's. His tents were luxurious, although the small elderly colonel already nicknamed King Collins concealed his considerable ability with unfashionable clothes.

Collins told Wellesley what he had learned at close range about Scindia and Berar. Their combined armies amounted to an indefinite number of thousands of fighting men; no one could precisely distinguish cavalry soldiers from *pindarries* who were no better than organized thieves, nor tell where the latter ended and camp followers began. In Mahratta armies everybody was mounted and armed after a fashion. Collins reported the Mahratta cavalry to number somewhere between 50,000 and 150,000, but dismissed them all from further consideration by saying, 'You may ride over them, General, whenever you meet them.'[2] Collins was far more complimentary about the Regular Battalions in Scindia's service. Wellesley and his officers already knew a good deal of them at second and third hand. During his Dhoondiah campaign Wellesley had actually corresponded with two Englishmen in Scindia's service.[3] No Regular Battalions had yet met British troops in battle and there was a considerable difference of opinion as to their worth in such a situation. Collins had seen these units every day for more than five months. He praised their weapons, regularity, discipline and ended with, 'Their infantry and the guns attached to it will surprise you.'

The ride home was hilarious; the general and his officers were not

---

[1] Budnapoor has grown and its walls have disappeared but other villages in the area still have a complete ring of substantial masonry, brick, and mud walls too high to be scaled without ladders.

[2] *Blackiston*, I, 144–5.

[3] *Supplementary Despatches*, II, 141 and 143. The officers were Captain Brownrigg (later killed in EIC service) and Colonel Sutherland.

above making fun of Little King Collins, his enormous wig and hat with a black ostrich feather, and his warning. They were full of animal spirits and anticipated a good dinner, a short war and prize money. The wealth that came to all those who helped in the taking of Seringa-patam was still fresh in their minds. Except perhaps for Wellesley himself, they were full of confidence based on their own condition, their equipment and the combat discipline they had displayed in many recent drills.

On the morning of 30 August the situation of the three armies, two British and one Mahratta, was unusual. Wellesley was at Aurungabad, the Mahrattas at Jalna and Stevenson at Kolsah about forty miles east of Jalna; all three were in line. Since Scindia and Berar were unencumbered by infantry and artillery, they could move faster than either British force. If they could cross the Godavery, they could plunder deep into Hyderabad and threaten the capital. Because of their swarms of irregular horse the Mahrattas were almost sure of their enemies' position at all times. Presumably they would be able to avoid them. Had Wellesley been in Scindia's place, he would have moved fast and deep into the territory of the new Nizam.[1]

At sunrise on 30 August Wellesley's army began to move east and then south from Aurungabad towards the Godavery. If Scindia was contemplating a real invasion, or even a raid into Hyderabad, Wellesley was going to be as close as possible behind him. He informed Kirk-patrick, the British Resident at Hyderabad City, about the holding out of Budnapoor and urged that the headmen of similar villages be told that the Mahrattas had no artillery and could not tarry long in any locality so that such resistance could be repeated time and again without great danger to the villages. Scindia could undoubtedly reach the Nizam's capital in spite of anything that either Wellesley or Stevenson could do, but if most villages held out a fast march would not be significant. If Scindia could not take Budnapoor, he certainly could not take Hyderabad with two EIC battalions inside. Wellesley's army probably could not catch Mahratta cavalry, but it could follow so closely that the enemy could do the country little damage.

In late August and early September there was a significant series of exchanges between Wellesley and Stevenson. Stevenson wanted to be conservative, but his young friend and commander would not let him. Wellesley was all audacity. 'Dash at the first fellows that make their

---

[1] The old Nizam died on 6 August 1803 and was succeeded next day without disturbance by his eldest son, Mizra Secunder Jah: *House of Commons Account*, 191.

appearance and the campaign will be our own. A long defensive war will ruin us.'[1] There was more of the same in almost every dispatch, but the two got on well in spite of the younger man's sharpness. Wellesley praised Stevenson in his communications to others. 'He has been exposed single-handed to united armies reported to consist of 200,000 men. Not a Mahratta horseman has entered the Nizam's territory. Colonel Stevenson, on the 23rd, played the Mahratta trick upon them by cutting off some of their supplies.'[2]

Stevenson's force was considerably larger than Wellesley's, although the latter was stronger in European soldiers. Two additional King's units, however, cannot have been responsible for a sharp variation in the amount of harassment the two armies received from the enemy light horse.

Somewhat to his surprise, Wellesley found that his own auxiliary cavalry, the Mahrattas under Goklah and Appah Dessaye and Bisna-ypah's Msore units, were better than Stevenson's Moguls. He wrote to Stuart on 8 September 1803 that the enemy 'appear to be much afraid of this division, and very little so of Colonel Stevenson's. They will not allow me to come within forty miles of them; I have not yet seen one pindarry. They have been very near to Colonel Stevenson, and their pindarries very troublesome to him. I imagine that the Soubah's horse [the Nizam's Moguls], although very fine, are inactive, and difficult to be moved out of camp; whereas, I believe the few Mahrattas I have are, or have the reputation of being, very active.'[3]

When Wellesley moved south from Aurungabad to follow the Mahratta cavalry in case of a dash for Hyderabad City, he ordered Stevenson to move on Jalna. The old colonel arrived there on 1 September 1803 and on the following day took the place by storm after breaching the walls[4] with his three iron siege guns, two 18-pounders and a 12-pounder. At Ahmednuggur Scindia had lost his only strong base south of the Godavery and was now deprived of the only fortified place he held south of the line of the ghauts.

On the day Jalna fell Wellesley again came to the Godavery near Rakisbaum. He found the river in fordable condition and crossed over to the right bank the next day. This was unheard of so soon after the rainy season, but was due, of course, to the failure of the monsoon.

[1] 17 and 20 August 1803, *Dispatches*, II, 210 and 219.
[2] *Dispatches*, II, 241.
[3] *Dispatches*, II, 284.
[4] Jalna is now a sprawling city. I could find no trace of its old fortifications, although according to Burton they survived into this century almost intact.

At Rakisbaum Wellesley learnt from his carefully organized intelligence system based mostly on three independent nets of local *hircarrahs* (Indians from Mysore and Madras were as conspicuous here as Europeans) that on 30 August Scindia had moved from Jalna southeast to Partoor where he had stopped. Apparently Scindia was as well informed about British movements as Wellesley was about those of the Mahrattas, hardly surprising as both were using essentially the same sources of information. The Mahratta chief heard of the march of Wellesley's army on 30 August, twenty-three miles in seven and a half hours complete with field guns, tumbrils of ammunition and four iron 12-pounder siege guns, and decided not to make a rush towards Hyderabad. He could march faster, but not fast enough to be safe or to do any real plundering. The Mahrattas stayed where they were.

Wellesley now conceived the idea of sending Stevenson against Berar's capital at Nagpoor. By now the veteran EIC colonel was well acquainted with Wellesley's theory of security through audacity, but this particular plan appeared to him extreme. He kept remembering the reverses suffered by British armies in India when he was young. Reluctantly Wellesley abandoned the plan, at least for the time being.

The cavalry of Scindia and Berar was still reported at Partoor on the night of 4 September. On the 5th and 6th Wellesley moved two marches down the Godavery so as to start even with Scindia if the Mahrattas did make for Hyderabad City. On the 6th, however, his separate groups of *hircarrahs* brought in information about sunset that the Mahrattas had withdrawn north and west towards Ajanta.

Stevenson failed to intercept the Mahratta army during this movement; it would have been a minor miracle if he had because of Scindia's thousands of *pindarries*, some of whom surrounded Stevenson's own camp. Wellesley wrote to Stevenson on 7 September, 'It appears to me that they press upon your corps too closely; and I am much afraid that you will find them inconvenient neighbours, unless you force them to keep at a greater distance. I am very anxious, therefore, that you should move out of your camp, and give them an alert; and to tell you the truth, I am of opinion that if you do not take this step, you will be attacked in your camp.'[1] Even before he received this letter, the stout old colonel was improving. He gave better than he received in two or three running cavalry fights and on the 6th surprised an enemy camp with a night attack causing casualties and capturing baggage. He cut off another convoy of enemy provisions on the 9th.

[1] *Dispatches*, II, 281.

Wellesley remained south of the Godavery until the 18th, covering a British convoy of provisions which reached him on that date. He now had seven EIC battalions with him, for both Dallas and Hill had joined. But two more battalions were needed at Poona as the rivers were now mostly fordable. He finally sent off the 2/18 Madras complete with its new commander, Lieutenant-Colonel Griffin, and added the 1/3 Madras under Captain P. H. Vesey. The second unit was chosen not because of incapacity on the part of either the unit or its commanding officer, but because one battalion had to go, and Vesey was an inveterate grumbler and complainer in writing.[1]

Stevenson was still near Jalna. On the 21st Wellesley encamped at Sailgaon, only a mile from Stevenson at Budnapoor. This was the closest the two British armies had been to each other since 15 April at Aklooss. Wellesley and his older colleague met to compare their information about the enemy. On 5–7 September Scindia and Berar had moved back to the area just south of Ajanta and had brought some of their infantry and artillery up the ghaut. The *hircarrahs* reported that at least two brigades of Regular Battalions, the troops Little King Collins had praised, were encamped with the Mahratta cavalry at Borkardan about thirty miles north of Budnapoor. There might be as many as three *compoos*, perhaps twenty Regular Battalions which would mean 20,000 disciplined sepoys with one hundred organic field pieces.[2] But Wellesley and Stevenson could surely handle them.

If the Mahrattas really were at Borkardan, the long awaited opportunity to beat them in battle might be at hand. Wellesley discussed local topography with Stevenson and others, both European and Indian. His plan evolved quickly and was to lead to one of the most important British victories in India, though the battle as fought was not as he visualized it at Budnapoor.

Before describing the battle of Assaye, we should briefly discuss recent events in other parts of the enormous Mahratta Confederation. So far Holkar had not joined Scindia and Berar against the British; the situation of these two princes was not enviable. Scindia held parts of Guzerat along the west coast, but had no field army there. The British strategy was, of course, to attack the enemy wherever possible. As we have seen, Wellesley was in charge of all British operations in the Deccan and Guzerat.

[1] *Supplementary Despatches*, IV, 179. Vesey was, however, the only captain to command a battalion for long during this period. He had done well in the *pettah* assault at Ahmednuggur.

[2] See Appendix II for the organization of these units.

Understandably, neither Governor Duncan nor Major-General Oliver Nicholls, the Bombay C-in-C, was pleased to have most of the Bombay army under an officer several years junior to Nicholls and not on the Bombay establishment, but they were not exceptionally unco-operative. Duncan was critical of Wellesley's suggestions, but at least one of them was carried out before Wellesley's rather warm reply could take effect.[1] An attack on Baroach, Scindia's principal stronghold in Guzerat, was organized at Baroda. A force under EIC Lieutenant-Colonel Henry Woodington of about 1,000 fighting men, European and Indian, left Baroda on 21 August, more or less according to Wellesley's plan, and reached Baroach on the 24th. There was a small-scale siege with the opening of a single battery for two guns, a breach and finally an assault. Baroach was taken on the 29th for a total loss of 69 British casualties, and the surrounding area taken over by the EIC.

At Baroda Wellesley had already nominated Colonel John Murray of the King's 84th Foot to command in Guzerat. After garrisons had been provided for, there was a field army of two King's and four EIC infantry battalions with the normal complement of artillery, but it was not to be used actively in this war.

The situation further north was more complicated; Scindia's dominions extended from Ahmednuggur to Agra and Delhi. The northern half of this territory had been assigned to Benoît de Boigne, a Savoyard adventurer and the most successful of all the European professional soldiers with the Mahrattas. Under his wise and generally unselfish administration the area had become semi-independent. De Boigne had enough of India, however, and in 1796 returned to Europe with a large fortune. A Frenchman by the name of Perron took his place and showed even more independence.[2] The one major issue on which the considerable body of French in Mahratta country saw eye to eye with the Mahrattas themselves was in their opposition to the British. Perron would surely co-operate with Scindia against the EIC. He faced an army that was commanded by General Gerald Lake, the British C-in-C in India. Lake had been awaiting instructions from

[1] Wellesley's letters to Duncan and Murray of 29 August 1803 are interesting. The Governor-General had placed his brother in a nearly impossible military position. The letter to Murray contains the passage, 'I am not afraid of responsibility, God knows! I am ready to incur any personal risk for the public service, but I should be mad if I were to order this plan to be carried into execution': *Dispatches*, II, 248.

[2] 'Scindia retains no effective control over M. Perron or his troops': *House of Commons Account*, 157.

Arthur Wellesley to start hostilities, but he began them independently on 6 August upon receiving orders to do so from the Governor-General.[1] The operations which followed will be summarized later.

We should also remember that the situation in the Peshwa's own dominions south of Poona was bad. The Mahratta chiefs in the area were not really under his control. As Arthur Wellesley said, they were 'either declared or concealed enemies of Bajee Rao'.[2] But they did not revolt or obstruct Wellesley's communications with Mysore. This state of affairs might change; the southern *jaghirdars* would remain friendly only so long as the British image of invincibility remained bright. Wellesley knew that all was well only as long as he made no mistakes. The Mahrattas as a whole, regardless of their feelings for or against the Peshwa, wanted to be on the winning side. Some of them must also have realized that if the British won the forthcoming war, Mahratta supremacy in India would be at an end, along with their predatory way of life. But Mahrattas probably hated their fellow-countrymen more than they did the English.

There was another area where a small British army could strike effectively. The dominions of the Rajah of Berar extended to the Bay of Bengal where he controlled about 200 miles of the coastline in Cuttack, an area which separated EIC possessions around Calcutta from the Circars, a part of the Madras Presidency. The Governor-General was taking even more personal interest than usual in an operation from Ganjam towards Juggernaut and Cuttack which began on 8 September. This east coast operation was nominally under Wellesley's command – the forces there are shown in his return for 1 January 1804[3] – but he appears to have exerted no control. The area was closer to the Governor-General. When the original commander of this expedition, Lieutenant-Colonel Alexander Campbell of the 74th Foot, fell sick, the Marquess sent his military secretary, Lieutenant-Colonel G. W. R. Harcourt of the 12th Foot, to take command. There will be more about these operations in a later chapter.

[1] The Governor-General's dispatch is dated 27 July 1803 and was based as much on the news of renewed hostilities with France, which had just arrived at Calcutta, as on the Mahratta situation.

[2] *Dispatches*, II, 318–19.

[3] *Supplementary Despatches*, IV, 308–9.

X

Assaye

The Budnapoor conference between Wellesley and Stevenson on the afternoon of 21 September 1803 produced a simple offensive plan. Stevenson's army was to move north-west and then north-east towards Borkardan at dawn on the 22nd. Wellesley and his units were to move east almost to Jalna and then turn north towards Naulniah, two short marches away. If all went well, they would attack Scindia's forces at Borkardan about mid-morning of the 24th. Naulniah was about three hours away from Borkardan; Stevenson was planning to spend the night of the 23rd a similar distance away at Hussainabad.

We should note that the two small armies were co-operating closely under Wellesley's direction, but they had never been united at any time. They were advancing separately to the east and west of a low mass of hills, partly to prevent Scindia and Berar from slipping past them on one road while they used the other, and partly because the movement of the two armies along a single route would have complicated and slowed down their movements intolerably.[1]

Wellesley's army marched eighteen miles to the village of Paugy in just over six hours, arriving about noon on the 22nd. Presumably

[1] More able writers than I have discussed Wellesley's 'dividing his army' before Assaye, but most of them have not had the advantage of first-hand inspection of the area, or even the superb one-inch Ordnance Survey maps produced in British India early in this century. The hills are inconsequential compared to the normal Indian ghauts and are everywhere negotiable, but they do form a reconnaissance barrier of sorts. The Mahratta army could have moved south by one route while a united British army moved north by the other. The joining of Wellesley's and Stevenson's forces would have meant a column several miles long. Each of the routes available consisted of a single road; the defiles mentioned by Wellesley (*Dispatches*, II, 338) were where these narrow roads went through villages. All wheeled vehicles would have had to go through some of them in single file.

Stevenson made an equivalent march and camped at the village of Khamgaon on a branch of the Purna river that same evening.[1] There was more news of the enemy for both British commanders towards evening. Scindia and Berar were still at Borkardan with all their cavalry and three *compoos* of Scindia's Regular Battalions. These were the units Collins had praised; one battalion had tried to defend the *pettah* at Ahmednuggur but had not accomplished much.

By this time Wellesley knew the approximate strength and composition of the enemy units. The largest *compoo* was Pohlmann's,[2] formerly under Colonel Sutherland, which consisted of eight battalions, each with a strength of about 800, including the artillerymen who handled four field guns and a howitzer. Pohlmann's cavalry probably numbered about 500 with a similar number of armed pioneers, so that altogether he had about 7,500 fighting men plus some attached scouts.

The semi-independent *compoo* of the Begum Somroo, a vassal of Scindia's, consisted of five battalions and twenty-five field pieces with similar support;[3] her units were considered to be first-rate. Filoze's *compoo* was the smallest of the three and apparently not up to the others in equipment and leadership. It consisted of four battalions and about fifteen field pieces with the usual cavalry, pioneers and other auxiliaries. Like Pohlmann's, Filoze's *compoo* belonged directly to Scindia.[4] The entire regular force numbered about 15,000 disciplined soldiers under

[1] I have been unable to discover the name of Stevenson's camp site for the 22nd, but this village is in the right position as regards distance, lies on the most probable route and is well supplied with water. As mentioned later, Stevenson was planning and did start to spend the night of the 23rd at Hussdinabad. This village and Naulniah are about equidistant from the town of Borkardan.

[2] Pohlmann was a former sergeant in a British Hanoverian regiment. He had considerable military ability and a flair for the dramatic; he travelled by elephant with an elaborately uniformed and armed personal bodyguard. He served later as an officer in the EIC army. The most important sources for details of the Regular Battalions and the men who organiezd and commanded them are *Regular Corps* and *Military Adventurers*.

[3] The Begum was the widow of Walter Rheinhart, known as Sombre, a nickname changed to Somroo by Indians. One of the early professional soldiers in Scindia's employ, he had become a feudal subordinate. His widow inherited his political position and had a succession of army commanders, including the extremely talented, if occasionally drunken Irishman, George Thomas. The Begum was extremely attractive physically even in middle life and also intelligent. Her *compoo* was commanded at Assaye by Colonel Saleur.

[4] Baptiste Filoze inherited the *compoo* from his father and brother, and was of mixed blood. His father was Neapolitan and his mother Indian. A fair number of officers of these Regular Battalions, including some with English names, were only half-European. Filoze was not present at Assaye but his four battalions were, under the Dutch Major John James Dupont.

European officers. They had some eighty field pieces plus a few battering guns.

The Governor-General made two efforts to get all subjects of the British Crown out of the Mahratta armies. He offered pensions or similar employment with no reduction in total income to those who gave up their positions voluntarily, and threatened those who remained with treason.[1] But there were still Englishmen in Scindia's army at the battle of Assaye.

Apart from the Regular Battalions, Scindia and Berar had other infantry, probably at least 10,000 to 20,000 men, but they were not nearly so formidable. The number of Mahratta cavalry is even harder to determine; there appear to have been between 30,000 and 60,000 armed horsemen, not counting camp followers. Finally, there was a considerable train of Mahratta artillery in addition to that in Scindia's *compoos*.

Wellesley's army marched at sunrise on the 23rd, every man alert. All realized how close they were to the enemy field army. Even the light cavalry from Mysore under Bisnapah and irregular Mahratta horse under Goklah and Appa Dessaye moved more purposefully. Several of these units were well out in front gathering information and shielding the British army from hostile observation. Wellesley was at the head of his European and EIC cavalry. The infantry column came next, headed by the pickets of the day. Wellesley's small siege train followed, with the extra ammunition in tumbrils, and then the baggage. Last of all there were the pickets of the previous day, a squadron of British cavalry and a Mysore unit of about 800.

Wellesley arrived at the village of Naulniah shortly before 11 a.m. on the 23rd after a march of fourteen miles. It was as far as he planned to go for the day; Borkardan lay between nine and ten miles further on. The camp was already being marked out and Blackiston, the young engineer, had begun his surveying. Other tasks were being done according to established procedures when a patrol of the 19th Dragoons brought in some *brinjarries*.

---

[1] *Regular Corps, passim* and 49. Smith, the author, himself drew 1,200 rupees per month, and lists thirty-six other pensioners getting a total of 15,525 rupees. I gather from Arthur's own words that he personally did not consider a Briton who continued to carry out his contract of employment a traitor, even though it meant fighting against his country: *Supplementary Despatches*, IV, 189. The exact status of these officers is not now easy to determine. The descendants of one of them, Colonel William Gardner who worked for Holkar long after the Governor-General's efforts to get Englishmen to leave and later organized Gardner's horse for the EIC, sat in the House of Lords.

Wellesley questioned these men in Hindostani and received disturbing answers. They intended to sell food in the camps of Scindia and Berar, which were not actually at Borkardan but spread over a considerable area to the east, thereof. This sprawling camp extended over a stretch of three *coos* – a bit more than six miles – along the northern bank of the Kaitna. This river flowed roughly from west to east and was less than five miles north of Naulniah.

Wellesley's army had unintentionally approached too close to the Mahrattas; Scindia's and Berar's *pindarries* were sure to discover his camp within the next eighteen hours. Wellesley could wait for Stevenson and attack on the morning of the 24th according to plan, but the odds were against their having anyone to fight by that time.

Wellesley made no decision until he had had a look at the enemy's position. He ordered his infantry to halt according to plan at Naulniah, along with his baggage, siege train and half his cavalry. He himself pressed on to the north, supported by the 19th Dragoons and the 4th Native Cavalry. The area was reasonably flat and nearly treeless, but did rise to a low crest about three miles to the north. If the enemy did not yet know that the British army was in the area, there was no reason to bring it to their attention. Wellesley quickly explained to Colonel Maxwell what was required: the British cavalry regiments were to follow Wellesley, Barclay and Campbell who were well mounted, but they were to stay about half a mile to their rear and avoid skylines.

The three then rode off fast to the west and then north to within a half mile of the Kaitna, a considerable stream during part of each year. Wellesley dismounted beside a tree at the top of a low hill. He had a quick look and then uncased his telescope, pulled it out to its maximum length, and focused on what lay before him. He scanned carefully the open rolling country north of the river. The Mahratta armies which were spread out over more than seven miles, from Borkardan to Assaye, must have consisted of 200,000 souls.[1]

One thing was clear after Wellesley's brief survey; there was no

---

[1] I spent two days in the locality both on foot and in a jeep trying to find a point from which Wellesley could have seen any considerable portion of the Mahratta camp area. There are several low hills from which this might have been possible, but the whole area contains too many trees now. Neither Assaye nor Borkardan can be seen from south of the river here today. It is possible that Wellesley saw neither place, only enough of the camp area between to visualize the entire enemy position. Remember, he was a gifted professional soldier and had been working for weeks with *hircarrahs* and local maps. He had a talent for imagining what lay on the other side of any hill.

need to worry about alerting the Mahrattas to the presence of a British army. They already knew and were breaking camp, either to fight or to run. Wellesley, Barclay and Campbell rode east parallel to the Kaitna in plainsight. Although enemy cavalry units were crossing the river at Kodully, they did not yet present a serious threat to the safety of the British officers who had better mounts and cavalry support.

Scindia's European-officered infantry and artillery were on the left of the combined Mahratta armies, encamped in a regular manner north of the river for two miles, from just west of Kodully to the east of another village which Wellesley knew as Taunklee.[1] The infantry-artillery teams appeared to be disciplined and in good order. As Wellesley watched from his second observation point, about two miles east of his first, the Regular Battalions were forming into line on some higher ground north of the river, with the guns of each unit in front. The rest of the Mahratta army was far less well organized. A great mass of cavalry lay to the west along the Kaitna towards Borkardan. There appeared to be a similarly unco-ordinated mass of cavalry and infantry well north of the river near the unusually large village of Assaye.

Wellesley realized that he had caught the enemy in camp. If he attacked immediately, Scindia and Berar could not get away, except by sacrificing guns and baggage. The chance to defeat this host depended, however, on striking within the next three hours. It would have been useful to have Stevenson's army close at hand; but was it absolutely necessary? The Hyderabad contingent of EIC units and the Nizam's army might or might not be at Hussainabad. Conceivably, they could arrive at the Kaitna within three hours of the first artillery fire, but a provident commander could not count on that.

Wellesley saw that numerical odds meant nothing. Mahratta cavalry and pindarries were so disorganized that one had only to contend with the men in the front of their formations; the rest could not influence a battle one way or another. But the Regular Battalions

[1] There are many problems in the contemporary spelling of Indian place-names, but the Assaye campaign area gives rise to the worst. Contemporary maps almost never agree with the one-inch Ordnance Survey maps. Modern spelling, where available in English, often disagrees with both. The names of villages sometimes vary so much that there is serious doubt as to their identity. Kodully is surely the Kodoli of 1912 and today; Taunklee is similarly almost certainly modern Takli. But Wellesley's Naulniah has become Naini Khurd and Naini Buzury on opposite sides of the Purna river. I have followed his spellings save where they would cause obvious confusion. For instance, he and his contemporaries used to spell the name of the battle 'Assye'.

29 (*Left*) The walls of
Waroor. 30 (*Below*)
Assaye from the south.
This was the area of the
greatest British losses

31 A defile on Wellesley's way to Assaye, where the main road used to go through the village of Longaon

32 The northern wall of Assaye

33 The village of Assaye looking east, seen from the roof of its tallest building

34 Cannon, said to have been taken at Assaye, now in front of the Collector's House at Aurungabad

35 The view north from the remains of the fortification at Parterly which Wellesley ascended to observe the Mahratta forces around Argaum

36 The battlefield of Argaum. Note the flatness of the land and the Gawilghur hills in the background

might be a different matter. Their composition and strengths were similar to Wellesley's fine EIC units; they were as strong in men and stronger in artillery.[1] The rest of the Mahratta forces must contain some useful units, especially in a defensive position. No one knew better than the British commander the consequences of a lost battle hundreds of miles within what would quickly become enemy territory.

Wellesley considered the alternatives for no more than a couple of minutes. The opportunity was just too good to be missed. He would attack. Any other decision appears inconceivable, especially when one considers what he had recently written to Stevenson.

Wellesley, Barclay and Campbell rode back fast to join the British cavalry pursued half-heartedly by some Mahrattas. By the time they reined in, Wellesley had finally decided on his initial moves. He ordered Maxwell to advance with his two regiments of cavalry to a low crest south of the Kaitna, deploy into line, and halt facing the stream. The cavalry commander was also told to bring up his other two units from Naulniah and use them to extend his flanks. Wellesley employed Maxwell's entire cavalry initially to form a screen from west of Kodully to east of Taunklee.

Wellesley then galloped back to Naulniah and divided his infantry. One of the five EIC battalions and the pickets of the day before would stay with the baggage, heavy artillery and reserve ammunition. A camp was already half formed. The EIC unit chosen was the 1/2 Madras whose commander, Lieutenant-Colonel J. M. Chalmers, was Wellesley's senior battalion commander. The Naulniah force, including half the pioneers with the army, set about improving and supplementing the defences of the village. Normally a British army camped in the open, but in an emergency such as this security was more important than comfort. Chalmers probably moved everything into the walled village, put up additional earthworks, and even emplaced the four iron 12-pounders.[2]

Wellesley sent off the infantry towards Barahjala, a small village south of Taunklee, and conferred briefly with his local guides, one or more of whom may have accompanied the three British officers during

---

[1] *Elphinstone*, 67, who probably helped Barclay with the day-to-day figures, computes '500 sepoys per battalion' mainly because of desertion and sickness.

[2] I inspected 'Naulniah' in April 1968. As I have said, there are now two villages with about the same name, one north and the other south of the Purna. The former appears to have been the more defensible and was probably the one chosen. The latter is now larger, but more open; it may not have existed in 1803. It is unlikely that Chalmers used both.

a part of their swift reconnaissance. Wellesley had resolved on attacking, but wanted to avoid a frontal assault across a river against infantry and artillery already drawn up in line. He had all the topographical details firmly in mind by this time, but needed information about the places where the Kaitna was fordable. The guides who were supposed to know said that the river was fordable only between Kodully and Taunklee. They all agreed that there was no ford suitable for infantry and artillery to the east of Taunklee. This information just did not make sense. Wellesley had been in India long enough not to believe everything he heard from sources of this type, especially if the information was not logical. The Godavery was a much larger stream than the Kaitna, but was fordable in many places. So far Wellesley had not ridden down to the Kaitna, but he had caught glimpses of it. He had also seen two villages (Peepulgaon and Waroor) opposite each other, one north and the other south of the river. With two villages situated as these were, there would surely be proper approaches to the stream practical for artillery from both sides. From his own observations Wellesley was almost sure that the Kaitna was not too deep and should be fordable where the bottom was reasonably flat.

Wellesley had been riding Diomed during the morning and during his fast reconnaissance south of the river. He now shifted to a fine bay horse and gave orders to his grooms to rub the magnificent Arab down with straw and bring him forward along with another horse for possible use later in the day.[1] Wellesley had a last look at the preparations that Chalmers was making to defend Naulniah if it should become necessary and galloped north to the head of his infantry-artillery column which was led, of course, by the pickets of the day; presumably Wallace's Brigade – composed of the King's 74th, the 2/12 Madras, and the 1/4 Madras – came next, followed by Harness's Brigade in reverse order – the 1/8 Madras, the 1/10 Madras, and King's 78th. This order would allow forming into line from column with a European unit on each flank. All six infantry battalions and the pickets had the normal two field guns each, making a total of fourteen with the infantry.[2]

---

[1] This is part conjecture, but also based on what was customary in India at that time and on Wellesley's letter quoted in *Malcolm*, I, 233.

[2] Variations in the number of British artillery pieces at Assaye given by different authorities are frequent. I can see no valid reason, however, for doubting that each unit had its proper allocation. The organization of Wellesley's army was near perfect. The 74th had two brass 12-pounder field guns, the 78th which came from Bengal via Bombay had two brass 6-pounders. The EIC battalions also had two brass 6-pounders each. All were bullock-

On his first ride north with cavalry only Wellesley had roughly followed the Naulniah–Kodully road. With the infantry, however, he turned off at Barahjala and headed for the twin villages of Waroor and Peepulgaon. Maxwell and his four regiments of British cavalry still held a line on the south side of the Kaitna from behind Kodully to the rear of Taunklee. They were just standing; their gallopers would fire occasionally, but the Mahratta cavalry showed no inclination to attack. Maxwell's mounted regiments tried to shield Wellesley's infantry movement from hostile observation.

The die was cast. Wellesley was attacking a much more numerous enemy, but from an unexpected direction. He had to march across the front of the opposing army in battle array, but the Kaitna was an even greater obstacle to the Mahrattas than to the British. Besides, Scindia was no Frederick of Prussia.

The success or failure of the battle plan depended, however, on crossing the river with infantry and artillery where the guides said it could not be crossed – between the two villages. Wellesley was at the head of the pickets and urged his horse into a canter for the last two hundred yards. The approaches to the river both from the north and the south were moderately easy and a little work by the pioneers would get all the guns across. Wellesley must still have been apprehensive about the depth of water; if the stream really was not fordable here, his army would be in trouble. Logic, common sense and quick reconnaissance are not infallible.

Wellesley was the first man into the river; the water was less than three feet deep. Logic had won the opening round. As more British approached the ford area, however, they began to receive fire from heavy Mahratta pieces to the north in the direction of Assaye. An 18-pound solid shot took off the head of Wellesley's orderly dragoon; his body remained wedged in his saddle for several seconds in spite of his horse's frantic efforts to get free of the burden.[1]

The ground north of the Kaitna in this area was open and fairly flat for several hundred yards, but gently rising to a skyline. The village of Assaye could not be seen. The enemy guns continued in action as the British column came down to the ford and began to cross,

---

[1] Several eyewitness accounts survive, but they do not agree as to the dragoon's position when he was hit. He was probably still south of the river.

---

drawn. The pickets of the day, like each of the four British cavalry regiments, had two 6-pounder gallopers. See Appendixes I and II for details of weapons and organization.

but their fire was inaccurate and did little harm. They soon retired beyond the crest and presumably all the way back to Assaye.[1]

The British army would now surely be able to get across the Kaitna and deploy on the north side preparatory to an attack on the right flank of Scindia's Regular Battalions. Wellesley had manœuvred these units out of their strong position by crossing the river well to the east. He was in the process of winning the second round.

As the British infantry column began to cross, Wellesley sent a staff officer to Maxwell with orders to bring his cavalry to the right, cross the river at Waroor, and form a new line north of that place.[2] He ordered Bisnapah, Goklah and Appa Dessaye to hold back the mass of Mahratta horse now south of the river and prevent them from interfering with the British rear. It would be nice if his allies could hold the enemy in this locality, but it was not imperative. The loss of communications with Naulniah now would do no serious harm.

Wellesley's initial impression after crossing the Kaitna was that there was insufficient space to the north of the river for six and a half battalions in line, especially with the Mahratta guns on his right flank. He went forward with EIC Lieutenant-Colonel William Orrock of the 1/8, who commanded the pickets of the day, and posted his force far enough north and west of the river crossing point to leave room for two lines of infantry with intervals for guns between the battalions. He also personally positioned the King's 74th, the next battalion, level with the pickets north and south, but about 150 yards to the east. The next two EIC battalions (2/12 and 1/4) were to follow the 74th and align themselves on them. Wellesley left Barclay at the 'ford'[3] to bring north the 1/8 Madras and subsequent units and form them on the pickets. Barclay was also to direct Maxwell to form the cavalry to the east of the column led by the 74th. The somewhat complicated shifting to battalions from what had been essentially a single-line arrangement

[1] I realize that authorities have said that Mahratta guns 'from Assaye' fired on British troops crossing the Kaitna, but this was not possible; the two places are not in sight of each other. I believe their first position was at or near the low crest between the two rivers, about 1,500 yards from the ford.

[2] The infantry crossing took an appreciable time. A column of six and a half battalions moving on a front of half companies at quarter distance with fourteen guns would have been more than 1,000 yards long, probably about 1,400 yards in an area like this.

[3] The stream was probably fordable at almost any point. The Kaitna here has a sandy bottom, which in March 1968 showed little variation in depth. I crossed often and easily on foot. During and soon after a normal monsoon, the river would everywhere be unfordable, but once a crossing is reasonably easy in one place, it would not be dangerous because of depth of water in others.

with European battalions on either flank was necessary in order to form an equally effective two-deep formation with the exposed northern flanks of both infantry lines protected by European units.[1]

Wellesley now spurred forward to the top of a low rise near the earlier position of the Mahratta guns. He had another look at the enemy while his small force was coming up and forming in accordance with his new orders. He sent off Blackiston, his topographical engineer, to the north-west to get an idea of what lay in that direction.[2] Wellesley then appears to have ridden almost precisely towards Assaye, a little west of due north. When he topped the rise in this direction, he was half way from the Kaitna to the Juah, the river which he knew flowed past Assaye. He found that the two streams were farther apart than he thought. He also saw the village of Assaye clearly for the first time; it was full of Mahrattas and circled by artillery pieces, but these were on the ground, not mounted on the walls.[3] The place was not a strong fortress, but it had a lot of firepower; it was surely a position to avoid until the battle had been won in the field.

Before Wellesley turned away, he saw how Mahratta Regular Battalions which were changing front began to link up with Assaye. As he galloped back to his army he was followed by a large disorderly group of enemy cavalry, but his bay horse easily left them behind. He was soon back with his own forces with a clear picture of the entire area that was presently to become a battlefield. His first stop was with his cavalry commander. Succinctly he told Maxwell that he and his four regiments were to move forward to the Juah and then form line extending north and south, but remaining just out of effective artillery range of Assaye.[4]

As Wellesley completed his instructions to Maxwell, Blackiston rode

---

[1] The pickets had only two half companies of Scots, but their EIC half companies would be on the inside.

[2] This young engineer has left an account of Pohlmann's infantry and artillery 'changing their front and taking up a new position with their right on the Kaitna and their left on the village of Assaye'. They performed this 'in the most steady manner, though not exactly according to Dundas': *Blackiston*, I, 161.

[3] Assaye is still almost encircled by the usual strong mud, brick and masonry walls of the larger Mahratta villages of that day, but there was no easy way to install artillery on these walls. The guns were undoubtedly placed outside the village and may have been partially protected by fascines and earthworks. There were probably units of irregular infantry armed with matchlock muskets in the village itself.

[4] The cavalry flank must have been at least 800 yards from the ring of defences around Assaye to be reasonably safe by range alone, but it could have been closer. There is some dead ground easily identified today where a trifling tributary runs north into the Juah in which it could have formed.

in from his reconnaissance further west and confirmed what his commander had already surmised. The enemy was indeed forming a new and perhaps formidable line and would extend from river to river with a powerful anchor at Assaye. But the flank march by the British army had taken away the enemy's initial advantage of being formed behind a river with reasonably steep banks.

Wellesley's own reconnaissance had suggested a way of attacking the new enemy line without running afoul of the Assaye hedgehog. There was after all enough space for the entire infantry to attack in a single line and to go forward without assaulting the village itself, or even coming within really effective range of its surrounding guns. He had this in mind when he instructed Maxwell. It was unlikely that the Mahrattas would make a move at the exposed flank of a British infantry line with British cavalry deployed just to the rear and ready to charge.

The young major-general quickly rode further south to his infantry and artillery. Some of the guns, including apparently those of the pickets and the 74th, had moved north-west and opened on the artillery of the Regular Battalions deployed in line in front of their infantry. Wellesley gave orders personally to each of his battalion commanders about their part in the next movement.

The infantry was to attack the enemy in a single line, Wellesley told Orrock to march obliquely to his right so as to leave enough space for two EIC battalions between his pickets and his own battalion, and then straighten up and move west. Orrock was to keep out of effective artillery range of Assaye on his extreme right. There was no need for him to worry about his flank; the 74th would move into line there. He was to move out as soon as he could recover his guns.

As soon as Orrock said he understood his orders, Wellesley was off again to Major Swinton and the King's 74th. This fine battalion was to follow the pickets until they straightened up into line. The 74th was then to move forward at the double on the right of the pickets, to form the right of the British infantry line. The 74th was to be well north of the Kaitna, but to attack Scindia's Regular Battalions. Again Wellesley emphasized staying clear of Assaye. He then rode to Lieutenant-Colonel Macleod of the 2/12 and Major Hill of the 1/4 and told them to oblique to the north in column and then to form into line on the right of the 1/8. He next visited the temporary commander of the 1/8 and Major Dallas of the 1/10 and gave them similar orders. They were to form from column into line and move forward on the flank of the King's 78th which would be next to the Kaitna. Wellesley at this time expected that Orrock and the pickets would move out first, followed by the 74th, because they had further to go, but the line of battalions was to position itself on the 78th which would be the first battalion in from the river. Wellesley stayed temporarily with the 78th which was likely to be engaged first.

While Wellesley explained his plan of attack to the seven unit commanders, the Mahratta Regular Battalion artillery and the guns of the British infantry were firing at each other. The duel was at medium range, but the less numerous British pieces, which appear to have moved forward into their positions after the enemy guns had opened fire, suffered considerably. Losses of horses and bullocks, drivers, gun lascars and European artillerymen prevented Orrock and Swinton from recovering their guns as soon as Wellesley had expected.

Time was essential now. Occasionally, when a Mahratta shot found its target and passed through a formation, the British infantry had severe casualties. Wellesley gave the order to go on without the guns.[1] Perhaps Wellesley had never left the 78th. If he had, however, he rejoined them when he saw Orrock begin to advance. He ordered the kilted Highlanders forward. Their left flank is usually said to have rested on the Kaitna.[2] Every British infantry soldier, from major-general to junior *puckalee*,[3] could soon see the line of Mahratta Regular Battalions with their guns in front deployed precisely from the Kaitna almost to Assaye. The field pieces seemed almost hub to hub with an unwavering line of muskets and bayonets behind them. The ordeal that lay ahead was what the British troops had prepared for through countless hot tiring hours of drill, manœuvres, and target and bayonet practice. Wellesley had come half way round the world and spent sixteen and a half years in the army getting ready to prove himself in the severest of all tests, an infantry battle.

The British did not know that the forces deployed against them were commanded by the senior European professional officer present, Colonel Pohlmann. Berar had already left with his women; Scindia was far out of range and about to follow his example, but Pohlmann had thirteen Regular Battalions in line behind sixty-odd field pieces plus

[1] Wellesley is said to have sent this order to Orrock. I believe it possible, however, that he rode north and gave it to him in person.

[2] It is difficult to visualize this being literally true because of a series of bluffs and gullies. The line probably moved over smoother ground about 200 yards north of the river.

[3] Indian water-carriers, but definitely on the strength. Gunga Din was a *puckalee*.

perhaps some heavier metal.[1] Pohlmann's battalions were formed not more than 700 yards from where the British units went into line and began to advance. Once the enemy gunners saw the thin red lines advancing – both King's and Company's infantrymen wore red jackets – their fire became heavy. Every enemy gun was being worked at nearly maximum rate; not a single British piece was answering.

This first British infantry attack was delivered slightly en echelon, left in front. The King's 78th had furthest to go but was the first to go from column into line and move out towards the enemy. Wellesley rode a few feet from their right flank. The Highlanders would strike the Mahratta lines where they reached the Kaitna. If they broke through Pohlmann's anchor here, the enemy would be forced to swing back across a wide plain.

Every soldier of the 78th was a giant by Mahratta standards. Their kilts were swinging in unison; their weapons and buckles were polished and their belts freshly whitened. Nobody who saw this magnificent regiment deliver its first assault at Assaye ever forgot it. At sixty yards from the enemy guns which continued to fire, they halted as if on parade, presented their muskets, fired, recovered and reloaded. Then they went on again with their bayonets gleaming.

Some Mahratta gunners who survived the volley stayed with their pieces and continued to work them until bayoneted. Others threw themselves on the ground between the wheels feigning death. The Scots burst through the line of artillery pieces with bloody weapons, re-formed and advanced in line on the infantry behind. Again the 'Halt! Make ready! Present! Fire!' The volley crashed out with practically every musket roaring.[2]

The Mahratta regular infantrymen were good soldiers, the best sepoys in India after those in EIC units. But they had seen their guns taken with astonishing ease by white giants whose kilts and feathered bonnets made them seem more gods than men. After the second volley the two anchor battalions of Pohlmann's line broke leaving only a few die-hards to perish on Scottish bayonets.

The superb performance of the 78th made it easier for the 1/10 to do a similar job to the north where it also took the line of artillery in fine style, re-formed, and smashed the infantry behind. Similar suc-

[1] Scindia had kept four of Begum Somroo's battalions for his personal security. The *compoos* always had 'siege guns' with them which were often used in the field by Indian armies, but Pohlmann may not have employed them.

[2] In the era of flintlocks, only well disciplined units were able to fire a full second volley. Often fifty per cent of weapons loaded in action by inexperienced soldiers misfired.

cesses were achieved in succession by the 1/8, 1/4, and 2/12, all properly spaced. The attacks were cumulative in effect. About 900 yards of the southern portion of Pohlmann's line was shattered and about forty pieces of field artillery taken.

Sepoys from the four EIC battalions were overcome with their victory and temporarily went out of control in pursuit. They slaughtered many who tried to get away. Fortunately for the British army, the 78th did not join them, but re-formed in column of full companies at quarter distance and was ready to move as required.[1] There were still at least 20,000 Mahratta cavalry north of the Kaitna.[1] The enemy horsemen came forward menacingly and might have charged the disordered sepoys had it not been for the formed and ready King's regiment. The two Bombay 6-pounders assigned to the 78th came up and opened on the Mahrattas. The EIC officers had time to rally their battalions.

Wellesley had his bay horse shot dead under him during the successful attack, apparently just in front of Pohlmann's guns, but he sprang off nimbly as the beast fell and was not pinned underneath as sometimes happened when an animal was killed by an artillery discharge at close range. After a brief and unremarked delay his groom brought Diomed back for his second tour of duty that day. Arthur must have felt better with the Arab charger between his legs. In those days a commander needed a good horse not only for mobility, but also to give him the advantage of height, especially in an infantry battle on nearly flat terrain.

As Wellesley remounted, he heard disturbing sounds from the direction of Assaye. He rode north fast across an area covered with killed and wounded from his own and Pohlmann's battalions.[2] Up to where the 2/12 had delivered its assault, everything was well. Beyond, however, he found a literally bloody mess.

Orrock had made one of those tragic and inexplicable battlefield mistakes that occur all too frequently in military history. The commander of the pickets had been told to incline to his right far enough to allow space for the 1/4 and the 2/12 Madras and then to straighten up and

---

[1] The rest were to the south of the Kaitna where they contended ineffectually with Wellesley's Mysore and Mahratta cavalry.

[2] We should note perhaps at this point that these Regular Battalions were not composed to any considerable extent of Hindoo Mahrattas, who were mostly in the cavalry where chances for plunder were greater. The infantrymen in the Regular Battalions were 'mostly drawn from Northern India and the artillery manned and commanded by Portuguese and Indian Christians': *Cambridge History*, V, 393–4.

attack on the flank of the 2/12. The King's 74th would then come forward on his right to complete the British line, all out of effective artillery range of the fortified village of Assaye.

Orrock misunderstood his orders, or missed his way, or both. He marched off in the proper direction, probably in a column of half companies at quarter distance, but kept going and did not incline back into his assigned position and form into line. He went straight ahead towards Assaye with three and a half companies against perhaps forty guns and 10,000 matchlocks. The King's 74th followed the pickets, at first waiting for them to wheel to the left into line. Had they done so, the 74th would, of course, have done likewise to complete the infantry assault by a line of seven units with a King's regiment on each flank. When Orrock continued north, Swinton and the 74th could either follow in support, or leave the pickets to their fate. However, the first half company in Orrock's column was from the 74th. Swinton could not watch his Scots and their fellows destroyed. He followed Orrock, probably in line.[1] Both units received the direct fire of all Mahratta guns around Assaye, and also the slant fire of Pohlmann's battalion guns not engaged with the five British battalions attacking the southern portion of their line.

The pickets were practically annihilated.[2] The 74th, in spite of an iron and lead hail of extreme intensity, reached a cactus hedge only about one hundred yards from Assaye, but could get no further. The survivors recoiled to their rear about 150 yards and rallied round their colours. They were soon attacked by Mahratta cavalry and probably by the two northernmost of Pohlmann's Regular Battalions.[3] The survivors of the gallant regiment formed a rough square and fought off their attackers. Rather than yield, they piled about them a low irregular

---

[1] I have no conclusive evidence that the pickets were in column of half companies and the 74th in line, but believe it likely. Orrock was an EIC officer; he had a composite command. Further, Wellesley said, 'for a man to *lead* a body into a hotter fire': *Dispatches*, II, 341. Orrock would have been unlikely to lead a line. But the 74th was a King's regiment and Swinton a King's officer. Lines were the normal formation for all attacks in the King's army at that time.

[2] The 1/2 Madras was at Naulniah guarding the fortified camp there, except for a half company with the pickets, a total of perhaps fifty men. Of these, forty-six were killed and wounded. This unit would have been third in Orrock's column, behind the two King's half companies but ahead of the other EIC units. The conclusion is inescapable: the pickets suffered about 90 per cent casualties, although Orrock led and survived.

[3] Wellesley wrote: 'My [wounded] soldiers say that they heard one English officer [in Scindia's service] say . . .': *Supplementary Despatches*, IV, 189. If an English officer in Scindia's infantry – there were no foreign officers in his cavalry – was close enough for wounded Scots to hear what he said, his unit probably attacked the remnant of the 74th.

rampart made of the bodies of their foes. Better troops than Mahrattas have failed to break a British square.

Patrick Maxwell came belatedly but on his own initiative to the rescue of the 74th.[1] He gave orders for his three northern regiments to charge and led forward the King's 19th Dragoons himself, flanked on his right by the 4th Native Cavalry and on his left by the 5th. All these troopers had seen the fate of the pickets and the magnificent fight of the 74th. Their blood was up; even their horses seemed willing to crash through anything in their path. The double line of disciplined horsemen came on with sabres flashing in the sun. Maxwell's lines rode right over the attackers of the 74th, the Mahratta cavalry they found in the open, the battalion guns beyond, and perhaps a formed infantry unit as well. They cleared the area around the 74th and smashed the northernmost portion of Pohlmann's line. The dragoons were particularly effective; their Sheffield steel blades sometimes cut through the *tulwars* before killing or maiming the man who held them.[2] The Mahratta horsemen faced bigger and better men on stronger horses who also had the priceless advantages of discipline and regular sword exercise. Pohlmann's battalion, or possibly two of them, were probably taken at a disadvantage because they had come forward with their own *compoo* cavalry to attack the 74th.

This British cavalry charge was magnificent; it cleared the Mahrattas before Assaye as completely as Wellesley's infantry had done north of the Kaitna. Then Maxwell's troopers went at least partially out of control and disappeared across the Juah, the river that ran just north of Assaye. Maxwell and his men were pursuing when they should have stayed on the battlefield.

Wellesley appears to have arrived at the northern combat area just in time to see his cavalry sweep everything in front of them and then go off themselves. The British forces were victorious on both flanks. Wallace was moving the survivors of the 74th to the south out of effective range of the guns around Assaye, although these were now mostly silent.

[1] *Welsh*, I, 178, says that the idea came from 'Captain A. Grant, an officer' who was temporarily Maxwell's brigade major, but the idea was implicit in Wellesley's original positioning of the cavalry. They were stationed here to prevent a Mahratta attack on the British flank.

[2] A *tulwar* is the characteristic Indian sabre with an ornate small straight grip terminated by a round 'bottom guard'. They were often made of poor quality metal, more like iron than steel. The wealthier Indians usually had European blades remounted in India. We should observe, however, that *Blackiston*, I, 179, says that the weapons of the enemy were often sharper because they never used them for practice.

Wellesley was faced, however, with a most unusual situation: field guns both British and Mahratta in the southern area where the first artillery fighting had occurred were now being fired at the rear of the British infantry which had passed over them. The Mahratta gunners, overrun in the first infantry assault and left for dead, were partly responsible, but there must have been others as well. British pieces still in their first position seem to have been taken by Mahratta cavalry which swept southward from around Assaye so far as to be out of the path of Maxwell's charge. These battalion pieces, including those of the pickets and the 74th, were being used against the remains of the 74th, perhaps mostly by amateur gunners.[1]

Wellesley took immediate counteraction. His four EIC infantry battalions were now re-formed and efficient; he could use the 78th elsewhere. He appears to have ordered Harness to bring the 78th back towards Waroor to recapture from the west the line of guns it had already taken once from the east. Harness was to leave the two EIC battalions facing Scindia's still irresolute cavalry and the other two EIC battalions facing Pohlmann's shattered infantry which was now beginning to take a third position just south of the Juah.

After giving this order, Wellesley rode fast south-east to the 7th Native Cavalry, the only mounted unit Maxwell had left on the field, and led them against the Mahrattas who had taken the British guns. These two attacks, the 78th from the west and the 7th NC from the east, restored the situation in the British rear, but Wellesley lost Diomed. The gallant beast was piked through a lung. Wellesley was almost certainly fighting with his own sabre at least for a short time. Normally an animal with such a wound would have been shot in the brain, but Wellesley ordered the pike to be pulled out to give Diomed his slim chance to live. Wellesley had his saddle and holsters shifted and mounted his third horse of the day.

He now left a squadron of the 7th N.C. to make sure that the entire central area remained firmly in his possession – a precaution especially against stragglers from across the Kaitna – and took the remainder of both units north-west towards Pohlmann's third position. This former Hanoverian sergeant was a better than average commander; while Maxwell went off to the north and Wellesley had to retake his guns, including the pieces captured earlier, Pohlmann had re-formed his

---

[1] The Mahrattas who fired the British battalion guns may have come from the south side of the Kaitna, having crossed to the south bank and then recrossed west of Peepulgaon: Blackiston, I, 172.

Regular Battalions. They were now facing south with their left flank again anchored in Assaye; their right was drawn back across the Juah. This flat crescent, about a mile in length, was by no means a poor position. At least three of Pohlmann's original thirteen Regular Battalions had not yet been seriously engaged; he had some artillery left also, but probably not more than fifteen field pieces.

As Wellesley rode north, he saw Maxwell and most of his cavalry returning to almost the precise point from which they had begun their first charge about forty minutes before. They had gone north-west across the Juah, then north after the fleeing enemy, and finally come back south to recross the river, this time east of Assaye. Wellesley posted the 7th N.C. complete with all the cavalry gallopers – none had gone off with Maxwell – to guard what was to become the British rear; he told Harness to re-form the infantry line of battle probably in the same order as in the first assault. He then galloped over to Maxwell, whom he ordered to reorganize his three regiments of cavalry and charge the eastern half of Pohlmann's new line. It had been broken twice before and was now insufficiently protected by artillery.

Maxwell quickly prepared for the new charge; he had only about 600 sabres at hand, but formed them as before with the 19th Dragoons in the centre and the 4th and 5th N.C. on either flank. Again he himself led the charge, but was fatally hit by a piece of grape. He appears to have tried to rein in, dropped his sword and threw up his right arm in an involuntary gesture before falling from his horse. Those who followed saw him fall and were shaken. Some appear to have believed he signalled for a halt. The charge did not go home and there was no actual contact.

Maxwell's gesture may have had some bearing on this result. His death certainly did not help. But the chief reason for the failure was that the attack was never properly aligned. Instead of forming his troopers parallel to the Mahratta line and smashing straight into and through it, Maxwell began his charge with the British cavalry at an angle of about forty-five degrees with its target. The extreme right flank of the 4th N.C. made contact first, in theory one man at a time. The troopers (or their horses) considered personal survival more important than precise alignment and gradually changed direction away from the enemy bayonets. In a few seconds the movement was communicated from trooper to trooper. Suddenly Maxwell's entire force was galloping parallel to, and not into, Pohlmann's line. The horsemen careened past several Mahratta units and took their fire before they sheered off to the south.[1]

If Wellesley had stayed with these mounted units this second cavalry mishap of the day could have had serious consequences. When it occurred, however, he was already bringing forward his infantry battalions en echelon left in front for another attack on Pohlmann's regulars. He himself was again at the right flank of the 78th. These kilted Scots were tired because they had marched about twenty-five miles since dawn and had been involved in severe fighting during the hot afternoon, but they were still full of fire and confidence. Their line was as precise and as menacing as it had been an hour and a half before. They were ready for another test against the best the enemy had.

Pohlmann's soldiers had no desire to fight the kilted giants at bayonet range again. In a few seconds this mood was communicated to everyone. Pohlmann, his officers and his sepoys appear to have gone to a 'right about' and moved away fast, abandoning weapons and equipment as they crossed the Juah. The battlefield, except for Assaye itself, was now left completely in the possession of the British army.

While British soldiers drank long and thirstily from the river, Wellesley organized an attack on the village. He had immediately at hand the 6-pounders of the 78th and perhaps some EIC battalions. He ordered north some of the cavalry gallopers stationed with the 7th N.C. These pieces were all advanced to within 300 yards of the village and fired a few rounds. But Assaye was no longer formidable. Its 'garrison', mostly Berar's irregulars, had seen the fate of their betters. Their guns which had caused so much trouble earlier hardly fired a shot. Two British battalions, one of them almost certainly the remnant of the 74th, took the place with only minor difficulty.

The battle was over. Wellesley may have sent the 7th N.C. in pursuit, but it was not continued far. Even this unit which was least fatigued by combat was exhausted from more than twelve hours in and out of the saddles and perhaps thirty-five miles of riding. Every Mahratta gun and ammunition tumbril actually engaged was in British hands.

Wellesley's Indian allies were reasonably fresh after an afternoon mostly spent in the exchange of hostile glares with the enemy.[2] The

---

[1] *Blackiston*, I, 170, wrote, 'I suddenly found my horse swept round as it were by an eddy current. Away we galloped right shoulders forward along the enemy's line receiving their fire. We took to our heels manfully.'

[2] *Elphinstone*, 75, says the Mysore and friendly Mahratta cavalry suffered only a single casualty in this area.

outcome of the battle between the rivers greatly strengthened the loyalty of Goklah and Appah Dessaye.[1] Bisnapah and his Mysore horse were not only loyal, but efficient as well. The allied cavalry alone could not, however, conduct a vigorous pursuit of an undamaged cavalry army still many times their strength.

Bisnapah did cordon off the battlefield, at least to some extent, mainly to prevent plundering by the camp followers of both sides. There was not much danger of an enemy surprise; the British 'camp' that night contained neither tents nor normal equipment. But Wellesley and his tired units probably took minimum security measures themselves; they knew that the men who were supposed to be on guard – the pickets – were mostly dead or wounded. The story of the major-general sinking down at the end of the battle (soon after 6 p.m.?) and sleeping with his head on his knee appears absurd.[2] An incident which indicates a very different post-combat attitude was described fifteen years after the battle (25 September 1818) by John Malcolm who wrote to Wellesley, 'My native aide-de-camp, Subadar Syud Hussein, a gallant soldier, owes his rise to that day. He was the leading havildar of the Fourth Cavalry in the charge; and he afterwards dashed into the centre of a party of the enemy's horse, and bore off their standard. His commanding officer, Floyer, brought him and the standard to you; and upon the story being told, you patted him upon the back, and with that eloquent and correct knowledge in the native language for which you were celebrated, said, "Acha havildar; jemadar". A jemadar he was made, and amid all his subsequent successes in Persia and in India which have raised him to medals, pensions, and a palanquin from Government his pride is the pat on the back he received at Assye.'[3]

Wellesley probably spent an unpleasant night on some straw in an enclosed farmyard in the company of other British officers, some wounded. He was troubled by nightmares due to physical and emotional exhaustion.[4] The next morning Bisnapah brought in the baggage from Naulniah which he had left long before daylight. An hour later Stevenson reported from Borkardan. He had broken camp

---

[1] There was a rumour that Goklah, Appah Dessaye and their men were going to turn against the British should they lose, a not unusual happening in Mahratta wars. Scindia was married to Appah Dessaye's niece, and remained highly respected by the uncle: *Supplementary Despatches*, II, 224. Wellesley was not worried by the report. Defeat at Assaye would have meant a total disaster whether or not his allies changed sides.

[2] The evidence for this appears to be a 'MS note in the India Office Library': *Biddulph*, 145.

[3] *Brett-James*, 82–3.   [4] *Lady Longford*, 93.

at Hussainabad as soon as the battle started and marched to the sound of the guns. He had received a note from Wellesley summoning him forward during the night, but had run into nearly impassable country between the Givia and the Purna rivers; he appears to have lost his way as well. His force had kept on throughout the night but finally arrived at Borkardan not much closer to Assaye than they had been fifteen hours before when they had begun to move. Stevenson hanged his chief guide. After an eight-hour rest the force marched to Assaye. They had tried their best, but were twenty-four hours late.

The victory at Assaye was as complete as it could have been under the circumstances, although the body count of the enemy killed is said to have been only 1,200. A total of 102 guns and all Mahratta ammunition had been left on the field, but most of the tumbrils containing the latter blew up after the battle, presumably because the Mahrattas had left burning slow-match inside. Every Mahratta unit with the courage to stand had been broken and driven from the field.

On the other hand, Wellesley's army had suffered grievously; casualties are said to have been more numerous than in any other previous British battle victory in India. The British loss was 198 Europeans and 258 Indians killed, and 442 Europeans and 695 Indians wounded; it amounts to a total of 1,594 out of a force which probably numbered about 5,800 actually engaged – more than 27 per cent.[1] An analysis reveals that the 74th and the pickets incurred a disproportionate share of the casualties. The 74th lost 124 killed and 277 wounded, 62·6 per cent of the total European loss in both cases. The pickets practically ceased to exist, but no other units suffered severely. For instance, the King's 78th lost 24 killed, 77 wounded, and 4 missing, but about half of these casualties were probably incurred in the half company of the 78th with the pickets. The most seriously hurt EIC battalion, the 2/12 Madras, lost 212 of all ranks, which was less than 20 per cent of its total strength if the half company with the pickets is excluded. The 2/12 had a graver loss than any other battalion save the 74th because Pohlmann's guns to the north – but not the guns from Assaye – took this unit in the flank.

As we have seen, the excessive casualties in the pickets and 74th were owing to Orrock's mistake.[2] But Wellesley left him in command of

---

[1] Of Wellington's battles only Waterloo approaches Assaye in the percentage of losses.

[2] This tallies with Wellesley's letter to Munro, a historian in the EIC forces at the time, *Supplementary Despatches*, IV, 211; 'our loss would not have exceeded half its actual amount if it had not been for a mistake of the officer who led the pickets'. The pickets

the 1/8 and even insisted that his name be left blank when the incident was referred to in Gurwood's Dispatches. The only suggestion of criticism I have found is the recording of a private conversation of Arthur with his secretary in which he is quoted as saying that 'through habits of dissipation and idleness, he [Orrock] has become incapable of giving attention to an order to see what it means'.[1]

We should also consider the possible errors of another officer, Patrick Maxwell of the King's 19th Dragoons. He came out to India as St Leger's brigade major[2] and took over command of Wellesley's cavalry when Dallas left the army at Poona. His first charge was successful, but he allowed his troopers to go out of control across the Juah. (This sort of behaviour was the primary failing of many British cavalry regiments which fought under Wellesley in Europe.) Would this have occurred if Dallas had still been in overall command? I believe it might not. Maxwell's second charge was professionally incompetent. Though his gallant death has usually saved this movement from criticism, his units were badly aligned initially and may not have been directed properly.

What about the men who commanded the infantry brigades? Like Maxwell, both were King's officers; Wellesley praised all three of them in his official report of the battle. I have been unable, however, to find out much about what Wallace and Harness actually did; similar difficulties arise in a study of Wellesley's larger European battles later. He did so much himself.

I believe that Harness initially handled the King's 78th and the 1/10 and 1/8 Madras. This would leave Wallace with his own regiment, the King's 74th, and the 2/12 and 1/4 M.N.I. He undoubtedly stayed with his two sepoy battalions and guided them flawlessly into the first line at the time Orrock led the pickets and the 74th to disaster. One might suppose that if Wallace had been alert he could have prevented Orrock's mistake, but there is no evidence to support this assumption. He probably reached his own Scots about the time they needed him

[1] *Elphinstone*, 80. William Orrock received his first EIC commission in 1778, was made a lieutenant-colonel in 1802, and died in that rank still on active duty at Seringapatam in 1810: *Dodwell and Miles*, 134–5.
[2] I have no reason to believe that Maxwell continued, or even shared originally, his old chief's alcoholic habits, but some officers in India being what they were in those days, it is possible.

and the 74th would have had some casualties even if used properly, but the loss in the 2/12 and perhaps other units would have been considerably less.

most. Wellesley appears to have considered him abler than Harness who was almost certainly already in poor health.[1]

The principal criticisms of Wellesley's conduct of the campaign and battle of Assaye are that he should not have separated his army at Budnapoor, nor have attacked alone on the afternoon of the 23rd. Both criticisms seem unjustified. There was never a single army; there were always two. It would have been logistically and strategically impossible to conduct this campaign with a single force. If Wellesley had united both armies, the combination would have been not only hopelessly clumsy and slow, but totally incapable of guarding the Peshwa's and the Nizam's territory and also of taking Ahmednuggur and Jalna. Even a temporary union would have produced the disadvantages already pointed out earlier in this chapter.

With regard to attacking alone once he discovered the enemy within striking distance Wellesley wrote, 'I determined upon the immediate attack because I saw clearly that if I attempted to return to my camp at Naulniah I should have been followed thither by the whole of the enemy's cavalry. . . . I might have been attacked in camp.'[2]

Wellesley was logical as always, but he wrote this explanation at leisure and to support a decision made quickly in a critical situation more than a month before. I believe that at noon on 23 September his own theory of the inevitable superiority of audacious tactics in India and the fact that he did not want the enemy to get away were more important than logic. On numerous occasions he laid down for his subordinates the principle of attacking immediately a chance for doing so was presented. He followed his own advice without exception while in India. A defensive attitude never succeeded there. The only limitation he would accept concerned attacking an Indian enemy in a position he had occupied at leisure. Such a position was inevitably strong, as Scindia's first position had been north of the Kaitna. But at Assaye Wellesley managed to eliminate the advantage by attacking from the flank.

There was a further significant consideration in favour of an attack. A British failure to attack, even if not accompanied by material damage of a military nature, would have enormously increased the enemy's self-confidence and morale. Even hesitating to attack would have been remarked by allies and enemies and might have had unfortunate repercussions in political situations throughout India.

---

[1] Nine weeks after Assaye at the battle of Argaum, Harness had to be removed from his command for mental incompetence. He died at Ellichpoor in January 1804.

[2] *Supplementary Despatches*, IV, 211.

Once Wellesley began his operations from Naulniah, his conduct of the battle is difficult to fault. He struck the enemy as soon as an opportunity was presented, but from an unexpected direction. His remarkable eye for terrain and his unerring common sense never served him better than in locating the place to cross the Kaitna. His brief personal reconnaissance from the high ground north of Peepulgaon enabled him to appreciate the real enemy situation. His first infantry attack, even though incomplete owing to Orrock's error, swept the Mahratta units who were actually struck completely off their feet. Wellesley had fitted his formation admirably to match the enemy and the terrain.

Although Orrock and the 74th did go astray, Maxwell, following Wellesley's orders, was in a position to save what was left of them. Wellesley managed the recovery of his temporarily disorganized EIC battalions perfectly. If his entire infantry force, including the pickets and the 74th, had delivered the attack as ordered, the victory would have come sooner and been more complete. An effective cavalry pursuit would have been possible.

Not the least of Wellesley's personal contributions to the victory at Assaye was his recapture of his own rear area and the British and Mahratta guns. He used his best remaining infantry unit for this, but only after it could be spared. He also employed the 7th N.C., the only regular cavalry unit left on the field. This situation was unusual, but drastic action was necessary before the enemy could take advantage of their opportunity.

Wellesley ordered Maxwell's second charge, but did not depend on it to break Pohlmann's third line. He used the time to complete the organization of his second infantry attack which did drive Pohlmann from the field and sealed the victory. He finally captured Assaye with a minimum of loss because he had already stripped it of support and brought up artillery to cover the assault. Fortified villages could be extremely strong when held by determined men, but Berar's soldiers lost heart when they saw infantry and artillery preparing to attack and cavalry moving perhaps to intercept their retreat.

We must not forget that for almost a year Wellesley had been arming, equipping, organizing and training his force so that it could fight precisely as it did at Assaye. He had given his small army mobility, stamina and the ability to respond to orders and to fight according to plans and training. The force was hundreds of miles from its base in Mysore, but still as effective as it would have been near Seringapatam.

Finally, there was Wellesley's personal example, so important especially in that time and place. Colin Campbell wrote two days later, 'The General was in the thick of the action the whole time. No one could have shown a better example. I never saw a man so cool and collected.'[1]

Without question Assaye was the greatest of Arthur Wellesley's Indian victories. We should consider this battle and the preceding campaign in the light of his later unbroken string of European victories. Military critics have often faulted Wellington because he appeared to lack audacity and offensive flair in Europe. This criticism is unjust even applied to his European campaigns, but at Assaye he showed the opposite. From 5 May 1799 until he left India Wellesley drummed into his subordinates the importance of seizing and keeping the initiative. When his own test came at Assaye he grabbed the opportunity with both hands and won with an astonishing display of offensive spirit, quick thinking, and tactical competence.

[1] *Supplementary Despatches*, IV, 186.

XI

Argaum

The British pursuit of Scindia and Berar began almost thirty-six hours after the battle of Assaye. On the morning of 25 September 1803 Stevenson's army, less most of the surgeons, moved north to the Ajanta ghaut and down it. They recovered four brass field guns abandoned by the enemy, but apparently failed to find a further fourteen which had been hidden during the retreat. Wellesley's *hircarrahs* reported 120 cannon in the Mahratta armies before Assaye, none of which appear to have got down the ghaut. The Begum Sumroo's four Regular Battalions certainly had their field pieces, probably sixteen to twenty of them, when they left the Borkardan camp before the end of the battle.

Even after thirty-six hours there were unmistakable signs of a panic. Bodies of men and animals dotted the road, especially down the ghaut itself which at that time represented a kind of border. The route was strewn with baggage and equipment, most of it useless. The people here were subjects of the Nizam. The Mahrattas had treated them as enemies and suffered for it on the night of the 23rd and all during the 24th. Villagers along the way killed wounded Mahratta soldiers who were unable to keep up, and collected abandoned personal possessions for their own use. They may well have buried the missing gun tubes; brass was and is valuable for many purposes in India.

Wellesley's first concern in connection with his own army was to care for his wounded. Some were collected into 'hospital' groups on the night of the 23rd, but most remained where they fell. There were not enough surgeons or medical supplies for more than 1,000 injured men. All that could be done for most of them on the 24th was to make them as comfortable as posssible on the ground, protect them from marauders and the burning Indian sun, and make sure that all had plenty of water. This treatment was neither as inhumane nor as harmful to the wounded men as it seems today. The weather was warm and dry. Casualties who did not bleed to death on the first night were often better off with wounds undressed. The surgeons had more knowledge and skill than we realize, but they worked with unsterilized instruments and bandages[1] and nature unaided often did a better job.

Once the wounded were collected, there was the problem of burying the dead and collecting equipment. The dead of both sides lay in irregular heaps, especially where the 74th had rallied round its colours. The pioneers were set to digging orderly graves for the British and allied casualties west north-west of Assaye near the Juah.[2] Enemy dead were counted approximately and then interred in multiple graves.[3]

The twenty-six iron guns captured around Assaye were burst by being double-charged and having shot wedged in their bores. They were destroyed because they were not worth moving, but the brass pieces were 'so good and so well equipped that they [some of them, at least] answer for our service'.[4] The British also secured thousands of small arms and other personal possessions of the enemy of some value.

Wellesley's next problem was to replace casualties. The King's 74th had been removed from the active roster. Every officer was either killed or wounded; all the survivors were needed to care for their wounded comrades. Maxwell of the cavalry was dead; so was Captain Hugh McKay of the 4th Native Cavalry. Mackay had been detached for months and was doing outstanding work in handling all the 'public' bullocks, including the magnificent Mysore draft beasts. He had asked Wellesley for permission to return to his squadron for the battle, but had been refused. He joined against orders, charged at the head of his

---

[1] *Blackiston*, I, 181–2, tells of 'A surgeon whose bandages had been exhausted', taking 'a fine long girdle of cotton cloth' from an enemy. 'Up sprang the dead man and away ran the doctor. This extraordinary instance of a doctor bringing a man to life, so opposite to the usual practice . . .' Can one imagine a less sterile bandage?

[2] The cemetery area can be identified today and is shown clearly on the one-inch Ordnance Survey map of 1912.

[3] Some, perhaps most, of the 641 British dead (198 European and 433 Indian) were also buried in multiple graves. Five Indian officers and NCOs of the same family from the 1/8 Madras NI, a Muslim unit that assumed the name 'Wellesley's Own', were interred in a single grave; their comrades refused to mourn for them because they died doing their duty: *Wilson*, III, 110.

[4] *Dispatches*, II, 371.

squadron and lost his life. There were other damaging losses: two of Wellesley's small staff were severely wounded.

The five EIC battalions had not lost enough rank and file to make them ineffective for combat, but the 1/8 had lost four and the 2/12 six European officers, including its commander.

Wellesley recalled the 1/3 Madras, one of the two EIC battalions sent away before Assaye to reinforce Poona. They were no longer necessary to prevent its capture because the enemy too had lost heavily, especially in the Regular Battalions. Perhaps Captain Vesey of that corps had learned his lesson.

Wellesley, who could not spare enough British soldiers for a fortified hospital without weakening his army excessively, wanted to accommodate his wounded in Dowlutabad. It was a strong, commodious fortress on a conical hill, and lay only fifty miles away with no major streams on the route. Dowlutabad belonged to the Nizam of Hyderabad, had an ample garrison and presumably enough supplies. Wellesley asked Stevenson to apply for permission to use the place through Rajah Mohiput Ram who appears to have been the senior officer in the Nizam's army under Stevenson's command. However, the *killadar* of the fortress refused to receive the wounded and their attendants. The garrison was unusually jealous of details of the fortress's construction and would not allow English officers to approach within 500 yards.[1]

There were only two other choices, Aurungabad and Ajanta. At that time Aurungabad was not a strong place, just a sprawling group of fortifications more or less connected and poorly garrisoned. Scindia's Regular Battalions – even the four which had not been destroyed at Assaye – could easily have taken it. Ajanta was better and closer than Aurungabad, only about twenty-three miles away. Fortress and town,[2] connected by a stone bridge, were smaller than Dowlutabad and Aurungabad, but comfortable and strong enough to offer some resistance even to a regular Mahratta army with artillery, but not sufficiently powerful for the Nizam's *killadar* to refuse to receive the British wounded. The journey north had to be slow and easy and was postponed until all wounded men had received the full medical amenities available. Their transfer was begun about 1 October and

---

[1] *Welsh*, I, 168, says he could not get close enough to sketch it.

[2] Ajanta – the *pettah* is more substantially fortified than usual – is in good shape today and remarkably as *Welsh*, I, 184, describes it. There are also 'caves with rock carvings' nearby.

apparently completed on the 8th, or perhaps a day or two earlier.

While the wounded were moving into Ajanta, both Wellesley and Stevenson had moved down the ghaut to the north. The two armies remained separate but would co-operate to defeat the enemy in battle where possible and capture his bases if he would not fight. It was known now that both Scindia and Berar had retreated to Burhampoor where some of the former's infantry had taken refuge. Stevenson was ordered to take the city and arrived there on 8 October.

The Mahratta cavalry had moved west from Burhampoor and threatened to raid the Peshwa's territory around Poona and further south. Wellesley consequently moved west from the bottom of the Ajanta ghaut to protect the area in case Scindia and Berar were serious in their intentions. He received information to the contrary, however, and was back in Ajanta on the 8th.[1]

The enemy again threatened to march on south. Again Wellesley moved in the same direction, this time above the ghauts. He was half-way back to Aurungabad on the 11th, only to receive intelligence that the two Mahratta armies had separated, at least temporarily. Scindia had retired west; Berar had moved back towards Burhampoor but was too weak to threaten the Hyderabad army seriously.

Stevenson took Burhampoor on 16 October without serious fighting and collected some money from the civilian population in accordance with Wellesley's orders.[2] He moved further north on the 24th and after a short siege captured Asseergurh, which was much stronger than Burhampoor and full of military supplies. These two places with Ahmednuggur, Jalna and Baroach had been Scindia's important military bases in the Deccan. Now all of them were taken.

Perhaps more important than the fall of the fortresses was the surrender of ten of Scindia's European officers who confirmed that Pohlmann's thirteen Regular Battalions had disbanded during the retreat after Assaye. One of the officers, Major John James Dupon (or Dupont) who surrendered or was captured in Burhampoor or Asseergurh, had commanded Filoze's four-battalion *compoo*.[3] However, there were

---

[1] I have followed in particular Burton's sketch 'Theatre of Operations of the War in the Deccan 1803' which lists places and dates. These are also shown in *Dispatches* and *Supplementary Despatches*.

[2] This levy was not strictly in line with the Wellesley ideal for British rule in India since it was enforced by the threat of a sack, but the amount was moderate and urgently needed if the British were to continue to give cash for their purchases and to pay troops regularly and prevent indiscipline because of hunger: *Dispatches*, II, 662–3.

[3] *House of Commons Account*, 291.

apparently still at least ten more such officers, eight with British names, in Scindia's service.[1]

We should note some manœuvring of the field armies during Stevenson's sieges. Wellesley moved north on 17 October to be within supporting distance of the Hyderabad force, and was at Ferdapoor, a day's march north-east of Ajanta, on the 19th. He made the move in case the Mahratta armies had reunited and were about to attack Stevenson. The enemy junction did not take place, however, so Wellesley moved no further. Stevenson was strong enough to beat either Mahratta force separately, a fact the two chiefs undoubtedly appreciated.

Berar did not try to save Scindia's fortress of Asseergurh, but instead marched south and east as if to raid the Nizam's territory. His army actually passed between the two British forces about 20 October. Wellesley learnt of Berar's movements and returned to Ajanta the next day. The following eight days saw some of the finest marching ever done by a British army in India. Wellesley moved south and east covering as much as thirty miles a day, siege train and all. At least once he came within sight of Berar's army. The Mahrattas are said to have been driven from five campsites in two days until finally Berar lost his nerve and moved north-east again towards his own capital.

We should note the significance of Wellesley's 'two army' strategy. He used Stevenson to capture places of importance while he himself prevented the enemy from raiding friendly territory. When the Mahratta chiefs moved with cavalry only, they were reasonably safe but could accomplish little. A force of cavalry alone could not even take a mud-walled village. Scindia in early September and Berar in late October could have made a dash for Hyderabad City, but they held back because Wellesley would have followed them. They might not have been caught but would have been prevented from plundering in their fashion. Since Mahratta cavalry served mostly for plunder, an arduous and dangerous raid deep into Hyderabad with small expectations of profit was not attractive.

Berar would not cross the Godavery with his cavalry only and retreated north to join his regular infantry and artillery.[2] Wellesley

---

[1] *Supplementary Despatches*, IV, 190 and 206.

[2] We know far less of Berar's Regular Battalions than of those in the employ of Scindia and Holkar. Berar did not have as many European professional soldiers in his army. In fact, I cannot be sure that he had a single one. There is no doubt, however, that he had two types of infantry, the older irregular units and the new battalions with guns assigned to each similar to those of Scindia. The latter were commanded by his brother, Manoo Bappoo.

learnt of this decision on 10 November and for a week stopped where he was, near Chicholi, fifteen miles north of the Godavery. Stevenson was to get ready to move on Gawilghur, the principal enemy fortress in the hills which separated Berar's country from Hyderabad. Wellesley had already decided that Gawilghur would be Stevenson's next objective.

On the 11th Scindia's *vakels* (negotiators) had arrived in Wellesley's camp asking for an armistice. Wellesley was not surprised; he had detailed information about General Lake's victories against Perron, Scindia's semi-independent French subordinate who ruled a vast area to the north, including Delhi and Agra. As has already been mentioned, Lake began hostilities against Perron independently of Wellesley's declaration against Scindia. He marched from Cawnpore on 7 August, one day before Wellesley moved on Ahmednuggur. Lake took several important fortresses, including Alyghur, during the next month. He won a battle at Delhi on 11 September and occupied the old Mogul capital. However, according to Wellesley's most recent information Perron's army was still undestroyed and active early in October. Lake's magnificent victory at Laswaree was still three weeks away.

Scindia would benefit from an armistice in his southern theatre of operations if he could quickly transfer any of his strength north against Lake. But this was hardly practical. The two theatres were too far apart for Scindia to shuttle units from one to the other. The journey would have taken nearly two months. Besides, Perron was not really subordinate to Scindia any longer.

Wellesley saw no harm in granting Scindia an armistice for a short time, if he could separate him from Berar. The British armies would then be able to take Gawilghur and move on against Berar's capital more easily. Wellesley agreed to a cessation of hostilities, but insisted that it begin only if and when Scindia moved his entire force fifty miles east of Ellichpoor. Thus his army could neither help Berar nor suddenly move against Poona or Hyderabad. Wellesley did not count on any good faith from Scindia, but he had nothing to lose and a good deal to gain if the armistice terms were met.

By then Wellesley's system of intelligence was functioning almost perfectly as regards any major enemy movement. Small Mahratta detachments were able to march without having their movements reported, but not the main armies. The British commander knew Berar had moved towards his own infantry and artillery at about the same time as the armistice agreement with Scindia's negotiators was completed. Scindia was moving in the same direction, either to unite with Berar and continue the war, or fulfil the conditions of the armistice agreement. Stevenson had begun his march for Gawilghur on 15 November. A day later Wellesley began his own to the north and east from the Godavery to join the older commander in that area. Since the four forces were converging on roughly the same point, something was likely to happen.

Wellesley's army was at Rajoora on the 23rd and at Akola on the 27th. He sent word to Stevenson that he would meet him near Parterly on the morning of the 30th. The two commanders met on schedule, conferred briefly, and then about noon climbed to the flat top of a fortified tower in Parterly. It was unusually large and well built and allowed an all-round view of the country from the top.[1] The Mahrattas, presumably both Scindia and Berar's forces, were in plain sight to the north. Bisnapah's Mysore light cavalry was expertly skirmishing with the opposition; he would undoubtedly report soon.

Wellesley got out his telescope and began to examine the area behind the skirmishing horsemen. He could see a large army to the north, beyond the village of Sirsoli but south of the village of Argaum. It was already formed into something resembling a line. Was another battle imminent? Wellesley's mind began to work like a computer on times, positions and probable speeds. If the Mahrattas had formed their line – and it certainly looked as if they had – they would be unlikely to retire before nightfall.

Though Berar had infantry and artillery with him, those of Scindia in the Deccan were known to be nearly wiped out. The Begum's Regular Battalions were north of the Taptee. The enemy forces could not be more numerous than at Assaye and probably not of such quality. Wellesley now had both British armies at hand. The only problem was one of fatigue: his own army had moved eighteen miles since dawn; Stevenson's appears to have moved hardly less; and it had been a hot day. Wellesley was once more faced with the choice of attacking with an exhausted army or allowing the enemy to slip away. Again the decision was to attack, and orders to that effect were given quickly.

The baggage and siege trains of both armies went into separate

---

[1] This tower is not only still in existence but still in good repair, and is used as a dwelling by a locally important family who graciously allowed my party to go up through their home to the top. The view to the north is good, but trees now interfere with a detailed observation towards Sirsoli even with modern binoculars.

camps sufficiently secure to be proof against Mahratta cavalry of any strength. As at Naulniah, Wellesley chose his camp guard carefully. It was composed of his favourite 1/8 Madras, the pickets of the day before, and about three squadrons of Mysore horse. The guard had several field pieces as well as the four 12-pounder siege guns.[1]

The British armies advanced north from Parterly apparently in four columns. Wellesley's cavalry was on the extreme right; his infantry came next. Stevenson's cavalry was on the extreme left with his infantry adjacent to Wellesley's. Stevenson's total British infantry force was only slightly, if at all, less numerous than Wellesley's because his one King's infantry and his five EIC battalions were stronger individually than Wellesley's two King's and five EIC battalions. Stevenson was weaker in British cavalry; he had only two EIC regiments against Wellesley's one King's and three EIC units, but he still had several thousand Mogul cavalry which were more numerous and more effective in battle than Wellesley's Mysore light horsemen. Wellesley's Mahrattas were marching separately at this time; his orders to them were carried by a messenger who 'missed his road' so 'they were not engaged during the 29th'.[2]

Stevenson's infantry column was led by his pickets of the day; his strong European infantry battalion, now officially the King's 94th Foot came next followed by his five full-strength EIC Madras battalions. I believe their order was the 2/2, the 2/9, the 1/11, the 2/11, and the 1/6. These battalions were fresher than Wellesley's; their order was undisturbed by their halt near Parterly.

Wellesley's infantry battalions were not in order, probably because one brigade had countermarched. His pickets of the day were in the lead, but were followed by the 2/12 and the 1/10 Madras. Then came the King's 78th, the King's 74th and three more EIC Madras units, the 1/2, the 1/3 and the 1/4.

The four British columns approached the village of Sirsoli and the plain of Argaum from the south. This area is in the black-earth section of Nagpoor State and is now noted for its production of wheat and cotton. At that time it was covered with millet, the individual stalks of which were seven to nine feet tall. A man on foot could neither see nor be seen. When Wellesley had observed the country from the tower

---

[1] The field artillery comprised the four 6-pounders of the two infantry units, now all bullock drawn, and probably two 5·5-inch field howitzers. Stevenson's camp was separate; he used as guards the 2/7 Madras with some of his Mogul infantry, cavalry and artillery.

[2] *Dispatches*, II, 559.

in Parterly, his elevation and the fact that the whole flat plain is slightly tilted up to the north had allowed a distant but unobstructed view of the enemy's Argaum line. Now he could see little from around Sirsoli even on horseback. The plain was still exceptionally flat, but it was cut almost haphazardly by deep narrow canals. A *nullah* or wet-weather river ran generally north and south from before Sirsoli almost to Argaum.[1]

Wellesley made a quick personal reconnaissance to the north and reached a spot from which he could see that the Mahrattas were still in place. The deep narrow canals caused him considerable anxiety. Almost certainly, the enemy had taken up a situation behind one or more of them. He did not like attacking a Mahratta army head-on in a position of its own choice, but there appeared to be no alternative unless he did not attack at all. There were only about three and a half hours of daylight left, enough for a careful assault, but not for any extensive preliminary manœuvres. Wellesley again decided on attack.

He returned to Sirsoli as the head of his infantry column passed the village. He ordered them to oblique slightly to the right to clear a bend in the central *nullah*; Wallace was told to guide his pickets of the day to the east for about 1,000 yards, enough space for seven and a half understrength battalions to form into line, with battalion guns between each unit. The infantry line was then to halt.

Wellesley met Stevenson near Sirsoli. The old colonel was too weak from sickness to mount a horse, but his mind was clear. He exercised all command functions from a comfortable seat in the *howdah* of an elephant. Arthur quickly explained his battle plan. Stevenson's infantry line would form in line with his own, but on the west side of the *nullah*. The colonel's cavalry under an exceptionally able EIC officer, Lieutenant-Colonel A. Sentleger of the 6th NC, was to protect the left or western flank of the entire infantry line with Stevenson's two EIC mounted regiments and presumably several thousand Mogul horse.[2] Wellesley's own cavalry was to protect the right or eastern flank.

---

[1] Plans of the battle generally mark only Sirsoli, Argaum and the *nullah*, all apparently following the contemporary sketch map made by someone in the 1/3 Madras and published opposite *Welsh*, I, 188, which shows the *nullah* as nearly straight. The course of the stream is now different and was so in the one-inch Ordnance Survey (1912); I believe it was too in 1803. My own map (p. 311) is admittedly rough, but the positions of the *nullah*, etc., are taken from the 1912 map. In March 1968 the *nullah* was actually a series of shallow pools and appeared never to go completely dry even on the surface.

[2] As mentioned previously, it is impossible precisely to determine the size and constitution of the Nizam's army and its degree of subordination to Stevenson. Its contribution to the forthcoming battle was extremely limited, perhaps mainly to glaring at the enemy.

So far everything appeared to be going perfectly. Another ten minutes and the British armies would be in formal combat alignment, a considerable accomplishment in view of the fact that the two commanders and their forces had been more than twenty miles apart at sunrise. But battles seldom go as planned. As Wellesley's pickets passed the *nullah*, changed direction and began to march east, they came clearly into the view of the Mahratta gunners south of Argaum; the millet did not grow in the semi-dry water course. The sight of the British column may have given the Mahratta commander the first sure evidence of the presence of a considerable British force.

In any event, the enemy guns opened fire, although the range was about 3,000 yards. In the era of solid-shot artillery a column almost in line was a tempting target regardless of range. A round ball from one of the Mahratta guns, frequently 18-pounders even for field service, could kill several men. As often happened in those days, the first rounds were more accurate than those which followed. The air overhead was filled with the awe-inspiring sound of the passage of large shot; perhaps many of them were visible too. One of the balls struck a British bullock-drawn 6-pounder.[1] The ten animals attached to it appear to have survived, but wheeled to the rear and went off in panic. Another gun team did likewise, although apparently it was undamaged.

The two runaway guns drawn by panicking bullocks careered back into the two King's and six EIC half companies which made up the pickets of the day. The Europeans dodged the guns and kept their position, but the sepoys unaccountably broke. A mass of 250 men, twenty bullocks and two guns pushed back without warning into the next two battalions. Although the sepoy units had fought valiantly at Assaye, they were also seized by the unreasoning fear that sometimes causes the best of soldiers to misbehave.[2] Fortunately, Wellesley himself was within 150 yards. He rode towards them and endeavoured to stop their flight. When this did not succeed, '. . . instead of losing his temper, unbraiding them, and endeavouring to force them back to

---

[1] The four light 6-pounder gallopers used by the pickets in Wellesley's army, two for those of the day and two for those of the previous day, had been horsedrawn before and during Assaye, but bullocks were substituted after that battle presumably because they were easier to procure than horses and just as good for duty with infantry.

[2] Wellesley wrote to Stuart on 3 December 1803 about this incident (*Dispatches*, II, 565): 'The fact was, that the 1st of the 10th, and 2nd of the 12th, and the native part of the piquets, broke and ran off, as soon as the cannonade commenced, although it was from a great distance, and not to be compared with that of Assaye.'

the spot from which they had fled, he quietly ordered their officers to lead the men under cover of the village.'[1]

Meanwhile, the King's 78th came up with pipes skirling,[2] past the temporarily disordered sepoys, every Highlander in perfect step and kilts snapping in unison. Red tunics, white belts, gleaming weapons and tall black bearskins[3] made them appear superhuman. The Madras sepoys were good soldiers too and clamoured for another chance. Wellesley took them to their places on the right of the line, made sure they were properly positioned with their battalion guns between each units and had them lie down.[4]

Once his own infantry was all in position, Wellesley ordered Stevenson and Wallace to take the whole British line forward cautiously. Wellesley personally galloped off to the head of his cavalry column which had halted for orders. He advanced with the four cavalry regiments – with Dallas sick and Maxwell killed,[5] they lacked an experienced field officer – and their eight gallopers into the flat, but canal-bisected area well to the east of the Sirsoli–Argaum *nullah*.[6] The cavalry could usually see over the millet; the enemy line opposite them stretched to the east for a considerable distance, more than the British cavalry could efficiently occupy. But this was unimportant; there was nothing in the rear for the enemy to attack save Bisnapah's Mysore cavalry which was more than capable of caring for itself.

Wellesley advanced to within 800 yards of the enemy and formed his cavalry into line, each unit slightly separated from the next. He ordered the troopers to dismount, but had the eight cavalry gallopers advance

---

[1] *Blackiston*, I, 198.

[2] At Assaye Wellesley had all musicians detailed as medical assistants, but the Scots protested so much after the battle that the pipers were left on active duty in combat thereafter.

[3] For details of uniforms I have followed photographs of three prints of 'The Storming of Seringapatam' kindly supplied by the museum at Camberley. These are obviously contemporary and carefully explained. The 78th definitely had tall black headgear which appears to be of fur rather than feathers.

[4] This is, I believe, the first instance of Wellesley's use of a procedure that later became standard. The sepoys were not only much smaller targets for stray shot, but would have found it more difficult to have left their places in line had any wished to do so.

[5] The senior officer appears to have been EIC Major R. J. Huddleston of the 7th NC, the date of whose commission was 17 June 1803.

[6] The battlefield of Argaum has often been poorly described because of its lack of commanding features. These random ditches or canals, seldom more than eight or ten feet wide by four to six deep, may or may not be in the same position as in 1803, but they are too numerous and haphazard for careful enumeration. In March 1968 most of them appeared to be man-improved, but some at least are certainly of natural origin and surely existed at the time of the battle.

another 200 yards or more until the gunners could see the enemy line clearly; they then opened fire. Wellesley instructed each unit commander separately. They were to wait until the 6-pounders made an impression on the enemy and then to attack, but Wellesley cautioned them not to charge headlong into a canal.

The British commander then returned to his infantry in the centre. He had ordered his own and Stevenson's battalions to advance in rough alignment while he was taking forward the cavalry. The infantry, which consisted of three fine King's regiments and ten veteran EIC units with a total of twenty-eight guns in pairs, placed in the intervals between the battalions and on the flanks, was no more than 1,000 yards from the enemy when Wellesley returned. Infantrymen could rarely see the Mahratta line because of the level ground and the millet, but every man knew it was there. The canals were not difficult to cross either on foot or mounted, but ranks had temporarily to be broken. Where necessary, field guns were unlimbered and manhandled over the narrow cuts and reassembled on the other side. All units had been kept roughly in line by Stevenson, Wallace and their own mounted officers.[1] The old colonel on his elephant had an advantage in this terrain.

The infantry had advanced for about 2,000 yards under desultory Mahratta fire but suffered only a few casualties because the enemy gunners were initially at almost maximum range. Later on they were fatigued. In the muzzle-loading era, even the best of artillerymen did not shoot well when they were tired and dirty and their pieces overheated. The Mahratta gunners were handling poorer weapons than Pohlmann had at Assaye, and their targets were mostly hidden by the millet.

Wellesley allowed his infantry to continue its slow advance until it was within 500 yards of the enemy. Then he gave a prearranged signal, perhaps with his hat. The white Mysore artillery bullocks, five pairs per team, wheeled to the rear and brought the gun muzzles to bear on the enemy. The European gunners, the *matrosses* and the Indian lascars unlimbered smartly, loaded and fired. The first rounds that day were aimed at the opposing infantry. Each piece was cool, clean and handled by a skilful, disciplined crew. They appeared not to hurry, but they

[1] Colonel Harness, Wellesley's other infantry brigade commander, tried to perform his duties at Argaum in spite of severe illness, but failed. Wellesley wrote on 10 June 1804 (*Dispatches*, III, 345): 'Colonel Harness was taken ill a day or two before the battle. He was so unwell as to be delirious; I was obliged to order him into his palanquin.' He died, probably of a heart ailment, on 1 January 1804: *Dispatches*, II, 624.

37 The central *nullah* on the battlefield of Argaum

38 The village of Argaum from the last British position before the assault

39 The outer fortress of Gawilghur from the north. On the left is the main gate. In the foreground is one of about ten surviving tanks, mainly within the walls, and above it the outer wall

40 Gawilghur: the undefended north-eastern area with the south-east wall in the background

41 *(Above)* Gawilghur, looking from the south-east 'balcony' of the Inner Fort. Fortescue says that Wellesley had a second breaching battery on the hog-back in the mid-ground.

42 *(Left)* Gawilghur: the third wall seen from the ravine separating the Outer and Inner Forts

43 *(Right)* Gawilghur: the south–west gate. 44 *(Below)* The surviving wrought-iron gun in the Inner Fort at Gawilghur (length 22 ft, bore $12\frac{1}{4}$ in)

were probably delivering three rounds per minute.[1] Round shot and grape tore into the Mahratta infantry and artillery.[2] By this time the enemy guns were so hot that they were almost useless.

Back to the British cavalry on the extreme right. Their eight 6-pounders were in action for ten minutes before they began to accomplish what Wellesley had anticipated. They probably knocked out any artillery the Mahratta cavalry might have had, and then sent solid shot ploughing through the semi-formed enemy horse. Field guns were important in cavalry actions in India; one shot often caused several casualties and had a tremendous effect on morale. Both Hindoos and Muslims had a fatalistic acceptance of death which made them extremely, but passively, brave. They could not, however, stand artillery fire and their units began to waver visibly. The commanding officers of the 19th Dragoons and the three Native Cavalry regiments, four corps that had been companions for many months of active campaigning, went forward individually and with caution. When each unit came within about 200 yards of the enemy and the ground was clearly practical for horse, they increased the pace to a full trot which was about the optimum speed for the proper employment of shock from momentum and weapons.

For a few seconds each British regiment had a real fight. The Mahrattas were good horsemen. Many were well armed and partially armoured. A few had the courage and ability with their *tulwars* to challenge British troopers individually. But they lacked the co-ordination of discipline and training and the uniform weapon efficiency that is the result of practice. British sabres were better because of the temper of the steel and the strong muscles of the men who used them. Hours of sword exercise produced skill, dexterity and power for cutting and thrusting. Most important of all, the British cavalry were in formation so that every trooper could use his weapons and to some extent support his comrades on either side.

The cavalry combats on the right flank were all successful. Berar's Mahrattas broke and went off in panic, leaving perhaps a few misfit artillery pieces and some other fairly useless equipment. The British

---

[1] Some experiments recorded by Lieutenant John Russell in a little book *A Series of Military Experiments . . . made in Hyde Park in 1802* (London 1806) indicate a maximum rate of fire of seven rounds per minute for a 6-pounder with a skilled crew, but these were roughly aimed shots and in a cool climate.

[2] At a range of 500 yards only the 12-pounders attached to the King's 74th would have been firing grape. Grape from 6-pounders was normally not employed at much above 300 yards. In both cases, 'grape' was technically 'case'; see Appendix I.

units did not immediately pursue, although some of Bisnapah's horsemen may have done so even at this early stage of the action.

In the centre where Wellesley was personally in command, the opposing Mahratta infantry probably had been unable to see the cavalry action just described, although it apparently was concluded before the central part of the battle began in earnest. Because of flat terrain, high grain and deep ditches, the battle appears to have been fought in three separate parts.

The artillery assigned to British infantry battalions did not find it easy to disorganize the enemy regular infantry.[1] The Mahratta commander in this area was the Rajah of Berar's brother, Manoo Bappoo, a braver man than either the Rajah or Scindia.[2] He kept his disciplined infantry steady and sent forward a unit of 1,000 to 1,500 Arabs, the best professional soldiers in India. They came on unsupported and attacked the two King's regiments in the centre of Wellesley's section of the British line. They fell almost to a man, mostly by the fire of the Highlanders and the British artillery, but some survived the hail of lead and iron to die on Scottish bayonets.

One wonders if Manoo Bappoo realized that both King's units of Wellesley's army were in the centre of his line; their normal places were on the flanks. At 500–600 yards one line of men in red jackets and white belts looks much like another, especially through growing millet. Manoo Bappoo's Arabs might have fared better against EIC units.

Perhaps a few minutes before, the two left flank battalions of Stevenson's section of the infantry line, the 1/6 and the 2/11 Madras, were attacked by Scindia's cavalry. The Mahratta horsemen came within about one hundred yards, but were already in the process of refusing to close when the two EIC battalions delivered their volleys. The action appears to have become little more than a feint.

Soon after the elimination of the Arabs, Wellesley sent the entire infantry-artillery line forward; the units moved individually and carefully, not in a line en echelon assault as at Assaye. The infantry guns were manhandled forward beside the battalions to which they belonged, keeping up a slow fire during the advance. Both infantry and artillery had

[1] The sketch map referred to on p. 311 shows fifteen units aligned in the same way as the British with about thirty-eight guns in front. The long rectangle behind labelled 'Large mass of Mahratta infantry' played no part in combat.

[2] Berar and Scindia left Assaye at an early stage; I have found no contemporary reference to either of them taking part in the battle of Argaum even at long range. But Manoo Bappoo did his utmost; as will be shown in the next chapter, he was a brave man.

to cross ditches in order to get at the enemy.[1] One battalion after another would cross a canal, form on the other side, and continue the attack.

Manoo Bappoo's regular infantry probably numbered no more than 15,000 including artillerymen. They were well posted and reasonably well led, but weakened by seeing the Arabs defeated and receiving perhaps twenty minutes of intermittent artillery fire. Some, though probably not all, units tried to exchange volleys of musketry with the British battalions. The battle in the centre was decided in these isolated infantry duels. In every case the King's and EIC units quickly won. Manoo Bappoo's men withdrew to the rear in panic. As often happened, once the better troops of an Indian army were defeated, the rest fled. The large body of enemy infantry in the second Mahratta line seems not to have fired a shot before it went to the right about and headed for safety. Victory in the centre came at least half an hour after Wellesley's cavalry had won on the right.

We know less about what happened on the British left, Stevenson's flank, mainly because there were only a handful of Europeans involved, none of whom wrote a surviving account.[2] Lieutenant-Colonel A. Sentleger competently commanded a composite EIC and Mogul cavalry force, but we do not know the details. I assume that he employed essentially the same tactics as Wellesley on the right.

Scindia's negotiators were still with Wellesley's army. They had tried unsuccessfully to persuade him not to attack their master because of the armistice, but Wellesley pointed out that the armistice was not to go into effect until Scindia had complied with its terms. Instead of going fifty miles east of Ellichpoor, he had actively joined Berar. Wellesley obviously had no choice except to consider him an enemy.

Scindia's army at Argaum was all cavalry and formed in two large divisions one behind the other. As already mentioned, Scindia's horsemen attacked early in Stevenson's advance. Sentleger's cavalry may have had a part in the action. Both EIC and Mogul mounted units appear to have had light field pieces attached to them which probably opened fire in the same manner as Wellesley's had done. They may eventually have charged, but the fighting on the left cannot have been severe. Stevenson's two EIC cavalry regiments lost a total of two

[1] The exact position of the main Mahratta force at Argaum cannot now be determined, but an irregular 'canal' does run east and west across the central *nullah* about 500 yards south of the present town. This appears the most probable position for the first line of Mahratta infantry.

[2] The European officers and sergeants of two EIC cavalry regiments would have totalled no more than 30 and 4 respectively, according to *Wilson*, II, 341.

Europeans and eleven Indians wounded, one Indian killed and one missing. Scindia's army certainly left the battlefield before Wellesley's infantry attack in the centre had been completed.

On the other hand, when the Mahratta centre finally did break, Sentleger as senior cavalry officer present seems to have taken over Wellesley's four British regiments as well as his own two and the Mogul horse and continued the pursuit of the unfortunate enemy infantry for two days.[1] Thousands of Mahrattas were killed, especially during the first moonlit night. Elephants, camels, horses and bullocks, many of them laden with baggage, were captured. Wellesley himself was in the saddle until midnight. The Mysore horsemen under Bisnapah went after the enemy throughout the hours of darkness. The Mahratta allies under Goklah and Appah Dessaye joined in the next morning.

The total casualties for both British armies appear to have been 361, with only fifteen European and thirty-one Indian deaths. The Mahratta losses may have been as high as 5,000 or even 10,000. They lost all their artillery, thirty-eight pieces, and their ammunition. Argaum was a magnificent victory won at relatively small cost.

One wonders why the Mahrattas fought here at all. They had lost at Assaye when they had Scindia's Regular Battalions instead of Berar's against a British force half as powerful. An obvious answer is that the Mahratta generals did not know that Wellesley and Stevenson had joined forces. Bisnapah and his Mysore light cavalry had covered the junction of the two armies splendidly and screened their subsequent advance. The tall millet may have been a contributing factor.

Another answer may be Manoo Bappoo's pride in his own regular infantry and his confidence in the Arabs. He probably had not been at Assaye and may not have seen British troops in action. Once he knew that he was opposing both Wellesley and Stevenson, his control of an enormous army may have been so faulty that a retreat from his carefully taken position was next to impossible.

The relative ease of victory should not tempt us to overlook either the sound professional performance of the British commander and his armies or the disadvantages under which they fought. As usual Wellesley's army had marched their eighteen miles by noon and moved on at least a further four miles to Sirsoli. Most units probably covered nearly twenty-four miles before they began to fight the battle. Stevenson's army probably covered about twenty miles. But all British units continued as required without complaint.

[1] *Wilson*, III, 118.

The British armies at Argaum did full justice to their training and their months of active campaigning. The artillery was particularly efficient; Wellesley praised both artillery commanders.[1] But the guns were a part of infantry-artillery and cavalry-artillery teams, not a separate arm. All units handled themselves well on an exceptionally difficult battlefield. Wellesley's two King's infantry regiments resoundingly defeated the ill-conceived attack of the Arabs, suffering moderately severe casualties.[2] Stevenson's 1/6 and the 2/11 Madras defeated Scindia's horsemen at long range; they suffered hardly at all; during the whole day only eleven sepoys were wounded.[3] The only unit in Stevenson's army to suffer moderately was his King's regiment, the 94th Foot, to use its new name. It lost two killed, thirty-seven wounded and two missing.

We should look again at the slightly unusual order of Wellesley's infantry battalions which may have contributed to the momentary panic at Sirsoli. The pickets led as usual, with two King's half companies at their head. Harness's Brigade under Lieutenant-Colonel Alexander Adams of the 78th came next, but with the battalions reversed. The 78th was at the rear, the 1/10 in the middle, and the 2/12 next to the pickets. Adams may not have realized at the beginning of the battle that he was in charge of the brigade. As mentioned earlier, Harness tried to carry out his regular duties, but Wellesley had to order him back into his palanquin. Had the 78th been in front, there would have been no panic except perhaps from six sepoy half companies. The momentary discomfiture, if it was caused by the battalion transposition, was more than made up for by the presence of Wellesley's two battalions of Scots in the middle rather than at the ends of the line when they defeated the Arabs in the only serious infantry combat of the entire battle.

Wellesley's personal contribution to the victory at Argaum began days before when he sensed that he and Stevenson should again move closer together. For only the fourth time in more than seven months,

[1] Praise was usually reserved for brigade commanders; the artillery commander in Wellesley's army was Captain Beaumont and in Stevenson's Captain Burke: *Dispatches*, II, 558.

[2] Thirteen of the fifteen Europeans killed in action and 86 of the 145 wounded came from the two Highland regiments.

[3] The presence of the 2/11 at Argaum can be questioned because the unit does not appear in Barclay's report as printed in *Dispatches*, II, 559, but *Wilson* and *Burton* confirm not only its presence but that (*Burton*, 177) it suffered ten men wounded. The 1/6 had only one casualty, an injured sepoy.

the two armies were in sight of each other. The first had been at Aklooss in mid-April; the second and third had been before and after Assaye.

At Parterly as at Naulniah, Wellesley was faced with the decision whether or not to attack with units which would undoubtedly not be at their best because of fatigue. Again he chose to fight immediately, because if he let the opportunity slip the enemy would surely have retired during the night. It should be clearly understood, however, that the British forces were not really over-tired. There is no indication that any unit was ineffective, and they were all in fine marching trim.

Wellesley's personal reconnaissance before Argaum involved less riding and included nothing as dramatic as the discovery of the 'secret ford' at Assaye. But during his ride north, apparently along the central *nullah* and then probably to the east of it, he was able to get the entire battle area firmly in mind and issue his orders on that basis. His rallying of two and a half battalions of sepoys may have been of extreme importance.

Once the infantry of both armies was in position, Wellesley left them with appropriate orders under veteran commanders to take charge of the cavalry himself. He personally positioned the four regiments and gave them definite and simple instructions. He then returned to the combined infantry line because the battle would be won or lost there. He was on guard against and finally overcame the problem of the 'canals' which might have defeated a less able commander. In a few minutes he evolved a shift in tactics to fit the unusual circumstances the ditches presented. He accomplished with fire from both artillery and infantry what he could not do with a single shock assault. He remained at hand to see that all went well.

In spite of his illness Stevenson made significant contributions to the victory at Argaum as well as to the successful campaign which it terminated. After a quarter of a century in India he had in 1799 come under the influence and intermittent command of a man almost young enough to be his son, but he never complained and did his level best. It cannot have been easy for him to learn a new strategy and new tactics; he had grown up in the 'God will provide' school of logistics under commanders who moved ponderously when they moved at all. By the time of Argaum, however, he had assimilated the ideas of his mentor about precise movement, efficient staff work and the importance of detail.

Stevenson had learned neither quickly nor painlessly; Wellesley's coaching was effective but not always pleasant. When Stevenson took counsel of his fears or allowed Mahratta *brindarries* to annoy him, he received prompt admonishment. But he persevered in the use of Wellesley's advice and found that it worked. On several occasions he became audacious and beat the enemy at their own game, but he did not go too far and bring on a battle when unsupported.[1] In fact, 'the colonel with great prudence and propriety halted'[2] so that the two armies could meet at Parterly at noon on the 29th.

Stevenson's movement towards Gawilghur – after he had equipped his army for the siege at Asseergurh – had brought on the battle at Argaum. He fought there propped up in the *howdah* of an elephant, but he fully deserved Wellesley's praise; he had definitely become what is quite rare in military history, a capable subordinate commander of a semi-independent army.

[1] After his heavy losses at Assaye, Wellesley was not so audacious himself. He wrote to Stevenson on 12 October 1803: 'I acknowledge that I should not like to see again such a loss as I sustained on the 23rd September, even if attended by such a gain. Therefore, I suggest to you what occurs to me on the subject of the different modes, either of bringing on, or declining an action.' *Dispatches*, II, 404.

[2] Wellesley's report on Argaum to the Governor-General, 30 November 1803, *Dispatches*, II, 557 and 558. He added later, with sincerity, 'I am much indebted to Colonel Stevenson for the advice and assistance I have received from him.'

XII

Gawilghur and the End
of the War

A resounding victory won at small cost solves many military problems. The war against the Mahrattas was going astonishingly well in Wellesley's immediate theatre of operations. After the battle on 29 November 1803 both British armies were in fine physical and mental condition. The enemy was still numerous, but Mahratta morale was low.

Elsewhere in India there was more good news. On 1 November General Lake won decisively at Laswaree in a battle comparable to Assaye in viciousness and in what it achieved. Perron was utterly defeated. As we have seen, Scindia had lost in Guzerat also; Baroch had fallen. Colonel John Murray of the King's 84th Foot had been engaged in a local conflict on behalf of the Gaikwar against a rival for the throne. Murray did better than expected and was able to consider an advance on Scindia's capital at Ougein.[1] Lieutenant-Colonel G. W. R. Harcourt of the King's 12th Foot had conquered Berar's entire province of Cuttack with a force of no more than 3,000.[2] This campaign was complicated by weather and terrain, but it did not involve a great deal of fighting. For the first time British controlled territory extended along the coast from Madras to Calcutta. The Mahratta Confederacy no longer touched on the Bay of Bengal.

[1] Wellesley wrote to Murray often about this small-scale campaign against Canojee and in connection with Murray's possible contribution to the larger conflict against Scindia. On 1 December 1803 he wrote, 'You will be so kind as to make all your preparations for moving forward upon Ougein . . . [when I send you orders]': *Dispatches*, II, 560.

[2] The Cuttack advance was at first under Lieutenant-Colonel Alexander Campbell who had been detached from the King's 74th for some time. Harcourt had been the Governor-General's military secretary until he took over because of Campbell's illness. Wellesley was theoretically in charge of this campaign, but the Marquess directed most of it himself: *House of Commons Account*, 190–1, 243–5.

The two British armies that had won at Argaum moved by easy stages carrying their wounded towards Ellichpoor. On 3 December Wellesley camped only fifteen miles south of Gawilghur and reported to Stuart in Madras that from the plain 'It does not appear to be as strong as many hill forts in Mysore taken by our troops.'[1] Even nowadays the resemblance to Nundydroog is remarkable when Gawilghur is observed from the south, though Gawilghur is much larger. The fortress town was thought to contain Berar's treasure and some of his family. He also used it as a kind of fortified hot-weather retreat.[2] But British armies in India usually had less trouble taking hill forts of all types than one would expect from looking at the places.

A hospital was established at Ellichpoor. Wellesley then apparently approached to within two miles of Gawilghur from the south south-east during a personal reconnaissance. The principal problem in attacking the fortress was one of getting close to it.

The approaches from the south consisted of two 'roads' leading to the fortress from the valley below. The easterly approach was so difficult that it would not even accommodate bullocks. It is still in use, but one must climb, not walk. The westerly road was narrow and steep, but moderately loaded carriage bullocks could go up. It was scarped on both sides at the top, however, and had the final disadvantage of passing for half a mile within point-blank range of the guns on the west wall of the Inner Fort.

If the fortress-town had been as inaccessible on all sides as it was from the south, the place might have been impregnable. Unfortunately for Berar's garrison, the two rocky hills on which the fortress had been built were connected on the north by a narrow tongue of land to a whole low range of flattened mountains of similar elevation (about 3,600 feet) which extended east and west for many miles. Since the place could not be taken from the south, it had to be besieged from the north. At Ellichpoor, which was part of Hyderabad and in possession of the Nizam's *killadar*, Wellesley learnt that the main approach to Gawilghur was from the north and lay along the narrow tongue of land.

The information available at Ellichpoor was meagre perhaps because Gawilghur, though only thirteen miles away as the crow flies,

---

[1] *Dispatches*, II, 565.
[2] The present small town of Chikalda just to the north is still a summer resort of sorts. There is usually a breeze and the altitude gives some relief from the heat, especially at night.

was in another country and much further by the only practical route which led through hilly jungle – a glorified path not wide enough for any wheeled vehicle. On the other hand, the jungle was not as impenetrable as that in India 'below the ghauts'. Madras pioneers with strong working parties from the infantry should be able to help the bullocks and elephants pull and push the artillery up the hills and then west along the more or less flat crests. The total distance was about twenty miles.

Wellesley began his operations from Ellichpoor on 6 December 1803. He sent Chalmers and the 1/2 Madras from his own army to clear Deogaum and the valley four miles south of Gawilghur. From Stevenson's army he sent Captain Alexander Maitland with the 1/6 Madras and two companies of the King's 94th 'to seize the fortified village of Damergaum which covers the entrance to the mountains'.[1] Both these detachments succeeded in their missions, although Mahratta strength in the area was considerable. By this time Gawilghur was known to contain not only its normal garrison, but most of the survivors of Manoo Bappoo's regular infantry. Enemy patrols were active in the foothills, so ample guards would have to be left at Ellichpoor for the hospital.

The two British armies moved out of Ellichpoor at sunrise on the 7th. Wellesley advanced only as far as the village of Deogaum, nine miles from his starting place and in a direct line between Ellichpoor and Gawilghur. A standard camp was established near the village. Stevenson's army, temporarily reinforced by two of Wellesley's iron 12-pounders and artillery and engineer personnel, had a much more difficult assignment. The troops began to climb the Gawilghur hills at Damergaum and continued into rugged country. They had to cut out trees and build roads with earth and rock, at one point filling in a chasm to save miles of additional road. After four days of exhausting work Stevenson's army complete with its battering artillery and ammunition reached the village of Lobada on the ridge level with Gawilghur.

From this side the fortress was not so awe-inspiring. Although it was built on the summits of two hills with deep and precipitous slopes almost all round, a corridor about 400 yards broad led from the hills to the northern wall. The tongue of land was not open to the wall; two-thirds of it was protected by a tank or artificial lake nearly full of

---

[1] *Dispatches*, II, 584. Also *Thorn*, 304. After considerable research in the area, I am not quite sure what this means. The modern road is good here and appears to follow the old route, but there are other ways of getting up into the hills.

water. There remained, however, a ribbon of meadow about 120 yards wide which led up to the double northern wall with an extremely complicated entrance system.

Wellesley was at Lobada on the evening of 10 December because Stevenson's health had not improved. For the next five days he was to divide his time almost evenly between the two armies. This involved a ride of just over twelve miles from Deogaum to Lobada over the rough new road, but he could probably cover the distance in about an hour and a half.[1]

During the night of the 11th a breaching battery was begun on the crest of a small rise overlooking the tank[2] only 250 yards from the outermost wall. Fire was opened on the morning of the 12th from two 18-pounders and three iron 12-pounders. There was an enfilading battery of less powerful pieces – two such batteries later on – set further back and to the east to keep enemy personnel from repairing the walls or retrenching the breach.[3]

The weather of India is hard on masonry. The stone used originally at Gawilghur was probably a by-product of scarping the hilltops on which the place was built, and was not good building stone. As at Ahmednuggur, the old solid-masonry walls appeared stronger than they actually were; 12-pounder and 18-pounder shot travelling at more than 1,200 feet per second caused extreme damage after a few hours. Almost every round brought down chunks of masonry. There were to be three breaches in all, a wide one in the lower wall and two in the upper structure.[4]

The fortifications of Gawilghur still are quite complicated. They were built to fit the terrain rather than according to any regular plan. Gawilghur had, therefore, a weakness common to all fortresses of India design; it had little or no means of delivering flanking fire. The outer defences extended for more than six miles and varied in strength in accordance with the designers' estimates of the inaccessibility to an enemy. In March 1968, for instance, I found one stretch of nearly a

---

[1] The distance has been given as considerably more, and the route made out to be more difficult than it was. Wellesley did not have to go through Ellichpoor; his camp at Deogaum may have been chosen partly because of this, although the position also covered the hospital.

[2] The site is still obvious although time has destroyed all traces of the works.

[3] Two brass 12-pounder field guns were used in the first battery together with two 5½-inch howitzers. The second had two brass 12-pounders only.

[4] *Elphinstone*, 100. His description tallies closely with what one sees today. The place has never been completely repaired.

mile on the north-east side of the Inner Fort where I could see no trace of any fortifications. In 1803 there might have been a palisade or a trench of some sort, but nothing substantial since the slopes below were unclimbable from a military point of view. Such gaps in the fortifications did not constitute a physical weakness and did not contribute to the ultimate fall of Gawilghur. But they may have undermined the morale of the defenders.

The enemy had more than fifty pieces of artillery on the walls and in cavaliers, concentrated where targets were likely to appear. Some of the guns were large. One is still there, an enormous wrought-iron gun mounted on a small mamelon on the north side of the Inner Fort which could fire through nearly 180 degrees at any target that appeared on, or south of, the crest to the north.[1] Another similar piece was mounted so as to fire into the valley to the south; its balls were said to carry for a distance of several miles, but accuracy would have been poor and a single plunging ball would have been most ineffective.[2]

Stevenson's army had only an imperfect knowledge of Gawilghur's internal design. No accurate plan or sketch was available. The British did not understand the communications between the smaller, but slightly higher, Outer Fort on the north-western hill and the Inner Fort on the larger south-eastern hill which was unapproachable except by way of the Outer Fort. The two flat peaks were separated by an irregular ravine up to 300 feet deep, but it could not be clearly seen from any accessible point to the north.[3] In addition to fortifications the Inner Fort contained a number of tanks and many solid buildings. It was at that time a considerable town.

In December 1803 Gawilghur had a garrison of 2,000–4,000 men under a Punjabi *killadar*, whose name may have been Beny Singh, and a civilian population of about 15,000–30,000. After Argaum Manoo

---

[1] This piece, which lies on the ground – its carriage has long since rotted away – is twenty-two feet long and probably weighs about eighty tons, but has a comparatively small bore, 12¼ inches. It is too big to be carried away for scrap and has not been damaged seriously by the weather over all these years. *Blackiston*, I, 213, says these pieces were 'the dread of the surrounding country for at least 20 miles'. This range is, of course, an exaggeration.

[2] *Elphinstone*, 100, points out, however, that a 'gun that enfiladed the battery killed four men and wounded two' on the morning of the 15th with one shot. The surviving piece is in the right place to have done this.

[3] The central ravine at Gawilghur is obvious today, but not the fortifications (if any) that closed its northern end. In spite of semi-contemporary plans which indicate the contrary, I believe these defences were temporary only, if in fact they existed at all. The 'third wall' referred to by several participants in the siege was apparently the north-west section of the Inner Fort.

Bappoo and some 4,000–6,000 of his regular infantry came in, accompanied undoubtedly by camp followers who in Mahratta armies were often semi-armed.[1] Gawilghur was naturally strong, well fortified by Indian standards and amply garrisoned. Weapons, ammunition and military equipment were plentiful. The tanks were still reasonably full in spite of the poor monsoon and there was plenty of grain.

Throughout history, however, sieges have depended more on skill and morale than on walls and weapons. Wellesley's engineers were well trained and veterans of similar operations in India. They had skilled pioneers to do their work. The gunners knew how to hit where their shot would be most effective and how to maintain their pieces in action efficiently.[2] The assault would be led by active and courageous British officers who were exceptionally capable with their personal weapons.

By contrast, the Mahratta leaders had little knowledge or skill in the defence of their fortress. They did not try to prevent Stevenson's army from approaching the 'isthmus' which was the only effective breaching ground. They made no effort to protect the wall with an earthen glacis or any form of outwork. They did not fire during the night of the 11th at the place where the main battery had to be located.

We should look briefly at what had occurred south of Gawilghur. Between 6 and 8 December Wellesley had driven in all the Mahratta pickets, but he did not endeavour to invest the enormous fortress. He kept the bulk of his troops in camp at Deogaum four miles away, though he had a forward concentration post in the small village of Baury at the junction of 'roads' from the south and the north-west gates. British patrols pushed north on both tracks to within a musket shot of the walls. The difficult eastern route to the south gate of the Inner Fort was the only one that could possibly be used to get artillery within range of the fortifications. The other road was better in that it could accommodate draft animals, but was commanded by fire from the guns on the walls of the Inner Fort.

EIC engineers had much experience in moving guns over impossible

---

[1] No one can say precisely how many Mahratta soldiers were in Gawilghur. *Fortescue*, V, 44, suggests 4,000. I believe this figure to be too low: *Blackiston*, I, 232, gives 'about 8,000'. There is also confusion as to the *killadar*'s name and even as to whether Manoo Bappoo was in command of the regular infantry.

[2] *Blackiston*, 221; 'Our batteries continued to play as rapidly as safety would permit; for under a hot sun the guns must be left to cool [between shots. If not they] become so heated as to occasion the cartridge to explode.' Another result of too rapid firing was excessive erosion of touch-holes.

terrain mainly by manpower. They attempted to get Wellesley's two remaining iron 12-pounders up the eastern route on the night of the 11th. The Indian and, perhaps, European pioneers were reinforced by working parties of muscular Scots from the 74th and 78th regiments. If the task was humanly possible, these men would accomplish it.

Early in the evening engineers, pioneers, artillerymen and working parties began their efforts. We should remember that they had to do their work without artificial illumination, and there was no possibility of dragging the pieces up complete with their carriages – the wheels would not roll over the small steep cliffs. Stripping the carriages was no problem, but each gun, in modern terminology the tube only, became a nine-foot fiend weighing 4,100 pounds (32 cwt) able to crush men with the smallest slip or roll. There was no way to secure tackle above, not even room for a team to pull from a distance. Elephants, which normally were used in all difficult gun movements, could not negotiate the terrain.

The job simply could not be done; the route was too steep and too uneven. After ten hours' labour, the men buried the pieces under debris and retired as dawn was coming. On the night of the 12th they did manage to get forward two brass 12-pounders and two 5·5-inch howitzers, much lighter pieces, which they mounted in a battery within 400 yards of the south gateway, but about 450 feet below it. The brass 12-pounders had to fire at an elevation of almost thirty degrees and did no serious damage. Their shot are said to have rebounded back to the guns themselves and perhaps into the valley below. The battery was more like a sheepfold than a normal emplacement.[1]

Stevenson's battering pieces did far better on the northern side. They opened on the 12th, and by the morning of the 14th the breaches were thought practical: an armed man could climb into the fortress. Wellesley had a close look with a telescope and decided on an assault the next day. Stevenson was in no better health, so Wellesley continued to direct both armies, giving verbal orders and discussing all pertinent details with Stevenson's corps commanders. He confirmed his instructions in writing later that day from his camp at Deogaum.[2]

Wellesley knew from his own inspection that Stevenson's breaches

<hr/>

[1] *Elphinstone*, 98. I climbed up and down this route in 1968. Getting even two brass 12-pounders into position from the valley below was a notable achievement. According to Adye's *The Bombardier and Pocket Gunner*, 154, such pieces had a tube weight of at least 1,150 pounds.

[2] *Supplementary Despatches*, IV, 298. Wellesley's instructions were in the form of General Orders and were dated 15 December 1803, but would have been written the day before.

into Gawilghur were moderately difficult; if the garrison worked hard at repairing the defences on the night of the 14th, they might be unnegotiable the next morning. A skilful fortress commander would surely do this and perhaps place mines and other obstacles in the way of the assault. To discourage such measures, however, a large gun loaded with grape was discharged at the breaches every twenty minutes throughout the night.

A dawn assault had some advantage, but not enough to outweigh a few hours' additional battering if it should be found necessary. Wellesley also wanted the enemy inside Gawilghur to see his two powerful British forces approaching from the south. The assault was set for 10 a.m.

Wellesley's attack from the south had no hope of taking the place, but some of the Mahrattas inside had surely heard of the British escalade of the *pettah* at Ahmednuggur. Wellesley was still relying on audacity. If the Mahrattas had fought skilfully and courageously, Gawilghur could hardly have been taken at all, at least not on the 15th. But the image of British invincibility was already established. Even Hindoos who did not place such a high value on their lives as Europeans could fight effectively only in an atmosphere of some hope.

Stevenson's attack through the northern breaches was to be led by Lieutenant-Colonel William Kenny of the 1/11 Madras with the grenadier company and two battalion companies of the King's 94th and the flank companies of three EIC battalions – his own, the 2/11 and the 2/7 Madras. There were also small units of pioneers and artillery, making a total of about 1,000 men in all.[1]

The force that would make the second assault through the breaches if the first should fail, or would follow into the Outer Fort if it succeeded, was commanded by Lieutenant-Colonel Peter C. Desse of the 2/2 Madras; he had the light and two more battalion companies of the King's 94th with the flank companies of the other three EIC battalions of Stevenson's army – the 2/2, the 1/6, and the 2/9 Madras. Desse also had pioneers and artillery for a total of about 1,000 fighting men.

Behind these two forces Major James Campbell of the King's 94th led the other four battalion companies of his corps, backed up by the battalion companies of the 2/7, the 1/11, and the 2/11 Madras under EIC Lieutenant-Colonel John Haliburton, who was senior to all officers except Stevenson in the army. We will hear more of Haliburton.

---

[1] *Wilson*, III, 119.

The assaults were to be pressed home regardless of cost; a total of about 4,600 first-quality fighting men were assembled in the four assault commands. Only EIC Lieutenant-Colonel H. Maclean with the other three EIC battalions less their flank companies was held in camp as a reserve.

Wellesley's two southern, essentially diversionary,[1] assaults were commanded by Wallace and Chalmers. Wallace was to take the steep route to the southernmost gate and had his own under-strength King's 74th, the right wing of the King's 78th, and the ever-reliable 1/8 Madras; Chalmers was to ascend by the less difficult, though far from easy, road which led round the west side to the Outer Fort and was commanded by heavy guns on the west wall of the Inner Fort. He had the left wing of the King's 78th and the 1/10 Madras.

Wallace and Chalmers began their movement on time, but the Mahratta *killadar* (Beny Singh?) apparently tried to negotiate for terms before the assault. Stevenson, in spite of his illness, was now at hand to take charge of such a situation. Nothing but surrender at discretion was acceptable and the Mahrattas were given only half an hour to decide. However, when the enemy was seen to be violating the truce[2] Stevenson ordered Kenny forward before the time had elapsed.

Stevenson's storming parties swept up the breach in the approved fashion of the time and apparently without serious difficulty.[3] The Scots, followed by the sepoy flankers, went into Gawilghur covered by a storm of grape from all three British batteries which lifted only as they began to climb into the line of fire. A few brave Mahrattas rushed forward to contest the narrow passages at the top, but with shock weapons only. No effort had been made to retrench, or to close the breach with gambions. There were many cannons and scores of wall-pieces, but none had been shifted to sweep the breaches. The greater physical strength and discipline of the Highlanders were too much for the enemy in the close confines of the breach itself and the passages which

---

[1] Wellesley instructed Wallace (*Supplementary Despatches*, IV, 296) 'to show his force so as to draw the attention of the enemy to this side of the fort'.

[2] *Blackiston*, I, 225. It would appear that the *killadar* and Manoo Bappoo did not agree on the truce. When the latter said the former was a coward, the negotiations were broken off.

[3] The best eyewitness account of the formal assault, complete with the forlorn hope and other trappings, was written by *Elphinstone*, 100-4. Elphinstone was a civilian, but served as Malcolm's replacement and Wellesley's secretary. He had charge of one of Wellesley's three intelligence 'departments' and fought at Assaye, Argaum and Gawilghur, but in civilian clothes. He was unusually faithful to his daily weapon practice and was probably good at it.

lay beyond it. Their bayonets and clubbed muskets quickly killed almost every man that ventured to oppose them. A single Mahratta is said to have fought on equal terms with the assaulters for a time, but he too was killed.

Kenny's party entered the Outer Fort with relatively minor casualties, but apparently then split up. Remember, no one in the British camp knew much about the lay-out of Gawilghur. One group which probably went through the right-hand upper breach moved slightly west of south pressing their enemies towards the gate Chalmers was approaching. This 'north-west' gate actually lay in the south wall of the Outer Fort. In an endeavour to escape from some of Kenny's men, the garrison opened this gate and ran head on into Chalmers and the left wing of the 78th. These unfortunate men had just escaped from Scots in trews and were faced with more in kilts. They were caught literally between two fires. Those who had already emerged from the gate were on a narrow scarped causeway blocked by red giants behind viciously gleaming bayonets. The Highlanders' blood was fired by the audacious ascent and the skirling pipes. The situation for the enemy, especially at the head of their narrow column, could hardly have been worse. Heavy bullets from Brown Bess muskets were ploughing into them, front and rear. The survivors had a choice between the bayonets and the jagged rocks below. This double-ended slaughter was soon over. Chalmers' column from the valley below entered the Outer Fort.

Kenny himself and some of his men probably used the left-hand upper breach, went straight south and then east of south towards the Inner Fort. They soon received the support of Desse's units which had cleared the breaches and moved in the same direction. For the first time the significance of the half-seen ravine between the two hills became apparent. The British columns had overwhelmed the Outer Fort, but they were as far from taking the larger and more powerful Inner Fort as on the day before. The most formidable defences in Gawilghur, the so-called 'third wall', lie south of the ravine. On this side the only entrance is through a series of five massive gates with long, steep and narrow angled passages between. The entire route was swept by fire from battlements along the top of each passage. This retreat route for the garrison in the Outer Fort was apparently prematurely closed which led to the slaughter at the 'north-west' gate.

The series of gates and passages from the Outer into the Inner Fort could probably have been forced by British infantry, perhaps with the aid of an artillery piece, but it would have been a long and costly fight. Fortunately, it was unnecessary. Kenny and Desse formed their twelve companies of sepoy flankers, or at least a major part of them, in line at the bottom of the ravine. They extended a distance of about 350 yards from east to west, filling most or all of the portion of the ravine between the Inner and Outer Forts. The sepoys were told to fire at any enemy heads appearing above the 'third wall' battlements. Kenny then led the three companies of Scots under his command at the succession of gates. He fell mortally wounded, but his units began to make some progress.

Meanwhile, there was another development. The 'third wall' along the north-west side of the Inner Fort is built along the top of a steep cliff. From the north-east – the only place from which much of it could be seen before the assault – this cliff seemed near impossible to climb. However, Captain Campbell[1] of the light company of the King's 94th had studied it and the wall above with a telescope, perhaps from well down in the chasm. He believed that it could be climbed and led his men up a route he had already chosen. They carried with them a single sturdy ladder, not more than fifteen feet long, and reached the base of the wall on the top of the cliff without being discovered. They were taking full advantage of the covering fire from Desse's sepoys. Kenny's assault on the series of gates and twisting passages undoubtedly occupied most of the garrison's attention.

Campbell was the first man up the ladder and leapt down inside, sword in hand, followed quickly by his men. For a few seconds the Scots had to fight for their lives. Again physical strength, discipline and courage was on their side. Once all eighty of them were inside, the local opposition lost heart. Campbell led his men east behind the battlements to the head of the line of passages and gates and started opening them one at a time from the top. There were several short, bloody clashes, but the Mahrattas were always over borne.

Ten minutes later Campbell and his men admitted the rest of the British force into the Inner Fort. All organized resistance collapsed soon thereafter. Elphinstone tells us that he and a small party, haphazardly collected, opened the southern gate so that Wallace's column could enter. The colours of Berar were replaced by those of the King's 78th for which an even higher spot was found.

---

[1] This Campbell should not be confused with Colin Campbell of the 78th's grenadier company who aided in the taking of the *pettah* at Ahmednuggur. I believe the Campbell of the 94th was Archibald, but there were six commissioned Campbells in this corps at the time.

Elphinstone gives, perhaps unintentionally, an interesting picture of Wellesley's own movements during the storm of Gawilghur. On the morning of the 15th, Stevenson asked the young civilian, 'Will you go down from the fort to the valley below, or ride round by Damergaum, to tell the General what happens?'

'Neither, Sir! We are going to meet inside.'

Wellesley was never again so far forward in action as at Sultanpetah Tope. He lost control of a whole situation there because he was leading in a physical sense, but he was not going to sit in his tent at Deogaum and wait for someone to bring him news of the assault on Gawilghur. He entered the Inner Fort with Wallace, probably between the right wing of the 78th and the 74th.

British casualties were light, a total of 126. The Mahrattas lost tragically. Wellesley was to write three weeks later that the loss of 'the enemy was immense. The *killadar*, all the principal officers, and the greater part of the garrison were killed.'[1] The *killadar* atoned somewhat for his military inefficiency by dying sword in hand. So did Manoo Bapoo who had aimed so high and failed so ignominiously at Argaum. The fighting at the breaches and both inside and outside the 'north-west' gate was excessively bloody. There were some other spots of extreme resistance which led to severe enemy casualties. Quarter was not normally given when fortresses were stormed in India; the danger was too great that prisoners taken would return to the fight.

Some historians have assumed that practically the entire garrison of Gawilghur perished because they could not escape. I disagree; the walls were never high nor was the descent into the ravine unmanageable. In my opinion an active man with a turban of tough material that could be used as a rope could leave Gawilghur at almost any point and get away safely. There still is, for instance, a way out from the extreme eastern corner where a middle-aged American can get out and back again even without a turban. I believe there were at least 8,000 fighting men inside Gawilghur, of whom more than half got away.

Gawilghur contained fifty-two cannon, including the big wrought-iron pieces already mentioned, and 150 smaller wall-pieces which apparently were ½-pounders.[2] The garrison had 2,000 new British Brown Bess muskets complete with bayonets, scabbards, belts and cartridge boxes. There were, of course, many other weapons, including matchlocks and bows and arrows, but Berar's entire regular infantry

[1] *Dispatches*, III, 8.   [2] *Thorn*, 307.

had modern arms, most of them made in Agra probably after the French pattern.

There had been rumours in the British camps that Gawilghur contained treasure of gold and silver coin, plate and jewels belonging to the Rajah of Berar. The treasure was not discovered, although the British found tons of copper coins together with some silver bowls and dishes worth less than 300,000 rupees in all. No other coins and no gold vessels were discovered, nor were any jewels captured for the public treasury, although individual soldiers undoubtedly did obtain some loot.[1] If the treasure ever had been kept in Gawilghur, and there seems to be little reason to doubt that some at least had been there, the Mahrattas got it out in time. The British armies neither tried nor could possibly have succeeded in surrounding the place. It is also possible that the treasure was hidden and recovered later. Gawilghur was too large for an efficient search.

British soldiers, particularly the Light Company of the King's 94th, performed superbly in the taking of Gawilghur. The routes from the valley below were extremely rough and steep. Had Chalmers not fortuitously found his gate open, the passages behind it appear defensible by boys with rocks. The same is true of the southern entrance to the Inner Fort.

Wellesley's own contribution was as much physical as mental. He directed both armies, which meant an average of at least thirty-five miles of riding each day, much of it over a bad new road. He made no mistakes in the siege and assaults, but the victory depended in about equal parts on the professional skills of his armies, especially the engineers and artillerymen, and on the dominance of the Scottish infantry already established on the plain of Argaum and in the rolling country between the Kaitna and the Juah. Wellesley was able to retain the initiative and keep pressure on the enemy. He won with a combination of military expertise, fighting efficiency and audacity.

A military victory again solved problems. The Rajah of Berar was now nearly defenceless and his capital at Nagpoor lay open to an advance from Ellichpoor only eighty miles north-east. For once, a Mahratta chief had no desire for diplomatic manœuvring. Berar

---

[1] Wellesley in several places records his satisfaction with the troops for not plundering. There was no long-sustained orgy as at Seringapatam, but the King's 94th was not blameless in this respect. *Blackiston*, I, 229–30, 'was told to get about my business for a meddling young rascal or they would put their bayonets into me; and that having entered the place by storm, the devil himself should not hinder them from having their right of plunder'.

wanted peace on any terms as quickly as possible. His *vakels* came the day after Gawilghur fell.

The Governor-General had given Wellesley command of all military forces and control of all British Residents in the Deccan; he had also granted him complete authority to negotiate with both Berar and Scindia. This appointment was of extreme consequence; Wellesley was authorized to deal with the two rulers not only over their territory in the Deccan, but in the rest of India as well. Nominally, Scindia had controlled territory far to the north around Delhi and Agra; Berar had ruled Cuttack (his littoral on the Bay of Bengal). Much of these areas had now been taken from them. In those days conquered territory was not often returned. But a peace treaty would have to state precisely each territorial gain for the EIC, the Peshwa and the Nizam, and every other condition in favour of the British and their allies. Wellesley was aware that the enemy was extremely capable at interpreting documents that were the least bit ambiguous in their interest. His military responsibility would cease with the restoring of peace, but the treaties he made might last for generations.

Few young professional soldiers have had such great political and diplomatic responsibility and none have handled it better. The Treaty of Deogaum was concluded with Berar three days after the fall of Gawilghur. The Rajah was to disband his army, to receive a British Resident, to give up all of Cuttack and to surrender to the EIC and its allies his domains to the west of the Werdah river. The treaty was extremely advantageous to the British administration in India, but left the State of Berar still in being. The Wellesleys did not want to destroy the old order completely, but just to mould it according to their own ideas. The Rajah would become a minor power within a few years, but his people would benefit from an imposed peace and what was likely to be a more comfortable and prosperous situation.

What appeared to be a simple, easily interpreted clause of the treaty gave rise to a problem. Wellesley had chosen the Werdah, a large and well defined stream, as a definite frontier between the territories of Hyderabad and Berar. As early as 24 October Wellesley wrote to the younger Kirkpatrick, who still was British Resident at Hyderabad, for a complete list of the Nizam's districts and villages, but none was furnished. However, he was told by the Nizam's chief representative in his camp, Rajah Mohiput Ram, that the Nizam had no territory east of the Werdah. After the treaty was signed, Wellesley discovered that the Nizam did in fact have three districts on that side of the river. Mohiput Ram had been disloyal to his master. On 9 January 1804 Wellesley wrote to the Governor-General, 'It is scarcely possible to believe that Rajah Mohiput Ram did not know that the Soubah of the Deccan had territories on the left bank of the Wurda, but he told me upon more than one occasion that he had none. But supposing him to have had a knowledge of the extent of his master's territories in that quarter, his conduct in deceiving me upon that subject is not more extraordinary than his having been the channel by which a present of five lacs of rupees was offered to me provided I would consent to make peace with the Rajah of Berar on condition of his ceding to the Company the province of Cuttack only.'[1] Treaty or no treaty, Wellesley had no intention of depriving the Nizam of territory that had been long in his possession, even though the new frontier became less workable.

Wellesley realized, of course, that a treaty signed by an Indian prince was valueless in itself. If Berar was not made to abide by the British interpretation of this instrument, he certainly would not do so. Stevenson was told to repair his gun carriages, return the men and material borrowed from Wellesley's army and return to Ellichpoor from Gawilghur by the route that he went up.[2] He was then to move east towards Nagpoor until Berar proved his sincerity, or at least complied because of his inability to do anything else.

Scindia was not personally involved in the siege and fall of Gawilghur. For reasons best known to himself he neither interfered with the British armies there nor tried to raid Poona or Hyderabad. Now he was even more anxious for peace than during the short-lived armistice before Argaum. Wellesley's victory at Argaum followed by the capture of Gawilghur put the British in as superior a position to Scindia as they were to Berar. The former had already lost heavily in Guzerat and might lose his capital to British forces operating from there. As we have seen, Murray was ready to march on Ougein on receipt of Wellesley's orders to do so.

By now Lake had defeated Perron completely. The area from south of Agra to north of Delhi was British; so was a considerable area to the south-east known as Bundelcund. With Berar and Perron defeated and Holkar neutral, Scindia was virtually helpless; British armies could

---

[1] *Dispatches*, II, 648.

[2] Captain Johnson of the Bombay Army, a capable engineer, said that the road leading down to the valley from the north-west gate was 'very bad and not practical for guns': *Dispatches*, II, 597.

attack his remaining territories in Hindostan from the south, west, east and north. Arthur could have dictated severe terms to Scindia, but the Wellesley policy was not to destroy Indian states, just to change them enough to make sure they fitted into their new concept of India. In many respects subsidiary treaties were better than extending the Company's direct control.

The treaty with Scindia was signed on 30 December 1803. He was to receive an EIC subsidiary force similar to those at Hyderabad and Poona. He was to give up a great deal of territory in the north, some in Guzerat and all his possessions south of the Godavery, including the magnificent fortress at Ahmednuggur, except for hereditary holdings of sentimental but small actual consequence. These were to be held for revenue only and not to be occupied by military units of any type.[1]

More humiliating, all disagreements between Scindia and the Nizam or the Peshwa were now to be arbitrated by the British. On the other hand, Wellesley refused to allow Mohiput Ram and his Hyderabad forces to keep some of Scindia's towns and villages taken after Assaye and Argaum which were not confirmed to the Nizam in the treaty. Scindia conceivably might be as good an ally in future as the new Nizam. The French officers in Scindia's Regular Battalions were eliminated – no foreigners unacceptable to the British were to be admitted to his territory.

At this time another political-military development was completed, the alliance between the British, the Peshwa and Amrut Rao. Amrut Rao joined Wellesley's armies with a considerable body of cavalry on 22 December. Negotiations had been going on for months. Amrut, the Peshwa's brother by adoption, had never completely gone over to Holkar. Whatever Amrut's intentions might have been, Wellesley's final rush for the Peshwa's capital in April had prevented him from burning the city. He had wanted to come over to the British since Wellesley's arrival at Poona. Loyalty to Bajee Rao was secondary to his desire to be on the winning side. Amrut Rao was abler than his adopted brother. Wellesley compared them in his dispatch to the Governor-General's secretary of 26 January 1804. Having complained of the Peshwa he continues, 'I do know that if I was to give the government over to Amrut Rao I should establish there a most able

[1] Territory lost in the north yielded an annual revenue of 15,000,000 rupees, in Baroach 100,000 rupees, and in the Deccan 70,000 rupees. (Ten rupees were then equal to a pound sterling.) This did not include, however, the territory ceded to the EIC for the support of Scindia's new Subsidiary Force: *Dispatches*, II, 624. *Roberts*, 31, says the EIC gained £3 million per year.

fellow, who, if he should prove treacherous, would be a worse thorn in the side of the British Government than the creature who is Peshwa at present can ever be.'[1]

British prestige in India had never been so high. Half a dozen armies had won quickly and decisively, sometimes against nearly impossible odds. The Governor-General's diplomacy had been extremely successful without sacrificing the reputation for fairness and honesty so coveted by all the Wellesleys. The change from the spring of 1798 to the beginning of 1804 is almost unbelievable. Shore had complied with his instructions from home and had allowed British prestige and power to decline. He refused to support his allies and quaked before potential enemies. The Wellesleys and their band of active young men had restored local dominance within the old British areas of influence around Calcutta, Madras and Bombay and carried the fight to their enemies. The French had been removed successively from Hyderabad, Mysore and the Mahratta countries. The Company's territory had been more than doubled. Hyderabad, Mysore and Baroda had become prosperous and happy allies. During the winter of 1803–4 Britain appeared to have no serious rival in India at all. The future seemed secure.

There was still some fighting to be done after Wellesley concluded his treaties, some of it because of them. When Mahratta armies were defeated as at Assaye and Argaum, massive desertions were usually one result. Further, under the new treaties both Scindia and Berar were required to disband their forces. Not all their men could return to peaceful pursuits as there were too many of them. Some had either to plunder or starve; they formed themselves into bandit groups around leaders who were able to direct their joint activities productively. Berar and Scindia both covertly encouraged these bands, especially in territory they had surrendered, but the British armies which had won against regular foes won against these irregulars with comparatively little trouble.

First in point of time, EIC Major-General Dugald Campbell, Wellesley's senior who commanded south of the Kistna only, pursued a new Dhoondiah Waugh who had appeared in his area and had a growing following. He was not, of course, the man whom Wellesley and his cavalry had finally caught and killed at Conaghul on 10 September 1800. The second Dhoondiah was really Mohamet Beg Khan,

---

[1] *Dispatches*, III, 19. Amrut Rao had not actually joined Wellesley by 29 November 1803, 'but he sent for orders as soon as he heard that I intended to attack the enemy' at Argaum: *Dispatches*, II, 559.

but he was trying to gain mystic strength from a name associated with the earlier leader.

Campbell began a rapid three-day pursuit on 28 December 1803 and caught the new King of Two Worlds on the 31st.[1] Mohamet Beg Khan and about 3,000 of his followers were killed. Campbell was using the organization, strategy and tactics already evolved by Wellesley in his pursuit of the original Dhoondiah Waugh. British armies in India would never again move like vast slow pastoral migrations as Cornwallis's and Harris's had done towards Seringapatam.

Early in 1804 Wellesley ordered Malcolm to procure from Scindia a letter disavowing one of his lieutenants, Mulwa Dada, who had started to operate in Scindia's name against territory belonging to Hyderabad, the EIC and the Peshwa. Once Wellesley had the letter, he informed Mulwa Dada 'that he is little better than a common thief' and threatened to hang him if he were captured.[2] The message appears to have been enough for Mulwa Dada; we hear no more of him.

The *killadar* who surrendered Ahmednuggur and then removed most of the valuable public property in his private baggage was of a different stamp. He continued to operate as a freebooter after the treaties; Wellesley pursued him twice without success. But accurate and recent information about the *killadar* reached Wellesley during the evening of 3 February while he was bringing his army back towards Poona. Wellesley selected a special force consisting of all cavalrymen whose horses were in good shape, the complete King's 74th, the whole 1/8 Madras (Wellesley's own), and 100 screened volunteers from each of the other five EIC battalions. There were also twelve guns, those attached to the complete units selected.[3]

This force began its march at 6 a.m. on 4 February and had covered eighteen miles by noon when they camped in accordance with Wellesley's usual marching procedure. The enemy was not alarmed by the movement. At 10 p.m. the special force recommenced the march and covered forty-two more miles in the next fourteen hours. They came up with the former *killadar* and his forces and utterly destroyed them.

These sixty miles were covered in a total of 30 hours, twenty hours

---

[1] Campbell had especial praise for the flank companies of Wellesley's own regiment, the King's 33rd, which was semi-active around Moodgul throughout the war: *Wilson*, III, 127.

[2] *Dispatches*, II, 632.

[3] *Fortescue*, V, 73, gives 'four guns', but I believe he did not include the eight cavalry gallopers.

of marching time.[1] Not a man dropped out. There were undoubtedly enough spare horses and bullocks to take care of any who fell lame. The physical condition and discipline of men and beasts must have been practically perfect. To march so far with a considerable proportion of the whole command infantry and then fight successfully, even against a disorganized enemy, is an almost incredible feat. It was a greater achievement than Wellesley's dash for Poona the year before, which was completed with cavalry only.

[1] Perhaps the infantry did not cover quite sixty miles. On 7 February 1804 Wellesley wrote to Malcolm, 'I think the infantry must have marched 60 miles'; *Supplementary Despatches*, IV, 342. Even the Duke was human; when he told Stanhope of this performance on 11 November 1831, the distance covered had improved with age to seventy-two miles: *Stanhope*, 16.

XIII

A New Mahratta Conflict

Early in 1804 British India had acquired territory and power undreamed of even a few months before. As recently as 1 July 1802 the Mahratta Confederacy had been larger in area and population than the EIC but now it was humbled. Subsidiary treaties had been negotiated with the Gaikwar and the Peshwa. Scindia, Berar and Perron had been utterly defeated in the field. Only Holkar remained. Militarily he was the most powerful of the Mahratta chiefs after 25 October 1802 when he personally commanded the army which defeated the combined forces of Scindia and the Peshwa outside Poona, but he had the good sense not to meet Wellesley in battle at or near Poona in April 1803. He retreated north instead and took no further active part in the campaigns of 1803.

Once war was declared in August, Scindia and Berar openly tried to get Holkar to join them against the British and the Peshwa appears secretly to have done the same. Holkar was suspicious of their intrigues and remained neutral throughout the year. On 5 January 1804, Wellesley wrote, 'Your conduct has been most wise and politic, and has been perfectly satisfactory to me. So long as you refrain from attacking the Honourable Company and their allies, the British Government will not interfere with you.'[1]

Early in 1804 Holkar appears to have realized that even though his territory and army were undamaged, his power would inevitably decline with peace and tranquillity. His soldiers served mainly for plunder which could not be obtained for long if most of the territories adjacent to his own were protected by British armies.[2] Even in

[1] *Dispatches*, II, 625.
[2] Wellesley wrote to Malcolm on 7 January 1804, *Dispatches*, II, 641, 'The consequence of tranquillity [for Holkar's] overgrown army, constituted as his is, must be its gradual dissolution.'

1803 he had raised money in the Nizam's territory by force and plundered Scindia's almost as if he himself had been an ally of the British.

Holkar was probably as much cleverer than his fellow chiefs as he was braver. Further, he had considerably more military ability. He grasped the significance of Pohlmann's defeat at Assaye by a smaller British force. The Mahratta infantry-artillery teams of the European type in which there were only a few European or half-caste officers and NCOs were valuable when Indian armies contended against each other, but they were not effective against the King's and EIC units. Mahratta armies would be more serious opponents for Wellesley and Lake if they used their old tactics of moving and fighting mainly with cavalry.[1]

Holkar drew an even more sensible conclusion late in 1803. He had seen at close range how Wellesley handled the 1803 war in the Deccan and wanted no part of him as an adversary. Holkar controlled territory from south of the Taptee to north of the Chumbul and could operate either in the north or in the south. He decided, however, that if he fought at all, it would be in Hindostan. So he went there and never returned south while Wellesley was in India.

Though Holkar remained friendly with Wellesley for the first months of 1804, he had his differences with Lake. The sheer necessity of finding new territory to plunder led Holkar across the boundaries between his own territory and that taken from Scindia by Lake, but not yet formally under EIC authority. An exchange of letters was found unsatisfactory by the British C-in-C who on 27 December 1803 began to move his recently victorious army fifty miles south-west from Agra. Holkar retired and claimed to have no warlike intentions.

Both the Governor-General and his brother did their best early in 1804 to keep Holkar in line, but it was probably impossible. The able Mahratta leader was obviously strengthening his alliances and military position. He was conciliatory in words only and decapitated three British officers in his service because they refused to fight against their countrymen.[2] Lake found him actively hostile in February and March.

Though Holkar had decided to fight in Hindostan against General Lake and not in the Deccan against Wellesley, he had territory in the

---

[1] Wellesley agreed with Holkar, *Supplementary Despatches*, IV, 588 and elsewhere.

[2] Captain Vickers, Dodd, and Ryan: *Thorn*, 326–7. Actually Thorn says 'Todd', but the alphabetical appendix in *Military Adventurers* lists 'Dodd'. He was probably the officer from the Bombay Army who murdered a goldsmith and absconded to avoid standing civil trial.

latter which would be subject to British attack if there was a war. As usual in India at that time, his holdings were neither contiguous nor precisely bounded. He had fortified bases at Chandore and Galna south of the Taptee and some other territory. Even more important, his capital at Indore lay open to attack from Baroda.[1] Holkar may have preferred Lake to Wellesley as an antagonist, but if he went to war at all he would be unable to prevent Wellesley from attacking both Chandore and Indore. He did not, however, weaken his northern forces to defend his territories in the south. In true Mahratta fashion, he sometimes claimed that he controlled only territory that lay 'within the shadow of his horse'.

In the spring of 1804 the Governor-General was negotiating with Holkar both directly and through Lake. Wellesley was hardly more than a distant spectator, although he received all information that either had to send him as soon as the communications of the day would allow.[2] His suspicion that Holkar was preparing to fight rather than to go into a slow decline was confirmed early in April by a letter directly from the prince. Holkar demanded certain provinces in the Deccan as the price of his not going to war. More interesting from a strategic point of view, he admitted to Wellesley that he could not oppose the British infantry-artillery teams on the battle-field, but that 'countries of many coos shall be overrun and plundered and burnt' and that General Lake 'shall not have leisure to breathe'.[3]

The Governor-General did not want another costly war. He deplored bloodshed because it was the opposite of his desires for India. But so often those who build run into opposition which can only be over-come by force. The Governor-General soon realized that Holkar had probably made up his mind and was delaying only to gain allies, and on 6 April 1804 Richard issued orders for hostilities to begin. This dispatch arrived at Lake's HQ in less than ten days, and on 18 April the C-in-C moved west towards Jeypoor and then south-west towards Holkar's vast army, though he made no firm contact with it.

Wellesley did not receive his orders of the same date until 7 May.

[1] A perplexing small problem is the association of Ougein, supposedly Scindia's capital, and Indore which had been Holkar's before it was plundered and burnt during their war in 1801. These two cities were interrelated and to some extent substitutable for each other: *Hamilton*, II, 8–10.

[2] Letters in India at this time were carried mainly by runners who (on a hopeful estimate) made about six miles an hour without intermission; this postal system was called *tappall* in some areas and *dawk* in others. The *hircarrahs* and camels of southern India were near twice as fast, but the system was apparently not practical in the north.

[3] *Thornton*, III, 423.

He was in Bombay at the time. Wallace was in command of his army near Aurungabad. Arthur was still in field command of the active components of the Bombay Army, especially the division under Murray in Gujerat. This consisted of two King's infantry regiments, the 65th and the 86th, and four EIC battalions at Cupperwungee, another EIC battalion at Baroda, and another of the same at Surat. Wellesley was already moving two more EIC battalions into Murray's area.[1] All units had their regular allotment of field artillery, but Murray had no British cavalry.

Wellesley ordered Murray to move east towards Indore and Ougein, but he could not be specific. His control of Murray was tenuous in the extreme since Cupperwungee was three hundred miles north of Bombay. Wellesley had never been into Gujerat.

War in the Deccan was going to be difficult. It was all very well for the Governor-General to order his brother to fight Holkar, but there were problems of where and how. Holkar had no field army even as far south as Ougein. Chandore and several dependent hill forts were roughly seventy to a hundred miles from Aurungabad. Under normal circumstances, these posts would have been easy to take. In 1803 Wellesley and Stevenson had demonstrated conclusively their ability to capture fortresses like Chandore with speed even when the enemy had two field armies in the area.

Unfortunately, circumstances were not normal. The previous year Wellesley and Stevenson had been able to move at will because both used *brinjarries* and protected EIC convoys to bring up the supplies they needed. The two armies, both horses and men, were fed on supplies brought forward by bullocks which lived on the forage growing in the territory through which they moved.

The monsoon of 1803 had failed more completely than any within living memory; as we know, the Godavery had been fordable in early September. The shortage of water, always the curse of India, meant famine. In Ahmednuggur alone fifty people a day were starving to death in spite of an EIC work programme.[2] Wellesley could cope with a scarcity of food for men and even horses. He had foreseen the shortage and bought up rice as far away as Mysore and Canara. Even though Governor Duncan of Bombay took back grain originally

---

[1] *Dispatches*, III, 236.

[2] The distress was made worse by the total absence of stores of food from previous seasons. For years, especially the last three, Mahratta armies had been moving around the northern Deccan seizing any food available.

purchased at Wellesley's request, there was no shortage of it from other sources; Wellesley's horses had been eating rice instead of gram for weeks. But the same conditions which brought famine to men also led to a scarcity of food for bullocks. There was no fodder for them in the area south of the Taptee. Wellesley's unique mobility finally depended on bullocks who in turn depended on the country for subsistence. If they could not live on the country, there was no mobility. Until the monsoon of 1804 brought forth grass the British armies in the Deccan were practically marooned where they were.[1]

At that time a partial breakdown in communications between the Marquess and his brother presented another problem. Both were extremely busy; the Governor-General was brilliant, but perhaps not as well organized as his brother. Richard certainly had a tendency to procrastinate, while Arthur seized opportunities 'to do the business of the day in the day'[2] as he said long afterwards. Richard was at best a poor correspondent, even with his superiors in London. One characteristic exchange between the brothers is well known. Richard: 'Why do you write to my secretary and not to me?' Arthur: 'Because it is probable that I will get an answer from your secretary!'[3]

In the spring of 1804, however, there was no humour in the situation. Wellesley wrote to Major Shawe, 'the time is now fast approaching, in which my ignorance of the Governor General's intentions and wishes, on many points, to which I have alluded in my letters to you and to him, since the beginning of January, will be very inconvenient; and I shall be much obliged to you if you will be so kind as to review those letters and let me have an answer.'[4] The most perplexing question was the subsidiary force for Scindia; only the Governor-General could decide on its composition and other details. So long as it was not assembled and assigned, Scindia would be a doubtful ally.

Wellesley's offensive planning for a war against Holkar depended on Scindia and his cavalry. Privately the Major-General wrote to the

---

[1] Wellesley discussed the whole situation in a letter to Malcolm of 20 April 1804, the first time in his *Dispatches* that he makes concrete mention of the conduct of a war against Holkar. He had Murray at Baroda 'fully prepared to move at an hour's notice' (*Dispatches*, III, 232), but he pointed out the difficulty of moving his own forces in the Deccan and the impossibility of going with them to the north.

[2] *Stanhope*, 70.

[3] This is, of course, a simplification, but the actual words are as severe: 'I have written to Major Shawe for two reasons: first, because it was probable I should get an answer from him; secondly, it was probable that his answer would contain intelligence of matters in Bengal which it was desirable that I should have': *Dispatches*, II, 700–1.

[4] *Dispatches*, III, 183.

lovable and capable John Malcolm, 'I should have no difficulty about a plan for the war, if I had an idea what the Governor General intended to do about a subsidiary force for Scindia.'[1] Murray had been ordered to move out from Guzerat with a strong army, including two King's infantry battalions, towards Ougein and Indore, but if neither the Gaikwar nor Scindia co-operated, the British army would have no cavalry.

Another problem was the rumour that Lake expected Wellesley to move his own army or Stevenson's – now under Lieutenant-Colonel John Haliburton, as Stevenson had gone home because of his health – across the Nerbudda. Lake wanted to stay in the north and have Wellesley attack from the south. A few weeks after the beginning of the monsoon such an attack would probably have been possible under Wellesley, though not under any other British commander who ever served in India. However, if either of the two British armies in the Deccan, or a substantial composite group from both, had left the territory which was still insecurely held by the Peshwa, the Nizam and the EIC under the recent new treaties, '50 little Holkars'[2] would immediately have come into being. The movement would have been entirely wrong in other ways as well. Wellesley's troops were from the Madras Presidency; they were still logistically and organically dependent on Madras through Mysore and Hyderabad. Lines of supply and command from Madras to Aurungabad, about 600 miles as the crow flies, were already stretched further than ever before. Wellesley would have had to extend them at least 400 miles over two great rivers and through hundreds of miles of the most anti-British territory in India. It would have created an unthinkable situation. Conjecture suggests another possibility: could Wellesley have left Wallace in command in the Deccan, gone to Baroda and taken over Murray's army? I believe that such a course of action would not have been practical; it may not even have been possible. Wellesley was on the Madras staff; Murray's troops were all Bombay or King's units. Wellesley's relations with Duncan and Nicholls were already strained. We should also remember that Wellesley was still responsible for Mysore, Malabar and Canara.

When Wellesley received the Governor-General's orders to act against Holkar, he immediately ordered Murray to move on Indore and Wallace to get ready to move on Chandore; he was planning personally to command Wallace's force. On 18 May he left Bombay

[1] *Dispatches*, III, 232.   [2] Wellesley to Stuart, *Dispatches*, III, 165.

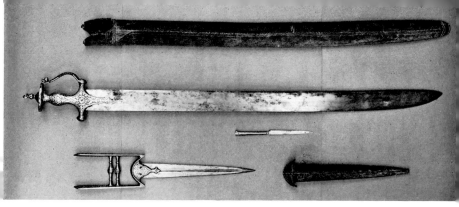

45 Tipoo's *tulwar*, dagger and knife. 46 Detail of firelock made for and used by Tipoo. 47-48 Details of a large EIC amusette or wall piece in the author's collection

49 Sir Arthur Wellesley and Diomed from an engraving after John Hoppner, 18

and on the 22nd joined his own army, but found that he could not move on Chandore until the following month.[1] There was not only a shortage of forage for the bullocks, but also of water for men and animals. Streams that normally had water in them either on the surface or just below it – which was reached by scooping out shallow wells by hand – were bone dry.

When June arrived, however, Wellesley decided against moving before the autumn. The rains were filling the streams, but the grass was weeks away. Chandore and the other hill forts were not worth any considerable sacrifice of fine Mysore draft bullocks. They represented a threat only if Holkar intended to use them as offensive bases. Intelligence from the north revealed that he had no such intentions, probably in part because of respect for Wellesley and his armies, but also because he too realized the famine conditions in the Deccan. Mahratta armies were dependent upon local supplies not only for animals but for men too.

For a while the new campaign against Holkar consisted only of a flow of dispatches that were often weeks out of date and increasingly full of bad news for the British. Then the situation changed radically. The Governor-General ordered his brother 'to break up his army' and come to Calcutta.[2] This meant returning the Bombay units to their own C-in-C. Wallace would continue to command Wellesley's Madras forces; Haliburton would remain in command of the Hyderabad subsidiary force which originally had been under Stevenson. If the two forces operated together, Wallace who was the senior lieutenant-colonel would take over the command.

On 24 June 1804, two days before the anniversary of his having assumed it, Wellesley gave up his commands in the Deccan. As he explained to Stuart on 20 June, he wanted to see him and the new Governor of Madras, Lord William Bentinck, before he saw the Governor-General.[3] He also wanted to talk with Purneah. The trip would not take a great deal longer by way of Seringapatam and Madras. He reached the former on 15 July and left again on the 19th. On the 26th he arrived at Fort St George and remained there until 2 August when he proceeded by sea to Fort William. The first com-

---

[1] Wellesley to Lake, 27 May 1804, *Dispatches*, III, 317.

[2] The Governor-General's order was dated 3 May 1804 and reached Wellesley on 19 June: *Dispatches*, III, 354–5.

[3] Bentinck arrived at Madras to replace Clive at the end of 1803. Wellesley wrote to both Stuart and Bentinck on 20 June 1804, *Dispatches*, III, 355 and 357.

munication from Calcutta to appear in either collection of his dispatches is dated the 14th, but he probably arrived two or three days
before.

Fort William, even then surrounded by the town of Calcutta, was
the control centre of British India. Arthur Wellesley was returning to
it for the first time since August 1799 when he left with the King's
33rd. At that time he had been a relatively unknown King's colonel
with a King's infantry battalion as his principal charge. During the
intervening six years his opportunities had been many and varied, but
he took full advantage of every one. He had worked out a system for
carrying out successfully many different tasks at the same time. He
was good at organizing and delegating, but kept all ultimate responsibility himself.

On his return to Bengal, Arthur Wellesley had a series of long
informal conferences with his brother Richard. They had not seen each
other for more than five years. Arthur certainly gave his brother
opinions based on his own observations in the Deccan and elsewhere.
He wrote memoranda on many different subjects. To a considerable
degree he became a part of the Government. One wonders, however,
why Richard brought Arthur about 2,000 miles to Calcutta. Some have
said that he needed Arthur's advice. The Governor-General had a high
regard for his brother's brain, his diplomatic ability, his military
competence and his common sense, but he was not the sort of man
who really needed advice or was unable to decide for himself. It seems
to me unlikely that Arthur was to be used only in an advisory capacity.

As early as 3 May 1804 the Governor-General had some reason to
be apprehensive about the conduct of the war against Holkar in the
north. Richard was no mean strategist. Perhaps his finest quality was his
ability to pick and chose subordinates. Lake and his primary subordinate, Lieutenant-Colonel the Hon. William Monson[1] of the
King's 76th, seemed less than ideal for operations against an army consisting predominantly of cavalry. They were certainly not as good a
team as Wellesley and Stevenson. The Governor-General may have
recalled the man whom history proved to be the most able military
commander in India at that time from an area where he could not be
particularly useful to within a few days' journey of where his military

---

[1] Unlike many King's officers in India, Monson had more than twenty years' experience
there. He came out in 1780 and commanded the light company of the King's 52nd at
Seringaptam in 1792. He was a fine combat leader, but in other ways had failed to impress
the Governor-General. He appears to have lacked the intellectual capability of most of
the Wellesley inner team.

capacity could have been employed to the highest advantage; it could have changed completely the achievements of the Wellesleys in India.

Richard already knew his brother's recommendations for a successful war against Holkar. Arthur had often suggested, 'If General Lake would only dash at him with his cavalry, it is my decided opinion that the war would not last a fortnight.'[1] He advocated for everyone, and used himself, a liberal measure of audacity backed up, of course, by sound logistics, organization and tactics. He had evolved his plan for this war through observation, study, actual experience in the field and common sense. He knew that Holkar was not going to rely primarily on European-type regular units as Perron and Scindia had done. He was committed by circumstances and his own deductions from the 1803 war to operate essentially like earlier Mahratta generals, to 'overrun, plunder, and burn'. His army numbered tens of thousands and had the mobility to accept or refuse a battle.

Wellesley put his finger on the principal weakness inherent in an army of this type. Whether it were defeated in battle or not, it could not withstand a fortnight of adversity and would go to pieces in retreat like the armies of Dhoondiah, Scindia and Berar. Men who came together for plunder would disband rather than suffer privation. Their morale fluctuated with their immediate prospects of stealing the property of others.

While Wellesley travelled from Bombay to Calcutta, south of Delhi, Lake and Monson were making a mess of things. Lake had gloriously defeated Perron because the Frenchman had been willing to fight battles, but Holkar would not follow this example. In late April and early May Lake tried to catch his enemy, but failed. He did not understand that he could win just as conclusively as in battle by resolutely driving Holkar south day after day.

On 8 May Lake stopped south of Tonga. His worst enemy was the climate. In this part of India the hottest season of the year was just before the monsoon. There were temperatures of 130 degrees Fahrenheit in the shade; European and even Indian soldiers died from the extreme heat and sometimes from lack of water. For a few days Lake supported Monson who was operating further south with five and a half EIC battalions and some irregular cavalry, but no European unit

---

[1] *Supplementary Dispatches*, IV, 397. The same day he forecast to Webbe, ibid., 395-6, 'If General Lake does not press upon him either with his own corps or some other, the affair will end in an insurrection in his own rear about Delhi, and our situation will become intricate'.

at all. Then the C-in-C with his main army retreated on Agra and Cawnpore largely because of heat and frustration; supplies may have been short, but there had been no real fighting.

Monson continued to move southward, not in pursuit of Holkar, but apparently to observe him. EIC Lieutenant-Colonel Patrick Don whose force now formed part of Monson's command, had captured Rampoora, Holkar's only stronghold above the Chumbul river. By the 28th Monson was south of the river at Kotah, roughly 200 miles from the nearest effective support. He moved nearly fifty miles further south through a steep, cramped pass and on 2 July took the fort of Hinglaisghur.[1] Then this small and poorly composed EIC army made another march to the south and stayed put for four days.

As we know, on 7 May Wellesley had ordered Murray to move forward from Cupperwungee and Baroda in the general direction of Ougein and Indore. Murray's force still included two King's infantry battalions, but no cavalry of importance; both Scindia and the Gaikwar had at the last moment failed to provide any. By 20 June the force was at Badnawar, less than three days' march from its objectives. Murray appears to have been a capable soldier, but his present mission could be carried out with complete success only by someone who also had diplomatic skill. He particularly needed to gain the confidence and co-operation of Scindia's brother, Bappojee Scindia, who commanded cavalry in this area. At the time Bappojee was favourably inclined to the British, but Murray appears to have failed to win him over.[2]

At Badnawar Murray heard that Holkar with his whole force was moving against him. He took counsel of his fears and moved west rather than east. He acquainted Monson with his decision – actually he only took up a strong position behind a bend in the river Myhie – but Monson construed the movement to be a retreat. Murray received other information the next day, reversed his march and on 8 July occupied Ougein.

At this time Murray and Monson were only seventy miles apart. Each was in command of a force too powerful to be attacked by

[1] 'An ancient and much-valued possession of Holkar's family': *Fortescue*, V, 80.

[2] Wellesley's dispatch to Murray written from outside Poona on 22 May 1804 (*Dispatches*, III, 298) explains the situation carefully and gives sound advice as well as indicating his own procedures. 'You have a great game in your hands, but all will depend upon your management of the Natives with whom you will have to co-operate. I have only to recommend to you to conciliate them as much as possible; to treat them with the greatest kindness and attention is the only mode of drawing from them any assistance. At the same time you must not lose sight of the fact that they are Mahrattas. No one of them can be implicitly trusted. Most probably, all are in correspondence with the enemy.'

Holkar's army which lay between them. Since he began his retreat from the north of the Chumbul, the Mahratta chief had lost tens of thousands of cavalrymen by desertion, though neither Murray nor Monson had made a bold or speedy move against him. Murray's intermittent advance had lacked confidence; Monson's force lacked power. The absence of even one European unit in the latter division appears inexcusable in the light of what British commanders already knew of war in India. We should note that, save in point of time, almost everything Arthur Wellesley prophesied had occurred. Two mediocre commanders had managed to reveal the essential weakness of Holkar's strategy; he had not been able to lay waste 'many coos' of territory friendly to the British because Murray and Monson had marched into his own heartland, forcing his armies to retreat before them. Two days of bold action would have brought the British commanders into contact with each other. Scindia's cavalry would have joined them with enthusiasm; Mahrattas always hastened to assist those who appeared to be winning.

Unfortunately Monson and Murray did not join forces. This time Monson took counsel of his fears. Brave as a lion in combat, he lacked a good commander's confidence when operating independently, not an unusual failing in military history. To do Monson justice, he was faced with many problems. He had only two days' food in camp, but in India this was not exceptional. He had learnt of what he considered to be Murray's retreat and believed that Holkar and his entire army were moving against him. He magnified out of all proportion the size and strength of what was left of Holkar's forces and considered his own weaknesses too seriously.

Instead of either maintaining a bold front or actually continuing to advance, on 8 July – the same day Murray took Ougein – Monson began a retreat to the north. His preparations were about as poor as can be imagined. He should have left a single well-disciplined EIC battalion as a rearguard and openly retreated in column; instead he tried to slip away under cover of an irregular cavalry screen.

Suddenly Holkar and his officers and men recovered their spirit. The British were retreating! Here was their chance. Holkar's entire cavalry army attacked and utterly destroyed Monson's rearguard save for some who changed sides. Remember, the rearguard was irregular cavalry, not EIC horse. Bappojee Scindia had finally joined Monson, but with only a token force. He brought with him news of the rearguard's defeat, and deserted to the enemy soon afterwards.

Nothing serious befell Monson's infantry and artillery until the 10th when they were passing through Mokundra Pass. About noon Holkar attacked, to some extent by surprise, from three different directions. Monson's EIC battalions behaved magnificently and beat back the Mahrattas in spite of cramped conditions. Monson continued his retreat northward and became desperate. He knew he was surrounded by Holkar's horde and feared being starved to death. On the 11th he went on in a driving rain, losing baggage and stragglers. When the Mahrattas attacked, however, the British sepoys beat them easily. Late on the 12th Monson arrived at Kotah; so far, the fighting ability of his command had suffered no serious damage except that he had lost all his cavalry.

Monson should have been safe at Kotah. Its Rajah was a British ally who had promised to give Monson logistic support. But such allies were quick to promise and slow to deliver food and other essential supplies. The situation was undoubtedly made worse by Monson's retreat; as already mentioned, Indian princes were likely to turn on any ally in trouble. Monson felt he had to continue his withdrawal because of the lack of food; he somehow crossed the Chumbul. One EIC battalion was cut off on the south side of the swollen stream, but turned on the Mahrattas who pressed them close and repulsed them with disciplined volleys and bayonets in spite of odds of twenty to one. Finally, this gallant EIC unit also got across, but without its guns.

Monson's troops went on over flooded roads with little food, surrounded night and day by Holkar's cavalry. They were forced to destroy the extra ammunition and on the 16th Monson abandoned his remaining artillery. He was now in country where a brook had become an unfordable torrent many yards wide. His force was demoralized to the point of complete disorganization when suddenly he decided to attack. He took a Mahratta camp on the 22nd and regained some respect. On the 23rd and 24th he crossed a flooded rivulet and on 27 July he arrived at Rampoora; there he found two fresh EIC battalions complete with artillery, some Indian cavalry under British officers, and some grain – all sent by Lake from Agra after he received the news of Monson's retreat. Rampoora was supposed to be the forward base of Lake's army, like Ahmednuggur in Wellesley's 1803 Deccan campaign. The only trouble was that Lake's field army was 300 miles away at Cawnpore.

Monson found Rampoora deficient in food and his efforts to collect reserve supplies were disappointing. Holkar's whole army, including infantry and artillery, was close at hand. Monson allowed himself to be semi-besieged for more than three weeks until on 21 August he continued his retreat. He was held up by another stream and on the 24th badly mismanaged a confusing fight on both sides of it. He was now fighting Holkar's artillery and infantry as well as his revitalized cavalry. Although Monson's sepoys continued to fight well, he lost his baggage and his wounded. Only able-bodied fighting men were able to get away in a hollow square with the enemy cavalry all round. On the evening of the 25th they arrived at Kooshalghur, a place of some strength and already in British hands.

But again Monson found himself surrounded. There was an even worse development: some of his Indian officers were found to be in communication with Holkar and two and a half companies actually deserted. The retreat continued and on the night of the 28th became a panic. Individuals, small parties and some fairly complete units reached Agra during the next two days, but all were in pitiable condition. 'By dawn of the 31st all the survivors had arrived. Twelve British officers had been killed, two more had been drowned, two more were missing, and five others had been wounded.' Monson had lost about half of his 'five and a half fine battalions through the sword, fatigue, and desertion. It was the heaviest blow that had fallen on the British in India since the destruction of Baillie's detachment.'[1]

Monson's retreat did irreparable harm. Holkar had not achieved any real military gains, but between 8 July and 31 August he had destroyed the image of British invincibility. Wellesley arrived in Calcutta in time to receive several interim reports of Monson's early troubles before news of the final disaster reached Fort William. One of his finest memoranda was devoted to this unfortunate campaign.[2]

All said and done, Monson failed because he advanced too far without proper logistic support and then lost his nerve. He was physically as brave as a man can be, but could not stand the strain of independent responsibility. He also lacked common sense.[3] Lake is not blameless. He was a gallant and effective battlefield commander, one of the best, but his qualifications as a strategist capable of properly evaluating

---

[1] *Fortescue*, V, 88.

[2] *Ward*, 44, wrote, 'For military historians the most instructive of his [Wellesley's] papers was an analysis of the faults committed by Monson in Malwa. Peel, who considered Wellington the most powerful writer in the English language, said it was the best military paper he had ever read.'

[3] Lake said of Monson, 'It really is somewhat extraordinary that a man brave as a lion should have no judgment': *Fortescue*, V, 105.

information may be questioned. His appraisal of the military situation was probably faulty in that he instinctively underrated an army like Holkar's because it would not meet him in battle. As C-in-C of all British India Lake made no effort to co-ordinate Monson's and Murray's forces. He appears to have been unable to see the larger picture and refused to accept responsibilities beyond his own army.[1] He was better at organizing and training than at logistics and best of all as a combat leader.

The Monson disaster went a long way towards changing the political situation throughout India. Basically, Richard Wellesley's government had been extremely successful because of an unbroken series of victories over Tipoo, Dhoondiah, Scindia, Berar and Perron. His diplomacy was brilliant because it was backed by strength. After Monson's retreat, however, all this changed. Bappojee Scindia had gone over to Holkar and Scindia himself became almost hostile. Even worse, the Jats under the Rajah of Bhurtpoor who had been securely allied to the British turned against them. British prestige fell out of all proportion to the size of this military fiasco.

Neither the Governor-General nor Lake tried to avoid personal responsibility by shifting the blame to Monson, although the Marquess probably had been apprehensive for months. He now had Arthur with him in Bengal and offered his brother's services to Lake. Understandably, Lake refused.[2] The Governor-General could not well override his decision in a military matter. The Baird episode was fresh in everyone's mind.

Lake had no intention of giving up his major battlefield command to a gifted junior. He was fully aware of the 'arrangements' made by Harris and Stuart to employ the Governor-General's brother in preference to his seniors. It would also appear probable that some of Arthur Wellesley's unflattering comments about Lake may have reached the C-in-C. Lake was not as self-sacrificing as Stuart; nor was he as convinced of Wellesley's military ability. He tactfully suggested that the younger general return to the Deccan with his old powers to act against Holkar from the south.

---

[1] He appears not to have answered Wellesley's communications on overall strategy: *Dispatches*, III, 315.

[2] Arthur Wellesley had anticipated this in his letter to Malcolm of 24 August 1804 (*Dispatches*, III, 443) when he wrote, 'You may depend upon it that the Commander-in-Chief will not allow me to undertake the settlement of affairs in Malwa [Holkar's country]; indeed it would be improper to propose such an arrangement to him, and unreasonable to expect that he would propose it himself.'

There was nothing the Governor-General could do but comply. On 9 November Wellesley was reinstated in all his central Indian authority, civil and military, subject only to the orders of Lake and Stuart. He immediately left Calcutta and on 21 November arrived in Madras. He continued to Seringapatam where he arrived before 1 December. However, he was held up for several days by a bout of fever. His illness appears to have caused him to think more about himself than he usually did. He had been in India for seven and a half years and was now past his thirty-fifth birthday. His health had been remarkably good for an Englishman in the East, but was finally showing the strain of maximum effort for months on end. At that time in India climate and disease killed one Briton out of two.[1]

When Arthur was better, there was good news from the north. Holkar had attached too much importance to Monson's retreat and had invaded northern Hindostan. He had been stopped at Delhi, however, by a magnificent defence under the Resident, EIC Lieutenant-Colonel D. Ochterlony. In spite of supply problems, Lake was in the field again with a new subordinate, King's Major-General John Henry Fraser who on 11 November won a battle at Deeg against Holkar's infantry and artillery, destroying them almost completely. On the 17th Lake himself surprised Holkar and his cavalry at Farruckabad. Holkar was not crushed, but he did suffer severe casualties and his prestige was badly hurt. India was beginning to forget Monson's retreat.

If Lake could defeat the Jats under the Rajah of Bhurtpoor, the turmoil in northern Hindostan brought about by Monson's misfortunes would be at an end. All that was necessary was to take two fortified cities, neither of which was considered as strong as Seringapatam or even Ahmednuggur. Deeg, where Holkar's infantry and artillery had already been defeated, was a relatively small place, though stronger than the large sprawling Bhurtpoor which was defended mostly by mud walls.

Wellesley remained in Seringapatam after his health improved. He appears to have had no intention of proceeding north unless there was something of importance for him to do there. In the last seven months he had covered 3,500 miles. The armies he and Stevenson had commanded in 1803, but now under Wallace and Haliburton,[2] had taken

---

[1] *Blackiston*, I, 23 wrote, 'Alas, of these my first companions [on the way out], above three fourths are [dead]'.

[2] The two officers were both lieutenant-colonels, Wallace being the senior, from 1 January 1798 to 24 July 1804. But Haliburton of the EIC was promoted on the latter date to full colonel. Wellesley tried to procure promotion for Wallace from Lake, but failed

all Holkar's forts south of the Taptee with only minor bloodshed. Chandore had fallen on 12 October.[1] Murray was far to the north, beyond the effective control even of Bombay.

Closer to Seringapatam, things were not as satisfactory as they had been. John Montresor had resigned his commission and died soon after he went to Prince of Wales's Island[2] for his health. Sir John Cradock had taken Stuart's place and wrote like a general officer who had just come out, which of course he was. In Madras Lord William Bentinck was not as effective a Governor as Clive had become.

[1] There is a good account of this minor campaign, including the capture of both Chandore and Galna, in *Welsh*, I, 212-34.

[2] Also known as Penang.

---

because of a technicality: *Dispatches*, III, 551-2. Wallace, a King's officer, served under an EIC officer who had been his junior until Haliburton's death in July 1805. I cannot help remarking that the same situation in reverse was more common and not so likely to have caused Wellesley to exert himself.

XIV

The Wellesleys Leave India

Arthur Wellesley worked harder in 1804 than in 1803 and achieved less. His dispatches record many problems great and small; he handled them with care, common sense and ever-growing ability. But the opportunities for dramatic service to Britain and the EIC that so closely follow one another in the earlier years passed him by. The restoration of the Peshwa and the victories of Assaye, Argaum and Gawilghur were followed only by an endless succession of dispatches and memoranda. His two brilliant treaties of 1803 were not even being carried out as he would have liked.

In 1804 Wellesley's commands were healthy, disciplined, militarily efficient and secure over an area about a third the size of western Europe, but there was no severe fighting. In May he sent Murray into Malwa with ample strength and general instructions to ensure Holkar's ultimate defeat, but the Mahratta chief had chosen to do the serious fighting in another area. As we have seen, Chandore and subordinate territory had been taken from him in October by Wallace and Haliburton who encountered a minimum of resistance.

There had been actual disappointments as well, like the largely unproductive 3,500-mile trip north. Lake had preferred to fight his own battles and direct his campaigns according to his own ideas without the services of a man so outspoken, efficient and acquisitive of responsibility. Even brilliant memoranda are poor substitutes for field command; a victory in battle may be the most rewarding of all human achievements.

As we have seen, Wellesley's health was beginning to fail. Seven years was enough. On 8 June 1804 he had written, 'I have served as long in India as any man ought who can serve anywhere else.'[1] He may have been only momentarily despondent, but since then things had built up. All three brothers had ample reasons not to be pleased with their recent treatment by the Government in London and the EIC.

On 4 January 1805 Arthur wrote to Richard's secretary, 'In regard to staying longer, the question is exactly whether the Court of Directors or the King's Ministers have any claim upon me strong enough to induce me to do anything so disagreeable to my feelings (leaving health out of the question) as to remain in this country.'[2]

By then it was known in India that Harris had been severely criticized by the Duke of York for employing Wellesley instead of Baird. The Court of Directors had given three subordinate officers the same reward Wellesley received for the elimination of Dhoondiah. The crowning insult from London, however, was that Stuart's appointment of Wellesley to the Staff in Madras had never been confirmed. When Major-General Smith arrived in India with such an appointment, the victor of Assaye would have been ousted by somebody virtually unknown. It was avoided only because General Fraser was mortally wounded at the victory of Deeg.

It was time for Wellesley to return home. The British victories in the north, especially Lake's at Farruckabad, made it possible. Malcolm – dear, able, muscular, good-humoured Malcolm, the sincere and close friend of all the brothers – agreed.[3] Arthur wrote to his agents at Madras to secure him a passage; in the days of sailing ships and prevailing winds he would have to leave by mid-March if he was not to waste many months on the way. All this was done as if he were a civil servant of small consequence going home on leave.

India did not let him get away so easily. The victor of Assaye received many testimonials and tokens of appreciation from those who knew best what he had achieved during his last months in India. His Deccan officers, having originally planned to present him with a gold vase worth 2,000 guineas, gave him a magnificent silver service

[1] *Dispatches*, III, 339.
[2] *Dispatches*, III, 593.
[3] 'I mistrust the judgment of every man in a case in which his own wishes are concerned. I have not come to this determination without consulting Malcolm who agrees with me.' *Dispatches*, III, 642. In the same communication he alludes also to a strong reason for his reaching England as soon as possible, to defend Richard against his enemies in the Government and outside it.

of the same value.[1] From the 124 British civilians in Calcutta he received a sword worth 1,000 pounds. The message which accompanied the sword was particularly appropriate, because it stressed not only military, but also concurrent political achievement. There were testimonials from the officers of the King's 33rd, the officers in Seringapatam and others.[2]

Perhaps even more gratifying to his feelings, the people of Seringapatam had told him simply, of their appreciation of his fairness, rectitude and efficiency: 'We the native inhabitants of Seringapatam have reposed for five auspicious years under the shadow of your protection. May you long continue personally to dispense to us that full stream of security and happiness which we first received with wonder and continue to enjoy with gratitude; and, when greater affairs shall call you from us, may the God of all castes and all nations deign to hear with favour our humble and constant prayers for your health, your glory, and your happiness.'[3]

He wound up his own affairs, packing up personal possessions, the accumulations of years, including his papers. He made provision for Salabuth Khan, Dhoondiah Waugh's son,[4] who had lived with him at the Dowlut Baugh. He went to Mysore City which was now flourishing and saw Purneah for the last time. When he rode back he passed the Sultanpetah Tope and the scenes of the great siege. He took his leave of Malcolm, Barclay and the others, as well as of familiar, loved places. Tipoo's garden palace had been the only home he had ever had.

On 9 February 1805 Wellesley began his last journey along the familiar road from Seringapatam to Madras. He went the same way he had come in 1799. The camp sites were still recognizable; the towns of Malavelley, Ryacotta, Amboor, Vellore and Arcot were the same, but

[1] The 'Assaye Plate', now on public display at Apsley House. This silver service is so definitely 'British India', and to my way of thinking the finest thing of its type ever produced.

[2] Wellesley replied to all. A sentence written on 2 March 1805 (*Supplementary Despatches*, IV, 501) to the officers of the 33rd expresses so much of his personality. 'I have only to recommend to you to adhere to the system of discipline, subordination, and interior economy which you have found established in the regiment, and, above all, to cherish and encourage among yourselves the spirit of gentlemen and of soldiers.'

[3] These people spoke out first on 16 July 1804, when Wellesley was first seriously considering going home: *Dispatches*, III, 419–20.

[4] Wellesley had adopted the boy after destroying his father. He deposited with the 'Magistrate at Seringapatam a sufficient sum for his education and maintenance'. The amount was 1,000 star pagodas: *Supplementary Despatches*, IV, 500. He also asked Purneah to see to his advancement: *Dispatches*, III, 663. The boy got on well as a youth, but was carried off by cholera in 1822: *Dispatches*, I, 219.

Wellesley himself was changed. Six years of almost unceasing activity had led to extraordinary self-development and to achievements beyond his fondest dreams, but now he was tired and unwell.

For three weeks he remained in Madras attending to unfinished business, much of it writing letters. There were celebrations that he can hardly have found welcome in his present condition. During this time he received notification of his appointment (on 1 September 1804) to the Order of the Bath, a considerably greater honour than after 1815 when it was expanded from twenty-four members into three classes with the first alone comprising seventy-two. The insignia was 'kicking about the *Lord Keith* which arrived ten days ago and discovered by a passenger looking for his own baggage'.[1] Sir Arthur sailed aboard the *Trident*, a vessel of the Royal Navy, at the special invitation of Admiral Rainier who was returning to England for the first time since 1794.[2]

The time at sea was astonishingly restorative to Wellesley's physical and mental state. The passage was no slower than usual – three and a half months from Madras to St Helena – and it made a new man of him. He still had memoranda to write, but nothing pressing. He had freedom at last from the responsibilities and the chores of command. The insects and the stench of India were gone. Clean fresh sea air, hard exercise, stinging cold salt water and simple food did the rest. He was still a young man: he celebrated his thirty-sixth birthday aboard ship. Once he got the malaria out of his blood and adjusted his system to only a normal load of daily problems, he would be fully recovered.

There was bad news at St Helena. His old and dear friend James Stevenson had died on the way home.[3] A flood of memories, both personal and military, must have come back. The finest was probably of the old cavalryman, mounted on an elephant, arriving at Argaum precisely on time. Wellesley was to win many complicated campaigns in the future, but would have only one other subordinate whom he could trust so completely and so safely. James Stevenson and Rowland Hill were each pre-eminent in their respective areas.

[1] *Supplementary Despatches*, IV, 496.

[2] He paid the customary and considerable forfeit to the captain of the East Indiaman for the accommodations reserved for him, but not used. He may have sent a lot of his possessions home in this vessel; the *Trident* would not have had room for them.

[3] Stevenson was promoted to major-general on 1 January 1805, but probably never knew about it. His widow, a young woman of considerable attractiveness, received 'a pension of 300 pounds a year'; *Supplementary Despatches*, IV, 512.

There was bad news of a different type from London. The political items were mostly unfavourable to him and his brothers. Richard had been superseded as Governor-General by the Marquess Cornwallis, a man far past his prime, but well known for his conservatism. Pitt, the Wellesleys' friend, had returned to power on 10 May 1804, but in declining health. He was unable to protect Dundas (now Lord Melville) or Richard. A new coalition with Russia, Austria and Prussia against Bonaparte was being attempted, but would it work better than the others?

Arthur's personal resiliency had obviously returned by the time he was ready to leave St Helena. He was already considering 'serving the public' in Europe; his ambitions may well have been returning. A letter to Malcolm, now actually Resident in Mysore, gives an indication, however, that his thoughts were not all in the future. 'Remember me most kindly to Purneah and Bisnapah and all my friends, black, white, and grey. . . . God bless you, my dear Malcolm.'[1] Perhaps the still rather junior major-general was a little homesick for India, the place he knew best.

A few words are in order about Henry Wellesley. He was the youngest of the five Wellesley brothers who survived into adolescence and the least spectacular of three who came early to public life. But being third to Richard and Arthur is hardly an indication of mediocrity. As we know, Henry came out as Richard's secretary in 1797–98. He returned to London to give a detailed account of the war against Tipoo, but was back in Calcutta early in 1801. He was too late, however, to prevent Richard from replacing Arthur with Baird.[2] Early in 1801 Henry Wellesley took on the unpleasant task of dealing with the Vizier and the territory of Oudh. There was a storm of disapproval: critics said the Governor-General had no right to appoint his brother. But Henry carried out his mission well and accepted only his salary as Richard's secretary. He returned home in 1802, although he continued to represent the Governor-General in London in a semi-official way.

Richard was the last of the brothers to leave India; none of them ever went back, although in 1827 Henry was offered the Governor-Generalship, which he refused. Had the Marquess come home at the end of 1803, he would have received nothing but acclaim, but the war

---

[1] St Helena, 3 July 1805: *Supplementary Despatches*, IV, 511–12.
[2] Henry wrote to Arthur on 22 April 1801, *Supplementary Despatches*, II, 364, 'Had I been here in time, I think I could have prevented his (Baird's) appointment.'

against Holkar had not gone well, although Monson's tragic failure had been rectified to some extent by the successful defence of Delhi, the victories at Deeg and Farruckabad and finally the capture of Deeg.

Before this good news had time to reach England, however, Lord Lake[1] mismanaged the siege of Bhurtpoor into another defeat as far-reaching in effect and as unnecessary as Monson's. His preparations were faulty and his first assault which might so easily have been successful was poorly co-ordinated. Lake's forces attacked and shifted position several times. The Jats inside gained confidence with every British reverse. On 21 April 1805 Lake finally abandoned the siege after about 110 days of fighting. Five separate grand assaults cost a total of 3,100 casualties, including 103 British officers killed or seriously wounded.[2]

Bhurtpoor did more for Indian morale than the Monson fiasco, even though the Rajah who was weary of the war proposed terms favourable to Britain, which were accepted almost immediately. The Mahrattas clearly perceived the shift in British objectives. The Wellesleys had been intent on building an empire; the new emphasis in London was on peace at any price. Scindia, Holkar and the rest now could gain more by talk than by their swords. The British armies in India were as good as ever, but the British Government and the Court of Directors were shifting their ground.

Let us look briefly at the reasons for the change; the chief cause was a lessening of confidence in the Marquess Wellesley and his team. The Board of Control stood solidly behind him so long as Henry Dundas was President. Richard and Dundas were both men of talent and had similar ideas for the future of India. They had served together on this same Board. But Dundas left it in May 1801. Addington's Government, which came in that year, did not support Wellesley's policies as Pitt's had done.

The Marquess wrote magnificent dispatches when he had something important to say, but remained silent for months when he had nothing, or even when what he did have to communicate was unpleasant. The old procedure of rule by 'Governor-General in Council' became a farce because the Marquess no longer attended most of its meetings; he considered them a waste of his time.[3] He governed Bengal and all India personally and encouraged the Governors in Madras and Bombay

[1] Lake had been created Baron Lake of Delhi and Laswarree on 1 September 1803. News of it arrived in India at the same time as Wellesley's knighthood.

[2] *Thorn*, 458 and *passim*.

[3] *Torrens*, 278, says he began this after he returned from Madras in 1799 and had the 'council proceedings communicated to him for approbation'.

to follow his example in their more limited spheres.[1] His leadership was such that nobody in India complained. The Board in London, however, reacted quite differently. So long as he was supremely successful, they could not replace him, but Monson's defeat was a valid excuse. Cornwallis was on his way out before news of the victories of Deeg and Farruckabad reached England. The additional defeat before Bhurtpoor appears to have been anticipated.

The Court of Directors had long been anti-Wellesley. The entire EIC at home was hostile towards the Marquess not only because their profits were reduced, but also because of rocketing costs. The debts of the EIC totalled seventeen million when Arthur Wellesley came ashore at Fort William in 1798; they had risen to thirty-one million eight years later. The directors and stockholders were more interested in profits than imperial conquest; after all, as far as the owners were concerned the EIC was still a trading company. Originally, it had acquired territory only in order to have a secure base for its mercantile operations.

Trade had to some extent been replaced by empire; the Wellesleys were more interested in the latter. But the profits of trade were still paying for a major part of empire building. The income or revenue from territory acquired in various ways never lived up to expectations. Because of changes in the mood of British politics, the Marquess Wellesley was at least partially 'supported in measures ten times more high-handed and dictatorial than those for which Warren Hastings had been impeached a dozen years earlier'.[2] But when he diverted funds from the purchase of goods destined for ultimate sale in Europe to defraying military expenses,[3] the Court of Directors were permanently antagonized.

Further, both Richard and Arthur Wellesley had read and absorbed the teachings of Adam Smith. They were known to be for Free Trade and against monopolies, even in connection with the carrying of merchandise and passengers between Britain, India and China. This was anathema in Leadenhall Street. The Directors felt with justification that the EIC had expended money as well as some blood and health to establish bases, procedures and a competent organization. They believed that others should not be allowed freely to profit by their work.

[1] Misra, 45, and passim.

[2] Lyall, 267-8.

[3] Oxford History, 607. Philips, 142, is even more severe. He says, 'the Directors, his masters by law, gave him not less than a million sterling annually to reduce the Indian debt', but he used it 'to develop a policy to which they were opposed'.

News that the ageing Cornwallis – he was in the sixty-sixth year of an extremely hard life – had been persuaded to accept again the dual responsibilities of Governor-General and C-in-C reached India unofficially by two overland letters to private individuals.[1] Rumours spread rapidly. The reign of the proconsul was nearing its end. On 29 July 1805 the Marquess Cornwallis arrived at Fort William and was greeted as a friend by Richard. The younger man had a sincere regard and even a disciple's veneration for his replacement. But the old nobleman was infirm of mind and body and not as gracious as he once had been. He could only complain of his new, too lavish quarters.[2]

Cornwallis came out intent on a policy of peace at any price. He was willing to give the Mahrattas, not only Holkar but others also, almost anything in order to obtain a cessation of hostilities. He was soon in such a poor state of mental health, however, that Lake and Sir John Barlow, the deputy Governor-General, put an end to his more absurd plans of giving up territory. The gallant old man slowly slipped into childishness and died on 5 October 1805. He was never a military commander or an intellect of the first rank, but a finer and more patriotic gentleman never lived.

Lake finally pursued Holkar as Arthur Wellesley had so often suggested. He drove him far to the north-west, practically out of India, and in December 1805 the ablest of the Mahrattas sued for peace on the Sutlej. Barlow cemented the peace in which he included all British enemies. He and Lake sacrificed some of the gains the Wellesleys and their dedicated group of young men had achieved in 1803, but retained far more than the British had in 1797.

A fortnight after Cornwallis arrived Richard sailed for England where he landed early in the following year. His return was not the triumph he expected and to which he was entitled when one considers the astonishing changes he had brought about in India. He was actually forced to stand charges in the House of Commons which were not finally dismissed until 1808.

Certainly he deserved better of his country, but the great Clive and Warren Hastings had stood similar trials. Some may censor his methods; Mountstuart Elphinstone only half-jokingly called him 'Old Villainy'. He really was not quite so virtuous and long suffering a statesman as his letters to Tipoo and the Mahrattas made out, but

---

[1] These came in May 1805: *Torrens*, 595.

[2] The Marquess Wellesley's Government House does appear to have been large and not well adapted to India.

he and his subordinates added enormously to British power in India and throughout the world. More important, in the time of Jena as well as Trafalgar, he had finally extinguished practical French ambitions in the East.

The Wellesleys did more in India than increase British power and gain an advantage in the world-wide struggle against France. They changed the predominant attitude of Englishmen towards public service there. Throughout the eighteenth century, the East India Company's morals with regard to money were low. Gifts were accepted freely in return for various trade licences and privileges. A biographer of Arthur Wellesley has said that in Mysore he could have made himself a quarter of a million pounds sterling 'while remaining within the law and the custom of the time'.[1] But on 14 June 1799 the young Colonel, even though still in debt, had written, 'I should be ashamed of doing any of the dirty things that I am told are done.'[2] He adhered rigidly to his own code of financial rectitude and influenced most of his countrymen with whom he came in contact. Henry Wellesley, who during his shorter period of administration in Oudh had similar opportunites of making money was equally strong-minded. As has been mentioned, he accepted only a single salary as his brother Richard's secretary, even though triple and quadruple place holding was common. Richard refused £100,000 from his share of the Seringapatam prize money. The example of the Wellesleys and their friends changed the accepted or popular motivation for most Britons in India from complete self-interest within the law to unselfish public service. My Indian friends say that this ideal still survives in the Indian Civil Service, even though British India is no more.

The Wellesleys worked and risked their lives for an empire which would benefit not only Britain but also its component peoples. Richard felt that the greatest blessing he could confer on the people of India was to bring them within the sphere of British justice, prosperity and tranquillity. He once replied to a congratulatory address by the citizens of Calcutta by saying, 'My public duty is discharged to the satisfaction of my conscience by the prosperous establishment of a system of policy which promises to improve the general condition of the people of India and to unite the principal Native States in the bond of peace under the protection of the British power.'[3] This regard for the governed was surely the best of British colonialism.

The Wellesleys left to India another legacy – to which Arthur

[1] *Aldington*, 97–8.   [2] *Supplementary Despatches*, I, 247.   [3] *Oxford History*, 605.

contributed more than Richard or Henry – the efficiency and audacity of British Indian armies. Before 1799 British units in India were brave and able in combat, but lacked the ability to move, a disadvantage which caused them to adopt an overall defensive strategy. The Wellesley armies in India were audacious not only because they had the spirit for it, but also because their daring was made possible by adequate training, organization and logistic support. Dugald Campbell caught the new Dhoondiah; Lake finally drove at Holkar and destroyed him completely. They were using essentially Arthur Wellesley's tactics.

The Board of Control, the Court of Directors and the Marquess Cornwallis could give back every acre of territory and every fortress that the Wellesleys added to British India, but the moral ascendancy gained by Richard's field commanders would have remained. This superiority applied to the King's regiments and also to EIC units. The amalgamations of officers of one race with ranks from another have not always been efficient, but in India they were – especially in units like the 1/8 Madras which called itself Wellesley's Own.

The Wellesleys changed India noticeably and permanently; India also changed the Wellesleys. In the next chapter we will discuss at some length what military knowledge Arthur gained in the East. First, however, we should briefly review other changes such as the personal relationships between the three brothers. Henry remained the good friend of both for life, but one wonders what Richard and Arthur felt towards each other during the last months of 1804 and in 1805. How did India figure in their final estrangement?

The Indian correspondence of Richard and Arthur is filled with discussions of many subjects, including the political situations in India and Europe. They were united in regard to the Treaty of Bassein and all that it entailed; Arthur defended Richard's entire Indian policy. They were eye-to-eye about honesty, integrity, public service and the advantages of British rule for the people of India. But there were differences also, small matters that arose mostly after the Baird trouble early in 1801. One of these was whether Scindia had lost the fortress of Gwalior by the treaty of December 1803. Arthur felt that the place should be left in Scindia's hands; Richard insisted that it be surrendered. In this connection Arthur wrote to Henry from Bombay on 13 May 1804, 'I differ in opinion with the Governor-General both as to the right and policy of keeping this fort: I have delivered my opinion to him regarding the latter, but have said nothing upon the former, as the question turns upon a nice point of the law of nations, which the

Governor-General has argued with his usual ingenuity; but I acknowledge I differ from him entirely. In fact, my dear Henry, we want at Calcutta some person who will speak his mind to the Governor-General. Since you and Malcolm have left him, there is nobody about him with capacity to understand these subjects who has nerve to discuss them with him, and to oppose his sentiments when he is wrong. There cannot be a stronger proof of this want than the fact that Malcolm, and I, and General Lake, and Mercer, and Webbe, were of opinion that we had lost Gwalior with the treaty of peace.'[1]

Richard was not perfect, although perhaps Arthur thought so even as late as December 1800. After that time, however, he began to voice serious criticisms especially to Henry and other third parties. The unfortunate Baird incident probably left wounds that were never entirely healed. One of the tragedies of human relations is that strong, self-reliant men, even brothers like Richard and Arthur who were close when young, tend to build up resentments. As they grew older and accomplished more, it was harder for each not to be critical of the other. Many people say that Richard was more brilliant than Arthur, but the older brother was also surely less stable and less well self-disciplined.

One wonders what happened between Richard and Arthur in the weeks they spent together in and near Fort William in 1804. Were they as cordial as of old? Had their personal habits changed so much that they were no longer able to enjoy each other's company? Did they discuss what must have been a mutual disappointment when Lake refused Richard's offer of Arthur's services? Was Arthur now too set in his ways to accept the tyranny of abundant wine after dinner?

Another change that India brought about in all three Wellesley brothers was their financial conditions. Richard had refused a share of the Seringapatam prize money, but received 5,000 pounds a year from the EIC as an annuity. He surely was better off when he returned than when he went out; so was Henry. Arthur Wellesley had less income in India than Richard, but was more careful with it. On 15 January 1805 he wrote, 'I am not rich in comparison with other people, but very much so in comparison with my former situation, and quite sufficiently so for my own wants. I got a great deal of prize money in the last war; which with what I got before, and a sum of money which the Court of Directors gave me for a service rendered to them in this country, and the accumulation of the interest upon those sums, have rendered me

[1] *Supplementary Despatches*, IV, 384–6.

independent of all office or employment.'[1] Arthur paid his debts and accumulated over 42,000 pounds,[2] every penny honestly earned.

Richard, Arthur and Henry withstood the Indian climate, diseases and military dangers astonishingly well. The two younger brothers were completely restored by the long trip home; Richard was left with a permanent nervousness, but this might also have come about in Europe. All three survived into old age in reasonably good condition.[3] As we have seen, many of their friends and colleagues were not so fortunate. Ashton, Allen, Sartorius, Montresor, Harness, Webbe, Haliburton, Dalrymple, Huddleston, Orrock and many others found Indian graves not connected with actual combat, while Fitzgerald, Maxwell, Mackay, Kenny and a disproportionate number of British officers serving in King's and EIC units died in combat or of wounds. Stevenson failed to make it home; Lake died of a cold and a weakened physical condition soon after he returned from India. Read who built the road through the Baramahal died in Malta on 19 May 1804. Lieutenant-General James Stuart who commanded the Bombay forces at Seringapatam and then served as C-in-C in Madras until 17 October 1804 returned to London in broken health. He lingered on unrewarded – he was not even knighted[4] – until he died early in 1815. He was a fine soldier and an able commander; his contribution to Arthur Wellesley's success in India can hardly be overstated. His extreme un-selfishness is unusual in every respect. Had he not used Wellesley instead of Baird and other senior generals, Britain might have had a succession of indecisive Coote-type victories in India and Corunnas in Europe rather than Salamanca, Vittoria and Waterloo. Stuart's death two months before Waterloo may have been unfortunate. He and Harris incurred the displeasure of the Duke of York for believing Wellesley to be a better military commander and diplomat than Baird. Harris who survived was created, as already mentioned, Baron Harris of Seringapatam and Mysore . . . on 11 August 1815!

Long years of life lay ahead for all the Wellesleys. They had done

---

[1] *Supplementary Despatches*, IV, 484.

[2] *Lady Longford*, 97.

[3] Their ages at death were: Richard, 82; Arthur, 83, and Henry, 74.

[4] Wellesley wrote about Stuart on 8 December 1804, 'I had no acquaintance with or claims upon him, excepting those of service; and I owe everything to his confidence, his favourable opinion, and his support. I feel for him an affection and gratitude which I cannot describe.' *Supplementary Despatches*, IV, 472. I believe that the victor of Waterloo may have been instrumental in Harris's peerage and might have asked that something be done for Stuart also. The Duke treated Stuart's grandson as one of his own: *Lady Longford*, 102 and 127.

their best work as a team in India. As individuals all three were to be reassigned elsewhere for the public good many times. Richard had already contributed his greatest achievement; Henry was to serve Britain in many political and diplomatic capacities, always carefully and well. Arthur's most important work lay ahead in Portugal, Spain, southern France and on a low crest in Belgium between Genappe and Mont St Jean.

XV
Arthur Wellesley at the Age of Thirty-six

'I understood as much of military matters when I came back from India as I have ever done since',[1] the Duke said long after Waterloo; it was an exaggeration. No man with a mind as acquisitive as Arthur Wellesley could fight as many successful campaigns against Napoleonic France as he did without learning a good deal more. His professional military skills were developed, however, to a maximum within Indian limitations while he was there. In India he acquired abilities to handle other problems that were not strictly military, like dealing with difficult allies and getting on with indigenous civilian populations.

The survival of Arthur Wellesley's writings – most of them published – allows a clearer picture of him as a young man than is available for any other great commander. Let us briefly review the qualities he had in 1805, which led to his later victories. Some were natural and some acquired, but most of what he did in Europe was foreshadowed by his campaigns in India.

Personal abilities are difficult to classify in the order of their importance in military operations, but surely one of Wellesley's most useful qualities throughout his military career was his own bodily efficiency and stamina. In the days when gentlemen often took pride in the amount of wine they could consume, and when fashionable generals frequently measured fifty or more inches around the waist, Wellesley was strong, lean and bright-eyed because he had learned that he functioned better with moderate amounts of food and drink.[2]

---

[1] *Stanhope*, 131.

[2] His advice to Henry in July 1801 was, 'I know but one receipt for good health in this country, and that is to live moderately, to drink little or no wine, to use exercise, to keep the mind employed, and, if possible, to keep in good humour with the world. The last is the most difficult, for, as you have often observed, there is scarcely a good tempered man in India': *Supplementary Despatches*, II, 501.

At the beginning of the nineteenth century those in India who did not do physical work frequently took no exercise. But Wellesley, Malcolm, Elphinstone, and several other young men of the Wellesley group worked hard to keep themselves in good shape. Wellesley took a vigorous walk immediately upon getting up in the morning; he rode often and far for recreation and travel. There is some evidence that he exercised with his sword and in other ways.[1] The correlation. between exercise, physical strength and agility on one hand and health on the other is not well established; temperate habits did not always prevent Indian maladies. However, in a country where sickness was normal and death by disease not unusual Wellesley was physically fit to an exceptional degree. The man who discovered the ford at Assaye and captured Gawilghur partly because of riding forty-five miles a day was at home in the saddle. He was accustomed to riding over all kinds of terrain. He could manage a spirited horse without having to devote his mind to it. In those days effective personal reconnaissance was of extreme value; it required ability, practice, fine horses and physical fitness. Wellesley had all four.

Wellesley's care of his mind was no less systematic. When he left England in 1796, he went further into debt to add to his library.[2] On his voyage out he disciplined himself to study for a certain period every day; his mind, once fully disciplined, actually seems to have enjoyed the careful absorption of detail. His standard procedure in dealing with a problem was first to gather every bit of information available and then to solve it. He was able to succeed more often than others because he had more facts and knew more about what had been done in similar situations in the past. He stored a great deal in his mind; he carried about with him in his 'tumbril for the commanding general's papers' what he might need in book form.

We have already discussed Wellesley's memoranda; they were written partly to inform others and in part to implant what he was working on firmly in his own consciousness. His logical, almost scientific approach is more mid-twentieth than early nineteenth

[1] For the well known '40 paces back and forth in front of his tent': Malcolm, I, 291. The sword exercise is not so well documented, but Elphinstone, Malcolm, and other Englishmen regularly threw spears, exercised with swords and fired pistols at marks: *Cotton*, 24. In India more than in Europe, an officer's life in battle depended on the strength and skill of his sword arm.

[2] A list of these newly-purchased books is given in *Guedalla*, 55–6. Twenty-eight of the thirty-nine titles – one title ran to twenty-four volumes – were about India. In addition, some of the books he already owned were in connection with the East.

century. He was drawing upon a fund of wide knowledge already assimilated. Whether he was writing at leisure or making critical combat decisions when seconds were vital, he had the knowledge he needed and could recall it immediately.

Wellesley once said 'that he could guess what was going on upon the other side of the hill better than most men'.[1] He certainly developed this facility while in India, but it was hardly 'guessing' as the term is usually understood. He evolved a unique system of intelligence that told him what was taking place in the enemy's camp. The heart and soul of this system consisted in Arthur being his own chief of intelligence. He was exceptionally good for his time at delegating work and responsibility, but he never delegated 'the collation and interpretation of information'. He was able intuitively to use his own background of knowledge, what he had gained in the past by reading, writing and talking to people along with his knowledge of what was happening and what was desired at the highest level. Throughout his long life he astonished supposedly better educated men by the amount, accuracy and diversity of his knowledge. But knowledge for its own sake was not important. He knew what Scindia was likely to do because he had initiated half the moves in the game already played. A subordinate lacks this familiarity.

If and when a problem developed, or even was likely to develop, Wellesley marshalled his previously acquired knowledge and put together the information he already had; there were usually bits and pieces from many places. Early in his career he seems to have learned the importance of calmly considering a problem with an initially blank piece of paper in front of him. Perhaps many such pieces of paper were filled up and thrown away, but some were not. The Second Duke, who edited the *Supplementary Despatches*, included one in connection with Wynaad, written about December 1800, and commented: 'These notes were written and re-written by Colonel Wellesley in a Book of Draft Letters and Memoranda. They afford a remarkable specimen of the manner in which he digested miscellaneous information, collected piecemeal from various sources, and relative to an almost unknown country, which was about to become the seat of war.'[2]

Once he had a firm hold on the background, he would generally take steps that would produce information of current value. One reason he wrote so much was to get replies which often contained news more valuable to Wellesley than to the man who wrote them. He also used

---

[1] *Oman*, VII, 96.   [2] *Supplementary Despatches*, II, 294.

hircarrahs, the long established spies and scouts of India, who for centuries had sold more or less correct military information to both sides. Everybody used them, but Wellesley managed to gain more from the facts he received. He paid promptly, generously and in gold, but he wanted the truth only. He developed the capability for cross-checking a good deal of what he was told. He kept his scouts on their camels, rather than allowing them to sit in bazaars and listen to rumours. Few Englishmen got on with Indians as well as Wellesley did. He was kind and seems to have realized intuitively how to appeal to their personal pride,[1] but he could be severe too. He did not like these *hircarrahs* to bring false or incomplete information and made it abundantly clear to them.

The best and quickest way to check facts delivered by *hircarrahs* and others was, of course, using common sense. Wellesley often refers to rumours that either could not be true or did not appear logical. Other Englishmen in India often believed such gossip, and sometimes came to grief. Wellesley warned Murray about this sort of thing in his letter of 26 August 1805 which said in part, 'Major Walker sends out Hircarrahs who return and tell him what they please; he writes the whole down and sends it off to Mr. Duncan by whom it is circulated. Major Walker discovers that his Hircarrahs have told him falsehoods; but I doubt whether they are punished, or rewarded[2] when they do well.' In order to avoid false intelligence as much as possible, Arthur developed 'Three distinct departments for intelligence, the heads of which communicated directly' to him. 'To each department he attached such a number of intelligence Hircarrahs, as rendered it certain that one [Hircarrah] would come in to each department from the enemy's camp on every day. The intelligence departments were kept by the Deputy Adjutant General [Barclay], by Mr Elphinstone who acted as Persian interpreter, and by Govind Rao, a servant of the Rajah of Mysore, who was used in the communications with the native sirdars.'[3]

Wellesley realized that more than 95 per cent of all information he received was useless. The personal drudgery of evaluating and collating

---

[1] Nicholls tells a story of Arthur giving a chief of *brinjarries* gold bracelets 'and enhancing the value by putting them on his wrists'. These things were more important in the East than in Europe: *Dispatches*, II, 372–3.

[2] *Dispatches*, II, 240.

[3] *Dispatches*, III, 539. This quotation is from a short memorandum on intelligence and was written by Wellesley at Fort William during the autumn of 1804; it is most informative.

it was a net loss in time and effort. But some of what remained was the material from which his victories were made.

Another part of his system of military intelligence was reconnaissance. We need not take time with his traditional use of patrols, probes in force and screens which sometimes were exceptionally effective, like Bisnapah's Mysore horsemen before Argaum. These were not usual. Wellesley had, however, one especially productive kind of reconnaissance, his own personal observation. His surveys at critical times were of extreme value and sometimes magnificent to the point of being unbelievable. We have seen him go off almost unprotected before Assaye and Argaum to get the lay of the land and to determine where the enemy was and what he was likely to do. But for every furlong ridden before these battles there were hundreds of miles of similar, though less essential, reconnaissance. British commanders in India before and after Wellesley frequently lacked physical fitness or riding ability; some perhaps could not afford the superb horses that made his extreme personal audacity relatively safe.[1] They also lacked the drive to practise on all kinds of Indian terrain in order to develop confidence and skill. Wellesley hunted for recreation, exercise and to learn exactly what each of his horses could do. He also developed an ability to tackle tough terrain. He and his mounts were in the habit of doing this sort of thing several times a week. Diomed could not only get quickly to places inaccessible to Mahratta horsemen, but also show them a clean pair of heels without even breathing hard. In his prime Arthur was probably as fine a practical horseman as ever lived.[2] He had strength, agility and all those thousands of hours in the saddle.

His intelligence system also produced information needed for his political and administrative responsibilities. He applied the same fund of knowledge, common sense and tightly controlled imagination to all problems from a treaty with Scindia involving millions of people to whether Sergeant Jackson was to be allowed to marry.[3] This attention to detail and willingness to do the drudgery of considering each prob-

---

[1] Wellesley is quoted by *Stanhope*, 182, as saying to an officer who complained that he had no way of finding out some information before he was personally in danger, 'you are mounted on a damn good horse and you have two eyes in your head'. The speed of a fine horse made close observation safe; Indians were seldom well mounted.

[2] Expert English hunters maintained that in middle life the Duke had a bad seat. I do not pretend to know what this meant in Buckinghamshire and around Walmer, but I doubt that most of those who made the comments could have followed at a walk where Wellesley rode fast and precisely. He was sometimes out to win a battle, not a fox's brush.

[3] Since 'he will certainly load himself with her' anyway, Wellesley was in favour: *Supplementary Despatches*, II, 537.

lem in the light of all available information is perhaps the quality most often associated with successful men. Wellesley appears to have done it as an exercise in self-discipline rather than as a means to an ambitious end.

Wellesley's relations with his officers became set in India and rarely varied thereafter. We have already discussed the sense of public trust and pecuniary rectitude the Wellesleys brought to India. Laws and regulations were less effective than examples.[1] Peculations were to occur during their time in India and after they were gone, but never again without censure by public opinion. Englishmen still served in the East mainly for money, but now they were concerned that it be honourably and honestly earned. Arthur expected British officers to behave like gentlemen. This concept is difficult to understand 170 years later, especially for an American, but it included several different patterns of behaviour. Indians were not to be beaten, cheated or otherwise taken advantage of; an officer was expected to win the respect of his men whether they be Europeans or Indians. Englishmen in responsible positions had to be a credit to their nation, even in small things like shaving daily and wearing clean linen.

Wellesley's relations with his subordinates were scrupulously respectful even when he was in fact blistering their hides with admonitions. 'I beg leave to suggest that it would be beneficial to the service in this country to send Lieutenant-Colonel Blank to join that part of his corps which is in Europe.'[2] In another instance his public admonition has a sort of delayed-action sting: 'He [the culprit] ought to have known that he is a part of a body of troops placed in this country to protect the inhabitants, and not to oppress them: having, however, forgotten his duty in that respect, and having been found guilty of conduct very improper in a British officer, a repetition of which would be highly prejudicial to the British interests and character in this country, he is hereby publicly reprimanded.'[3]

He was especially careful of the personal feelings of his subordinates. He regularly used words like 'be so kind as to' and then gave an order. He wanted officers, especially senior subordinates, to speak and write freely to him, and was less than normally interested in preserving his

---

[1] Wellesley wrote to a subordinate who had passed on to him the offer of a payment for a privilege, 'In respect to the bribe offered to you and myself, I am surprised that any British officer should not have given the Rajah to understand that the offer was "an insult" ' *Supplementary Despatches*, III, 548.

[2] *Dispatches*, II, 568.

[3] *Supplementary Despatches*, II, 520–1.

own dignity. Every Englishman in India, even the drunken Major Allen who had shot Ashton,[1] had inalienable rights.

This considerate treatment was more than just a habit and a means towards personal safety when senior officers could not with honour refuse challenges from their juniors. It was a true expression of the young commander's carefully considered opinion of the proper way to behave. His dispatches often contain something like, 'We are friends and will get along, but you must do better in regard to so-and-so.' As already mentioned, Wellesley did not blame subordinates. He kept Lieutenant-Colonel Orrock in command of the 1/8 Madras even after his tragic blunder at Assaye. He had reason to complain of Dalrymple in the spring of 1799 and of the younger Kirkpatrick[2] in 1803–4, but he was not excessively critical. By comparison with other senior officers in India at that time, Wellesley was not hard to get on with.

On the other hand, Wellesley lost no time in taking over immediately all responsibility to which he was entitled. He and his brothers were not democratic nor did they lack self-confidence. They did not believe in committees; when they wanted to get things done, they chose teams formed with clear lines of responsibility and strong personal leadership. Arthur was a dutiful and respectful subordinate and a faithful colleague. Except for his brother Richard, he fell out with no one for whom or with whom he worked, not even Baird.[3] He was willing to co-operate and often appeared to be doing so even when he had authority to command. He was conscious, however, of the dangers of divided responsibility in a crisis.

In his personal intercourse with his officers, he was reserved almost to shyness, save in the privacy of his own military family. His friends were Ashton, Close, Stevenson, Montresor, Malcolm and the younger members of his own staff, especially West, Barclay and Colin Campbell. Malcolm was ultimately the closest; he was of the same age, but below him in rank as was usual with King's and EIC officers.

[1] As we know, Major Allen of the King's 12th Foot challenged his commanding officer and killed him, as related briefly in Chapter III. Feeling against him ran high; Ashton was Wellesley's close friend. But Wellesley ordered the officer in charge of Allen to 'allow him every freedom consistent with safety': *Supplementary Despatches*, I, 170.

[2] Wellesley made a memorandum on 26 September 1800 of a conversation with Meer Allum that included, 'Major (James Achilles) Kirkpatrick, by dressing himself in the garb of a native and by the adoption of their manners, had made himself ridiculous, and was detested for his interference with their women.' *Supplementary Despatches*, II, 178.

[3] Baird and Wellesley were always on the best of terms personally. The former told Malcolm in Hyde Park in 1813 that he never had cause for personal enmity: *Brett-James*, 32. Their direct exchanges of letters were always cordial.

Malcolm had unusual ability as well as an almost unique capacity for friendship. He did more for Britain and the Wellesleys during their years in India than could have been expected from a man of his rank.[1]

One wonders about Arthur Wellesley's lady friends; he certainly was not a hermit. Not much real information survives, although Elers indicates that he flirted with married women, especially with those whose husbands did not mind.[2] We do know that his indiscretions, if any, were never flagrant.

Few Englishmen have ever been able to get on as well with Indians as Arthur. He followed no careful plan, but just treated them as he would have done if their skins had been white. There was far less separation between the different races in India at that time than later. Purneah, Bisnapah, Govind Rao, Meer Allum and even the Peshwa were his friends. General Wellesley spoke the vernacular of his day and knew intuitively how to appeal to Indian soldiers. He was from the first scrupulously careful as to relations with Indian civilians. In his area of responsibility he would not let EIC or King's soldiers misbehave. He was for law and order, the proper procedures of courts martial and the like; but when the discipline of his army or the general peace and well-being of territories under his control were concerned he punished serious offenders immediately and drastically. He was quick to flog or hang anyone who flagrantly misbehaved, regardless of whether he was one of his soldiers or a local civilian. Wellesley's swift and sure punishment ensured good behaviour on both sides.[3]

Early in his Indian career he appreciated the importance of paying all civilians fairly and honestly not only to keep alive the British reputation for rectitude, but also in order to receive a continuous flow of goods and services. He always tried to use coins current in the particular area in which he was operating, although the monetary systems of India were often difficult.[4] He stressed that every officer

[1] Malcolm's commission as a major was dated 6 June 1803, more than a year later than Wellesley's as a major-general.

[3] *Elers, passim,* appears to have been something of a gossip. He tells of an estrangement between Wellesley and his first ADC, Captain Francis Ralph West of the King's 33rd over Wellesley's attentions to Mrs Freese to which Captain Freese made no objection. He also suggests that Wellesley and Mrs Stevenson may have been intimate.

[2] 'If my Mahratta allies did not know that should I hang anyone that might be found plundering, not only should I have starved long ago, but probably my own coat would have been taken off my back.' *Dispatches,* II, 563.

[4] There were two basic systems of coins current in India at that time, one Hindoo or southern Indian, and the other Muslim. The gold pieces of the two systems were *pagodas* and *mohurs,* both broken down into four or five other units. Hundreds of mints struck

and European soldier must treat Indians with respect and honour their rights not only in body but in property. We should remark briefly on his tendency towards vehemence of expression and exaggeration that is obvious in isolated quotations of the following kind: 'The natives are the most mischievous, deceitful race of people I have seen or read of. I have not yet met with a Hindoo who had one good quality and the Mussulmans are worse. They are all most atrociously cruel.'[1] In his sweeping criticisms which were never intended for the public Wellesley often voiced stronger sentiments than he would have set down on reflection. The above words were obviously not meant to apply to Purneah, Bisnapah and the many other friends 'black or grey'; they are not dissimilar from a statement made after Vittoria about British soldiers being 'the scum of the earth'. Both statements may have been true in specific situations, but are too strong for quotation later.

All army commanders of the eighteenth and early nineteenth centuries had trouble with their troops looting in captured towns. The stormers of Seringapatam were out of control for more than twenty-four hours. Two sepoys were hanged beside the gate used by the British to get into the *pettah* of Ahmednuggur. As we have seen, at Gawilghur the King's 94th did not behave as well as Wellesley thought. Common soldiers and many officers considered all civilians and their property in a city taken by storm to belong to those who did the taking. Misbehaviour in India was hardly worth mentioning, however, compared to what lay ahead in Spain.

Let us look at Wellesley's use of his infantry, cavalry and artillery in combat to understand the foundation upon which his success depended. A commander who can do everything well except fight is obviously useless, while one who is good in combat can sometimes cover up many deficiencies. Wellesley learned his trade in India; he was clever enough later to adapt his training to Europe.

[1] Wellesley wrote this on 12 July 1797, when he was only five months in India: *Supplementary Despatches*, I, 16. It should be balanced against his lavish praise of Bisnapah and his Mysore soldiers who served under him against the Mahrattas. In his application for a full rather than a half-pay pension for Burry Khan, he said, 'he was always a man of good character and well connected in his corps [the 1/8 Madras]. He received the wound at Assaye': *Supplementary Despatches*, IV, 495.

coins more or less according to one system or the other; Mysore used both. But coins of the same name did not have the same value because of variations in weight, purity and local acceptance. Numismatically, India was extremely complicated. There were, for example, five different types of *pagodas*, four of *mohurs*, and at least three rupees in the bazaar at the same time: *Dispatches*, II, 419–20.

At first he used standard British tactics in India. As we have seen, he prided himself on making few changes. He operated in strict accordance with regulations, even the complicated EIC regulations. He modified no part of the standard drill or fire discipline of his infantry which fought in lines two ranks deep and stressed firepower from efficiently handled muskets. Proportionately more enemy soldiers died on British bayonets in India than in the Peninsula or at Waterloo, but shock was still secondary to firepower. It should be emphasized, however, that Wellesley managed to make his battalions more effective because of his concentration on training, his management of them before contact and his leadership in and out of battle.[1]

Wellesley used cavalry more often and more effectively in India than in Europe because it was better trained and more controllable in the East. As we have seen, however, Maxwell was not blameless at Assaye; this going-out-of-control in a charge was the curse of the British mounted arm in the Peninsula and at Waterloo. Wellesley's cavalry was better handled at Argaum, perhaps because he positioned his units himself and left Huddleston, an EIC officer, in charge. The best of all his Indian cavalry exploits was his single-line charge against Dhoondiah Waugh at Conaghull where the quality of the enemy soldiers was probably better than at any action he fought in the East. Nearly all of them were veterans from Tipoo's Muslim units.

Artillery was more important in India than in Europe for two reasons. First, the pieces were more deadly because they were used at closer range. Second, artillery casualties produced a greater effect because enemy discipline was less trustworthy. The sudden spectacular jets of smoke and the smashing noise of guns proved useful by themselves. Artillery as used by Wellesley in India was not really a separate arm, but a partner to both the infantry and the cavalry. In most situations on major battlefields and equally where a single unit was operating alone, two 6-pounders increased the combat potential of an EIC infantry battalion by at least 50 per cent. Detachments of smaller size often had a single gun which greatly improved their firepower and the respect they received from the enemy. Cavalry units benefited from attached artillery in a similar way. In India Wellesley learned to use his artillery in small units and at close range. In contrast, the Mahrattas around Assaye and at Argaum used their cannon in much the same 'grand battery' way as the French were to do at

---

[1] The reader's attention is directed to Appendix II: Organization and Tactics. There is a discussion of infantry, cavalry and artillery as usually employed by Wellesley.

Waterloo, and with roughly the same result. Occasionally shooting at long range caused a few casualties – it could cause panic as at Argaum – but it was not normally effective against disciplined troops.

Throughout his Indian career Wellesley stressed the importance of using all arms in combination. Individual bravery and combat effectiveness were desirable especially in storming places, but in the field unit discipline and co-ordinated fire and movement were more important. The combat efficiency of infantry, cavalry and artillery used together was greater than the sum of their individual potentials. This combination increment applied to small forces also. Wellesley was quick to praise actions of this type. On 31 October 1803 Captain Baynes with three EIC companies, two 3-pounders and 400 Mysore horse beat 5,000 Mahrattas because of the young officer's presence of mind and ability to manœuvre.[1] Even more important, on 10 October 1803 Wellesley devoted a General Order to EIC Captain O'Donnell and a mixed detachment which used a ruined village as a base for offensive operations against a much larger enemy.[2] Small independent forces of all arms able to stand off many times their own number were the means by which convoys moved safely.

One of Wellesley's outstanding advantages over Bonaparte was his ability personally to command forces of any size and composition quickly, flawlessly and with complete confidence. One did not learn this sort of thing as a general officer, nor in half a dozen drill sessions. Wellesley developed his abilities slowly, first with his own King's 33rd and later with other units both singly and together. He went to special trouble to see that every unit he had could drill and manœuvre impeccably. He tested them himself to check on his battalion officers and for his own practice. He was careful to stress the importance of infantry battalions and cavalry regiments operating together under a variety of conditions, especially their forming into lines with their artillery. Wellesley and his units manœuvred well because they manœuvred often. The French Emperor could not drill even a battalion; his artillery background and his phenomenally rapid rise up the military ladder prevented him from developing this skill.

Wellesley wanted professional competence at all levels among his soldiers and usually got it. Officers and men were volunteers who served for many years in India. Almost all of them got better with practice; the weapons and drill of the era were simple. Most young officers could become effective if they practised reasonably conscien-

[1] *Dispatches*, II, 465–8.   [2] *Supplementary Despatches*, IV, 196–7.

tiously. Older men, especially EIC field officers who were getting on in years, did present problems at times, but Wellesley developed a facility for placing such men in jobs for which they were best qualified.[1]

We should look at some of the tactical 'firsts' scored by Wellington in Europe which have obvious Indian origins. The most important one, of course, was the use of the 'thin red line', the two-deep infantry formation stressing firepower over shock. In India this practice was not new; nor was it actually new in Europe either, although most of Wellesley's opponents thought it was;[2] Wellesley became accustomed to it in India and never deviated from it. If men had the strength to hold it and the training to continue their volleys effectively, the inherent advantage of this arrangement was obvious. At Assaye Wellesley learned that even Scindia's Regular Battalions could defeat fine cavalry if they held their line formation with confidence.[3] Another 'first' probably traceable to India was the way the Royal Artillery used their guns at Waterloo, the procedure of making the enemy take them over and over again. This tactic came from Wellington's resourceful military mind, but was almost surely based on the manner in which Scindia's guns were actually handled at Assaye. When British infantry swept over Pohlmann's artillery, the gunners took shelter under their pieces or feigned death, or both; then they came alive, turned their guns around and continued the fight. The Duke modified this arrangement so that the guns only were 'taken'; the gunners were sheltered under the bayonets of infantry squares nearby.

In Europe, Wellington won with his infantry at small cost partly because half a world away, near Sirsoli, two and a half EIC battalions panicked. After restoring them, he had them lie down. This manœuvre may not have looked well, but it had obvious advantages. The physical protection was important, especially for a nation with limited manpower and a voracious Navy. At Argaum, Wellesley learned too that even good troops are sometimes subject to unreasoning fear, but he also learned how best to control it. The famous 'flat of the sword' treatment and similar manifestations of a senior commander's anger may be

---

[1] As already mentioned promotion in the EIC armies was by seniority only and at least to some extent within regiments. An infantryman once commissioned, if he lived and kept out of serious trouble, was going to command a battalion about twenty-five years later. The disadvantages of this system may be one reason why years later Wellington preferred limited purchase of promotions.

[2] *Fortescue*, V, 346–50.

[3] Maxwell's second charge was surely defeated, in part at least, by the resolution of Pohlmann's Regular Battalions.

gallant, but they are seldom useful. Wellesley's method at Argaum was better. He did not have to use it often, but on 18 June 1815 it was of vital importance.

In India Wellesley also developed the habit of doing as much battle-field direction as he possibly could. He would probably have followed this procedure anyway, but Orrock's tragic mistake at Assaye convinced him of the danger inherent in communications under combat conditions. Not all men were as cool as he was, or able to think clearly when enemy round shot were bouncing about. Wellesley must frequently have considered how he could have managed his first infantry attack at Assaye and still have handled Orrock's column as well. He went with the King's 78th because these kilted Highlanders had to do the more difficult and most critical task. He could not have been in two places at once. In his future battles, however, he managed to avoid orders being misunderstood to a greater extent than at Assaye. Where possible, he personally handled all important movements, or at least saw them well started, before he went on to the next.

Most of Wellington's later military troubles were also foreshadowed in India. At Assaye Maxwell's cavalry pressed their first charge too far and went clean off the battlefield. This type of behaviour was not common in British India where cavalry was usually, better handled because of strict discipline and thorough drilling, but for British mounted units in Europe it was the rule rather than the exception.

Wellesley had some trouble with Stevenson and Murray who had the human tendency of many subordinate commanders to take counsel of their fears. The personal relationship between him and Stevenson was sufficiently close so that after a few, not quite tactful, admonitions the older man learned to correct this fault. Murray did not have this advantage and contributed to Monson's tragedy. Ten years later Picton and Cole retreated past one strong position after another until they were near to letting the French relieve Pamplona. As at Quatre Bras on 16 June 1814, Wellington arrived at Sauren just in time.

Now about sieges. In India Wellesley was blessed with competent engineers, a force of professional pioneers and an adequate siege train. He took every place he attempted, though some assaults were delivered without any preliminary preparations. The garrisons were neither strongly motivated to resist nor skilfully commanded. The garrisons of Burgos, Ciudad Rodrigo, Badajos and San Sebastian were braver, better soldiers and more competently directed. We should not forget, however, that Lake failed to take Bhurtpoor and suffered almost as many casualties as Wellington did in his successful siege of Badajos.[1]

We should now consider strategy. We have already pointed out Wellesley's audacity in the East as opposed to his more cautious behaviour later in Europe; both attitudes were based on sound thinking and common sense. The position of the British in India depended on maintaining prestige, the image of invincibility. A few thousand Englishmen could not rule millions of Indians on any other basis. However, after Assaye there was a certain change in Arthur's attitude to audacity even in India. He cautioned Stevenson about fighting another such battle and avoided one himself. His Assaye casualties would have been cut by half if Orrock had moved correctly, but Wellesley knew that mistakes are inherent in battles. In terms of casualty percentages, he was to win all his later victories in the field far more cheaply; only Waterloo was close to Assaye.[2]

Wellesley's greatest single contribution to Indian warfare, strategic mobility, has been discussed at various points. It was based on common sense and attention to details, and the fact that his armies complete with a siege train could move 600 miles and be more effective than at the start. When necessary, his infantry and field guns could march sixty miles in thirty hours. Wellesley did not normally advocate the attacking of Indian armies in a position of their choosing, because they were clever in their selections and frequently had strong artillery. We have discussed his indirect approach at Assaye and his cautious advances to prevent embarrassment of his units by the local canals at Argaum. Orrock's attack on the village of Assaye was, of course, exactly what Arthur wanted to avoid. On the other hand, a British army in Mahratta territory could not stay on the defensive. The enemy would have used its vast numerical superiority in cavalry to surround and cut off, the sort of thing that happened to Monson. The alternative to attacking the enemy in position, or remaining on the defensive, was to engage during or immediately following manœuvre, before the enemy was set. This was best because of the superiority of British organization and articulation, especially under an able combat leader like Lake or Wellesley himself.

In connection with Wellesley's strategy in India, we should note

---

[1] Lake lost about 3,700 at Bhurtpoor; Wellington's casualties at Badajos were 4,157. The Duke's loss at San Sebastian was 3,700 and at Burgos 2,059.

[2] The Assaye casualties were slightly more than 25 per cent of those engaged; Waterloo cost the Anglo-Dutch army about 16,000 out of about 67,000 or a trifle under 24 per cent.

also his frequent use of a semi-independent force which operated under his control, but beyond immediate supporting distance. As long as British forces of infantry, cavalry and artillery retained their confidence and discipline, they could move almost as they chose in India. Stevenson's army, for instance, was not likely to be overwhelmed suddenly, or even brought to battle disadvantageously. Two allied armies operating at a distance from each other could accomplish far more than a single army of twice the size. One could prevent offensive action by the enemy while the other took places valuable to him.

In India Wellesley developed a group of qualities, most unusual for that time, that had to do with the care of his troops; he was perhaps the outstanding young commander of this type since Alexander of Macedon. Wellesley acquired the habit and the ability to look after his men both in barracks and in the field. His dispatches abound in orders like 'tents must be provided', 'Madras troops must have rice', 'a veranda and secure doors and windows are necessary to keep men healthy', and literally hundreds of similar statements. Pay, new clothing, arrack, food for Europeans, medicines, ammunition of regular and special types and many more commodities were all necessary. So were exercise, discipline, cleanliness, training and that indefinable but vital element, morale.

Providing for troops in Vellore or Seringapatam was easy once the EIC regulation processes were set up and working; John Company had plenty of money. But in order to restore the Peshwa Wellesley had to march 600 miles into what would have been enemy territory for any other commander. He marched hundreds more before he beat Scindia and Berar. As already mentioned several times, his strategic success was based on his ability to move fast and relatively continuously without loss of efficiency, something that required good logistics and personnel management.

The magnificent Mysore bullocks, large female elephants to assist them with artillery and fairly paid *brinjarries* were a great help, but the most important reason for the improvement was Wellesley's logical and detailed forethought and planning. An arrack keg needed to be filled with water once the arrack was out, or the sun would destroy it. Spare wheels and carriages for the field pieces were available when required. The pontoons from Bombay did not move a full day's march, but Wellesley made his own basket boats and had them available when required, as Caesar had done 1,850 years before. Wellesley formed his boats into bridges when necessary, and often left them in place under guard for considerable periods,[1] a considerable improvement on Caesar. The boats gave freedom of movement across rivers during the monsoon, something never available in India before.

The ability to cross Indian rivers expeditiously was of extreme strategic importance, but it was only one of many problems in regard to the movement of men, animals, artillery and a minimum of baggage absolutely necessary to keep Europeans and Indians in good physical condition. Before 1800 such difficulties were insurmountable in India[2] – 140 years later they were not too well handled in Burma – but Arthur's men rarely missed a meal and never lacked ammunition. The simple personal wants of that time were fully provided for over hundreds of miles of marginal roads through territory that might have been hostile save for Wellesley's diplomacy and prestige. He did all this with a staff of astonishingly small size.[3]

His accomplishments in Portugal, Spain and southern France were similar. From 1808 to 1814 Wellington had carts for his oxen and ports into which the mercantile strength of Britain could deliver almost everything required, but he used the logistic skills he had learned with Indian bullocks mostly carrying their loads on their backs and without much seaborne assistance.

We should not forget Arthur Wellesley's debt to many individuals in India. He was serving with professionals; most EIC field officers had twenty years of active duty behind them. Wellesley possessed the gift of all great commanders, of learning from others. These men had given him facts and ideas; they assisted in developing techniques and tactics. Arthur matured in the company of senior officers like Harris, Stuart, Stevenson, Montresor, Close and Read. He also learned from junior officers like Malcolm, Mackay, Macleod and many others. He was assisted by professionals like Barclay, Vesey, O'Donnell, Baynes and Colin Campbell. He had his kilted and unkilted giants and EIC units like the 1/8 Madras who refused to mourn their Assaye dead because they found their end doing their duty.

Soon after Wellesley set foot on English soil in September 1805 a

[1] Brett-James, 75.

[2] Guns taken to Seringapatam by Cornwallis and even Harris were left there because they could not be profitably taken away. Wellesley's siege pieces could move eighteen miles in six hours for days on end along with an adequate supply of ammunition: Dispatches, III, 435.

[3] Barclay's detailed analysis, dated 1 January 1804, of the forces 'under Major General Wellesley' total 58,483 fighting men from 'Mysore, Malabar, Canara, Goa, Wellesley's personal command, Hyderabad Subsidiary Force, Poona, Hyderabad, Guzerat, & Cuttack' with a staff of eight including two chaplains: Supplementary Despatches, IV, 308–9.

meeting took place which may be significant. For the first and only time he met his fellow Knight of the Bath, Horatio Lord Nelson.[1] In many ways the two men were as dissimilar as day and night, but both knew their jobs because they had served a rigid apprenticeship far from their native shores. They had survived where many others died, or were found wanting. Both were professionally competent and possessed at least potential greatness. For one of them the final proof came only a month later, at Trafalgar, but Waterloo was still far over the horizon.

Bonaparte called Wellington a sepoy general, something Wellesley surely was in 1805 and for as long as he lived. He had learned slowly and stored away bits and pieces of knowledge and know-how from India that were to be useful in the Peninsula and at Waterloo. He had developed the ability to do the right thing quickly under widely varying conditions of terrain and opposition.

Arthur Wellesley did not really know as much of military matters when he returned from India as he did later. In India, however, he had worked out combat procedures and tested them in battle. He had the knowledge, the physical strength, the courage and the coolness under fire to win in the East or the West. Eventually he was able to take on the best enemy there was anywhere and remain continuously victorious.[2] If in 1812 the sepoy general had been the Emperor of the French, the Grand Army in Russia would have been well fed, clothed and housed.

---

[1] Wellesley had been created a supernumerary K.B. Eventually, he took Nelson's place on the permanent roster.

[2] The misfortune at Sultanpetah Tope was probably gone from all minds save Wellesley's own, but this experience was also useful.

Appendix I
Ordnance in India, 1798–1805

With some slight adjustments to be discussed presently, British cavalry, infantry and artillery in India between 1798 and 1805 had arms of the same standard type as issued in Britain. There were a few minor differences between King's and EIC units.

On the other hand, the ordnance used against British armies in India varied enormously. Indian weapons included types not then used in Europe as well as many other exotic or antique arms. I have been able to piece together some details with the assistance of English friends, but do not claim any specialized knowledge in the Indian field.

Let us first discuss what is best known, the arms used by King's regiments of British infantry. These came out with muskets, bayonets and leather cartridge boxes containing fixed (paper-wrapped) ammunition and spare flints. The NCOs sometimes had halberds, swords and, perhaps, spontoons; the officers had fusils, pistols, swords and again, perhaps, spontoons. All these weapons were also used in Europe.

The standard Brown Bess musket of the British Army was the Model II, a strong heavy flintlock smoothbore arm with a 42-inch iron barrel. It was cal. .75 or slightly larger, and brass mounted. This weapon was normally carried in good units, and was handsome as well as being reliable. The iron and brass were polished and appeared to advantage against the deep brown of the well oiled stock and the white of the leather carrying sling.

The Brown Bess was not noted for accuracy; 'her sight was not long'.[1] But the weapon was not intended for precision. The only

---

[1] From a delightful but little known poem 'Brown Bess' written by Rudyard Kipling in 1911. It also contains the words, 'So she followed her Redcoats, whatever they did, from the heights of Quebec to the plains of Assaye.' I am indebted to Colonel Rixon Bucknall for this poem in MS form.

front sight was the bayonet stud at the top of the barrel; there was no rear sight at all. The weapon, as fired by an average infantryman could hit a stationary man almost every time at fifty yards and an enemy unit in line at a maximum of about 150 yards. In the hands of well-trained infantry it could be fired reasonably fast, up to four shots per minute. Its 480-grain spherical bullets would shoot through any body-armour.

Bayonets had triangular blades approximately sixteen inches long and sleeves to mount them around the end of the musket barrel. The fit had to be adjusted from time to time to keep an individual bayonet tight on a particular musket. There were no safety catches, but an infantryman could not lose his bayonet if he pulled it straight out.

EIC infantry had similar muskets and bayonets as their principal weapons. The East India Pattern[1] Brown Bess weapons – those purchased in Britain by the EIC – are of the same general description as those used in King's units save for 39-inch barrels, slightly lighter construction and simpler brass mountings. They used the same ammunition and could take the same bayonets. The EIC Pattern musket was the forerunner of the Model III 39-inch barrel muskets used in the British Army before Waterloo which continued in service until the end of the flintlock era.[2]

British officers serving in India often made important personal contributions in combat. Those in King's regiments used any weapon they considered appropriate, although a sword, probably of their own choosing, was by far the most usual. According to regulations EIC European officers used only swords and pistols.[3]

British cavalry in India, both King's and EIC, was armed predominantly with sabres of the curved British light cavalry type. (The King's units sent to India were 'light' cavalry in Europe, but they became 'heavy' by comparison with Indians and their mounts.) This sabre is excessively curved and lacks protection for the hand, but was much better than most comparable enemy weapons. British cavalry also had carbines and pistols. Fortescue in discussing a pursuit writes,

---

[1] The actual 'pattern musket' with the EIC cipher and dated 1779 on both lock and barrel, from which others were copied, is preserved at the Tower of London. Three similar ciphered and dated arms are at the United States Military Museum at West Point.

[2] All the British infantry at Waterloo is sometimes said to have had Model III weapons. I hesitate to disagree, but the Model II battlefield recoveries still preserved in private and public museums are too numerous in my opinion to be explained by their having been in the hands of Hanoverian militia and King's German Legion units only.

[3] *Buckle*, 108, says that on March 1788 fusils and spontoons were 'replaced by swords'.

'This is the only time I have found that British cavalry actually used their firearms' – to shoot enemies out of trees.[1] It may be significant that on 21 November 1802, when Wellesley was first preparing the expedition to restore the Peshwa, he ordered the casting of 500,000 musket balls and only 20,000 for carbines and pistols.[2]

EIC cavalry firearms were also made in Britain. They were similar to the flintlock smoothbore pistols and carbines used in King's cavalry regiments, a statement that does not mean much since British cavalry firearms were never really standardized. There is an EIC ciphered pistol in the India Museum at Sandhurst marked 1798, which may be typical of those used in Company units in India. It is carbine bore and slightly lighter than most contemporary King's cavalry weapons. I know of no EIC carbine made before 1806. Apparently most arms purchased for use in India that actually went out were destroyed through use over many years.[3] EIC sabres were also made in Britain and of the standard light cavalry type. There is on exhibition at the Tower of London, however, a *tulwar* (sabre) with a British-made blade and a typically Indian grip. Could this have been regulation issue in Native Cavalry units at one time? The best available Indian weapons were almost certainly used by EIC units in emergencies.

Before discussing British artillery material, let us briefly consider the cavalry and infantry weapons used by Wellesley's enemies between 1799 and 1804. They varied enormously not only from army to army, but also within the same unit. 'It is probable that no national or private collection in Europe contains any arms which might not be [found in Mahratta armies]. The Parthian bow and arrow, the iron club of Scythia, sabres of every age and nation, lances of every length and description, matchlocks of every form, and metallic helmets of every pattern.'[4]

On the other hand, the Mahratta Regular Battalions and similar units maintained by the Nizam before 1798 appear to have been armed with European muskets and bayonets or good copies of them made in India. As we have seen, Berar's men in Gawilghur had almost 2,000 EIC Brown Bess muskets. There were small arms manufactories at Agra which produced French pattern weapons said to be the equal in

---

[1] *Fortescue*, V, 99n.

[2] *Dispatches*, I, 380.

[3] A fair number of ciphered wall pieces dated 1793 survive, but they appear to have remained at the Tower after the Company turned over its arms in storage and production to the Government soon after the beginning of the war with France.

[4] *Nolan*, II, 432 quoting *Wilks*. Lances were not issued to British units at this time.

appearance and workmanship of the originals except that the locks did not last well.[1] Before Mornington's subsidiary treaty there were manufacturing arsenals in Hyderabad that produced arms for both Raymond and Piron.[2]

Indian infantry without contact with European officers or manufactories used almost anything; bows and arrows were still encountered occasionally. Various types of matchlock gun which were cheaper and easier to produce than flintlocks were more common in the hands of Indians; good matchlock muskets were superior to 'firelocks', the term given to flintlocks in those days when the weather was dry and everyone had time to get ready.[3] Indian cavalry also used *tulwars*, sometimes with European-made blades, and occasionally had lances. Artillerymen were armed with pikes. Both cavalry and infantry had a bewildering array of javelins, axes and daggers.

We should also discuss what was then a typically Indian weapon, the rocket. Light infantry and sometimes cavalry armed with rockets were frequently encountered in Mysore; the Mahrattas also used them, but less frequently. Rockets are often mentioned in the original records of the period and had no European counterpart until later. Today we think of them as artillery, but then a rocket was predominantly a small arm, usually just a mechanical javelin, although small explosive heads were used occasionally.

The Indian rocket was not like the British Congreve type used against Bayonne and at Waterloo, for it was normally handheld. It was less accurate, but had more power and range than Indian bows.

The pieces of artillery used in the British armies were almost all standard Woolwich types. Only the carriages were made in India.[4] Wellesley's field cannons were light and made of brass: 3-pounder, 6-pounder and 12-pounder guns, and 5.5-inch howitzers.[5] He used 3-

---

[1] I have followed a tradition that the French were paramount in these units, but 'Major Sangster, a Scot, cast cannon and made muskets at Agra and elsewhere': *Military Adventurers*, 387–8. Why would he have followed the French pattern?

[2] Malcolm praises these and sent one of the firearms produced there to the Governor-General: *Malcolm*, I, 68.

[3] 'The fire of a matchlock battalion is heavier than that of a musket battalion': *Military Adventurers*, 65.

[4] Some guns were cast at Fort William in the eighteenth century, but not enough to be of significance. Occasionally a captured Indian piece or one cast in France would be used.

[5] Tube weights were roughly a hundred times the weight of the solid shot fired, or a trifle more, although *Buckle*, 176, mentions a 6-pounder which weighed only 4¾ cwt (522 pounds). He says, however, that the 6-pounders employed after 1800 weighed 6½ cwt (725 pounds). *Adye*, 154, says that the 'light' 12-pounder weighed only 984 pounds

pounders mainly for detached service, but for a time Stevenson had them with his cavalry. Both 12-pounders and 5.5-inch howitzers were especially useful for secondary batteries in sieges; they cleared the breaches of defenders during an assault or prevented repair. Two 12-pounder field guns were sometimes attached to King's infantry battalions. As we have seen, Stuart wanted 12-pounder gallopers – the term as used in India will be explained presently – for his cavalry, but Wellesley did not consider them worth the extra weight which limited mobility.[1] On 12 July 1804, when setting forth artillery requirements for the Peshwa's subsidiary force, he listed 22 field pieces, 18 of them 6-pounders.[2] This reduction of brass pieces above 6-pounders for a field army was unusual; Stuart had wanted 'four brass 18-pounders and two 8-inch Howitzers' for the force he assembled in northern Mysore early in 1803.[3]

Field carriages used in Wellesley's campaigns in India present an identification problem. Here I have relied heavily on the advice of General Hughes at Woolwich.[4] The best diagrams for this period are in *Buckle*, No. 1, No. 2, and No. 3, but they show only a side view. Without General Hughes's guidance I could have learned little from them. The first is a Muller or 'bracket'-type carriage with a double trail; the check pieces run back parallel to each other and are joined only by brackets or a transom. This old form of carriage was used by the Bengal artillery until about 1810.

About 1800 the Madras artillery produced a solid or beam trail carriage, the type usually associated with nineteenth-century muzzle-loading artillery. Although no records exist, the latter type were probably made by Wellesley and Captain Scott at the Seringapatam arsenal.

Before the introduction of mechanical recoil absorbing devices the basic problem for all artillery carriages was one of weight and size vs. durability. In India this was aggravated by the extremely fast drying

---

[1] 'The six brass 12-pounders . . . are entirely useless. By sending these away from the army a gain would be made of 310 bullocks for guns, ammunition, and spare carriages.' *Supplementary Despatches*, IV, 3.

[2] *Dispatches*, III, 511: The others were two 12-pounders and two 5.5-inch howitzers for sieges and not attached to individual battalions for field service.

[3] *Supplementary Despatches*, IV, 5.

[4] Major-General B. P. Hughes, C.B., C.R.E., chairman of the Royal Artillery Institution in a letter to me dated 6 August 1969.

---

which may account for the excessive breakage of the carriages both in Wellesley's and Stevenson's armies in the latter half of 1803.

out in the long periods of intense heat and sunlight. In 1801 both brass
and iron cheek pieces were tried,[1] but wood was better. All iron axletrees for brass 12-pounders tried out by Wellesley 'broke in less than
a quarter of an hour's firing'.[2] These pieces were also notoriously hard
on carriages. At Gawilghur Stevenson's and Wellesley's artillerymen
'broke the axletrees [type unspecified] of every 12-pounder carriage
we had'.[3]

A long heavy carriage would stand up under more firings than a
short light one. Something had to absorb the recoil or the carriage
would break, especially when the piece was elevated even five degrees.
All these pieces ran back on discharge, but this was not sufficient. This
basic compromise between weight and efficiency in carriage design
still continues. A light piece is easier to move, but not so effective in action.

Galloper carriages used in Europe at that time were for small guns
and had permanently split trails. These formed without adjustment to
the shafts which were used to attach a single large strong horse to the
piece. Sometimes another horse was attached in tandem; drivers usually
rode these animals. A light 3-pounder might have been mounted in
such a carriage, but the usual limit was a 1.5-pounder with a tube
weight of 150 pounds.

The Indian gallopers were certainly not of this type. Out there the
term was used merely to designate the type of animals for which the
carriage was rigged at that particular time. Gallopers were horse
drawn, but with the usual limber; the animals were not attached
directly to the carriage. According to the Indian definition even
12-pounder gallopers were obviously possible. As mentioned in
Chapter XI, Wellesley had 6-pounder gallopers for his pickets through
Assaye, but replaced the horses with bullocks before Argaum as
replacement bullocks were easier to obtain. Ten powerful Mysore
bullocks could pull a light 6-pounder complete with carriage and
limber as fast and as far as infantry could march.

All this artillery was of brass and for use in the field or for secondary
siege batteries. Throughout his campaigning in India Wellesley also
carried siege pieces which were much heavier than field guns of the
same bore size and were made of iron rather than brass on account of
the cost.[4] He preferred 12-pounders which had a tube weight of 32

---

[1] *Buckle*, 170.   [2] *Dispatches*, II, 565.   [3] *Dispatches*, III, 30.

[4] A student of artillery can find many comparisons over the years of iron and brass
for use in gun tubes. There were several small advantages on the sides of both metals,
but initial cost appears to have been the deciding factor in favour of iron for heavy
artillery.

cwt, although Stevenson had two 18-pounders. Wellesley's pieces were drawn by forty or more bullocks[1] assisted by a large female elephant for each pair of guns; all four could keep up with the infantry even in moderately rough country.

These heavy, high-velocity iron guns were mounted in a carriage with both firing and travelling positions for the trunnions so that, when being transported, some of the weight of the tube would be transferred to the limber wheels.[2] The men, bullocks and elephants who handled these must have been well trained and skilful to cover ground fast in practically roadless terrain.

During this time Indian artillery was far less uniform and generally less efficient. Guns were being cast at Seringapatam and at Hyderabad during the period of French ascendancy. Scindia's pieces, most of them probably cast at Agra, were better, but they were by no means uniform.[3] None taken at Seringapatam were fit for British use; those captured at Assaye were.[4] British artillerymen considered the Assaye weapons to be first rate, although some pieces had unusual ornamentation.

A few words should be said about the extraordinary types of Indian artillery. Mahratta guns not assigned in regular battalions, such as those which defended the village of Assaye and fired at too long a range at Argaum, were '. . . of all sorts and dimensions; and, having the names of their gods given to them, are painted in the most fantastic manner; and many of them, held in esteem for the services they are said to have already performed for the state, cannot now be dispensed with, although in every respect unfit for use. Were the guns even serviceable, the small supply of ammunition with which they are

[1] *Supplementary Despatches*, IV, 109. Jasper Nicolls wrote in his journal, quoted by Gurwood in *Dispatches*, that on several occasions iron 12-pounders were 'drawn by forty-four bullocks, nine sets (of four each) formed abreast, and four pairs of leaders': *Dispatches*, II, 585. This same entry throws some light on 6-pounders also: 'The infantry have all 6-pounders, but of different weight and length; the Madras guns are old and short. The heavy guns (Nicolls is still referring to 6-pounders) have twelve bullocks, the others ten.' Nicolls was a captain and may have been on Wellesley's staff from after Assaye until after Gawilghur: *Dictionary of National Biography*, XIV, 495.

[2] A carriage of this type is described by *Buckle*, 179, and illustrated, 579; it was known as 'Colonel Duff's Pattern'.

[3] There were fourteen different sizes of guns and howitzers among the seventy-six brass pieces captured on 23 September 1803. They varied from 1-pounders to 18-pounders for guns and from 5-inch to 8-inch for howitzers: *Wellesley's Notes*, 282. *Thorn*, 117, says that pieces of the French type were cast at Ougein and Muttra also.

[4] Wellesley wrote on 3 October 1803, 'Scindia's ordnance [is] so good and so well equipped that it answers for our service. We never could use Tipoo's.' *Dispatches*, II, 371.

provided has always effectually prevented the Mahratta artillery from being formidable to their enemies.'[1]

There were also splendid, typically Oriental pieces which were sometimes more than twenty feet in length. The Great Gun of Agra, if it could have fired a cast-iron ball, which I doubt, would have been a 1,500-pounder. The large wrought-iron gun at Gawilghur is approximately a 150-pounder. During the siege of Seringapatam '. . . one of those enormous engines, called Malabar guns, was fired at our works. The man stationed on the flank of the battery for the purpose [observation], seeing the flash, gave the usual signal, "Shot!" A moment or two afterwards, seeing a large body taking its curving course through the air, he corrected himself by calling out "Shell!" As the ponderous missile (for it was an enormous stone shot) approached, he could not tell what to make of it.'[2]

In spite of the lucky shot described by Elphinstone which killed four men and wounded two at Gawilghur, these enormous weapons were, of course, almost useless. They had considerable range, but fired only a single solid projectile and would only have been effective against fortifications, but were too heavy to be moved. The Gawilghur piece which was beautifully finished is made of wrought iron and carefully built up. It has survived where it is because even during World War II it proved too big to be moved for its scrap iron value. The Great Gun of Agra which was cut up and melted long ago is said to have been made mostly of copper and tin, with the addition of precious metals.

We will now briefly discuss artillery ammunition. As in Europe, British field guns used solid and case shot. Howitzers fired shell and case, the latter being greater than the one in the guns.[3] Siege pieces fired solid shot for breaching, but could also use grape if it was available. During this period British ammunition for field guns and howitzers was all of the fixed type; the solid shot, shell, or can of case was secured to one end of a wooden sabot and the powder charge in a varnished cloth container or equivalent to the other.

---

[1] *Nolan*, II, 436–7.

[2] *Blackiston*, I, 138.

[3] I use the term 'case' because the term 'grape' is not technically correct. Mention of the latter is, however, far more common in contemporary records. I believe it unlikely that the 'true grape' of a later period, usually three layers of three balls each rigidly held together before discharge, was used at all. Howitzers normally used smaller balls than guns because their muzzle velocities were lower which meant less effective range. The smaller balls would have had more close-in effectiveness.

A peculiarity of British Indian ammunition was that 12-pounder guns sometimes fired shells. Wellesley had shells for 4.5-inch howitzers, a size he did not use, strapped into 12-pounder cartridges. They were employed probably more for psychological effect than for producing casualties.[1] A shell of this type was hardly more than a powerful hand grenade, unworthy of a piece that had to be drawn by at least twenty pairs of bullocks.

Scindia's regular battalion artillery used ammunition of the European type contained in tumbrils and limber chests. Some Indian gunners probably loaded similar cartridges, but others scooped powder from open barrels and were blown up when an error was made.

A mention should be made of Indian wall pieces, an intermediate type of weapon between artillery and small arms. There were two types, miniature cannons mounted in a yoke attached to a swivel and overgrown matchlock muskets with a hook to secure against the outside edge of the wall.[2] These fired either a single iron ball weighing from less than half a pound to more than a pound, or a number of smaller shot, made of iron or lead.

Body armour was used in India to some extent, although no King's or EIC units are known to have had it, except for the 'helmet' of the King's dragoons. Most Indian horsemen wore turbans containing yards of narrow but strong woollen cloth which were almost sabre-proof. Plate and chain metal armour was sometimes used as well as Chinese type quilting. This seems to have been effective when the Indians fought each other, but was not so good against Europeans with better sabres and stronger and more skilful arms.[3] None of it was proof, of course, against a ball from a Brown Bess musket, and must have hampered a fighting man's movements in a hot climate. It was particularly inconvenient to swim in; some of Dhoondiah Waugh's followers drowned trying to cross a river in their armour.

[1] Wellesley suggested to Stevenson who was advancing on Burhampoor, 'If they should hesitate about giving you a contribution possibly a shell or two from your 12-pounders . . . would accelerate their decision.' *Dispatches*, II, 418.

[2] According to *Ayde*, 154, an 'amusette' was an artillery piece weighing about 300 pounds. Whether the EIC wall pieces mentioned on p. 281 n. 3 of this Appendix are *amusettes* or not is debatable. They are about six feet long, have 1-inch bores, and weigh forty-five pounds. Similar weapons were used in the field during the American Revolution, but I have found no mention of their active field service in India.

[3] *Blackiston*, 207-8, mentions the practice common in the King's 19th Dragoons of removing the turban of an antagonist with the point and then slashing the bare head.

Appendix II
Organization and Tactics in India, 1799–1808

In broad outline the British military organization in India was similar to that at home, but there were points of difference. There was not a single British army in India, but two: one composed of King's units loaned to the EIC and supported by the Company from the time they left Britain until they returned; the other the EIC Army. The co-operation of the two armies with no more friction than there was – and there was a good deal of it at various times – is remarkable.

Although the EIC was active in the East from the early 17th century, its military forces were organized at company level only for approximately 150 years and functioned as a type of police force for the protection of EIC mercantile establishments known as factories. When France took Madras in September 1746, British land forces in that Presidency consisted of 200 Europeans and 2,000 Indians. The latter were not then under European officers and drill sergeants and the majority were still armed with bows and arrows.

The Court of Directors of the EIC was faced with a choice of having a real army or losing in India. They could either abandon their long-established concept of 'trade but not territory', or have the French take over everything. They chose the lesser of two evils and began to build an empire which required a military establishment larger and more complicated than a factory security force. The EIC Army is said to have begun with the arrival at Madras in January 1748 of Major Stringer Lawrence. He was nearly 51 years old, and a surviving portrait shows him as unusually fat even for that time. He began, however, to build immediately and combined the seven independent EIC companies of European soldiers into a single battalion later known as the

Madras Europeans.[1] Lawrence also began the organizing, training, disciplining and arming of Indian soldiers after the British fashion under European officers and sergeants,[2] although these units did not grow to battalion size until 1759. The Bengal and Bombay Presidencies followed the lead of Madras in regard to both European and Native battalions.

The first King's Regiment was sent to India in 1754. It was then known as Adlercron's (its colonel's name) but was to become the 39th Foot. Eyre Coote was a subaltern in it until gazetted a captain on 18 June 1755; he and some of his 39th were with Clive when he won his great victory at Plassey. The second regiment to go out to India was the 84th Foot; this was raised by Coote especially for service in the East. He was a lieutenant-colonel at this time and appears to have bypassed the rank of major.[3] The contribution of King's Regiments to the British effort in India after Plassey was considerable. There were at least seventeen of them present in India during the Mahratta War, although some were below strength.[4]

The first King's Regiment of cavalry to go to India was the 23rd, later designated the 19th Light Dragoons. This unit arrived in Madras without horses in October 1782 and for sixteen years was the only King's cavalry regiment in India. The extreme usefulness of this unit against Tipoo between 1790 and 1792 led to the raising of Native Cavalry units similar to it, although there had been Native Cavalry troops or companies as early as 1700. James Stevenson was one of the first Madras cavalry officers.

The EIC artillery organization in each Presidency was rudimentary until the middle of the eighteenth century. Companies of artillery were formed (presumably on paper) 'in each Presidency on 17 June 1748. That in Bengal was probably lost in the Black Hole trouble, but re-formed to fight at Plassey.'[5] The twelve British pieces used at this 1756 battle may have been naval pieces on travelling siege carriages which were manned by personnel most of whom had no previous field experience. True field guns of the Muller type appeared later, although the pieces themselves were mostly assigned to infantry

---

[1] Still later this unit was known in succession as the Madras Fusiliers, the 102nd Foot, and the 1st Battalion, Royal Dublin Fusiliers.

[2] European NCOs were never numerous and were used mainly as drill instructors.

[3] At the time of Plassey he is often referred to as Major Coote, but if he held this rank, it was conferred temporarily by Clive: *Coote*, 47: *National Biography*, IV, 1084.

[4] House of Commons Account, *passim*.

[5] A letter from General Hughes to the author dated 10 December 1969.

battalions in actual campaigns, or even in the smaller garrisons. From 1798 cavalry regiments also had pairs of assigned field guns.

EIC artillery personnel in the upper grades – i.e. officers, NCOs and gunners – were almost all European.[1] Gun lascars were, of course, Indians, but normally they only handled drag ropes and performed minor functions during firing. When pieces were assigned to single infantry units, EIC artillery officers did not accompany their guns:[2] the artillery came directly under infantry officers who were not gunners.

We should note, however, that artillery companies of ten guns were often assigned intact to five battalions operating together. There was definitely something of a dual responsibility: the individual two-gun sections assigned to a battalion would have been responsible to the commanding officer of that unit in action, but to the artillery unit for day-to-day operation. Both Wellesley and Stevenson had chiefs of artillery who undoubtedly kept a close check on all artillery pieces and personnel with their respective armies regardless of their temporary assignment to other units.

INFANTRY ORGANIZATION AND TACTICS

Infantry was the predominant arm in India; in order to understand combat out there in Wellesley's time it is necessary to know how foot soldiers were organized and how they moved and fought. Both King's and EIC infantry battalions were organized in the same manner. Strength depended on casualties, health and replacements from home for King's units. Native battalions could be recruited more easily if suitable replacements were available locally, but frequently they were not. Throughout his military career Wellesley preferred to have under-strength units rather than reduce quality by adding untrained, undisciplined personnel. Full roster strength was from 900 to 1,100 but numbers below this were common. During Wellesley's time there

---

[1] Native artillery units were tried from time to time, but appear not to have worked out. A Native artillery company was raised in Madras in 1799, but reduced in 1802: *Wilson*, III, 71. One reason for this was the feeling that trained Native gunners might desert and become skilful enemies. Even Wellesley, who advocated the training of sepoys as auxiliary gunners, said 'care should be taken to select men who are known and distinguished for their attachment to the service': *Supplementary Despatches*, IV, 502–3.

[2] The only exception seems to have been when two EIC 6-pounder gallopers went to serve with a King's cavalry regiment. An EIC lieutenant fireworker, two European gunners, and twenty-three Natives manned these: *Wilson*, II, 342.

was at least one instance of an EIC battalion which had 1,600 men in it.[1]

Each battalion, regardless of size, was divided into ten companies, two of which were the flank companies. In King's battalions, the flank companies were the grenadier company,[2] which was normally on the right of the line, and the light company on the left. The better soldiers were usually, although not always, in these flank companies. The bigger men were grenadiers; the smaller, more active soldiers were generally in the light company, so long as they qualified in other ways. To some extent these flank companies had special, or perhaps additional training. As they were detached from the rest of the battalion, they were able to operate more efficiently alone than the other eight line companies.

There were no light companies in Wellesley's EIC battalions; both flank companies were grenadiers. In his opinion, Natives were poor skirmishers. Even with the best sepoys, control, which was of paramount importance, was not possible when units were spread out.[3]

During Wellesley's time Native Infantry regiments normally consisted of two battalions, but these units served separately more often than together. Even as late as 1793 an EIC battalion was normally commanded by a captain and had only 'a European adjutant, an assistant surgeon, and six or eight subalterns attached to it'.[4] A captain cost the Company less than a major or a lieutenant-colonel. By 1799, however, the number of European officers had increased to about twenty-seven per battalion at full strength, a condition rarely achieved. The normal rank of a battalion commander was lieutenant-colonel,[5] although Captain Vesey was in charge of the 2/3 Madras Native Infantry for months in 1803 and 1804.

Both King's and EIC infantry battalions habitually formed in lines two ranks deep; the unit of manœuvre was generally a half company. A battalion column was normally twenty half companies, one behind the other. The extreme width of a half company at full strength was

---

[1] A Bombay battalion under Murray in Guzerat: *Dispatches*, III, 236.

[2] The throwing of grenades had been discontinued long before; there were no hand grenades in British India: *Dispatches*, I, 108.

[3] 'The sepoys must not be employed upon these light troop duties; they are entirely unfit for them': *Dispatches*, II, 363. General Lake endeavoured to organize and train light companies in his Bengal Native Infantry, but apparently without success. 'Both flank companies of each Native battalion then and for some years afterwards consisting of grenadiers': *National Biography*, XI, 413. There were no light companies in the EIC armies as late as 1809: *Nineteen Movements*, VIII.

[4] *Welsh*, I, 15.

[5] Wilson, II. 290.

about twenty-five men shoulder to shoulder, a little less than fifty feet, but too wide for any road in those days. British infantry in India did not use roads except in unusual circumstances, or at least did not confine itself to them on the march. The length of a battalion column varied with the distance between half companies; these units did not march one behind the other with only a single pace separating them. If the entire battalion was likely to have to go from column into line just by having each unit wheel 90 degrees, the individual units were 'at full deploying distance'. This meant roughly fifteen yards of open space between half companies.

Forty ranks of soldiers, two in each half company, with nineteen gaps of fifteen yards between each half company would have occupied about 215 yards in depth, too much for compact strength. Half and quarter distance columns, with eight and four yards separating the half companies, were more common and obviously led to shorter columns. A 1,000-man battalion in column of half companies at quarter distance would have occupied a space about fifteen yards wide and ninety yards deep. It could form line facing one flank or the other reasonably quickly and regularly, but personnel would have had to move laterally at one or both ends.

Close order drill was then the very essence of infantry tactics. Battalions manœuvred on the battlefield precisely as they did on parade. By the time the Wellesleys arrived in India, Dundas had standardized these procedures.[1] Both King's and EIC battalions followed the system known as the Nineteen Movement; by using them infantry could go through all their evolutions precisely and without confusion. It should be emphasized that British units in India performed these manœuvres well because they practised them often for exercise, discipline and in order to be ready for combat.

In battle, British infantry fought in line; enemy cavalry in India was not sufficiently strong to make squares necessary. A two-rank line allowed maximum firepower, because both ranks could fire at the same time because the muskets of the rear rank were long enough to extend well past the faces of the men in front. Advancing with a whole battalion in line over a considerable distance has always been difficult, but it was done in India as well as it ever had been in military history.

[1] This Dundas (Colonel and later General Sir David) should not be confused with the President of the Board of Control, Henry Dundas, first Viscount Melville. They appear to have been unrelated. David Dundas wrote not one book but several. *Principles of Military Movements Chiefly Applied to Infantry* . . . appeared in 1788, *Rules and Regulations for the Movement of His Majesty's Infantry* was issued in 1792.

Malavelley, Assaye and Argaum were won by British infantry battalions advancing in line.[1]

British infantry in India created more enemy casualties with bullets than with bayonets. Both King's and EIC battalions were good with their muskets because they practised with them. Live firing was limited throughout the world at that time by the relatively high cost of ammunition, but the EIC had money which the Wellesleys spent freely. But the ever-present threat of British bayonets supported the firepower; one without the other would have been less effective. British bayonets in India gained, actually as well as psychologically, because of the physical superiority of the Europeans. To some extent this advantage rubbed off on the British Native battalions deployed nearby.

Assaults on fortified places were less formal than battles. When possible, a portion of the British infantry engaged would cover the other portion with fire. But generally the first few men who mounted a breach or got over a wall had to use their personal weapons to kill some of the defenders and overawe the rest. Bayonets and swords wielded by men confident of their skill, strength and ability to support each other were more important than bullets from muskets and pistols, although undoubtedly maximum effectiveness was reached when shock and firepower were combined.

Battles and assaults were, of course, of paramount military importance. We should not forget, however, the almost endless series of small infantry actions in India – fought to protect camps, convoys, depots of boats and the like – that sometimes did not even include friendly casualties. Wellesley's emphasis was always on maintaining discipline and order, while taking advantage of all favourable circumstances. A single company which could continue to manœuvre, fire and use its bayonets when necessary could defeat easily a thousand semi-organized enemies.

CAVALRY ORGANIZATION AND TACTICS

As we have seen, there was only one King's cavalry regiment in India until 1798. In Cornwallis's war against Tipoo the effectiveness of the

[1] Although Arthur Wellesley stressed the value of training manœuvres in which more than one battalion formed a single line, he appears to have used in each instance battalion lines only. At Malavelley and Assaye, his battalions advanced en echelon; at Argaum, they went forward independently.

19th Dragoons was so considerable, however, that the EIC began to organize similar Native Cavalry regiments almost immediately. After some experimenting, the regimental organization was standardized at nineteen Europeans – two of them drill sergeants – and 498 Natives, divided into three squadrons of two troops each. A troop at full strength contained two or three British officers, three Indian officers, eight Indian NCOs, a trumpeter, a water carrier and seventy privates or troopers.[1] Where terrain would permit, a cavalry regiment could go through complicated evolutions by means of troop or half troop units.

In India British cavalry was employed effectively in combat in only one way. It charged at controlled speed and used its sabres – sometimes the threat of a charge was sufficient. Other tactics were secondary. If terrain permitted, charges were normally delivered with squadrons and troops in line – two ranks of horsemen advancing with an interval of about fifteen yards between the front and rear rank. A 500-man regiment would occupy, including the intentional gaps between squadrons and troops, a front of about 300 yards. As already mentioned, at Conaghull against Dhoondiah Wellesley formed all his cavalry into a single rank, but had two King's cavalry regiments along with the 1st and 2nd Native Cavalry.

In 1782 there were not enough horses in Madras sufficiently strong to bear Europeans. In this connection, we should again note that Light Dragoons counted as heavy cavalry in India. These troopers were effective partly because of their discipline and training, but in part because they and their horses[2] were physically more powerful than their opponents. To some extent at least, this advantage also worked in favour of EIC Native Cavalry who were probably no larger than the men they fought, but who through exercise had developed more strength and skill with their weapons. The comparative heaviness of British cavalry, even of Native units, was not a complete advantage. They were not good at light reconnaissance and screening, or at operating against Mahratta *brindarries*. Wellesley was fortunate, however, in having Bisnapah's *silladar* horse from Mysore as well as his Mahratta allies for these responsibilities. The term *silladar* implied

---

[1] *Wilson*, II, 340–1.

[2] A horse that could carry a European and his equipment cost sixty pounds, a large sum in those days; in addition to its rider each animal normally had two men to care for it. Prices of really good horses in India were astonishingly high, as much as 300 pounds or even more. An ensign earned less than fifty pounds a year.

that each trooper furnished his horse, horse keeper and weapons, and was paid accordingly.

ARTILLERY ORGANIZATION AND TACTICS

We have already discussed the unusual arrangements in regard to European and Indian artillery personnel and the dual responsibility of the two-gun sections assigned to battalions and cavalry regiments. It may be significant that the authority on the Madras Army, Lieutenant-Colonel W. J. Wilson,[1] does not tell us how artillery and infantry officers were supposed to share responsibility for these assigned units. A company of artillery obviously consisted of five two-gun units, each commanded by a sergeant with a corporal, two European gunners and a fairly large number of Indians; these units were assigned to infantry battalions. One unit, serving with a battalion many miles from any other unit, would have been totally dependent upon the battalion commander, but what happened when two or more battalions were together?

Field artillery tactics in India were normally based on the proper employment of one or more two-gun sections. Wellesley made no effort to get any sort of grand battery into operation. In battle each battalion had the support of its two 6-pounders which gave the infantry more firepower, especially within the range of grape; they also gave the intangible advantages associated with artillery in India. Without its guns, a battalion was always subject to the near approach and consequent harassment from enemy cavalry and rocketeers. The two 6-pounders gave a battalion enough long-range punch to inspire respect; this pair of pieces could also clear jungle which might or might not be occupied by enemy infantry. EIC gunners were genuine professionals and skilful in handling their weapons.

Siege artillery in India was competently handled because both officers and gunners were skilful veterans. Most European soldiers took their profession seriously; artillerymen learned how to handle guns both in the field and against fortifications. The pieces were different, but the personnel was the same. The gunners who opened the actual breach at Seringapatam in less than three days knew what they were about, and the British artillery at the sieges of Ahmednuggur and Gawilghur did professional jobs with far less material. Lake's tragic failure before Bhurtpoor came from improper planning, poor logistics

[1] Referred to as *Wilson*.

and inferior leadership during the first assault, rather than deficient artillery skill.

Field pieces could also be employed against fortifications 'to open the gates', a technique that has not been explained as clearly as it might have been. I believe that for this purpose the pieces used should have been loaded with powder only.[1] Wellesley wrote on 14 October 1803, 'I think that General Lake's capture of Allyghur is one of the most extraordinary feats that I have heard of in this country. I never attacked a fort that I did not attempt the same thing, viz., to blow open the gates, but I have never succeeded. I have always taken them by escalade, which appears to have been impossible in this instance.'[2]

THE REGULAR BATTALIONS IN NATIVE ARMIES

Native princes were quick to appreciate the superiority of European military weapons, organization and tactics. There is always a tendency for those who lose a war to imitate the victors. As soon as Stringer Lawrence, the great Clive and their French counterparts began to form sepoys into European-type battalions with European arms partly under European officers, the Indian rulers began to do likewise. This process began in Mysore and Hyderabad, but the Mahrattas spent more money over a longer period and had considerably more Regular Battalions. The units of this type raised by Scindia and Holkar were the best in organization, weapons and discipline. Some of them were also well along towards developing unit pride. Pohlmann's brigade had not been defeated before Assaye; they were all-conquering against ordinary Indian units. At the battle of Poona in October 1802 the fighting strength of both Mahratta armies lay in their Regular Battalions.[3] These units did not meet British armies until 1803, and only Holkar realized that they probably would not be effective against King's and EIC troops.

Benoît de Boigne of Savoy was the best known and most successful of the European professional soldiers who raised Regular Battalions for the Mahratta chiefs. He began his career with them in 1781 and was

---

[1] *Blackiston*, I, 129, says of the attack on the *pettah* at Ahmednuggur, 'the artillery officer (in charge of the field gun so used) had been firing shot at it, instead of running up his gun and blowing it open'.

[2] *Dispatches*, II, 414. See also *Thorn*, 97–8.

[3] Dawes, who commanded Scindia's regular units, might well have won the battle had he not been killed. As mentioned, Harding fell at Holkar's side during the final decisive cavalry charge.

a competent officer of courage and high professional ability. What is more unusual, he appears to have been honest and public spirited as well. He was one of the hardest workers in India and spent his days much like Arthur Wellesley.

This Savoyard even anticipated Richard's subsidiary treaties. In 1793 he took over territory for the support of his troops as the EIC did later on. When he began to administer territory, he made many of the improvements in regard to justice and internal economy that the Wellesleys were to adopt a few years later. De Boigne not only had a clause in his contract that relieved him from ever fighting the British himself, but earnestly advised Scindia never to fight them either and if necessary to disband his army to prevent a rupture of friendly relations with the EIC.[1] In 1797 he returned to Europe at the age of forty-six with a fortune of 100,000 pounds, and married a girl of seventeen. He bought himself an estate in his native Savoy and survived for more than thirty years, kind and generous to all.

There were other professional officers as colourful as de Boigne, notably a huge, and in many ways admirable, Irish sailor by the name of George Thomas. He could neither read nor write, but he might have won a large part of India had he been able to conquer his desire for drink. Most of these men were able and some were honourable. They came from several European countries and America, although a fair number were half-castes.[2]

Early in the nineteenth century it became the fashion for English writers to imply that most of the European officers serving with the Native princes were French. This was more or less true in Raymond's army in Hyderabad and towards the end of Perron's time in northern Hindostan, but certainly was not accurate for other units in other places. 'Englishmen', a term which included other British, were at least twice as numerous as Frenchmen. Usually these officers had left King's or EIC units under a cloud, or to better themselves from the ranks. Sutherland was cashiered from the King's 73rd Foot as a young officer; Finglass was quartermaster of the King's 19th Dragoons. Pohlmann was a sergeant in a Hanoverian regiment in the British Army. Colonel J. P. Boyd, who served the Peshwa, was an American. As we have seen, some of these European officers, including Englishmen,

[1] This was Madhojee Scindia; his adopted son, Dowlut Rao Scindia, succeeded him on 3 March 1794: *Wellesley's Notes*, 4.
[2] The best sources of information about this most unusual group of men are *Military Adventurers* and *Regular Corps*.

continued to serve Scindia and Holkar against their countrymen in 1803 and 1804 in spite of generous offers from the Governor-General to abandon their employers.

One of these Regular Battalions in the Wellesley's time consisted of about forty Native officers and 700 enlisted men. They were organized after the EIC pattern[1] and were supposed to have roughly the same tactics. There were two main differences. First, one of these battalions, although slightly smaller than a similar EIC unit, had five rather than two field pieces, supposedly four 6-pounder guns and a 5.5-inch howitzer as well. A full complement of artillery ammunition consisted of 300 round shot and 100 cartridges of grape for each gun. There were 50 explosive stone shells and 50 charges of grape for the howitzer.

The other major difference was the extremely small number of Europeans in a Regular Battalion. Two white or partly white officers and six 'Portuguese' gunners were about the maximum per battalion; Perron, who took over from de Boigne and finally lost to Lake, is said to have run 40 battalions and 380 guns with only 300 Europeans, including those supervising his manufactories for small arms, cannon and ammunition.

Four to eight Regular Battalions were organized into brigades or *compoos*. There were both cavalry and heavier artillery at *compoo* level and apparently some additional irregular infantry as well as the inevitable swarm of camp followers of all Indian armies. In good units morale was high. Indian soldiers were often more attached to their European leaders than to the Indian prince who paid them.

ORGANIZATION AND TACTICS IN NATIVE ARMIES

The Regular Battalions in the various Native armies were strongly influenced by European tactics, organization and discipline; other units were modelled on them to a lesser degree. As we have seen, Tipoo took considerable advantage of the Frenchmen who were either in his employ or allied to him; other Native armies did so to a smaller extent.

On the other hand, weapons, organization and training all cost money and time, much more than was required to put infantry and cavalry of the old Indian type in the field. We know far less than we would like to about purely Native organization. The cavalry tended

---

[1] The French influence may have led to a reduction in number of companies per battalion at least in some units: *Military Adventurers*, 64 and *passim*.

to group around individual chiefs and sub-chiefs, but there must have been something more definite than this; even irregular cavalry cannot operate without some internal organization for movement, subsistence and control. Similarly, Indian infantry units must have been organized, even though we lack details. Thousands of men cannot march, cross rivers, camp, build fortifications and do the dozens of other normal military activities without some sort of internal division and subordination.

We are on firmer ground with regard to tactics. The Mysore cavalry under Bisnapah Pundit had no European officers or drill sergeants, but appears to have been remarkably proficient in light cavalry responsibilities of every sort, except delivering a controlled charge on a battlefield. The same was probably true of the Mogul horse which Wellesley commanded on the way to and at Seringapatam. It was informally armed and organized, but capable of exerting considerable individual pressure on an enemy by means of their weapons efficiency. Their charges would probably not amount to much more than a simultaneous attack by many individuals, but if the enemy was no better organized, they could be effective. The Mahratta cavalry could not apply shock by means of discipline and momentum either. They were superb horsemen, however, and some of them were fair swordsmen. They performed remarkably well against Monson.

Native infantry without any European influence tended to be better on the defensive. It could not manœuvre in the open or attack effectively in daylight. As Wellesley said, the Mahrattas were able to choose extremely strong positions, take them efficiently and hold them well. Even the King's 74th with Orrock's pickets in front was unable to take the village of Assaye, and the Jats were able to defeat Lake at Bhurtpoor. Offensively, Indian forces were at their best in irregular actions like night surprises against British forces that thought themselves far removed from danger. In October 1802 a mad rush against sleepy semi-armed men had worked well at Pancoorta Cottah in Wynaad. Another type of Native offensive that proved effective was the cutting off and surrounding of a British force. Defensive lines could be advanced to such an extent as to encircle a better organized enemy. Baillie suffered a disaster of this type on 10 September 1780. Fear of a similar event caused the Monson fiasco. Wellesley warned Stevenson that 'he would be attacked in his camp'. The Mahratta cavalry had an unusual facility for surrounding and cutting off an enemy with greater combat potential.

Wellesley's decision to attack at Assaye may have been caused in part by his own fear of a situation like this. To be cut off in one's camp was the crowning indignity. It may also have been the only way the enemy could win offensively, but the tactic is difficult to apply without help from the opposition. Baillie, Munro and the French commanders at Dien Bien Phu had to help Hyder, Tipoo and Giap. An army with both strategic and tactical mobility was not likely to be caught. The Mahrattas especially developed the cavalry raid by tens of thousands of horsemen which succeeded if the opposition lost its head and/or lacked manœuvrable strength in the field. Cavalry alone could accomplish little against even a much smaller force of integrated arms if it could also move and fight cohesively.

Appendix III

Order of Battle, British Forces against Tipoo Sultan of Mysore in 1799

I MAIN ARMY, LIEUTENANT-GENERAL HARRIS:[1]

Cavalry, Lieutenant-General Floyd:

1st Brigade, EIC Colonel James Stevenson
King's 19th Dragoons, 1st Native Cavalry, 4th Native Cavalry
2nd Brigade, EIC Colonel John Pater
King's 25th Dragoons, 2nd Native Cavalry, 3rd Native Cavalry
   Total Cavalry strength: 884 Europeans, 1,751 Natives

Right Wing Infantry, EIC Major-General Thomas Bridges:

1st Brigade Major-General Baird: King's 12th Foot, King's 74th
   Foot, King's Scotch 'Brigade' (later the 94th Foot)
3rd Brigade EIC Colonel Francis Gowdie: 1/1st, 1/6th, and 1/12
   Madras Native Infantry
5th Brigade, EIC Colonel George Roberts: 1/8th, 2/3rd, and 2/12
   Madras Native Infantry

Left Wing Infantry, Major-General William Popham:

2nd Brigade, Colonel John Cope Sherbrooke: King's 73rd, Regiment
   de Meuron[2]
4th Brigade, Lieutenant-Colonel Gardiner: 1st, 2nd, and 3rd Battalion
   Bengal Volunteer Infantry

---

[1] George Harris, John Floyd and James Stuart were all King's officers and territorially restricted lieutenant-generals. Harris and Floyd were advanced to this rank 'in the Army' on 1 January 1801, with Harris seven spaces senior. Stuart reached this rank on 29 April 1802.

[2] The Regiment de Meuron was Swiss and had been in Ceylon in the service of the Netherlands. After the capitulation of the island to British forces in 1796, the entire regiment took service with the EIC. It was all-European, but not British.

6th Brigade, Lieutenant-Colonel Scott: 2/5th and 2/9th Madras Native Infantry

Total Infantry strength: 3,650 Europeans, 10,695 Native Artillery: This army contained 608 European gunners and 1,483 Indian gun lascars to handle 56 field pieces. These gunners had dual functions, however, and would man the siege pieces also. The field artillery consisted of two brass 18-pounders, eight brass 12-pounders, 38 brass 6-pounders, eight brass 3-pounders and four brass 5·5-inch howitzers. The siege artillery consisted of two iron 24-pounders, 30 iron 18-pounders, eight iron 12-pounders, and three 8-inch brass howitzers.[1] Engineers and Pioneers: there were European engineer officers and NCOs plus about 1,000 Indian pioneers under European officers. EIC Colonel William Gent was in command of these.

Total fighting men (15 February 1799), 20,071.

II BOMBAY ARMY, LIEUTENANT-GENERAL STUART:
Right Native Brigade, Lieutenant-Colonel John Montresor:
1/2 Bombay (653), 1/4 Bombay (672), 1/3 Bombay (663)	1,988

Centre European Brigade, Lieutenant-Colonel Dunlop:
King's 75th (233), Bombay Europeans (528) or King's 103rd,[2] King's 77th (693) — 1,454

Left Native Brigade, EIC Lieutenant-Colonel John Wiseman:
2/3 Bombay with additions (717), 1/5 Bombay (663), 2/2 Bombay (675) — 2,055

Artillery, EIC Lieutenant-Colonel George A. Lawman (166 Europeans + 344 Natives) — 510

Engineers and Pioneers, EIC Lieutenant-Colonel J. C. Sartorius and EIC Captain B. Moncrieff — 423

Total Fighting Men (11 February 1799) — 6,430

III BARAMAHAL ARMY, EIC LIEUTENANT-COLONEL
ALEXANDER READ
Infantry, Europeans 109, EIC Native 1,123	1,232
Nizam's under Major Grant	1,973
Cavalry, EIC 47, Nizam's 1,584	1,631
Artillery, EIC 108, Nizam's 139	247
Pioneers	24
Total fighting men (12 April 1799)	5,107

[1] See Appendix I for details of field and siege artillery.
[2] This unit is found listed both ways in surviving records. The actual transfer came about 1800.

IV COIMBATORE ARMY, EIC LIEUTENANT-COLONEL
ARCHIBALD BROWN

Infantry:

Five (5) companies of the King's 19th Foot	386
Madras	617
Detachments from 2/1, 1/2, 1/3, 1/13, and 2/13 Madras Native Infantry	3,198

Cavalry:

Artillery: 99 Europeans and about 300 Natives	399
Pioneers and Engineers:	200
	————
Total fighting men (20 February 1799)	4,800

V NIZAM'S ARMY INCLUDING SUBSIDIARY FORCE AND THE
KING'S 33RD FOOT (COMMANDED BY MEER ALLUM BUT
WITH THE ADVICE OF COLONEL ARTHUR WELLESLEY)

Infantry:[1]

King's 33rd Foot	788
1/10 Bengal Native Infantry	993
2/10 Bengal Native Infantry	1,008
2/2 Madras Native Infantry	1,051
2/4 Madras Native Infantry	998
1/11 Madras Native Infantry	989
2/11 Madras Native Infantry	1,037
Artillery: 142 Europeans + 318 Indians with 14 guns	460

There were also additional units of infantry, cavalry, and artillery 'in
the Nizam's service', but some of these had English officers. Total
strengths are usually given as:

Infantry, 3,621 under EIC Captain John Malcolm

Cavalry, about 10,000 under advisory command of EIC
   Captain Patrick Walker

Artillery, 350 gunners and lascars with 26 guns

Total fighting men (20 February 1799) at least	21,000
	————
Grand Total fighting men about	57,000[2]

---

[1] The King's 33rd was commanded by Major John Shee; the subsidiary force (six
EIC battalions) were commanded by EIC Lieutenant-Colonel James Dalrymple.

[2] This total is suspect especially because of problems in enumerating the Nizam's own
units. Some of these may have been counted twice.

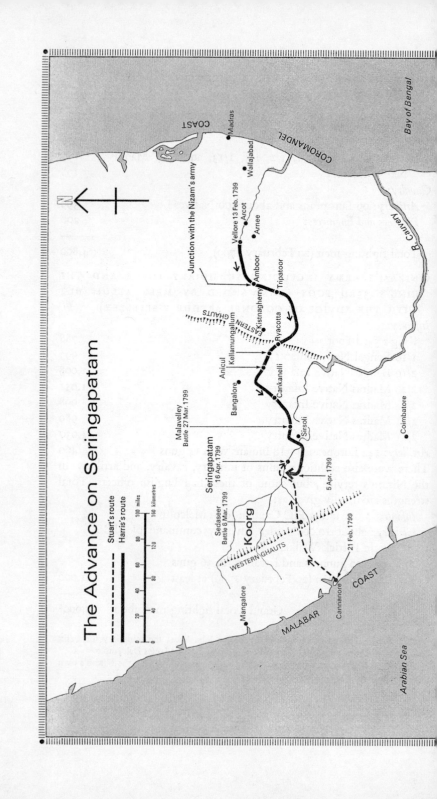

The Advance on Seringapatam

Stuart's route
Harris's route

0   20 40 60 80 100 miles
0   40 60 80 120 160 kilometres

N

Bay of Bengal

Madras

COAST

Wallajabad

COROMANDEL

Arcot
Arnee

Vellore 13 Feb. 1799

Junction with the Nizam's army

Amboor
Tripatoor

Kistnagherry

EASTERN GHAUTS

Ryacotta

Kellamungallum
Anicul

Cankanelli

Bangalore

Malavelley
Battle 27 Mar. 1799

Sirsoli

Seringapatam
16 Apr. 1799

5 Apr. 1799

Sedaseer
Battle 6 Mar. 1799

Koorg

WESTERN GHAUTS

21 Feb. 1799

Mangalore

MALABAR

COAST

Cannanore

Arabian Sea

Coimbatore

R. Cauvery

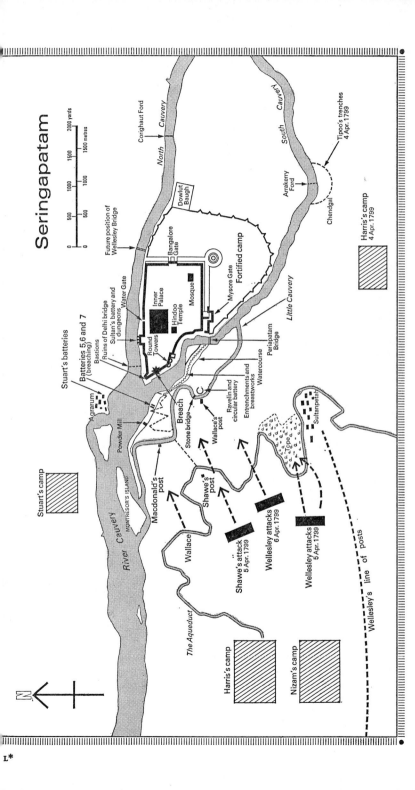

Seringapatam

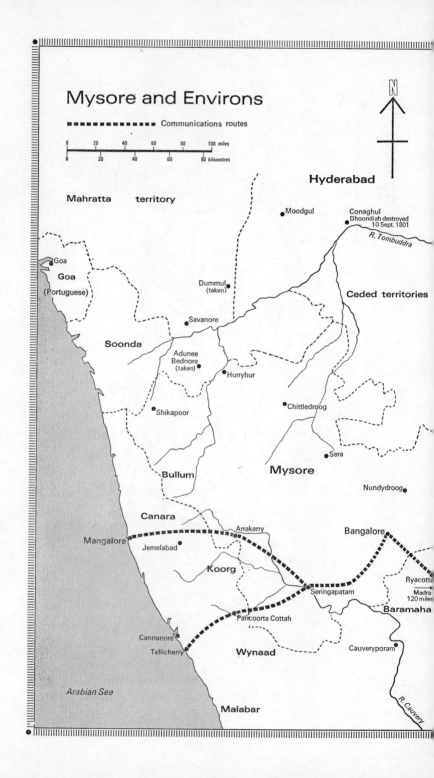

Mysore and Environs

▪▪▪▪▪▪▪▪▪▪▪ Communications routes

0 20 40 60 80 100 miles
0 20 40 60 80 kilometres

N

Hyderabad

Mahratta   territory

• Moodgul

Conaghul
Dhoondiah destroyed
10 Sept. 1801
R. Tombuddra

•Goa
Goa
(Portuguese)

Dummul•
(taken)

Ceded territories

•Savanore

Soonda

Adunee
Bednore•
(taken)   •Hurryhur

•Chittledroog

•Shikapoor

•Sera

Bullum   **Mysore**

Nundydroog•

Canara

Arrakerry

Bangalore

Mangalore   •Jemelabad

Ryacotta
Madra
120 miles

Koorg

Seringapatam

Baramaha

Pancoorta Cottah

Cannanore
Tellicherry

Wynaad   •Cauveryporam

Arabian Sea

Malabar

R. Cauvery

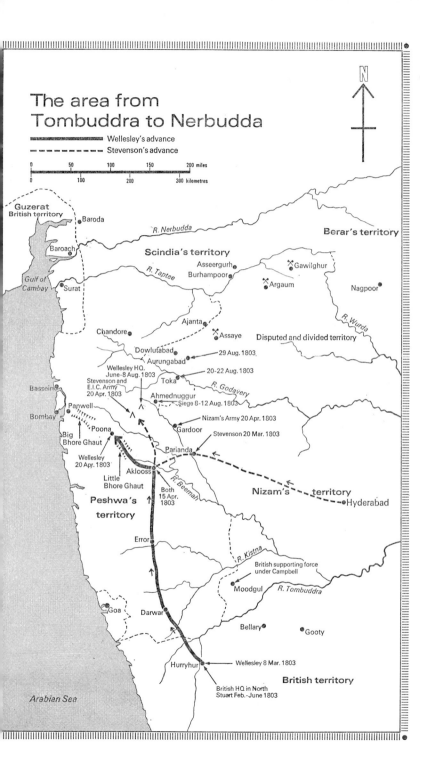

The area from Tombuddra to Nerbudda

▬▬▬▬▬▬▬ Wellesley's advance
– – – – – – – – Stevenson's advance

| 0 | 50 | 100 | 150 | 200 miles |
| 0 | 100 | 200 | 300 kilometres |

N

Guzerat
British territory

Baroda

R. Nerbudda

Berar's territory

Baroach

Scindia's territory

Gulf of
Cambay

Surat

Asseergurh
Burhampoor

Gawilghur

Argaum

Nagpoor

R. Wurda

Chandore

Ajanta

Assaye

Disputed and divided territory

Dowlutabad

Aurungabad

29 Aug. 1803

Wellesley HQ.
June-8 Aug. 1803
Stevenson and
E.I.C. Army
20 Apr. 1803

Toka

20-22 Aug. 1803

R. Godavery

Bassein

Ahmednuggur

Siege 8-12 Aug. 1803

Bombay

Panwell

Gardoor

Nizam's Army 20 Apr. 1803

Big
Bhore Ghaut

Poona

Stevenson 20 Mar. 1803

Wellesley
20 Apr. 1803

Parianda

Little
Bhore Ghaut

Aklooss

Both
15 Apr.
1803

R. Beemah

Nizam's – – – territory

Hyderabad

Peshwa's
territory

Error

R. Kistna

British supporting force
under Campbell

Moodgul

R. Tombuddra

Goa

Darwar

Bellary

Gooty

Hurryhur

Wellesley 8 Mar. 1803

British territory

British HQ. in North
Stuart Feb.-June 1803

Arabian Sea

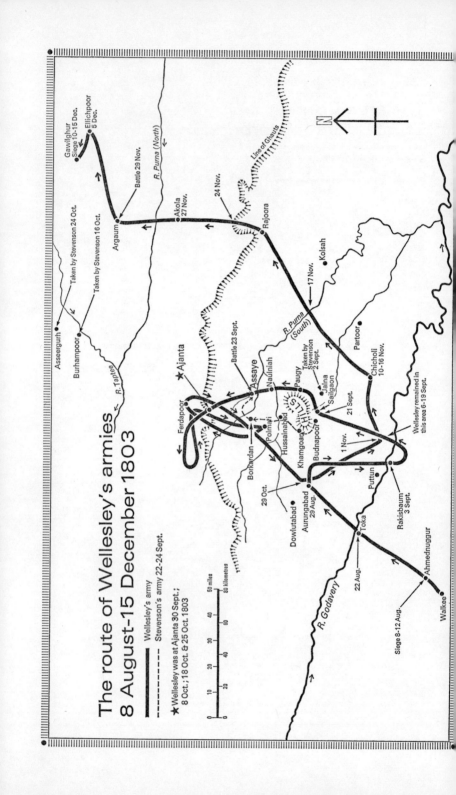

The route of Wellesley's armies
8 August–15 December 1803

—— Wellesley's army
------ Stevenson's army 22–24 Sept.

★ Wellesley was at Ajanta 30 Sept.;
8 Oct.; 18 Oct. & 25 Oct. 1803

N

Gawilghur
Siege 10–15 Dec.
Ellichpoor
5 Dec.
Battle 29 Nov.
R. Purna (North)
Akola
27 Nov.
24 Nov.
Line of Ghauts
Argaum
Taken by Stevenson 24 Oct.
Taken by Stevenson 16 Oct.
Asseergurh
Burhampoor
R. Taptee
Rajoora
17 Nov.
Kolsah
R. Purna (South)
Battle 23 Sept.
Ajanta
Assaye
Nadiniah
Paugy
Taken by Stevenson 2 Sept.
Talna
Partoor
Chicholi
10–16 Nov.
Ferdapoor
HILLS
Saligaon
21 Sept.
Polmai
Borkardan
Hussainabad
Khamgoan
Budnapoor
1 Nov.
Wellesley remained in
this area 6–19 Sept.
29 Oct.
Dowlutabad
Aurungabad
29 Aug.
Puttun
Rakisbaum
3 Sept.
Toka
Ahmednuggur
R. Godavery
22 Aug.
Siege 8–12 Aug.
Walkee

0 10 20 30 40 50 miles
0   20   40   60   80 kilometres

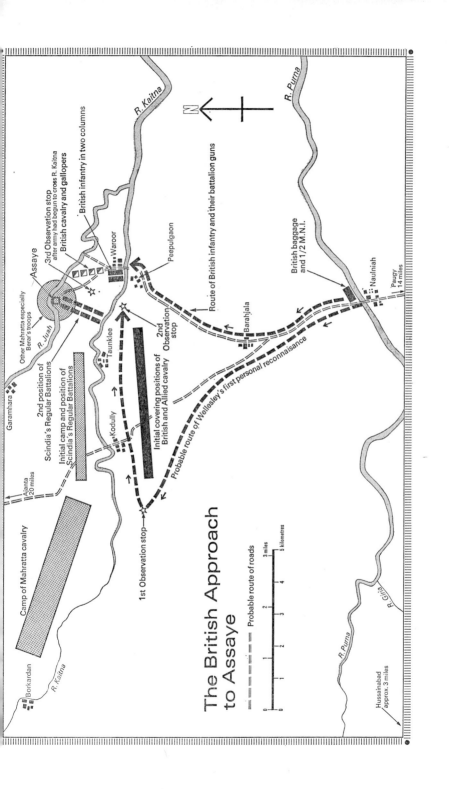

The British Approach to Assaye

Borkardan

R. Kaitna

Camp of Mahratta cavalry

Ajanta 20 miles

Garamhara

Other Mahratta especially Berar's troops

Assaye

R. Juah

2nd position of Scindia's Regular Battalions

Initial camp and position of Scindia's Regular Battalions

Kodully

Taunklee

3rd Observation stop
after army had begun to cross R. Kaitna
British cavalry and gallopers

British infantry in two columns

R. Kaitna

Waroor

Peepulgaon

2nd Observation stop

Initial covering positions of British and Allied cavalry

1st Observation stop

Probable route of Wellesley's first personal reconnaisance

Route of British infantry and their battalion guns

Barahjala

R. Purna

British baggage and 1/2 M.N.I.

Naulniah

Paugy 14 miles

Probable route of roads

0 1 2 3 miles

0 1 2 3 4 5 kilometres

R. Purna

R. Gitla

Hussainabad approx. 3 miles

N

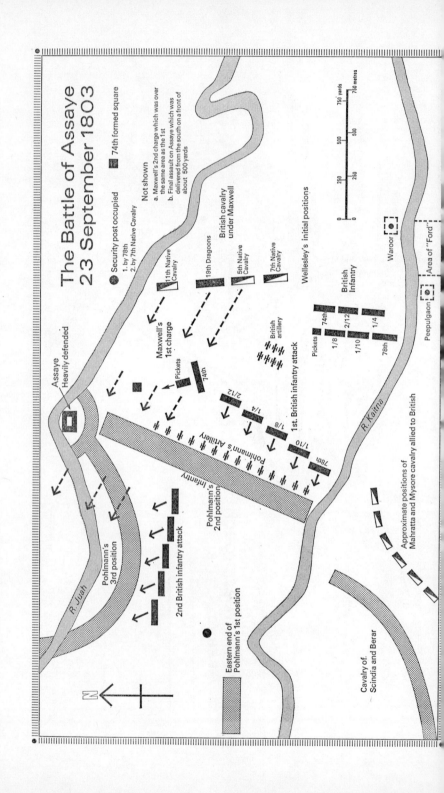

The Battle of Assaye
23 September 1803

● Security post occupied
  1. by 78th
  2. by 7th Native Cavalry

■ 74th formed square

Not shown
a. Maxwell's 2nd charge which was over the same area as the 1st
b. Final assault on Assaye which was delivered from the south on a front of about 500 yards

11th Native Cavalry

19th Dragoons

5th Native Cavalry

British cavalry under Maxwell

7th Native Cavalry

Maxwell's 1st charge

Wellesley's initial positions

British artillery

British Infantry

Pickets

74th

74th
2/12
1/4
1/10
78th

Pickets
1/8
2/12
1/4
1/10
78th

Assaye
Heavily defended

Pohlmann's Artillery

Pohlmann's 2nd position

Infantry

1st. British infantry attack

R. Juah

Pohlmann's 3rd position

2nd British infantry attack

Eastern end of Pohlmann's 1st position

R. Kaitna

Approximate positions of Mahratta and Mysore cavalry allied to British

Cavalry of Scindia and Berar

Waroor

Peepulgaon

Area of "Ford"

0   250   500   750 yards
0   250   500   750 metres

N

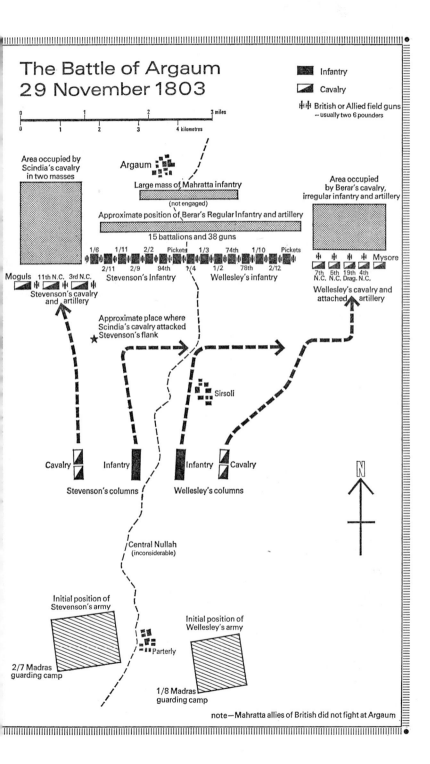

The Battle of Argaum
29 November 1803

| | Infantry |
| | Cavalry |

⊞⊞ British or Allied field guns
— usually two 6 pounders

0   1   2   3 miles
0   1   2   3   4 kilometres

Area occupied by Scindia's cavalry in two masses

Argaum

Large mass of Mahratta infantry
(not engaged)

Area occupied by Berar's cavalry, irregular infantry and artillery

Approximate position of Berar's Regular Infantry and artillery

15 battalions and 38 guns

1/6 1/11 2/2 Pickets 1/3 74th 1/10 Pickets

2/11 2/9 94th   1/4   78th 2/12

Stevenson's Infantry   Wellesley's infantry

Moguls 11th N.C. 3rd N.C.

Stevenson's cavalry and artillery

7th 5th 19th 4th
N.C. N.C. Drag. N.C.

Mysore

Wellesley's cavalry and attached artillery

Approximate place where Scindia's cavalry attacked Stevenson's flank

★

Sirsoli

Cavalry   Infantry   Infantry Cavalry

Stevenson's columns   Wellesley's columns

N

Central Nullah
(inconsiderable)

Initial position of Stevenson's army

Initial position of Wellesley's army

2/7 Madras guarding camp

Parterly

1/8 Madras guarding camp

note—Mahratta allies of British did not fight at Argaum

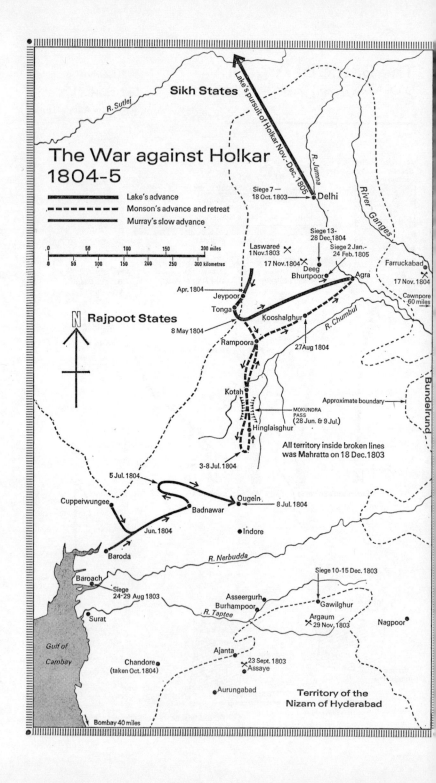

The War against Holkar 1804-5

Lake's advance
Monson's advance and retreat
Murray's slow advance

Sikh States

R. Sutlej

Lake's pursuit of Holkar Nov.-Dec. 1805

R. Jumna

River Ganges

Siege 7 — 18 Oct. 1803 • Delhi

Siege 13- 28 Dec.1804
Siege 2 Jan.- 24 Feb.1805

Laswaree 1 Nov. 1803 ✕

17 Nov.1804 ✕

Farruckabad
17 Nov. 1804

Deeg
Bhurtpoor • • Agra

Cawnpore 60 miles

Apr. 1804 • Jeypoor

Rajpoot States

Tonga

Kooshalghur

R. Chumbul

8 May 1804

Rampoora

27 Aug 1804

Kotah •

MOKUNDRA PASS (28 Jun. & 9 Jul.)

Approximate boundary

Hinglaisghur

All territory inside broken lines was Mahratta on 18 Dec.1803

3-8 Jul. 1804

5 Jul. 1804

Cupperwungee •

Ougein • ← 8 Jul. 1804

• Badnawar

Jun. 1804

• Indore

• Baroda

R. Nerbudda

Baroach •

Siege 24-29 Aug 1803

Siege 10-15 Dec. 1803

Asseergurh •
Burhampoor •
R. Taptee

• Gawilghur

Argaum ✕ 29 Nov, 1803

Nagpoor

Surat •

Gulf of Cambay

Chandore • (taken Oct. 1804)

Ajanta

23 Sept. 1803
✕ Assaye

• Aurungabad

Territory of the Nizam of Hyderabad

Bombay 40 miles

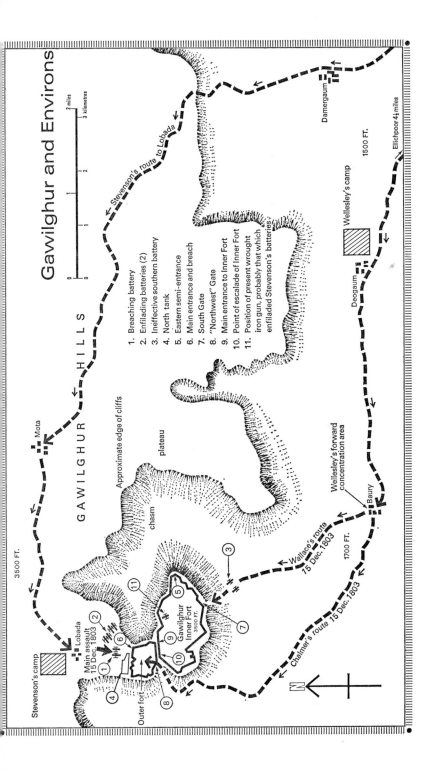

Gawilghur and Environs

1. Breaching battery
2. Enfilading batteries (2)
3. Ineffective southern battery
4. North tank
5. Eastern semi-entrance
6. Main entrance and breach
7. South Gate
8. "Northwest" Gate
9. Main entrance to Inner Fort
10. Point of escalade of Inner Fort
11. Position of present wrought iron gun, probably that which enfiladed Stevenson's batteries

GAWILGHUR HILLS

3500 FT.

Mota

Approximate edge of cliffs

plateau

chasm

Stevenson's route to Lobada

Stevenson's camp

Lobada

Main assault 15 Dec. 1803

Outer fort

Gawilghur Inner Fort 3600 FT.

Wallace's route 15 Dec. 1803

Chalmers' route 15 Dec. 1803

Wellesley's forward concentration area

Baury

1700 FT.

Deogaum

Wellesley's camp

1500 FT.

Damergaum

Ellichpoor 4½ miles

N

0 1 2 3 kilometres
0 1 2 miles

AFGHANS

Delhi

Agra

Oudh

Nepal

Mahratta

Ougein
Indore

Baroda

Surat

Confederacy

Nagpoor

Bengal
(Presidency)

Calcutta

Bombay
(Presidency)

Poona

Hyderabad

Hyderabad

Circars

Masulipatam

Goa
(Portuguese)

Mangalore

Mysore

Seringapatam

Cannanore
Tellicherry

MALABAR COAST

Arcot

Madras

Madras (Presidency)

CORMANDEL COAST

Pondicherry

Tanjore

Carnatic

Travancore

Bay of Bengal

Ceylon

British since 1796, but
not part of India

Arabian Sea

British India
March 1805

British territory in 1795

Territory added by the
Wellesleys by July 1805

| 0 | 100 | 200 | 300 | 400 miles |
| 0 | 100 | 200 | 300 | 400 | 500 | 600 kilometres |

Bibliography

I had the privilege of discussing this book with the present Duke of Wellington during its early stages. I asked him what material I ought to study. We discussed a number of titles and he suggested that by far the most valuable would be the three volumes of the first Duke's *Dispatches* and the four volumes of his *Supplementary Despatches*, including their indexes. After months of study, I completely agree. These nine thick volumes and the maps of the *Supplementary Despatches* have given me more than 90 per cent of my raw material.

They give in readily accessible form practically all Wellington wrote that is of military and political value from about the age of twenty-seven to the age of thirty-six. I know of nothing similar in connection with any other commander. The Great Duke is revealed by his daily thoughts and activities; at the time he wrote he had no idea that his letters and orders would be read by anyone other than the recipients. He expressed himself clearly and completely. I am grateful for my two years of association with him in mind and spirit through what he wrote.

A word of caution is in order, however, about these dispatches. The India volumes are not easy to read or comprehend. In spite of editorial explanations and some other documents included by Colonel Gurwood and the second Duke (the editors of the *Dispatches* and the *Supplementary Despatches* respectively) many terms can be made meaningful only by context, and careful research is often needed to determine the post of the addressee. Some of the letters are clear in phraseology, but not in overall purpose. There are many Hindostani terms. In fact, until one gets a fair knowledge of India in Arthur Wellesley's era, his dispatches are likely to be somewhat boring. One of his contemporary biographers praised the India dispatches, but his next sentence proved that he had not read them. The omissions are exasperating at first and the dispatches can only be fully understood by referring to the originals in the present Duke's possession at Apsley House.

There are, of course, other fairly accessible original records. Malcolm and Elphinstone were part-time professional writers. Lushington's biography of his father-in-law, Lord Harris, and Beatson's work are well and carefully written by eyewitnesses and contain much 'official correspondence'. The House of Commons Account and Wellesley's Notes are excellent, but difficult to obtain.

I found three valuable works of reminiscences by men associated with Wellington. These are Elers, Welsh and Blackiston. Perhaps Hickey should be included, although his close association with Arthur Wellesley was brief.

There were several contemporary histories written by men in India, including Duff, Wilks and Thorn. There are also some useful military manuals. But one can soon become buried in extraneous material, especially at the India House and in the War Office Library.

I must mention one series of volumes that I have not had at my disposal. *The Indian Dispatches of the Marquess Wellesley* are similar to those of Wellington. I have tried to buy the five volumes for years without a single offer and have had access to them only briefly, while in Britain. I have both Owen and Pearce, but they are not entirely satisfactory substitutes. Micro-filming something of the length of Wellesley's *Dispatches* and then reading it all and referring to several rolls of microfilm later would be almost impossible. Fortunately, most of what the elder brother wrote that is important to a narrative primarily devoted to Arthur is available elsewhere, usually in several places.

Secondary references are headed in my opinion by Lady Longford's magnificent first volume. She has had the industry and the specialized knowledge to interpret and review carefully, for perhaps the first time, all the unpublished 'Wellington' manuscripts at Apsley House.

Other biographies are weak as far as India is concerned, although Guedalla's research into Wellington's early libraries is of real value. Alexander is better for this era than some of the later writers. The portion of Ward referring to India is of extreme interest; his mind is astonishingly able to get to the heart of things. His concern with Wellington in India, however, is so short as to be misleading. Aldington also is useful.

Earlier secondary works on the subject of Wellington's campaigns and battles in India are limited. Fortescue lacks detail, although his overall appreciation is valuable. Burton's work has obvious value because he too was in the Indian Army, although a century later. Wilson's account is perhaps the best, but he is primarily concerned with the Madras Army.

Now for the background: there are many books, but none able to give the feel of India painlessly in a few hours. I read those listed below with a growing sense of despair, the sort of frustration one might build up reading a one-volume anthology of English Literature or an *Encyclopaedia Britannica* account. Hamilton's *East India Gazetteer* and both editions of Rice's Mysore books are in the same category. The East India Military Calendar constitutes the three most disappointing volumes I have; they contain many short biographies, but only about three of them are useful. I wish, for instance, that the authors had included Stevenson, Montresor and Stuart.

On the other hand, *Dodwell and Miles* has been a true blessing; every EIC officer I have looked for is there. I wish I could tell these two how much I am in debt to their compilation. I have used the Army Lists for King's officers not quite so satisfactorily. *The Dictionary of National Biography* is always good, but contains only the top few. I could go on for pages, but in descending relevance. The *Dispatches* and *Supplementary Despatches* are essential; everything else is secondary.

I make no claim to completeness in this area; the two bibliographies below, with the single exception of Wellesley's *Dispatches*, include only books that I own and have used either in the flesh or on microfilm. The first is composed of all those titles referred to specifically in my notes and references which are listed alphabetically by their short titles. The second group includes only titles which contributed some material for my reference cards prepared during this study, although nothing survived from them in the final notes and references. I had to choose between keeping notes and references within bounds and having them at the bottom of the pages or giving more and relegating them to the end. I have not often referred, for instance, to *Dodwell and Miles*, the Army Lists, and *D.N.B.*, although all have supplied much detail.

I should explain about the procurement of my sources; the India House Library is head and shoulders above everyone else. I wish to thank the people there – there have been more than half a dozen in all – for extremely helpful assistance in every single matter in which they could help. They gave me while I was in London the use of their efficient facilities and microfilmed quickly and accurately everything we requested. This book would have been impossible without their map reproductions, over a hundred sheets in all. The British Museum strove valiantly in spite of their enormous work load, and I want particularly to thank Mr T. A. Corfe of the Map Room. The Princeton University Library was as helpful as it could be, but military history in India is beyond its scope.

I also want to thank Maggs, Francis Edwards, and Kegan Paul. My India Want List contained titles more difficult to find than most of those required for the Peninsula and Waterloo, but each firm came up with some books of great importance. Microfilm extends the field of knowledge enormously, but the books themselves are easier to use.

SHORT TITLES USED IN FOOTNOTES

Adye	ADYE, RALPH WILLETT. *The Bombardier and Pocket Gunner*. London, T. Egerton, 1809.
Aldington	ALDINGTON, RICHARD. *The Duke*. New York, Viking Press, 1943.
Alexander	ALEXANDER, SIR JAMES EDWARD, K.L.S. *Life of Field Marshal, His Grace The Duke of Wellington*. 2 vols. London, Henry Colburn, 1840.
Beatson	BEATSON, LT.-COL. ALEXANDER. *View of the Origin and Conduct of the War with Tippoo Sultaun. Comprising a Narrative of the Operations of the Army of Lieutenant-General Harris and of the Siege of Seringapatam*. London, W. Bulwer and Co., 1800.
Biddulph	BIDDULPH, COLONEL JOHN. *The Nineteenth and Their Times, being an account of the Four Cavalry Regiments in the British Army that have borne the number Nineteen and of the Campaigns in which they Served*. London, John Murray, 1899.
Blackiston	BLACKISTON, MAJOR JOHN. *Twelve Years' Military Adventures in Three-quarters of the Globe, or, Memoirs of an Officer*. 2 vols. London, Henry Colburn, 1829.

Brett-James   BRETT-JAMES, ANTONY. *Wellington at War,*
1794–1815. London, Macmillan and
Co. Ltd., 1961.

Buckle   BUCKLE, E. *The Bengal Artillery.* (No title
page reproduced.)

Burton   BURTON, MAJOR R. G. *Wellington's Campaigns
in India.* (Division of the Chief of the
Staff Intelligence Branch.) Title page gives
title only.   Calcutta, Superintendent
Government Printing, India, 1908.

Cambridge History   DODWELL, H.H., M.A. *Cambridge History of
India. British India,* vol. V. Delhi, S.
Chand and Co. 1963.

Coote   SHEPPARD, E. W. *Coote Bahadur, A Life of
Lieutenant General Sir Eyre Coote, K.B.*
London, Werner Laurie, 1956.

Croker   CROKER, JOHN WILSON. *The Correspondence
and Diaries of The Late Rt Hon John
Wilson Croker, LL.D., F.R.S.,* Secretary
to The Admiralty from 1809 to 1830.
Edited by Louis J. Jennings. 3 vols.
London, John Murray, 1885.

Dispatches   GURWOOD, LT.-COL. *The Dispatches of The
Field Marshal The Duke of Wellington
during his various campaigns in India, Den-
mark, Portugal, Spain, the Low Countries
and France.* 12 vols., plus Index. London,
John Murray, 1837–1838.

D.N.B.   STEPHEN, SIR LESLIE AND LEE, SIR SIDNEY
(Eds.). *Dictionary of National Biography.*
22 vols., 5 supplements. Oxford, 1917.

Dodwell & Miles   DODWELL (EDWARD) and MILES (JAMES
SAMUEL). *Officers of the Indian Army.*
London. Longman, Orme, Brown, and
Co., 1838.

Duff   DUFF, JAMES GRANT. *A History of the Mahrattas.*
3 vols. London, Longman, Rees, Orme,
Brown, and Green, 1826.

Elers ELERS, GEORGE. Edited by Lord Monson and George Leveson Gower. *Memoirs of George Elers, Captain in the 12 Regiment of Foot (1777–1842).* London, William Heinemann, 1903.

Elphinstone COLEBROOKE, SIR T. E., BART, M.P. *Life of The Hon. Mountstuart Elphinstone.* 2 vols. London, John Murray, 1884.

Fortescue FORTESCUE, HON. J. W. *History of the British Army.* 13 vols. London, Macmillan and Co., Ltd., 1899–1930.

Fortescue's Life FORTESCUE, HON. JOHN, LL.D., D.LITT. *Wellington.* London, Williams and Norgate Ltd., 1925.

Glover GLOVER, RICHARD. *Peninsular Preparation: The Reform of the British Army, 1795–1809.* Cambridge University Press, 1963.

Guedalla GUEDALLA, PHILIP. *The Duke.* London, Hodder and Stoughton, 1931.

Hamilton HAMILTON, WALTER. *The East India Gazetteer.* 2 vols. London, John Murray, 1815.

Harris LUSHINGTON, THE RT. HON. S. R. (Harris's son-in-law). *The Life and Services of General Lord George Harris,* G.C.B., *Baron of Seringapatam and Mysore, during his Campaigns in America, the West Indies, and India.* London, John W. Parker, 1840.

Hickey SPENCER, ALFRED. *Memoirs of William Hickey.* 4 vols. London, Hurst and Blackett, 1925.

Hook HOOK, THEODORE. *The Life of General, The Rt Hon Sir David Baird, Bart., G.C.B. K.C., E.T.C.* 2 vols. London, Richard Bentley, 1832.

Hooper HOOPER, GEORGE. *Wellington.* London, Macmillan and Co., Ltd., 1913.

House of Commons *House of Commons Account, Bengal, Fort St. George and Bombay Papers presented to* the House of Commons, Pursuant to their orders of the 7th of May last, from the East India Company, relative to the Mahratta War in 1803. Printed by order of the House of Commons 5th and 22nd June, 1804.

Lady Longford   LONGFORD, LADY ELIZABETH. *Wellington. The Years of the Sword.* London, Weidenfeld and Nicolson, 1969.

Lyall   LYALL, SIR ALFRED, P.C., K.C.B., D.C.L. *The Rise and Expansion of the British Dominion in India.* London, John Murray, 1910.

Malcolm   KAYE, JOHN WILLIAM. *The Life and Correspondence of Sir John Malcolm, G.C.B. Late Envoy to Persia and Governor of Bombay.* 2 vols. London, Smith, Elder, and Co.; Bombay, Smith, Taylor and Co., 1856.

Marshman   MARSHMAN, JOHN CLARK. *The History of India* (From the earliest period to the close of Lord Dalhousie's Administration.) 2 vols. London, Longmans, Green, Reader & Dyer, 1867.

Maxwell   MAXWELL, SIR HERBERT. *The Life of Wellington.* London, Sampson, Low, Marston and Company, Ltd., 1907.

Military Adventurers   COMPTON, HERBERT. *A Particular Account of the European Military Adventurers of Hindustan from 1784 to 1803.* London, T. Fisher Unwin, 1892.

Misra   MISRA, B. B., M.A., PH.D. *The Central Administration of the East India Company 1773–1834.* Manchester University Press, 1959.

Nineteen Movements   ANONYMOUS. *The Nineteen Movements as ordered for the British Army.* By an Officer. Calcutta (printed for author), Mirror Press, 1809.

Nolan   NOLAN, E. H., PH.D., LL.D. *The Illustrated History of the British Empire in India and the East from the Earliest Times to the Suppression of the Sepoy Mutiny in 1859.* 2 vols. London, James S. Virtue. (No date.)

Oman   OMAN, CHARLES, K.B.E. *A History of the Peninsular War.* 7 vols. Oxford, Clarendon Press, 1930.

Owen   OWEN, SIDNEY J., M.A. *A Selection from the Despatches, Treaties and Other Papers of The Marquess Wellesley, K.G., during his Government of India.* 2 vols. Bangalore, Mysore Government Press, 1877.

Oxford History   SMITH, VINCENT A., C.I.E. *The Oxford History of India, from the Earliest Times to the End of 1911.* Oxford, Clarendon Press, 1919.

Pearce   PEARCE, ROBERT ROUIERE. *Memoirs and Correspondence of The Most Noble Richard Marquess Wellesley, K.P., K.G., D.C.L.* 3 vols. London, Richard Bentley, 1846.

Petrie   PETRIE, SIR CHARLES, BART. *Wellington: A Reassessment.* London, James Barrie, 1956.

Philips   PHILIPS, C. H., M.A., PH.D. *The East India Company, 1784–1834.* Manchester University Press, 1968.

Regular Corps   SMITH, MAJOR LEWIS FERDINAND. *A Sketch of the Rise, Progress, and Termination of the Regular Corps formed and commanded by Europeans in the service of the Native Princes of India with the Principal Events and Actions of the late Mahratta War.* Calcutta, J. Greenway, written 1804.

Roberts   ROBERTS, GENERAL LORD. *The Rise of Wellington.* London, 1895.

Stanhope   STANHOPE, PHILIP HENRY. *Notes of Conversa-
                            tions with the Duke of Wellington*. London,
                            Oxford University Press, 1888.

Supplementary Despatches   WELLESLEY, ARTHUR, DUKE OF WELLINGTON.
                            *Supplementary Despatches and Memoranda
                            of Field-Marshal Arthur, Duke of Welling-
                            ton*. Edited by his son, the 2nd Duke of
                            Wellington. 15 vols. London, John
                            Murray, 1858–72.

Thorn   THORN, MAJOR WILLIAM. *Memoir of the War
                            in India, conducted by General Lord Lake,
                            Commander-in-Chief, and Major-General
                            Sir Arthur Wellesley, Duke of Wellington.
                            From its Commencement in 1803, to its
                            Termination in 1806, on the Banks of the
                            Hyphasis*. London, T. Egerton, 1818.

Thornton   THORTON, EDWARD. *The History of the British
                            Empire in India*. 6 vols. London, Wm. H.
                            Allen and Co., 1843.

Torrens   TORRENS, W. M., M.P. *The Marquess Wellesley,
                            Architect of Empire*. London, Chatto &
                            Windus, 1880.

Vibart   VIBART, MAJOR H. M., Royal Madras Engin-
                            eers. *The Military History of the Madras
                            Engineers and Pioneers*. 2 vols. London,
                            W. H. Allen & Co., 1881.

Ward   WARD, S. G. P. *Wellington*. London, Batsford,
                            1963.

Wellesley's Notes   ANONYMOUS. *Notes on the War in India 1803*
                            (on spine); *Notes relative to the Late Trans-
                            action in the Mahratta Empire*. Fort William
                            (no publisher named), 15 December 1803.

Welsh   WELSH, COLONEL JAMES. *Military Reminis-
                            cences Extracted from a Journal of Nearly
                            Forty Years Active Service in the East
                            Indies*. 2 vols. London, Smith, Elder &
                            Co., 1830.

323

Wilks   WILKS, COLONEL MARK. *Historical Sketches of the South of India, in an attempt to trace the History of Mysoor: from the origin of the Hindoo Government of that State, to the extinction of the Mahommedan Dynasty in 1799.* 3 vols. London, Longman, Hurst, Rees, Orme and Brown, 1817.

Wilson   WILSON, LT.-COL. W. J. *History of the Madras Army.* 5 vols. Madras, printed by E. Keys at The Government Press, 1882.

OTHER WORKS

BARNES, MAJOR R. MONEY, *A History of the Regiments and Uniforms of the British Army.* London, Seeley Service and Co., Ltd, 1954.

BELL, DOUGLAS, *Wellington's Officers.* London, Collins, 1938.

BIDDULPH, COLONEL J., *Stringer Lawrence: The Father of the Indian Army.* London, John Murray, 1901.

BLACKMORE, HOWARD L., *British Military Firearms, 1650–1850.* London, Herbert Jenkins, 1961.

BOWRING, LEWIN B., C.S.I., *Haider Ali and Tipu Sultan and the Struggle with the Musalman Powers of the South.* Oxford, Clarendon Press, 1893.

COTTON, J. S., *Mountstuart Elphinstone* (in *Rulers of India*). Oxford, Clarendon Press, 1892.

CRAIG, WILLIAM D., *Coins of the World, 1750–1850.* Racine, Wisconsin. Whitman Publishing Co., 1966.

DUNDAS, COLONEL DAVID, *Principles of Military Movements Chiefly Applied to Infantry.* London, T. Cadell, 1788.

ELPHINSTONE, THE HON. MOUNTSTUART, *The Rise of the British Power in the East.* (Edited by Sir Edward Colebrooke, Bart.) London, John Murray, 1887.

FORTESCUE, JOHN, LL.D., D.LITT., *Six British Soldiers.* London, Williams and Norgate, Ltd, 1928.

FOSTER, WILLIAM, C.I.E., *A Guide to the India Office Records.* London, H.M.S.O., 1966.

FRASER, SIR WILLIAM, BART, *Words on Wellington.* London, John C. Nimmo, 1902.

GLEIG, G. R., M.A., F.R.G.S., *The Life of Arthur, Duke of Wellington.* London, Longman, Green, Reader, and Dyer, 1865.

HENDERSON, A. J., M.A., PH.D. and HOWARTH, O. J. R., M.A. (eds.), *Oxford Survey of the British Empire.* 6 vols. Oxford, Clarendon Press, 1914.

HENDERSON, J. R., *The Coins of Haidar Ali and Tipu Sultan.* Madras, Government Press, 1921.

HUTTON, W. H., *The Marquess Wellesley.* Oxford, Clarendon Press, 1893.

KAYE, JOHN WILLIAM, *Administration of the East India Company; A History of Indian Progress.* 2nd Ed. London, Richard Bentley, 1853.

LUNT, JAMES, *Scarlet Lancer.* Rupert Hart-Davis, London, 1964.

MALLESON, COLONEL G. B., C.S.I., *The Decisive Battles of India from 1746 to 1849 inclusive.* London, W. H. Allen and Co., 1883.

—— *Seringapatam, Past and Present.* Madras, Higginbotham and Co., 1876.

MILL, JAMES and WILSON, HORACE HAYMAN, *The History of British India.* 10 vols. London, James Madden. 1858.

MUIR, RAMSEY, *The Making of British India.* Manchester, The University Press with Longmans, Green, & Co., London, 1915.

MULLER, WILLIAM, *Elements of the Science of War.* London, 1811.

PERCIVAL, VICTOR, *The Duke of Wellington, A Pictorial Survey of his Life (1769–1852).* London, H.M.S.O., 1969.

RICE, LEWIS, *Mysore and Coorg. A Gazetteer compiled for the Government of India.* 2 vols. Bangalore, Mysore Government Press, 1877.

ROBERTS, P. E. *History of British India under the Company and the Crown.* London, Oxford University Press, 1958.

—— *India under Wellesley.* London, G. Bell and Sons, Ltd, 1929.

Royal Military Calendar, East India Military Calendar: Containing the Services of General and Field Officers of the Indian Army. London, Kingsbury, Parbury and Allen, 1823.

RUSSELL, LIEUTENANT JOHN, *A Series of Military Experiments of Attack and Defence Made in Hyde Park, in 1802.* London, T. Egerton, 1806.

SMITH, CAPTAIN GEORGE, *An Universal Military Dictionary, or a Copious Explanation of the Technical Terms, etc. used in the Equipment, Machinery, Movements and Military Operations of an Army.* London, J. Millan, 1779.

SMITH, MAJOR LEWIS FERDINAND, *The Mahratta and Pindari Wars.* (No title page reproduced.)

STUBBS, FRANCIS W. (MAJOR), *History of the Organization, Equipment, and War Services of the Regiment of Bengal Artillery.* 2 vols. London, Henry S. King and Co., 1877.

WELLER, JAC, *Wellington at Waterloo*, London, Longmans, Green & Co., 1967.

—— *Wellington in the Peninsula, 1808–1814*. London, Nicholas Vane, Ltd., 1962.

WELLESLEY, *The Indian Despatches of The Marquess Wellesley*. 5 vols. London, 1836.

WHITWORTH, GEORGE CLIFFORD, *An Anglo-Indian Dictionary*. London, Kegan Paul, Trench and Co., 1885.

Index

General Index

References to plates are given at the end of entries in italic numerals

Mohiput Ram, Rajah, 197, 227–9
Monson, Lt.-Col. the Hon. William,
240–6, 254–5, 274, 275, 299
Montresor, Lt.-Col. John, in Mysore,
51–2, 97; journey to Ceylon, 104;
Malabar command, 124, 127, 128,
137, 141, 148; ill-health and death,
248, 260; friend of Wellesley, 268,
277
Monypenny, Lt.-Col. Michael, 70–1,
97
Mulwa Dada, 231
Murray, Col. John, 168, 214, 228, 236,
238, 242–3, 246, 248–9, 265, 274
Munro, Sir Hector, 14, 15, 85, 300
musnud, 15, 45, 145
mutiny of EIC officers, 6
Mysore Commissions, 47, 85
Mysore Silladar cavalry, 141, 161, 172,
178, 189, 201–2, 205, 208, 210, 266,
294, 299

nairs, 128
Nana Furnavese, 133
Nelson, Horatio, 36, 278
Nicholls, Maj.-Gen. Oliver, 120n, 168,
238
North, the Hon. Frederick, Governor
of Ceylon, 105–6, 109
nullah (aqueduct), 60, 61–7, 68, 203–5,
212

Ochterlony, Lt.-Col. D., 247
O'Donnell, Capt., 272, 277
Ogg, Major Samuel William, 104,
114n
Orrock, Lt.-Col. William, 178, 180–1,
183, 190–1, 193, 260, 268, 274, 275,
299

peons, 17, 159, 163
Perron, 168, 200, 214, 228, 233, 241,
241, 246, 297–8
Peshwa, the, *see* Bajee Rao
Picton, Major John, 34–5
Picton, Sir Thomas, 34n, 274
pindarries, 162–3, 165–6, 173–4, 213
Piron, 24, 282

Pitt, William, the Younger, 2, 7, 19,
253–4
Pohlmann, Col., 171, 181–8, 190, 193,
198, 206, 234, 273, 296–7
polygars, 89–90, 92, 94, 121
puckalee, 181
Purneah, Dewan of Mysore, 82, 83n,
86–9, 91, 94, 97, 100, 101, 117, 119,
121; Bullum and Wynaad campaigns, 124–6, 128, 148; friend of
Wellesley, 115, 129, 239, 251, 253,
269–70
Pyche Rajah, 92–4, 124, 127–8, 148

Rainier, Admiral, 36, 106, 252
Raymond, Col., 23–4, 282, 297
Read, Lt.-Col. Alexander, 16, 17, 43,
44, 47, 49, 69, 74, 86, 260, 277, 302
regiments mentioned in campaigns:
1st Bengal Volunteers, 67
2nd Bengal Volunteers, 67, 71
3rd Bengal Volunteers, 67
1/4 Bombay Native Infantry, 127
King's 19th Dragoons, 67, 124, 140,
153, 161, 172–3, 185, 187, 191, 207,
289, 294, 297
King's 25th Dragoons, 53–4, 66, 67,
150
King's 12th Foot, 33, 34, 62, 64, 74,
78, 113, 169, 214
King's 33rd Foot, 1–3, 7, 9, 33, 141,
240, 251, 272; expedition to
Penang, 10–14; return to Calcutta, 14; mission to Madras,
28–30, 34; joining Hyderabad
force, 46; Mysore campaign, 49–
81; Mysore resettlement, 88–100
King's 39th Foot, 5, 289
King's 65th Foot, 236
King's 73rd Foot, 67, 69–70, 71, 75,
77, 150, 297
King's 74th Foot, 56, 66, 68, 71–2,
75, 140, 154, 156, 161, 169, 176,
178, 180–1, 184–6, 188, 190–1,
193, 196, 202, 220, 222, 225, 231,
299
King's 75th Foot, 52
King's 76th Foot, 29, 240

Index of Places